THE IMPERIAL THEME

The Imperial Theme

FURTHER INTERPRETATIONS OF SHAKESPEARE'S
TRAGEDIES INCLUDING THE ROMAN PLAYS

BY

G. WILSON KNIGHT

Emeritus Professor of English Literature in the University of Leeds
Formerly Chancellors' Professor of English, Trinity College, Toronto

> Two truths are told,
> As happy prologues to the swelling act
> Of the imperial theme.
> MACBETH, I. iii. 127.

> Look down, you gods,
> And on this couple drop a blessed crown!
> For it is you that have chalk'd forth the way
> Which brought us hither.
> THE TEMPEST, V. i. 201.

LONDON

METHUEN & CO LTD

*Originally published by the Oxford University Press
in October 1931
First published (third edition) by Methuen & Co Ltd
in 1951
Reprinted with minor corrections 1954, 1958, 1961
Reprinted 1963
Reprinted with minor corrections and additional notes and
first published as a University Paperback 1965
Reprinted three times
Reprinted 1979
ISBN 0 416 68740 7*

*Printed and bound in Great Britain by
J. W. Arrowsmith Ltd, Bristol*

1004 010531

PREFATORY NOTE

THIS, my second main Shakespearian volume, was first published in 1931 and went out of print some ten years later. In re-issuing it I shall not preserve the original preface, which was unnecessarily burdened by references to other writers of the moment, not, for the most part, as acknowledgments, but prompted rather by the desire to feel my own investigations as part of a general movement. I have, however, been since forced to realise that they constituted a more lonely statement than that preface suggested, and one which is even now subject to a number of misunderstandings. It may therefore be as well, from a later perspective, to attempt a general clarification of their relationship to the work of others.

As I have recently suggested in my 'prefatory note' to the enlarged re-issue of *The Wheel of Fire*, these investigations can be considered to lie directly in the tradition of A. C. Bradley's *Shakespearean Tragedy*, which is too often wrongly supposed to have been limited to the *minutiae* of 'characterisation'. But they also offered something new, particularly in what might be defined as the willingness, or even will, to find in great literature significances that may best, to challenge the opposition and avoid all misunderstanding, be called 'mystical'. The new patterns unrolled with suddenness and inevitability; but it is right to record here that the thought-atmosphere in which this happened may be related to the early writings of Middleton Murry, and in retrospect I subscribe to the general acknowledgment made on the appearance of my first published work —except for articles—*Myth and Miracle* (1929; afterwards incorporated into *The Crown of Life*). The reading of the Final Plays presented in *Myth and Miracle* was itself new, and had before that been searching, without success, for recognition; but Mr. Murry's general approach and militant support during those years of what

might be called the *religious* content of great poetry served
as a stimulus and an encouragement, if not more. Indeed,
my final understanding of the positive impact of *Antony
and Cleopatra* owed something to an article of his in *The
Times Literary Supplement*; and my stress on its theme of
'loyalty' to an essay in *Discoveries* (see pp. 264, 326
below). There were, however, certain serious divergences, and these quickly appeared. I favoured a new
precision in the handling of imagery and symbol that was
repellent to the more romantically minded, who felt that
I was in danger of reducing mystery to dogma. I have
on occasion wondered that my insistence on the unity of
the Shakespearian play has not been criticised—especially
where the theory of production is the argument—as an
attempt to turn a romantic dramatist into a writer of
classic form. But, though 'intellectual' in technique, my
work was never so in either origin or purpose. It has,
it is true, been sometimes associated with what is often,
if inexactly, called the 'Cambridge' school of literary criticism, headed by such names as T. S. Eliot, I. A. Richards
and, later, F. R. Leavis, if writers so different may be
grouped together; and my first main volume enjoyed the
favour of Mr. Eliot's introduction. I would, however,
emphasise once again that poetic 'interpretation', as I see
it, is to be firmly distinguished from 'criticism'. The
critic is, and should be, cool and urbane, seeing the
poetry he discusses not with the eyes of a lover but as an
object; whereas interpretation deliberately immerses itself
in its theme and speaks less from the seats of judgement
than from the creative centre. It deliberately aims to write
of genius from the standpoint not of the reader, but of
genius itself; to write of it from *within*. So, while the
critic stands on his guard against the lure of the unknown
and prefers not to adventure too far from home, interpretation, it must be confessed, is happiest among the vast
open spaces of what is, nevertheless, a severely disciplined
speculation.

Such a work of 'disciplined speculation' was Colin

Still's book on the symbolism of *The Tempest* called *Shakespeare's Mystery Play* (1921; revised and re-issued under the title *The Timeless Theme*, 1936), which remains today a too little recognised land-mark in Shakespearian studies. Still's book was brought to my notice by himself on the appearance of *Myth and Miracle* in 1929, and thenafter it remained part of my general equipment. Years later I found among my papers a jotting on a review of its first appearance; so his thesis, at least in outline, had apparently been in my mind yet earlier. I would take this opportunity of again drawing attention to a neglected study.

My present remarks are prompted by fear of misunderstanding. Mr. Stanley Hyman, writing in *The Kenyon Review* for Winter 1948, has recently been at pains to argue that my work from *The Imperial Theme* onwards owed much to the imagistic studies of Caroline Spurgeon. As I pointed out in my reply (Winter 1949), this was never so. Her pamphlet *Leading Motives in the Imagery of Shakespeare's Tragedies* appeared in the same year, 1930, as *The Wheel of Fire*, followed by another, *Shakespeare's Iterative Imagery*, balancing *The Imperial Theme* in 1931. Though I should probably have preferred not to, it seemed a duty to read her work as it appeared, and whenever any detail of her discovery lay within the area of my own rapidly unfolding interpretations, I tended to see it—as, variously, on pages 176, 208 and 244 below— as a debt. This was the more natural since our relations were most friendly. She had written to me on the publication of *The Wheel of Fire* a letter which gave it a rank among Shakespearian studies which manners forbid me to publicise. It is a pleasure to record this example of unselfish encouragement from an older and established authority to a new-comer and potential rival. For that early encouragement and example I remain, as I have said elsewhere, deeply, and for ever, in her debt.

The year 1930 saw yet a third work of similar argument: Mgr. F. C. Kolbe's *Shakespeare's Way*, which, as

my original preface to this study recorded, may have
brought to my more detailed notice certain pieces of 'disorder' symbolism in *Macbeth* used in the following pages.
Three studies in one year had thus advanced a similar
thesis: namely, that Shakespeare's plays showed significant coherences that could be, provisionally, discussed in
their own right in loose dissociation from the story; they
had, as it were, key-*motifs*. With Caroline Spurgeon these
were necessarily 'images'; with Kolbe, they might be
images, ideas, or just things, as with the moon in *A Midsummer Night's Dream*. But both studies were limited;
they were always in danger of calling some minor strand
in the texture *the* leading motive. Though both came
near to defining what my introduction to *The Wheel of
Fire* called the 'spatial' quality of the Shakespearian play,
their results remained linear, or stringy, with no such
revelation of an imaginative *area*, or field of significance,
as you find even in Bradley's discussion of 'atmosphere'.
It would seem that I was myself sometimes too readily
content with a few cross-sections in *The Wheel of Fire*;
whereas in this volume the technique is more fully conscious, deliberately aiming, as in my analyses especially of
Julius Caesar, *Macbeth* and *Antony and Cleopatra*, to
capture as many as possible of the interlocking and
interthreading recurrences.

Kolbe's study was, as far as it went, sound, though with
a value varying greatly according to his insight into different plays, some being treated far more fully than others.
Of Caroline Spurgeon's work there is more to say. Her
two pamphlets were precursors to the major volume on
Shakespeare's imagery that appeared in 1936. On her
results in general a warning may be offered. Her subject
of analysis was 'imagery' in a very limited sense, and any
negative inferences therefore likely to be misleading.
Since *Julius Caesar* is poor in 'imagery', she writes it
down as lacking excitement in composition; whereas no
single work of Shakespeare so tingles with vivid, fiery and
—to use Masefield's word—'startling' life. The truth is,

the pervading atmosphere of 'fire' is here generated mainly by events and descriptions more important than any imagery. 'Imagery' by itself is—in so far as we make such distinctions at all—always a minor accompaniment, and by itself as likely as not merely to modify, even sometimes, in the way of art, to tend to contradict, the central interest, as with the pastoral similes in Homer and Vergil. Nevertheless, the central interest remains, in spite of all counter-checks, central; and it is fatal to forget it. Besides, metaphor and simile are used to make comparisons, and there is no point in comparing anything to itself. Therefore, though Shakespeare's dominant imaginative impression is the 'tempest', yet, since, being so important, it is expressed as much, or more, in event, extended passages of description and stage direction, as in metaphor, it eludes Caroline Spurgeon's especial method almost completely; and the material presented in my book *The Shakespearian Tempest* accordingly complements, but does not clash with, hers. It is really remarkable how little clash there ever was. The two contributions were from the start basically different both in method and in result. Her positive results hold, as all positive results must, a high value; her negative statements tend to mislead us in exact proportion to the extent of the evidence on which they are based.[1]

My own studies have attempted to offer interpretations of the whole art-form, in all its ramifications, story, persons, atmosphere in—as near as may be—a single, swift, act of the mind. That is, to enrich and fill out our instinctive acceptance of the story and its people with the far less

---

[1] In any considered account of these movements emphasis would necessarily be laid also on Wolfgang Clemen's important study. Here I am only attempting a personal note. Ignorance of the German language has so far hindered my appreciation of Dr. Clemen's work, but it is good to know that an English version is shortly to appear.

Mention might also here be made of Roy Walker's studies of *Hamlet* and *Macbeth*, *The Time is Out of Joint* and *The Time is Free*, as probably the most important recent developments, in England anyway, of the tendencies we are discussing.

instinctive recognition of spatial significances. That such significances often prove extremely hard to realise is clear from the strange reception my own studies have experienced. And here a word or two may be in place regarding certain recent correspondence to which I have been, as I see it, forced. I refer—over and above my letter, already noticed, in the *Kenyon Review*—to three letters in, respectively, *The Review of English Studies*, Oct., 1946; *Scrutiny*, Dec., 1949; and *The Times Literary Supplement*, 21 April, 1950. These were concerned outwardly with the simple matter of professional acknowledgment among investigators in the same line of business. The facts adduced must not, however, be supposed my only, or even my main, reason for so coming into the open with a complaint; there was more remaining, as Hamlet puts it, 'behind'; and it is only because I believe that the whole matter goes far deeper than one might suppose, that I return to it now.

It would seem that the reactions that worry me, and which have often, in reviews and elsewhere, risen to a quite irrational anger [1] and misrepresentation, are vitally important symptoms of a general unease. My interpretations, in Shakespearian and other fields, have, with all their faults and ineffectualities admitted,[2] nevertheless been labouring towards a new and more direct understanding of poetic art. Now, just as a new work of genius itself often antagonises the very recipient who is later to

[1] See, in particular, the revealing correspondence 'Shakespeare's Angels' in *The Times Literary Supplement*, 14 Sept.; 19 and 26 Oct., 1946.

[2] I take this opportunity of drawing attention to a serious blunder—the only one of such magnitude that I am aware of—in my discussion of *Pericles* in *The Crown of Life* where, on pages 47 and 63, I have regarded as authentic two stage directions devised by Malone. How such a mistake, against the danger of which I was at the time on my guard, arose I cannot well recollect: it may be I was relying on the Arden edition which I certainly referred to for other reasons and which strangely makes no note of Malone's hand in these directions. It is my hope that library copies of *The Crown of Life* may be corrected for the sake of students. My thanks are due to Prof. Allardyce Nicoll for drawing attention to the error.

be most influenced by it, so these interpretations appear
to have antagonised many of their recent followers.[1]
Since it is part of their purpose as intellectual interpretations to lift the awareness of poetic truth from the unconscious to the conscious, one must perhaps regard a merely
indirect, or twilight, response as the measure of a certain
failure in exposition. But the fault is not merely in the
books themselves. There is in the human mind a strong
reluctance to face, with full consciousness, the products of
poetic genius; and this often takes the form of an attempt
to reduce them to something *other*, to read them either in
terms of some lesser attribute within themselves more
readily assimilable to an intellectual enquiry, or in terms
of their age; that is, of modern histories and of forgotten,
and comparatively non-significant, works. This, our
natural academic tendency, is of appalling, and insidious,
strength. Whereas a vital interpretation trying to do
justice to Shakespearian poetry in its wholeness and its
power must always be suspect, approval awaits anyone
who more safely reduces it to characterisation, or stage-
technique, or statistics of imagery, applying to such parts,
or aspects, a scholarly precision that *looks* very effective,
but which has nevertheless, by concentrating on a part
and forgetting the whole, quite failed to do justice to the
essential life and amplitude of the work concerned. Such
scholarship receives a ready, if ephemeral, acclamation
denied to the more authentic and comprehensive approach. Even when certain generous and kindly gestures
are made, they are usually—in my experience—accompanied by some reservation or disclaimer, as though to
say, 'Please do not suppose that I wish myself to be
associated with the more daring fancies in these books.'
Disagreement on details is inevitable and distrust of the
fanciful salutary. All would clearly be well were it not for
the uncomfortable suspicion that it is too often the very

[1] E. M. W. Tillyard's valuable essay on *Troilus and Cressida* is a typical
example based on incorrect quotation from *The Wheel of Fire*. See my
letter in *The Times Literary Supplement*, 21 April, 1950.

essence of poetry, the liquid fire of its veins, which we are being asked to suppress. One cannot define it without metaphor. It may, indeed, appear to be mainly a question of style. Such critics want a cold statement of what is—and this applies especially to the poetry treated in this volume—in essence startling and apocalyptic. A true interpretation should and must—it is the very signature of its success—return saturated and glittering from those elixirs. But for this living impact neither our academic, nor perhaps our critical, traditions have much liking: they want things watered down and diluted.

The inhibiting motive is a fear. Consider the recent attempts to clothe the naked substances unearthed by the new interpretation in a well-cut, twentieth-century, suit of Elizabethan learning; and yet there was a time when we were told that all these philosophic universals could not be in Shakespeare, since the learning of his day and circle had no room for them. Once discovered, a contemporary philosophy is unearthed to fit them; but the discovery came first from a plain inspection of the Shakespearian poetry, not from a studious research into lesser authors. I would therefore urge that the academic instinct to regard such authors as a *necessity* of interpretation offers violence less to my own efforts—for what would that matter?—than to the majestical works they claim, in all humility, to serve. Let me yet once again emphasise that the correct procedure is to interpret an age in the light of its great books and men of visionary genius, not the men of genius in the light of their age. Our academic tradition has got it the wrong way round; and if this seems an extravagant statement, one has only to adduce the great analogy from Christian theology, where it is, surely, a platitude to observe that history is to be interpreted in the light of Christ, and not Christ in the light of history. What is true with the great prototype of all genius is, if we have any respect at all for hierarchies of value, true also, in its degree, of lesser men. Here our whole educational tradition is at fault: it stands itself with great composure, it is true, and much dignity, on its head.

We must feel the great works of human genius not only as themselves giving significance to, interpreting, and pronouncing judgement on, the events and thought of their, and other, times; but also as part of a great company, speaking to each other, like mountain peaks breathing an atmosphere unknown to the valleys. Therefore, though little profit comes from studying Pope's *Essay on Man* in relation to its supposed 'background' of Bolingbroke's philosophy, the comparison of it with *Thus Spake Zarathustra*, as is, I think, satisfactorily demonstrated throughout my *Christ and Nietzsche*, illuminates and enriches both. It is accordingly to be questioned whether the reference of Shakespeare to minor writers of his day, theological, philosophical, psychological or historical, does him or us any very valuable service, since what is most important in his work is best compared, not with his contemporaries, but with his great peers across the centuries; with Aeschylus before, with Byron after.

Something is certainly happening in our study of poetry that has not happened before; something very closely concerned with the spatial qualities of art; that is, with the 'eternity' dimension. Though the adventure very naturally arouses a certain fear, it must not be refused. We have surely no great reason to be content with ourselves, as we are; but there are voices speaking to us, offering to lead us into new and strange waters, and among new heights.

In this re-issue the original references have been as far as possible adapted to the Oxford Shakespeare. The exigencies of photography have prevented an absolute accuracy, but all references will be found to be within two or three lines of the Oxford text.

1951   G. W. K.

1965: I have made an adjustment on p. vi and tidied some ugly mannerisms in my main text.

CONTENTS

I

ON IMAGINATIVE INTERPRETATION

THE following essays are concerned primarily with what I have termed 'life' themes. By this I intend themes which are positive and optimistic and consistently related throughout Shakespeare to images suggestive of brightness and joy. In the sombre plays such themes lend point and meaning to the negative principles there predominant: there is a clash of positive and negative. Often, however, one positive 'life' theme may conflict with another. Thus, in my present treatment I analyse two of the sombre plays with especial regard to their more positive and happy effects; and the three Roman tragedies as an interplay, not of assertion as against negation, but rather of one positive value against another. Therefore for my present purpose a clear understanding of these Shakespearian positive 'values' and this suggestive imagery is most important. Neither can be appreciated whilst we confine our attention to logical analysis of plot and subtle psychologies of 'character'. Both are essentially transmitted imaginatively to the imaginative consciousness. From that we must work. And thence we shall discover many necessary readjustments when we return to inspect plots and persons in the plays. First, I shall note the Shakespearian 'values', drawing my examples primarily from Shakespeare's earlier plays; next, offer some remarks on imaginative interpretation in general; then notice certain recurrent imaginative effects; and, finally, consider the order of the plays analysed in my following essays.

By 'values' I mean those positive qualities in man, those directions taken by human action, which to the imaginative understanding clearly receive high poetic honours throughout Shakespeare. While analysing the sombre plays I have already observed two main values: war and love. My purpose here is not to multiply those values but merely to indicate a certain expansion of the first into three closely related divisions, and a necessary addition to the second. We are still left with two main values: in this, as in other, matters, the Shakespearian universe can be shown to possess an impregnable and rock-like simplicity beneath a superficial appearance of complexity. Now nearly all the plays before *Julius Caesar* and *Hamlet* are either war-plays or love-plays. But a passage from a recent important article by Dr. Hugh Brown[1] will make it evident that 'war' alone is too limited a label: 'At the beginning of his career Shakespeare's aim was to express himself through his hero. His natural ambition as a poet was to obtain absolute control over his own mental world, at this time a very turbulent dominion. His hero would therefore appear as a heroic and successful king.' This 'kingly ideal', as he termed it, is important. The historical plays leave a powerful impression of kingly glory, kingly responsibility. We must here be guided by imaginative, not purely logical, impressions. Kingship may be all but idealized to divine proportions:

> Not all the water in the rough rude sea
> Can wash the balm off from an anointed king;
> The breath of worldly men cannot depose
> The deputy elected by the Lord.   (*Richard II*, III. ii. 54)

Such reverberations of poetry are significant. Here, and often elsewhere, the typical Shakespearian 'infinity' metaphor of ocean is applied to kingship. 'Value' in Shakespeare is ever 'infinite', a thing of intuition, emotion, spiritual apprehension: not to be limited by any too material considerations of intellect. Through the long historic succession we find kingship presented as fraught with temptations, dangers, insecurity; wrongly and rightly possessed; sometimes strongly idealized. But it is always important to the action: a theme of high human splendour and tremendous imaginative significance. Kingship holds an infinite burden of care. Henry VI (*3 Henry VI*, II. v), Henry IV (*2 Henry IV*, III. i), and Henry V (*Henry V*, IV. i), all repeat in noble cadences the same story of anxiety,

[1] 'The Divine Drama', *The Hibbert Journal*, Oct. 1930.

responsibility, unrest: as though mortal man were too small and weak to bear so heavy-royal a weight upon his brow. Yet, at the end, the furthest splendour of kingship is embodied in Henry V. He includes, and surpasses, the best of the others, as Cleopatra includes and surpasses all other ideals of love. Henry V knows the divine assurances of Richard II, the kingly unrest of Henry VI and Henry IV; even the sense of unrightful position that continually urged Henry IV to a crusade of expiation. So he prays before Agincourt:

> Not to-day, O Lord,
> O, not to-day, think not upon the fault
> My father made in compassing the crown!
> *(Henry V*, IV. i. 309)

He is deeply religious throughout—indeed, 'the mirror of all Christian kings' (*Henry V*, Act II, Cho.), supreme in mortal humility and divine authority, wisdom, and all manly and kingly excellence. And he is successful in action. This is essential to the perfect king; the kingly ideal being necessarily a worldly and temporal ideal, which must stand the test of action, however sanctioned by the divine and overweighted with infinite care: wherein it differs clearly from the other great ideal, 'love'. *Henry V* marks the culmination of the historical plays; and the protagonist the highest splendour of kingly beauty.

Henry V wars against France for his own, and his country's 'honour'. Now 'honour' is a value close-twined with 'kingship' and 'war'. The concept is continually found at the heart of action, its motive, purpose, and justification. Thus Henry V admits that 'if it be a sin to covet honour' he is 'the most offending soul alive' (*Henry V*, IV. iii. 28). That is a typical Shakespearian thought. But it is clear that desire for 'honour' may equally fire the rebel. So Hotspur speaks the fine extravagance:

> By heaven, methinks it were an easy leap
> To pluck bright honour from the pale-faced moon,
> Or dive into the bottom of the deep,

Where fathom-line could never touch the ground,
And pluck up drowned honour by the locks;
So he that doth redeem her thence might wear
Without corrival all her dignities!

(*1 Henry IV*, i. iii. 201)

Two 'honours' may often be opposed to each other. All is, superficially, a seeming flux of unreliabilities. Bolingbroke deposes Richard II and then expects to receive proper allegiance as rightful king: and the poet partly sanctions this attitude.[1] 'Right' and 'wrong' are ever dangerous formulations in the dramatic world, and the historical plays constantly illustrate divided allegiances, contesting candidates for kingship, violent quests for 'honour'. Yet from out this welter, emerging from our total series, it is clear that both 'kingship' and 'honour' may, and, indeed, from their frequent recurrence and importance must, be regarded as principles of positive value, although they may take different and sometimes dangerous forms. The varying intricacies of plot should not prevent our understanding of them as powerful Shakespearian values. Logically, we might feel that Hotspur's 'honour' was to be condemned; imaginatively, we shall attend rather to the striking imagery by which, in the passage I have quoted above, 'honour' is associated with an infinite splendour of purpose.

I have quoted passages idealizing both kingship and 'honour'. My purpose here is to indicate certain directions of Shakespearian thought, not to prove them by detailed

---

[1] This has been well emphasized by Mr. Middleton Murry in a note on *Richard II*, 'Shakespeare and Order', *The New Adelphi*, Sept. 1928. Here Mr. Murry, observing York's transference of loyalty to the new king, writes: 'Carlisle is loyal to the divine right of a king; York is loyal to the divine principle of *order*': which is relevant to my understanding of Claudius in *Hamlet*. Mr. Murry writes: 'Order is God's will; and York's sense of the Divine—more nearly Shakespeare's own, I think—stands against Carlisle's and Richard's.' But we must remember that Richard's story does not end with his play. Not till Henry V's beautiful prayer before Agincourt do we feel England's throne cleansed of his sacred blood.

quotation. Similarly, I shall shortly notice the idea of 'soldiership', closely related to the other two. It, also, may be vividly idealized:

> I saw young Harry, with his beaver on,
> His cuisses on his thighs, gallantly arm'd,
> Rise from the ground like feather'd Mercury,
> And vaulted with such ease into his seat,
> As if an angel dropp'd down from the clouds,
> To turn and wind a fiery Pegasus
> And witch the world with noble horsemanship.
>
> (*1 Henry IV*, IV. i. 104)

'Horsemanship' is frequently associated with soldiership. Now in the history plays action in cause of values is expressed mostly by war. Therefore war, or warriorship, is itself almost an ideal. It is perhaps rather an aspect of the others in purposive action. It is not in fact easy to find many instances where 'kingship' or 'honour' maintain themselves strikingly without a correspondent stress on war. King John for England's sake is to 'glister like the god of war' (*King John*, v. i. 54). The king who shows little warriorship, like Richard II, tends to fail as king. So the perfect king, Henry V, is compact of warriorship and assertive 'honour', and his play blazes with an imaginative optimism and glorified boast of power which we find again, with differences, in the effects of *Antony and Cleopatra*. And, though Dr. Hugh Brown has well observed that the kingly ideal is attacked by the spirit of humour, and though with this ideal we can, remembering Falstaff, clearly include those of 'honour' and 'war', yet we see that all maintain themselves to the last. War, honour, kingship all blend in Henry V.

But these values are wide in scope. The ideal of war, for example, clearly suggests practical efficiency and manly power in general. Such vague qualities often become crystallized and defined in the Shakespearian world in the form of warrior excellence. So, too, 'honour', though usually applied to action military, yet clearly suggests a quality which extends further and may be applied in any

age or place, in war or peace. The equivalent to-day might
well be a form of business competition. Which sounds a
queer transposition. Yet there is Shakespearian sanction for
it. Hotspur, the greatest of 'honour' experts, considers that
a purely business proposition calls his honour in question:

> I do not care: I'll give thrice so much land
> To any well-deserving friend;
> But in the way of bargain, mark ye me,
> I'll cavil on the ninth part of a hair.
>
> (*1 Henry IV*, iii. i. 137)

So, too, with the kingly ideal. It is of all these the most
universal, and suggests (i) the essence of order, and (ii) the
extreme grandeur of world-glory.

Kingship must be related closely to 'order'; and this
concept is of profound importance in Shakespeare. Most
of the history plays and many of the tragedies present a
plot of conflict and disorder. Disorder in man, party, or
state is a recurring theme. It is often related to images of
'disease'. Sometimes we find concise disorder-symbolism to
direct our understanding: weird phenomena in sky or
earth foretelling change and disaster. Such occur in *King
John*, iii. iv. 153–9; iv. ii. 182–7; *Richard II*, ii. iv. 8–15,
and, applied to the black magic of the rebel Glendower, at
1 Henry IV, iii. i. 13–57. Such symbols blend with
'tempests': they, roughly, stand for 'disorder', 'tempests'
for 'conflict'. The opposite to these is 'music', which accompanies, induces, or suggests, peace, concord, and love.
Clearly, the king is himself an order-symbol, being both
heart and head of the organic body of the state. So a close
attention to the exceeding importance of Shakespeare's
'order' and 'disorder' thought will explain the almost
superhuman importance of his kings, the continued
emphasis on fidelity and allegiance as the purest forms of
'honour', and the consequent hatred of treachery, seen in
an extreme instance in the plot against Henry V, where it is
shown to merit sixty-five lines of vigorous and withering
reproof prior to the offenders' execution. By viewing the

king as a symbol of order we may often focus in the individual speech, act, or play a more than local and individual significance.

Next, there is the thought of world-glory or ceremony. It is the shell of kingship, the outward form of supreme authority. It is given magnificent expression in *Henry V*:

> No, thou proud dream,
> That play'st so subtly with a king's repose;
> I am a king that find thee, and I know,
> 'Tis not the balm, the sceptre and the ball,
> The sword, the mace, the crown imperial,
> The intertissued robe of gold and pearl,
> The farced title running 'fore the king,
> The throne he sits on, nor the tide of pomp
> That beats upon the high shore of this world,
> No, not all these, thrice-gorgeous ceremony,
> Not all these, laid in bed majestical,
> Can sleep so soundly as the wretched slave . . .
>   (IV. i. 274)

There it is in all its Shakespearian splendour of imaginative appeal and all its essential limitation. Such 'ceremony' may clearly be grand as the caparison to true kingliness: but surrounding unrighteous or unwise authority it has no prolonged life, no value. Richard III, moved by power-lust and desire for selfish glory, calls poetic vilification on his head and speedily wrecks himself. King John is far from being a good king, yet as lord of England he receives fairly high poetic approval. Richard II, careless of responsibility, trusts in his idealized kingship without recognizing that he himself is no real king: hence his fall. Henry IV gains his throne more or less unjustly, and yet by care and anxiety solicits our regard, and at times comes close to the essence of true kingship. But the issue is not decided until *Henry V*. Henry V is the Messiah of true kingliness. He is both wholly responsive to the divine responsibility he holds and also wholly glorified by temporal success. The others often possessed the 'ceremony' without the soul of kingship. He has both in full measure. And even he feels wearied by the burden of his responsibility: yet, because he knows that 'ceremony' is but a poor requital for his infinite anxiety, because he is the soul of 'honour' and 'warriorship', because he ever puts faith in God, he is shown as a perfect king. There are no short-cuts to kingly peace in Shakespeare. It will be clear, then, that the world-glory of kingship, the 'tide of pomp' on which it puts to sea, is both a positive good and a potential lure to evil and disorder. Joined to essential wisdom and integrity, it is one aspect of a high ideal; divorced from those, it is an unreality, a tinsel thing of tawdriness for which rash men sacrifice the order of nations. Exactly the same association and contrast obtains with 'love' and 'gold'. Love is frequently compared with gold, jewels, or valued merchandise; it is also contrasted with such precious things. Gold, however valuable in terms of worldly bargains, remains a thing temporal and of slight worth; whereas love is divine and eternal. It is the same with kingship. World-glory is endued with imaginative splendour as the sign and emblem of greatness. But it remains an emblem.

All these may be classed as 'earthly' values in comparison with 'love'. True, they surpass the limits of material things, of trivial reason, and appeal to the deeps of the human soul, which in turn expresses them in imagery which suggests the divine and infinite. All, being 'values', are 'infinite' in comparison with 'reason'—this is clearly stressed by the Trojan argument on values in *Troilus and Cressida* (II. ii. 25–68). But, though the distinction is certainly not clear in Shakespeare except from a comprehensive view of his whole work, we can clearly admit that values of warrior proficiency, honour and reputation, kingly nobility, and even communal order, may be classed as more closely earthbound than the divine ethereality of love. I need not stress the fact that love is a powerful 'value' in such plays as *Romeo and Juliet*, *A Midsummer Night's Dream*, *The Merchant of Venice*, and *Twelfth Night*. Love is clearly autonomous throughout such romantic plays. And here again we find 'tempests'. In the history plays 'tempests' suggest division and conflict: the ideal is victory and consequent peace under a perfect king, and, finally, a consummation in that king's successful love. That is the theme of *Henry V*. The tribulations of earthly life are shown as surpassed, the ideal of kingship and peace attained: next, the whole hierarchy of world values is crowned by the finer value, love—which is not, however, here presented with much fire: Henry V proves a prosaic wooer. However, the love theme serves to blend personal desire with national concord: which two are often at variance. Elsewhere we sometimes have a love-honour contrast: notably in *1 Henry IV*, where 'honour' draws Hotspur from Lady Percy (this is repeated in the Brutus-Portia relation in *Julius Caesar*), and breaks into the newly wedded happiness of Mortimer. Love finds no easy home in the history plays. It is often crushed—as in the parting of Richard II and his wife—by the travailing necessities of world-order. It is the same with *Romeo and Juliet*: the sacrifice of love here is exactly caused by state-division, and its life-blood, as Mgr. Kolbe notes, is poured out to create a final harmony in Verona. Love is sacrificed to 'order' (we should observe a powerful love-honour conflict in Romeo during the middle action). In the histories 'tempests' stand for conflict, and the opposite of 'tempests' is state 'order'. But in the romantic comedies the opposite of 'tempests' is personal 'love'. There political 'order' is usually taken for granted, or, if it enters at all, it is a background only, as in *As You Like It* and *Much Ado*. We are concerned mainly with personal love-themes. 'Tempests' are things of severance and division, the ideal is union of families, union of lovers. Now, though 'tempests' always suggest, and indeed are, the same metaphysical reality—'conflict' and 'division' being ultimately the same—yet their opposites, 'order' and 'love' are by no means always in practice synonymous. They may themselves conflict, to make more 'tempests'. In *Troilus and Cressida* the Trojans, love-idealists, are opposed to the Greeks, intellectuals: and from the latter we have

Shakespeare's longest 'order-speech'. In the first half of Shakespeare's work each has its own world where it is supreme. In the history plays the poet starts from a deliberate poetic realism, showing the place of personal love in world affairs, showing it necessarily sacrificed to more imperious demands; in the romantic comedies he starts from a purely fanciful apprehension of a magic land—Illyria or Arden or Belmont—where the soul's dreams come true, and sets off his themes of romance against the 'tempests' of temporal existence. The one group shows unity in state as the ideal; or at least, since that is rarely attained, shows its reflections, 'honour', noble kingship, righteous war, as a trinity of ideals. The other limits its territory to the magic land of the soul's personal longing. In this sense the romances are the more religious, whereas the histories are rather worldly in subject matter, the poet's attitude, and the ideal towards which the action moves.

Romance is, certainly, close to religion in Shakespeare. This is the value which I suggest may be added to and finally blended with 'love'. But in the history plays it is also recognized that there are religious facts, religious duties to which the clangour of warring strokes is, or ought to be, alien and abhorrent. Prince John addresses the Archbishop of York:

> My Lord of York, it better show'd with you
> When that your flock, assembled by the bell,
> Encircled you to hear with reverence
> Your exposition on the holy text
> Than now to see you here an iron man,
> Cheering a rout of rebels with your drum,
> Turning the word to sword and life to death.
>
> (2 *Henry IV*, IV. ii. 4)

The Archbishop is not only a soldier: he is a rebel. And probably the thought of rebellion is the stronger. Yet we may note the clear contrast of 'holy text' with the phrase 'an iron man'. Elsewhere, bishops and archbishops join in state intrigues, often plot rebellion or urge the king (as

in *Henry V*) to war. The divine interthreads the earthly in
these plays: in the king the earthly becomes all but divine.
Both divinities are juxtaposed and entwined later in Prince
John's speech, and their irrational conflict stressed:

> Who hath not heard it spoken
> How deep you were within the books of God?
> To us the speaker in his parliament;
> To us the imagined voice of God himself,
> The very opener and intelligencer
> Between the grace, the sanctities of heaven
> And our dull workings; O, who shall believe
> But you misuse the reverence of your place,
> Employ the countenance and grace of heaven,
> As a false favourite doth his prince's name,
> In deeds dishonourable? You have ta'en up,
> Under the counterfeited zeal of God,
> The subjects of his substitute, my father;
> And both against the peace of heaven and him
> Have here up-swarm'd them.   (*2 Henry IV*, iv. ii. 16)

Notice the metaphoric figure by which the Archbishop is a
'favourite' and 'heaven's grace' his 'prince'. And, again,
observe how an earthly king is God's 'substitute'—even
though he may have dethroned another such substitute,
here Richard II, 'the deputy elected by the Lord' (*Richard
II*, iii. ii. 57). The co-existence of kingly and episcopal
divinity is subtle throughout these plays, in comparison or
contrast. In *King John* the contrast of Church and State is
developed in detail.

The romantic plays show powerful themes and figures
of religion, directly associated with love. In *The Comedy
of Errors* Aemilia, thinking her husband lost at sea, becomes an Abbess, living at Ephesus. The secluded life is
thus her shelter from love's tragedy. (We are reminded of
the 'chapel' and 'temple' associated with Hermione and
Thaisa in the Final Plays.) Often we find Friars helping
distressed lovers. In *The Two Gentlemen of Verona* Silvia
is helped to escape by Sir Eglamour, who is asked to meet
her 'at Friar Patrick's cell' where she intends 'holy

confession' (IV. iii. 43). This clearly forecasts the more prolix development of the same idea in *Romeo and Juliet*: there Friar Laurence is an important and carefully drawn person in the play, and the action depends largely on his decisions. In both these plays the Friar helps love's distress. Which happens again in *Much Ado About Nothing*. Here the Claudio-Hero tale is an early pattern of those similar plots which succeed each other in the Final Plays: love's tragedy, death, and surprising resurrection. And here this particular mechanism of amazing revival is worked by Friar Francis. In addition, we may note the ill-fated marriage ceremony and beautiful chapel-scene in which Claudio offers votive song and music to the wronged Hero, supposed dead. In all these plays the Friar is, so to speak, 'in the secret'. He knows more than the others. There is just a suggestion of divine omniscience to be expanded later in the person of the Duke in *Measure for Measure* when disguised as a Friar. Something similar recurs in *Twelfth Night*, where Olivia brings a Priest to her love, Sebastian:

> Blame not this haste of mine. If you mean well,
> Now go with me and with this holy man
> Into the chantry by: there, before him,
> And underneath that consecrated roof,
> Plight me the full assurance of your faith;
> That my most jealous and too doubtful soul
> May live at peace. He shall conceal it . . .   (IV. iii. 22)

It is the Church that knits lovers in a holy bond. Again, in *Twelfth Night*, the Priest speaks of

> A contract of eternal bond of love,
> Confirm'd by mutual joinder of your hands,
> Attested by the holy close of lips,
> Strengthen'd by interchangement of your rings;
> And all the ceremony of this compact
> Seal'd in my function, by my testimony . . .   (V. i. 159)

The love-theme in *The Merchant of Venice* is also associated with images of holiness. Portia pretends to Lorenzo that, whilst Bassanio is away, she will obey a 'secret vow' to 'live

in prayer and contemplation' (III. iv. 27) at a monastery
nearby. We might compare Helena in *All's Well*, or the
'hermitage' of *Love's Labour's Lost*, v. ii. 805. Later we
hear that Portia

> . . . doth stray about
> By holy crosses, where she kneels and prays
> For happy wedlock hours. (v. i. 30)

She descends from her magic home, Belmont, into the dust
and turmoil of human tragedy at Venice, like an angel
come to earth: and there, we might add, she tends to
represent the fine Christianity expressed by her mercy-
speech. Nor must we allow our sight to be blurred by what,
to us, appears her somewhat unchristian attitude later. We
need to observe with elastic sympathies: to see Shylock
with the tragic intuition demanded by *Macbeth*, to understand Portia by the different intuition of fanciful romance.
Not till the Final Plays are these two Shakespearian intuitions perfectly blended. For the present, we may, then,
suggest that 'romance' and 'religion' are closely associated
in these plays. This religion is Roman Catholic. The
Protestant representatives of religion are, it seems, less
important. Sir Nathaniel, in *Love's Labour's Lost*; Sir Oliver
Martext in *As You Like It*; Sir Hugh Evans in *The Merry
Wives*—all serve a comic rather than a richly imaginative
purpose. To them we may add Sir Topas as impersonated
by Feste; and remarks about Puritans generally. Moreover, often religious phraseology directly blends with the
rhetoric of love. A Romeo-speech is sufficient to indicate
this tendency:

> She speaks;
> O, speak again, bright angel! for thou art
> As glorious to this night, being o'er my head,
> As is a winged messenger of heaven
> Unto the white upturned wondering eyes
> Of mortals, that fall back to gaze on him
> When he bestrides the lazy-pacing clouds,
> And sails upon the bosom of the air.
> (*Romeo and Juliet*, II. ii. 25)

She is a 'dear saint' (II. ii. 55). This is quite usual in

Shakespeare. The height of feminine purity is shown us
in *Measure for Measure*, where Isabella aims at the perfected
sanctity of a nun's life: which ideal is there presented in
order to be attacked by a profounder wisdom. We might
compare the lovely lines on the 'blessed' vocation of the
nun in *A Midsummer Night's Dream* (I. i. 67–78), where
it is contrasted with the 'earthlier happy' ideal of wifehood.
The ideal of womanly sanctity in all its forms is strong in
the early plays: motherhood (as with Constance in *King
John*), wifehood, maidenhood.

I have sketched roughly the main 'values' outstanding
from Shakespeare's earlier work. Though the comic
spirit may, as Dr. Brown aptly observes, attack the kingly
ideal—and, as I have noted, both 'honour' and 'war' as
well—yet humour is not itself a value, except to the professional jesters, Feste and Touchstone; and yet it may
blend with a value, especially love, so that both mingle
to create a world of laughing joy. Humour and tragedy
are perhaps rather twin mediums of poetic expression,
rather an attitude towards 'value' than values themselves:
thus humour may often, like tragedy, be negative with
reference to values, as in the wit campaign against love in
Much Ado. But the values, as I have noted them, are
maintained fairly safe throughout the first half of Shakespeare's work. They are contrasted, associated, opposed
in conflict, blended in harmony. The value of personal
faith to a master may touch both allegiance to a king or
love of a friend. Love of man for man may be strong as
the love of women: in *Timon* there are hardly any women,
and those in Act I disguise themselves as Amazons. Love
and soldiership are contrasted often, especially in *Much
Ado*, in Benedick's speech on Claudio's transformation and
Claudio's own words (I. i. 306–15) earlier. Love and
kingship may be associated. Love is a spirit 'high' and
'imperious' (*Two Gentlemen of Verona*, II. iv. 130). A lady
may be 'empress of my love' in *Love's Labour's Lost*, IV. iii.
56. Love is compared with 'sovereignty' in the same play
(IV. iii. 234). Love's presence is like majesty:

> What peremptory eagle-sighted eye
> Dares look upon the heaven of her brow,
> That is not blinded by her majesty?
>   (*Love's Labour's Lost*, IV. iii. 226)

This thought is repeated in *Troilus and Cressida*:

> Even such a passion doth embrace my bosom:
> My heart beats thicker than a feverous pulse;
> And all my powers do their bestowing lose,
> Like vassalage at unawares encountering
> The eye of majesty.   (III. ii. 37)

Troilus's state of mind is similar to Bassanio's when, like Troilus, at the moment of success in love he draws a picture of the buzzing multitude clustering round a 'beloved prince' (III. ii. 181). A fine phrase occurs in *All's Well*:

> Now, Dian, from thy altar do I fly,
> And to imperial Love, that God most high,
> Do my sighs stream.   (II. iii. 80)

In such passages the more spiritual is expressed in terms of the more material reality: which is the usual poetic process. For love is the soul's true emperor, the soul's quest, the ultimate peace and imperial theme of life. Clearly then it blends with the divine, and hence the love office of Friars in the romances. We have observed how, in Prince John's speech, 'heavenly grace' is imaged as the Archbishop's 'prince'. So elsewhere the most perfect religious peace may well be compared, or contrasted, with kingship. The saintly Henry VI speaks:

> My crown is in my heart, not on my head;
> Not deck'd with diamonds and Indian stones,
> Nor to be seen. My crown is called content;
> A crown it is that seldom kings enjoy.
>   (*3 Henry VI*, III. i. 62)

In which the ultimate statement of Shakespeare as given in *The Tempest* is beautifully, at that early date, crystallized.

In the sombre plays these values are attacked by negations: hate, evil, death. Not that those negations are quite new. They occur fleetingly often before, especially in the earliest plays or poems, where *Lucrece* and *2 Henry VI*[1] clearly forecast *Macbeth*, and *Titus Andronicus King Lear*. Metaphors, passages, or scenes frequently remind us of the later plays. But not till the period introduced by *Julius Caesar* and *Hamlet* is there a prolonged and careful analysis of these negative forces. To understand these plays then, we must, evidently, be prepared to observe the 'values' which are to be questioned and attacked. Hence my outline of the Shakespearian 'values' here. In *Hamlet* we find evil undermining the royal throne of Denmark and the nobility of Hamlet. There is the contrasted warriorship of Fortinbras and fine vigour in revenge of Laertes. Claudius lives up well through the greater part of the play to the kingly ideal, in spite of his previous crime. But that deathly crime works in his conscience refusing, through Hamlet, to allow him to attain perfected kingliness and love. He flies from the play, conscience-stricken, his court in chaos, like Macbeth at the feast, and later has to descend to treachery to save himself. In both Hamlet and Claudius an evil, a death—whether in conscience or pure apprehension—cuts into the typical values. Here, and in many of the following plays, love and all 'honour' values are ranged together against the instruments of darkness. War and love are grouped side by side in *Troilus*, and related to 'honour', especially the 'infinite' honour of Priam, King of Troy. The Greeks, on the contrary, are disordered, blasted by a vague evil most clearly apparent in Thersites. In that state of consciousness, the very idealism of Agamemnon makes him a futile king: we are in a world—or camp—of intellectual contradictions. Like the Duke in *Measure for Measure*, Agamemnon fails as king through a profound intuition. Both are aware of the purely temporal and worldly aspect of apparent success or failure. Ulysses' reason shows Agamemnon to be wrong, neglecting, as he does, the

---

[1] I have analysed the clustering resemblances to *Macbeth* in this play in *The New Adelphi*, Sept. 1927 (now in *The Sovereign Flower*, App. D).

universal principle of 'order'. The idealistic Trojans recognize and practise intuitively the fine values of kingship, allegiance, honour, warriorship, and love. They show an orderly world. The Greeks argue at length and are in disorder. The Trojans have values, the Greeks, as a whole, are indecisive. Among them any profound intuition—such as Agamemnon's tragic philosophy—can be shown to be absurd. They recognize the need for 'order', but do not attain it. 'Order' is powerfully stressed by Ulysses in his long speech to Agamemnon and his dialogue with Achilles about 'the soul of state' and Polyxena. In *Measure for Measure*, his fine ethical intuition makes the Duke too profound an individualist to be a practically successful ruler and order-force: he is rather by nature a prophet. So he naturally distrusts all shows of world-glory, of 'ceremony':

> I'll privily away. I love the people,
> But do not like to stage me to their eyes:
> Though it do well, I do not relish well
> Their loud applause and Aves vehement;
> Nor do I think the man of safe discretion
> That does affect it. (I. i. 68)

It is exactly this distrust of shows—such as Angelo's—that is at the root of this ethic. Thus the kingly ideal is here questioned by a profound individualism. So, too, is that of feminine purity. Is not such purity, considered as an absolute, in an extreme instance only a limitation of human nature?—a weakness, not a strength? Such ideals begin to appear ludicrous here, especially in the scene where Angelo's love for Isabella matures. There is nothing to prevent a normal wooing. But both equally have regarded sexual love as a hideous vice, and both know, presumably, the other's professed views on sex. Hence their reciprocal violence from the start. It is profoundly comic. Such 'purity' contradicts human life. In *Othello*, the negative forces oppose Cassio's efficiency as a soldier, his honour and 'reputation', and Othello's warriorship and love. *Macbeth* shows us an apotheosis of kingship in Duncan and the English King. Macbeth, or the evil, drags kingship down to hell. Warriorship, 'degree', honour—all are tormented by the evil. Here order is inverted to an idiot chaos. In *Lear* again we find disorder, yet not chaos exactly: 'all ruinous disorders follow us to our graves'. There is disorder in the soul, the family, the state. Again the negative forces are embattled against kingship and love; though the blending here is close between negative and positive and there is no such violent opposition as in *Othello* or *Timon*. In *Timon* love suffers, and the warrior Alcibiades avenges its failure. Timon's curses are long essays on the typical Shakespearian idea of 'disorder', closely equivalent to Ulysses' speech: all temporal forms, and therefore all 'order', are repudiated by him. Timon, we are told, like Hamlet, the Duke in *Measure for Measure*, Lear, and the other protagonists, has been a good soldier. In all these plays kingship, warrior-honour, and love are positive forces, grouped together, and often related to 'order'. The negations oppose them. And yet sometimes a positive spiritual power may be opposed to order, as I have observed in Agamemnon and *Measure for Measure*. This positive conflict is clearly apparent in the Roman plays. In them we find a different pattern. They witness no powerful negations; if at all, negations themselves the result of the antagonism of positive values. Positive forces conflict. 'Honour' is opposed to 'love' and imperial glory in *Julius Caesar*: there is disorder in Brutus' mind and the state, his 'honour' conflicting with his 'love', and forcing him to oppose Caesar's kingship. Antony, the lover, brings peace and order back to Rome; and Cassius is finally justified by love. Brutus' 'honour' appears to fail, love to excel. In *Coriolanus* warrior-honour is raised to its extreme, isolated, and allowed to express itself in action: so exaggerated and consequently dangerous, it begins to assume a deathly horror. It is related to state 'disease' and disorder. Love is victorious here: womanhood in its three forms—mother, wife, maiden—save Rome. Personal love is here an 'order' force. In *Antony and Cleopatra* love is again victorious over warriorship, honour, and imperial power and responsibility: the power here being not exactly kingship, but something even more tremendous, since the triumvirs are continually shown as princes, not of a state, but rather of a world. In no play is the imperial theme of government more magnificently presented; in none is it more vividly silhouetted as transitory against the infinite brilliance and imperial theme of love.

By such considerations of 'value' must we attempt to interpret these later tragedies. Shakespeare plays many variations on certain universal ideas, certain symbolic images. There is re-grouping and re-arrangement, but essentials persist. Such essentials, however, will only be apparent to an imaginative response. Imagination will, having observed a striking 'honour' speech, allow other 'honour' thoughts to attach themselves, clustering round the original nucleus, until they form a compact unit of such ideas throughout Shakespeare. Imagination is synthetic, continually at work to make new wholes. But, while we attend only to 'characters', and view each person as a single person of isolated human actuality and refuse to complicate our reading by giving free rein to the imagination, we deliberately shut from our understanding the only elements in Shakespeare which will lead us from multiplicity and chaos toward unity, simplicity, and coherence.

To devote excessive attention to 'characters' is, truly, fatal. The 'character' cannot be abstracted from those imaginative effects of poetry and poetic-drama of which he is composed. That is to abstract him from himself and thus create a pure abstraction. Hence criticism of 'character' often leaves pages of commentary with few references to the Shakespearian text; whereas an imaginative interpretation will always be interwoven with numerous quotations. By the number of such quotations all interpretation must, to a large extent, be judged. The persons of Shakespeare are compact of poetic colour, poetic association, and are, moreover, defined as much by what happens to them or is said of them as of what they do and say. In *Measure for Measure* we must, for example, be ready to observe the importance of Lucio's continuous words slandering the Duke to his face during his disguise. The Duke's ethic is born of his knowledge of evil potential in himself. His sees his philosophy of lenience proved right by the drastic results of pharisaical righteousness in Isabella and Angelo. And his remembrance of his own evil—which is crucial to his ethic—is kept alive by Lucio chattering of his supposed vices at his side. Lucio is as the Duke's repressed self, alive at his elbow. And here we observe how close the Duke, Lucio, and Isabella are to Othello, Iago, and Desdemona. Iago causes Othello to distrust his ideal of purity by suggesting its impurity; Lucio underlines the Duke's distrust of such purity as Isabella's by continually suggesting that such an ideal is a form of insincerity. The two triangles may thus be shown to bear a close relation to each other. But while we regard only persons as individual people, irrespective of the dramatic pattern, such similarities cannot appear. Now *Measure for Measure* is unusually ethical and psychological in theme. Ethical interpretation is here necessary, provided always it be subordinate to the whole pattern. Often, however, a superficial ethic may blur our sight of the finer imaginative suggestion. The action is not decorated with images: the images are the action. A play of Shakespeare is, as a rule, primarily imaginative, not psychological or didactic: and often has some striking imaginative effects, which criticism usually ignores, considering them outside its province. For example, after listening to Lucius' music, Brutus is disturbed by Caesar's ghost. The full value of this scene, will not, to the desultory reader, emerge from pure reading. Stage representation will be necessary, where, if the production be careful and correct, the purely imaginative effects of Shakespeare may be extremely powerful. Interpretation should be soaked in the dramatic and visual consciousness.

Then it will see here something far more valuable than that provided by the average ethical commentary. For the criticism or interpretation that is limited to Brutus' 'character' will praise, first, Brutus' kindness to his boy, and second, his courage when confronted by a supernatural apparition: and no more will, very likely, be said. If, however, we allow ourselves to be truly receptive to the imaginative impact, we shall note a happy artistic contrast. We shall see temporary peace, love (Brutus' for Lucius), music (love's voice—the usual Shakespearian association), healing and restorative: next, the sudden irruption of an 'evil' spirit, shattering that dream of love in one who has spurned all love for 'honour'. The contrast is vivid. Ethical criticism, regarding only Brutus' reaction to this or that event, and quite neglecting the quality of the events to which the poet subjects him, sees, indeed, certain aspects of his personality, but quite fails to find that essential poetic vision unlimited to any one 'character' or event, but rolling its fine frenzies from earth to heaven to explore the mysteries of reality, natural, human, or divine. And often that vision, when understood, forces us to reinterpret 'character' in a new light. Here it will force us to see a powerful 'evil' in Brutus who, to a purely and primarily ethical judgement, must assuredly appear immaculate. Ethical criticism judges a man by his intentions, in literature or life. Imaginative criticism judges rather by results, by the tree's fruits, not its roots. No Shakespearian protagonists have purer original intuitions than Brutus and Hamlet: both suffer inward division and disorder, and so pave hell with their actions.

If we grant that such a contrast as we find here in *Julius Caesar* is worth more than the minutiae of 'character', we immediately find a whole world of similar imaginative effects throughout Shakespeare unrolling profound significances. Nor will attention to such be disloyalty to Shakespeare as either poet or dramatist: we risk only disloyalty to pass commentary. For in the theatre we are surely concerned rather with imaginative effects than ethical problems. We see things as light or dark, happy or sad, peaceful or turbulent. To such simplicities we there respond intuitively. So, if we are to find an intellectual meaning for any play or scene, we should, as far as possible, keep as close as we can to the visual or aural imagination. In *Othello*, for example, music, always suggestive of unity and love, preludes the middle action where Iago instils his poison in Othello, the action where shortly 'chaos is come again' in the soul of married love. How often has this exquisite effect been observed and stressed? So, too, music accompanies love's distress in tragedy in Desdemona's and Ophelia's songs, and in *Julius Caesar*, as I have just noted, where it may be compared with the music which accompanies Caesar's happy glory in Act I. Music in *Lear* and *Timon* is similarly important. Interpretation, as I have said, must be soaked in the dramatic consciousness; and the more we attend to such elements, the more often we shall find ourselves directed instinctively to form groups of imaginative themes, poetical colourings, throughout the plays. The dramatic persons and their names change from play to play: but the life they live, the poetic air they breathe, the fate that strikes or the joy that crowns them, the symbols and symphonies of dramatic poetry, these are not so variable. They are Shakespearian. More, they are Shakespeare. Not without primary attention to such imaginations can we remain true to Shakespeare as poet or dramatist: certainly not true to him as both.

But there is, nevertheless, a 'good' and an 'evil' in the world of the imagination. This is not quite the ethical 'good'. The 'good' in this sense is rather, aurally, the musical as opposed to the tempestuous; or the 'light' as opposed to the 'dark' in visual suggestion. Certainly in Shakespeare this may be considered a fair approximation. Often the imaginative will roughly correspond to the ethical 'good': but the correspondence is rough. Macbeth's crime is clearly an extreme evil from whatsoever point of view we regard it; and the play's colourings are correspondingly dark. But the Ghost and Hamlet themes in *Hamlet* are also dark, although the protagonist and his father's spirit tend to enlist our ethical sympathies. And we must then be prepared to modify our ethical response till it is in tune with our imaginative vision. That does not mean that we must exclude ethical considerations. But we must use ethical phraseology in subjection to imaginative effects, as part of our interpretation of the imaginative whole. Not till then do the profounder levels of *Hamlet* reveal their content. 'Right' and 'wrong' baffle us, appear to change places. Which is as it should be. The good Ghost was in purgatory, suffering for his 'crimes'. It is, surely, remarkable that, although numerous books and essays have been devoted to Hamlet's 'character', comparatively little has been said, certainly hardly any exact analysis has been attempted, of the most powerful acts of imagination in the play: the ghost scenes. They have, it seems, not as yet been properly understood in all their deathly portent and unnatural horror: despite the fact that the poet emphasizes these elements to excess. Thus, to the imagination, there is much of 'evil' in the Ghost and Hamlet himself. We must see Hamlet as a dark force. True, we do not, in the theatre, feel inclined to blame him: but neither do we, in the theatre, blame Macbeth, or, if we do, our blame is far from the essence of our response. Our response is purely an intuitive perception of dramatic or poetic power containing elements of ethical knowledge, but never subject to the ethical judgement. Again, we may regard *Antony and Cleopatra*—a valuable antithesis to *Hamlet*. Cleopatra has been often exposed to ethical criticism. She has led a frankly immoral life, and set an example of licentiousness from the very throne of queenship. How may this be endured? And yet, what shall we say of Enobarbus' inspired description of her on Cydnus, and her own magnificent self-immolation at the end? Commentary has constantly been forced into the weakest expedients: such as the suggestion that love is not an easy theme for Shakespearian tragedy, as though Shakespeare blundered into the fifth act by mistake; or that Shakespeare shows a crude morality by so extravagant a sublimation of his heroine. Such commentaries result from an inability rightly to place the ethical judgement in an imaginative criticism. For the process is clear. We have abstracted from the play, that is from Cleopatra's words and acts and the words spoken of her by others, certain words stressing her immorality. These form, probably, about one-tenth— that is liberal—of the total poetic effect which we may call 'Cleopatra'. Having been spontaneously drawn to these ethical considerations, because they lend themselves to ethical interpretation, the commentator next proceeds to analyse the whole theme in their light—or, rather, fog. A true interpretation will, however, recognize that Cleopatra's final speech is the outstanding effect in the whole play: dramatically and poetically. If we must be guilty of bias, it would be safer to start with such poetic splendours and remain true to them at the risk of lesser infidelities. Yet there is no need for that. We can find our legitimate pieces of 'ethic' and fit them into our whole picture quite easily—but only if we allot them a secondary, not a primary, attention; if we remember to read the parts with reference to the whole, not the whole with reference to one, arbitrarily chosen, part. In the language of imaginative interpretation Cleopatra is wholly 'good': that is she, and her play, are aureoled in completeness, assertion, brightness, all things positive and happy. Hamlet, to the imagination, becomes 'evil', unhappy, negative, and dark. Such is our ethic of the imagination: it will often be found to bear remarkable correspondence to that of Christ.

The Cleopatra-Hamlet contrast is quite vital to our understanding of Shakespeare. It is not my purpose to destroy the conventional Hamlet, the courtly prince and gentle humourist of popular appreciation, without putting something of greater value in its place. True, we must not be blind to the beauties of *Hamlet*. But then all poetic tragedy draws equally on the wells of serene loveliness. *Macbeth* is beautiful, for therein we make contact with

the essences of reality. But yet I would stress this significant 'good' and 'evil' within the vision of poetry: the
'light' and the 'dark' of imaginative statement. And
herein we find, clearly, Hamlet to be dark, a death-force;
whereas Cleopatra is light, a life-force. Nor has the poet
himself failed to support his vision with those images
proper to its own nature, those images, I should say, of
which his vision is itself composed. In the *Hamlet*-world
there is ever an emphasis on death and disease, in *Antony
and Cleopatra* on forces of life and health. Such suggestive
images are important. Throughout Shakespeare there are
numerous major or minor effects correspondent to life-
themes, health-themes. I have already outlined the main
'values' of love and honour and those others to which they
are related. Next I shall note some of the more obvious
effects of imagery and suggestion which correspond to
these values. Here I shall confine my remarks mainly
to the greater tragedies from *Julius Caesar* and *Hamlet* to
Antony and Cleopatra.

'Sun', 'moon', and 'stars' are frequently used to suggest
an infinite splendour and universal justification. Usually,
they bear relevance to love, as in *Hamlet*, *Julius Caesar*,
Coriolanus, and *Antony and Cleopatra*. Sometimes they
relate to an idealized imperial power or kingship as with
Julius Caesar and Duncan, or, once, to warrior-prowess
in *Coriolanus* at IV. v. 115 (we might recall Hotspur's
honour-moon association). A kindred infinity-suggestion may be expressed by reference to great and
historic mountains: Olympus, Pelion, Ossa. Such are
found in *Hamlet*, *Julius Caesar*, *Othello*, and *Coriolanus*.
The infinity of any 'value' is continually expressed by
'ocean' metaphors, which usually contain powerful suggestion of purely personal emotion. Images from nature
abound and are very exactly used. Nature and animal
references are generally our readiest approaches towards
understanding of a play's dominant colour and note.
Nature is defiled in Hamlet's confession of melancholia—
'a pestilent congregation of vapours'; distorted in *Macbeth*;

variously grim and kindly in *Lear*; idealized in *Antony and Cleopatra*. Air-life or water-life may be used to suggest something strangely beautiful as in Ophelia's death and *Antony and Cleopatra*; and we might compare *Much Ado*, III. i, where images from life in both elements help to raise an especial lyric note harmonizing with human love. Air-life, again, may be presented with more evil meaning in *Macbeth*, where it yet suggests a spiritual ethereality which makes contact with *Antony and Cleopatra*. Nature's productiveness, the thought of procreation, contrasts with death and destruction in *Macbeth*, and is closely related to themes of human birth; is otherwise suggested once in *Coriolanus*, v. iii. 162–4, and fully glorified in *Antony and Cleopatra*. Flowers indicate natural sweetness, often accompanying love: as in *Hamlet* and the latter scenes of *Lear*, where they bear relevance to Ophelia and Cordelia respectively. We might compare *Twelfth Night*, I. i. 40–1. Conversely nature's harshness may be stressed, as in *Lear* and *Timon*, where it is nevertheless considered less cruel than human civilization. Earlier examples occur in *The Two Gentlemen of Verona* (v. iv. 1–6), and often in *As You Like It*. On the human plane we may further observe interesting variations played on the thought of 'feasting'. It is usually a positive life-force. It is aptly related to Claudius in *Hamlet*, is there smirched with evil suggestion, and incurs the protagonist's disgust. Similarly, it is twined close with Timon's bounty, and incurs the satire of Apemantus who confines his own feasting, like Timon later, to 'roots'. It may be misused by the dark forces. The Greeks in *Troilus and Cressida*, who here are nearer darkness than light, feast Hector, only to subject him to Achilles' repeated insults and feed the satire of Achilles' cynic remarks in soliloquy later. In the same way Iago and Lady Macbeth use drink to further their own purposes. But Iago understands the true nature of drink which he observes to be 'a good familiar creature if well used'. In *Macbeth* the feasting-idea is extremely powerful throughout, directly opposed by the dark forces. Conversely, it forms integral part to the life-vision of *Antony and Cleopatra*. Feasting is important for the Menenius-Coriolanus contrast, and in the scene where Coriolanus offers himself and his services to Aufidius. It is vivid and important throughout *Julius Caesar*. Miss Spurgeon has observed numerous metaphors of food frequent throughout *Troilus and Cressida*, and also notes the preponderance of disease-metaphors in *Hamlet* and *Coriolanus*. I have already elsewhere referred to disease-metaphors in *Macbeth*. In these plays, and throughout Shakespeare, they suggest often national sickness and are to be related to the 'order' concept. 'Disorder' and 'sickness' are mutually suggestive in Shakespeare: Timon imprecates both on mankind. Rich metals, gold, and jewels are scattered throughout the plays. The most usual association is that of love and jewels. The loved one is continually a 'jewel' in Shakespeare. In *Othello* once the whole world becomes a rich stone, 'a chrysolite', unworthy to buy love's treasure. Lovers give 'jewels' to each other. Love is the consummation of the soul's longing, the loved-one herself the 'soul' of the lover: hence the individual's soul may be 'mine eternal jewel' in *Macbeth*. Gold-symbolism is powerful in *Timon*. But greed for rich metals for their own mercenary sake is villainous. The gold of love and the gold of worldly riches may be either associated or contrasted. The 'jewel' thought may also be related to the magnificence and bounty of kingship, as with Claudius' 'union' or Duncan's 'diamond': and elsewhere the imperial theme of love is close to the imperial splendours of kingship. All these rich metals are thus highly electrified by the positive currents of Shakespearian value. Conversely rock, stones, iron constantly suggest hardness of heart: 'iron' is thus important throughout *Coriolanus*. 'Fire' is of vivid importance in *Julius Caesar* and *Antony and Cleopatra* and glimmers intermittently throughout *Macbeth*. It may, with reservation, be associated with the idea 'spirit'.

That is but a rough list, far from exhaustive. Such

effects may be observed and related to 'atmosphere', action, and dramatic persons. They may occur in images or may themselves be intrinsic to the action. We must be prepared to regard any play, or scene, as an interplay of 'values', pictorial images, or persons. Most usually, we find, and should analyse, a complex pattern of all. The Shakespearian play is a drama of action: but the contestants are imaginative, not purely personal, forces. Often they may be closely related to one or more persons, may act through persons: they are not always confined in and limited by them. The death-force in *Hamlet* is most closely related to Hamlet himself. But it is also related to Claudius' original crime: hence Claudius, in a time of remorse, knows he has a 'bosom black as death'. The Ghost overstands the drama, a portentous death. The evil in *Macbeth* envelops, but is not limited by, Macbeth himself. It acts through his wife, originates in the supernatural. Such imaginative forces built of 'values', all vitalized imagery, all suggestion of death and darkness or light and life, demand our closest attention. But such examination must ever be elastic, and our sensibility to the Shakespearian imagination must never crystallize into rigid codes. For example, music is a consistently applied dramatic effect, generally, nearly always, to be related to love or concord in some form or other. But Cassius, whose love is an important strand in *Julius Caesar*, 'hears no music'. Our interpretation will take this into account, but will not therefore be blind to his love. The final explanation will be simple enough. Cassius is a blending of envy, conspiracy, loneliness, and longing for love. At the beginning his envy, at the end his love, is predominant. His 'hearing no music', therefore, applies rather to his office as dramatic conspirator than to his eventual sublimation as lover. For, just as 'tempests' and other 'disorder' symbols are opposed to both social and individual 'order', so music, the exact opposite of 'tempests', accompanies those two realities. Hence music may be the 'food of love' in *Twelfth Night* (i. i. i), but 'the man that has no music in himself is fit for treasons, stratagems, and spoils' in *The Merchant of Venice* (v. i. 85). But, clearly, public sedition and personal love are not incompatible. I have already shown that personal intuitions and political 'order' often conflict. In fact, that is the most profound dramatic conflict in Shakespeare, except for the 'tempest'-'music' opposition itself, which is ultimate. Hence 'music' may as justly be opposed to the one Cassius as it might be—actually it is not—associated with the other. At the start he is unmusical: but he might possibly have enjoyed music later.

'Music' and 'tempests' are of all our most important symbols. Their interplay is the axis of the Shakespearian world. Style of verse, types of play, imaginative themes, 'character', veins of imagery—all pass in turn, alternating, changing, blending, as the great planet swings over: but all revolve on the 'tempest'-'music' opposition. Those two correspond to the most fundamental of ideas necessary to natural, human, or divine realities: conflict and concord; evil and love; death and life. And though these may form difficult combinations, such as the frequent apparent incompatibility between a personal love and the state's order, which vitalizes many plays and especially *Antony and Cleopatra*, yet 'tempests' and 'music' themselves are changeless metaphysical realities, however Protean and kaleidoscopic the human forms they take. And not only Shakespeare, but all tragic literature, all poetry, has its tempests of division, its unity of poetry's music. A line of poetry delights by its resolution of divided and conflicting words and concepts in the single music of harmonious utterance. So, too, in poetic tragedy. The ultimate dualisms of joy and grief, good and evil, life and death, are unified within the harmonies of the tragic intuition. We watch the process in Shakespeare's greater plays, where 'tempests' and 'music' are nearly always explicitly actualized. Two truths are told, and given tragic resolution in the sombre plays, as happy prologues to the imperial theme of *Antony and Cleopatra* where tragedy itself is transcended, and the final unity built of duality takes crystal and exact form before our eyes. In that vision, tempests are stilled, and music alone directs and tunes our understanding. But usually 'tempests' and 'music' are firmly juxtaposed or finely blended. They take different forms, are clothed in different plots, themselves ultimate. Through them we see into the heart and essence of Shakespeare's work.

I conclude with some remarks on the order of the plays treated in the following essays. I print my essays in an order corresponding to the plays' probable order of composition, with the reservation that *Coriolanus* may have succeeded *Antony and Cleopatra*. Two of the 'sombre' plays appear again, analysed mainly in respect of life-themes, and may be taken here to suggest the whole group. But, since the three Roman plays are close together in many important qualities, we may ask why *Julius Caesar* should be so far and so significantly separated from the other two. The Roman plays cannot be called 'sombre'. Negations are not powerful therein. *Julius Caesar* witnesses a poetic attitude of keen and delighted vision. In this play, says Mr. Masefield,[1] Shakespeare 'saw life startlingly'. The phrase is exquisitely apt. *Julius Caesar* presents a complex and startling vision of human life, containing many favourite themes—imperial power, honour, love. It is presented, it is true, partly on the *Macbeth*-pattern and with a corresponding 'evil' to be related to Brutus, but the whole is so alight with erotic perception that the vision remains optimistic, vivid, startling. Towards the close there is, in the sublimation of Cassius, a forecast of the life-in-death victory of *Antony and Cleopatra*. In its optimistic vision it thus contrives to forecast the opposite poles of Shakespeare's tragic intuition, together with all the Shakespearian 'values'. It has four protagonists. No play of Shakespeare is so

[1] In 'Shakespeare and Spiritual Life', The Romanes Lecture, 1924. I would acknowledge a general debt to Mr. Masefield's suggestive lecture in my work on *Julius Caesar*, and elsewhere.

crammed with 'themes'. Why did *Hamlet* and the sombre plays follow—if they did follow—*Julius Caesar*? This may be a question to leave unanswered. Or we may say, with Mr. Masefield, that *Hamlet* is 'a questioning of vision'. A questioning of this startling, complex, and happy vision given poetic form in *Julius Caesar*. That may apply, roughly, to the whole group. And *Antony and Cleopatra* could scarcely have been written without the long succession of distressful plays from *Hamlet* to *Timon*. The poet, perhaps, only attains the heights at the cost of sounding the depths. In my previous volume we were concerned mainly with those deeps of lonely suffering: here our employment is more joyful, and leads us directly to the Everest of Shakespearian drama, *Antony and Cleopatra*.

Additional Note, 1965: My phrase on Cleopatra as 'wholly good' on p. 24 should be read strictly in terms of my commentary on pp. 309–10 and 316–18 below.

In his comments on *Julius Caesar* Mr. Masefield (p. 30, note, above) was perhaps the first to offer an *interpretative* approach to Shakespeare's tragic symbolism.

II

THE TORCH OF LIFE:
AN ESSAY ON JULIUS CAESAR

THE style of *Julius Caesar* is extraordinarily simple and naïve. It lacks the metaphoric richness which so often gives power and complexity to Shakespeare's poetry, and seldom touches the deep solemnities we meet in *Timon*. Here is an example:

> He had a fever when he was in Spain;
> And when the fit was on him I did mark
> How he did shake . . . (i. ii. 119)

Again,

> If we do lose this battle, then is this
> The very last time we shall speak together . .
> (v. i. 98)

That is usual, not exceptional, here. We miss the packed and blazing associative language of *Henry V*: the vital image wrenched from its habitual usage to do exact metaphoric service in bringing the abstract and spiritual essence in moving splendour before our eyes, metaphors turned out

> In the quick forge and working-house of thought.
> (*Henry V*, v, Cho. 23)

But deep notes are yet within the compass of this simplicity:

> You are my true and honourable wife;
> As dear to me as are the ruddy drops
> That visit my sad heart. (ii. i. 288)

And,

> O that a man might know
> The end of this day's business ere it come!
> But it sufficeth that the day will end,
> And then the end is known. (v. i. 123)

Yet, though simple in point of metaphor, the play is far

from simple in other kinds of imaginative colour. The imagery of idea, simile, description, and incident presents a complex pattern of interthreading, dividing, and blending colours. The whole imaginative vision is extremely rich, ablaze with a vitality not found in previous plays. I will notice first two main elements: animal-suggestion and metals.

We have a fine menagerie of beasts. They are mostly picturesque and, if not, often presented with a vivid and visual sense-perception that all but makes them so. There are many dog references, such as letting 'slip the dogs of war' (III. i. 273), 'base spaniel fawning' (III. i. 43), the dog 'baying the moon' (IV. iii. 27), Casca 'like a cur' stabbing Caesar from behind (V. i. 43), Caesar spurning a suitor 'like a cur' (III. i. 46). Besides these horses are vividly mentioned and compared in point of fiery vitality and spirit with human beings by both Brutus and Antony (IV. ii. 23–7; IV. i. 29–36). Horses, so often idealized in Shakespeare, contribute powerfully, as in *Macbeth*, to the ominous disorder-symbols (II. ii. 23). Caesar and danger are like 'two lions litter'd in one day' (II. ii. 46). We hear of a lion that 'glared' and 'went surly by' (I. iii. 20–21); 'a lioness', says Calpurnia, 'hath whelped in the streets' (II. ii. 17). Cassius compares Caesar to a 'lion' (I. iii. 106). Two eagles perch on Cassius' ensign and fly away, giving place to ravens, crows, and kites (V. i. 81–7). The bird of night sits 'hooting and shrieking in the market-place' (I. iii. 26–8). Says Antony over Caesar's body:

> How like a deer, strucken by many princes,
> Dost thou here lie!   (III. i. 209)

He is a 'hart' (III. i. 207). The conspirators showed their teeth 'like apes' and fawned 'like hounds' (V. i. 41). There is elsewhere direct reference to the lamb, ass, unicorn, bear, elephant, hind, wolf, sheep, lamb, adder, Hybla bees; and, moreover, suggestion of others: 'ferret and fiery eyes' (I. ii. 186), 'waspish' temper (IV. iii. 50) and the falcon (I. i. 77–8). Now this list is dominated by a single quality:

vivid and picturesque perception. Often the comparison
with men is important. Throughout we shall observe a
peculiar sensitiveness to human appearance and human
'spirit': a vivid apprehension of human life. This apprehension extends to the animals, often, as in some of the
above examples, both animal and man deriving a heightened
and startling visual reality by a skilful comparison. The
play, as a whole, works within the limits of our animal-list:
it is startling, picturesque, vivid.

The flash of metals illumines the action. Sometimes
they are heavy, dull: the conspirators' swords have 'leaden
points' to Antony (III. i. 173), sleep lays his 'leaden mace'
on Lucius (IV. iii. 268). More often they are vivid,
spiritualized things. Swift anger is carried 'as a flint bears
fire' (IV. iii. 111). Thus fiery spirit is associated with a 'flint'
and 'fire'. The spirit-metal association occurs again in:

> Nor stony tower, nor walls of beaten brass,
> Nor airless dungeon, nor strong links of iron,
> Can be retentive to the strength of spirit.   (I. iii. 93)

For spirit is stronger, keener, than the metal it employs—
'I know where I will wear this dagger then' (I. iii. 89).
Terrible news is like steel: Cassius' death to Brutus will be
as 'piercing steel and darts envenomed' (V. iii. 76). A
lover's heart is gold:

> There is my dagger,
> And here my naked breast; within, a heart
> Dearer than Plutus' mine, richer than gold:
> If that thou be'st a Roman, take it forth;
> I, that denied thee gold, will give my heart.
>
> (IV. iii. 100)

As so often in Shakespeare, heart's-gold is compared with
gold metal. Again, we have a dagger here. Daggers,
metals, gold, are scattered throughout. Spirited action uses
swords or daggers for its purpose. There are the daggers
that murder Caesar, and Brutus has the same dagger for
himself when his country needs his death (III. ii. 52).
They are vivid, alive things. 'Here, as I point my sword,
the sun arises' (II. i. 106). 'Here, take thou the hilts', says

Cassius to Pindarus at the moment of his death (v. iii. 43), and

> Caesar, thou art reveng'd,
> Even with the sword that kill'd thee.   (v. iii. 45)

'I held the sword' says Strato of Brutus' death, 'and he did run on it' (v. v. 65). These are a few instances: but swords and daggers are important throughout, dramatically and imaginatively. The use of them is vivid, spirited. And there are other rich metals, 'coronets' (i. ii. 239), 'a kingly crown' (iii. ii. 101). Brutus talks of coining his 'heart' and selling his 'blood for drachmas' (iv. iii. 72–3). Again a heart-gold association, as in *Timon*. I return to it later. We hear of an ass bearing gold (iv. i. 21). Brutus' countenance will be as 'richest alchemy' to glorify the murder of Caesar (i. iii. 159). This assortment of metallic suggestion points us to two ideas: (1) spirited action—'daggers', and (2) the gold of man's heart. Throughout we shall observe a certain positive life-force firing the play's action. The keen metal of spirited purpose and the deep gold of love—vivid in the 'drachmas' left to Roman citizens in Caesar's will—blend, contrast, and support each other in this world of spirit, fire, and love.

Those words I intend to justify. The vision throughout is both 'sensuous' and 'spiritual'. 'Sensuous' I use to indicate a vivid apprehension of physical detail, especially in man's facial appearance; 'spiritual' to suggest a dynamic energy in man, a fiery blood and fiery vitality which enrich the action from start to finish. Although many elements of gloom, death, sickness, and sleeplessness occur, yet our whole vision is rather a life-vision and a love-vision than one of negation: there is no cloud of cynicism over the action.

There is continual reference to very ordinary things which would not normally be expected to take part in high tragedy. These are natural enough in a Roman play: Caesar's parks and walks, city walls, battlements, towers, windows, chimney-tops, chariots, statues, pulpits, porches, robes, parchment. But it is more surprising to find napkins, tapers, wax, clocks, kerchiefs, hats, Caesar's 'closet', his nightgown, Brutus' 'closet', Caesar's gown—very vividly described—Brutus' gown, the leaf of Brutus' book turned down where he left off reading (IV. iii. 273), 'nightcaps' (I. ii. 248), Brutus' 'wholesome bed' (II. i. 264). Yet such are integral to the poetic statement here. In this play of fine action, where world-issues so tremendous are being decided, we yet face a vision which notices these details. There is a warm, sympathetic, and emotional apprehension of such things, articles themselves warm with the touch of human personality. So sympathetic a human realism thus inter-penetrates our theme. This sympathy is still more rich in human detail. References to personal appearance are everywhere. The countenance, in joy or grief or excite-ment, is frequently observed. Brutus has 'veil'd his look' to Cassius and turns 'the trouble of his countenance' only upon himself (I. ii. 37-9); he will construe to Portia 'all the charactery' of his 'sad brows' (II. i. 308). The con-spirators come to Brutus with 'half their faces buried in their cloaks' (II. i. 74). Upon which Brutus soliloquizes:

O conspiracy,
Sham'st thou to show thy dangerous brow by night,
When evils are most free? (II. i. 77)

Therefore they must hide treachery's 'monstrous visage' in 'smiles and affability' (II. i. 81-2). He tells them to 'look fresh and merrily' (II. i. 224). Fear is vividly described: 'a hundred ghastly women transformed with their fear' (I. iii. 23). So, too, Cassius tells Casca:

You look pale, and gaze,
And put on fear, and cast yourself in wonder.
(I. iii. 59)

Dangers will vanish when they see Caesar's 'face' (II. ii. 12). Here is a vivid, visual touch:

Cassius, be constant;
Popilius Lena speaks not of our purposes,
For, look, he smiles, and Caesar doth not change.
(III. i. 22)

Romans came 'smiling' in Calpurnia's dream to bathe

their hands in Caesar's blood (II. ii. 79); mothers, says
Antony, will but 'smile' to see their children slaughtered
(III. i. 267). Before the murder the conspirators showed
their teeth 'like apes' (v. i. 41). Again,

> If we do meet again, why, we shall smile.   (v. i. 118)

Brutus tells Strato to 'turn away' his 'face' as Brutus runs
on his sword (v. v. 47). Cassius tells Pindarus to strike
'when my face is covered, as 'tis now' (v. iii. 44); so, too,
Caesar fell 'in his mantle muffling up his face' (III. ii. 191).
Cassius has 'a lean and hungry look' (I. ii. 194):

> Seldom he smiles, and smiles in such a sort
> As if he mock'd himself and scorn'd his spirit
> That could be moved to smile at any thing.   (I. ii. 205)

Here is a striking piece of such pictorial writing:

> But, look you, Cassius,
> The angry spot doth glow on Caesar's brow,
> And all the rest look like a chidden train:
> Calpurnia's cheek is pale; and Cicero
> Looks with such ferret and such fiery eyes
> As we have seen him in the Capitol,
> Being cross'd in conference by some senators.
> (I. ii. 182)

'Eyes' are, indeed, especially frequent. There is Brutus'
and Cassius' conversation on 'eyes' (I. ii. 51–8). 'Why
stare you so?' asks Cicero of Casca (I. iii. 2). 'Set honour
in one eye, and death i' the other' and Brutus will regard
them indifferently (I. ii. 86). Caesar's 'eye' lost 'its lustre'
during his fever (I. ii. 124); the lion in the Capitol 'glared'
on Casca (I. iii. 21); Brutus asks Lucius if he can hold up
'his heavy eyes awhile' to play music (IV. iii. 256). 'Eyes'
are vivid:

> Shall I be frighted when a madman stares?   (IV. iii. 40)

Brutus would not wrangle before the 'eyes' of the army
(IV. ii. 43). Seeing the ghost, he cries:

> I think it is the weakness of mine eyes
> That shapes this monstrous apparition.   (IV. iii. 276)

Nor are 'eyes' the only physical details so vividly observed.
Parts of the body are frequently mentioned. Cassius
recognizes Casca by his 'voice':—'your ear is good', says
Casca (I. iii. 41–2). Later, he knows Cinna by 'his gait'
(I. iii. 132). The conspirators' hats are 'plucked about their
ears' (II. i. 73). Says Caesar:

> Come on my right hand, for this ear is deaf. (I. ii. 213)

There is mention of Ligarius' ear (II. i. 319). Casca stabs
Caesar 'on the neck' (V. i. 44): he is the first to 'rear' his
'hand' (III. i. 30). The citizens, if they realized his love,
would 'beg a hair of him for memory' (III. ii. 139). The
conspirators kissed 'Caesar's feet' before stabbing him (V.
i. 42). Cassius' faults are cast into his 'teeth' (IV. iii. 99).
'I kiss thy hand' says Brutus (III. i. 52); and Cassius: 'As
low as to thy foot doth Cassius fall' (III. i. 56). We hear of
the Senators as 'greybeards' (II. ii. 67), of Cicero's 'silver
hairs' (II. i. 144), Caesar's wounds are 'dumb mouths' with
'ruby lips' (III. i. 260), and when Caesar was ill 'his lips did
from their colour fly', his 'tongue' cried for drink (I. ii. 122).
'Tongue' is frequent (II.i.313; II.iv.7; III.i.261; III.ii.232;
v. i. 46; v. v. 39). Caesar was loath to lay his 'fingers' off the
crown (I. ii. 243), the citizens 'clapped their chopped hands'
and uttered such 'stinking breath' that Ceasar fell down, and
Casca dared not laugh for fear of opening his 'lips' and
receiving the 'bad air' (I. ii. 245–53). Caesar 'plucked me
ope his doublet and offered them his throat to cut' (I.ii. 267).
Cassius cries:

> There is my dagger,
> And here my naked breast.   (IV. iii. 100)

Brutus talks of 'this breast of mine' (I. i. 49), and
Cassius bares his 'bosom' to the 'thunderstone' when the
lightning opens 'the breast of heaven' (I. iii. 49–51). It is
time to close our list which is not exhaustive. But these are
important touches. They witness a certain intimacy in
the poet's treatment of his persons, an intimacy reflected
in the reader, so that we experience a vivid awareness of
these persons' bodies and appearances, a certain emotional

sympathy with them as physical beings. We regard them as one we love, whose 'eyes', 'hands', 'feet', are important, spiritualized, dynamic to our senses.

Besides actual body-references there are many thoughts of body-nourishment, the life-forces of eating, drinking, sleeping. The play opens at 'The Feast of Lupercal'. Caesar, in his fever, called 'Give me some drink, Titinius' (I. ii. 127), and Cassius gives as reason for his equality with Caesar that they both 'have fed as well' (I. ii. 98):

> Upon what meat doth this our Caesar feed,
> That he is grown so great? (I. ii. 149)

Cassius asks Casca to a meal:

> *Cassius.* Will you sup with me to-night, Casca?
> *Casca.* No, I am promised forth.
> *Cassius.* Will you dine with me to-morrow?
> *Casca.* Ay, if I be alive, and your mind hold, and your dinner
> worth the eating. (I. ii. 292)

Referring to this blunt wit of Casca's, Cassius says:

> This rudeness is a sauce to his good wit,
> Which gives men stomach to digest his words
> With better appetite. (I. ii. 304)

Brutus' melancholy will not let him eat, talk, or sleep (II. i. 252). Portia is only wanted to keep with him 'at meals' and comfort his bed (II. i. 284). Caesar is to be carved as a 'dish fit for the gods' not 'as a carcass fit for hounds' (II. i. 173-4). The conspirators are invited to 'taste some wine' with Caesar before they go to the Capitol 'like friends' (II. ii. 126-7). Hence Brutus' act, like Macbeth's, is a desecration of hospitality, conviviality: an evil opposed to a life-force. Cinna the poet dreamed that he feasted with Caesar (III. iii. 1), Cassius is told to 'digest' the venom of his spleen (IV. iii. 47), Brutus and Cassius celebrate their new-cemented friendship with a bowl of wine (IV. iii. 158): an association again suggesting the usual Shakespearian connexion between the sacrament of feasting or drinking and love. Eagles perched on Cassius' standards 'gorging and feeding from our soldiers' hands' (V. i. 82). Now these 'feeding' references are not peculiar to this vision: they recur with equal force in *Antony and Cleopatra* and *Macbeth*, where in the one they are triumphant life-forces, in the other desecrated by evil. Yet, since this play contains the beginnings of both those, these elements are to be observed. They suggest health, happiness, love—they are positive life-forces: either they accompany and blend with love (as the bowl of wine) or they are sharply contrasted with some evil, enemy to life, as in Brutus' mental unrest which will not let him 'eat', or the desecration of Caesar's hospitality. Here, too, they harmonize with the peculiar domestic and intimate note I have already observed. Portia complains how Brutus arose 'yesternight at supper' to muse and sigh distractedly. 'Ungently', he has stole from her bed (II. i. 237–8). And sleeping, sweet restorative to anguish, is recurrently suggested here: Brutus' anguish, like Macbeth's, is one bound with sleeplessness. At the centre of the play the impending evil wakes families, units of peaceful life, from their beds. So Portia and Brutus, Calpurnia and Caesar, the latter in his 'night-gown', rise unrestfully, disturbed by unruly thoughts or fears. This element I have noticed in detail elsewhere. Thus we have not only a powerful apprehension of the human body, but also recurrent suggestion of that which nourishes and refreshes the body. The disorder forces are seen to oppose these forces of life. There is also frequent suggestion of the opposites: disease, infirmity, weakness.

In this matter *Julius Caesar* is pre-eminent. Nearly every one in the play is ill. Calpurnia is 'barren'. Cassius bases his arguments against Caesar mainly on points of physique. He tells how he and Caesar tested their swimming powers in the Tiber, 'stemming it' with 'lusty sinews' (I. ii. 107–8); but Cassius eventually had to save the 'tired Caesar' from sinking. Then he vividly describes Caesar's 'fever' that made him 'shake', observing its effect on his 'lips', 'eye', 'tongue', and 'voice' (I. ii. 119–31). Why should a man of such 'feeble temper' sway the 'majestic' world? Caesar swounds, he has 'the falling sickness' (I. ii.

257). He is deaf, too (I. ii. 2 1 3). Calpurnia wants to tell the
Senate that Caesar is 'sick' (II. ii. 65). At first he will not
agree, but finally gives way—'Mark Antony shall say I
am not well' (II. ii. 55). Cinna the poet suffers from
nervous apprehension (III. iii. 2). Calpurnia cries out in her
sleep (II. ii. 2) and is, like Portia, at the point of break-
down. 'O I grow faint' cries Portia (II. iv. 43). Hearing of
Portia's death, 'Upon what sickness?' asks Cassius (IV. iii.
152). Brutus pretends to be physically ill to hide his
mental anxiety:

> Is Brutus sick, and is it physical
> To walk unbraced and suck up the humours
> Of the dank morning? What, is Brutus sick,
> And will he steal out of his wholesome bed
> To dare the vile contagion of the night,
> And tempt the rheumy and unpurged air
> To add unto his sickness? (II. i. 261)

Later, Portia tells how he 'went sickly forth' (II. iv. 14).
Primarily it is his soul, his 'state of man' that is ill; but
this, as with Macbeth, includes his body. Ligarius comes,
broken by fever and ague:

> By all the gods that Romans bow before
> I here discard my sickness! (II. i. 320)

To be weak or thin meets observation and often reproach.
Cassius blames Caesar for his physique. So also Caesar
blames Cassius:

> Let me have men about me that are fat,
> Sleek-headed men and such as sleep o' nights.
> Yond Cassius has a lean and hungry look;
> He thinks too much. Such men are dangerous.
> (I. ii. 192)

Physical weakness is here twined with the recurrent idea
of sleeplessness. But Lucius is always sleepy, in Act II
and Act IV. Lepidus is 'a slight unmeritable man' (IV. i. 12),
and, 'Away, slight man' (IV. iii. 37) cries Brutus in anger to
Cassius. Cassius is short-sighted—'my sight was ever
thick' (V. iii. 21). Often, then, we observe these enemies

to physical fitness: 'Caesar was ne'er so much your enemy as that same ague which hath made you lean' (II. ii. 112). Which sickness in our persons is more than once related to the wider sickness, or supposed sickness, of the state (I. ii. 259–60; II. i. 327). All the chief persons but Antony are physically or mentally unwell. Antony alone gives any suggestion of robustness. But even he 'revels long o' nights' and so sleeps late (II. ii. 116). Yet all the persons convey an impression of fiery strength and ardour. The spirit is fiery, the body is weak: which contrast is vivid in Cassius' arguments against Caesar, whose power bears no proportion to his physique, in Caesar's words on Cassius, and Ligarius' access of spiritual strength conquering his physical weakness. We often find an important body-spirit contrast. The association of 'body' and 'spirit' occurs powerfully in Brutus' speech on swearing:

> Swear priests and cowards and men cautelous,
> Old feeble carrion . . .   (II. i. 129)

Such, he says, are to be contrasted with the 'spirit' of the conspirators. The body-spirit thought is fundamental, whether in association or contrast.[1] I return to it later. For the present, I emphasize only the recurrent suggestion of physical appearance, the 'feeding' references, the many illnesses. We have a vivid apprehension of physical life, viewed with a strange intimacy and emotional sympathy; which sympathy is usually noticeable between the persons themselves. Emotion, too, is an important strand:

---

[1] Throughout Shakespeare there is a strong suggestion of a body-soul dualism in association especially with destructive acts, such as murder, or with deception, whereby the outward appearance conflicts with the inner fact. Often the 'body' is imaged as a building for the indwelling 'life', 'soul', or 'spirit'; often, too, the 'body' may be compared with 'city-walls'. See *Romeo and Juliet*, III. ii. 73–85; III. iii. 106–8; *Cymbeline*, III. iv. 70; *King John*, III. iii. 20–1; *Macbeth*, II. iii. 72–4; III. iv. 105. But they are numerous everywhere. And, as usual in Shakespeare, the metaphoric image may be expanded into the plan of a whole play. There is never a rigid distinction between Shakespeare's matter and manner. (I have dealt further with this body-soul dualism in 'The Shakespearian Metaphysic', *The Wheel of Fire*.)

especially 'weeping'. These spirited Romans are not only physically weak: they are excessively given to tears.

'Weeping' is indeed a valuable part of our emotional texture. Flavius orders the citizens to

> Weep your tears
> Into the channel, till the lowest stream
> Do kiss the most exalted shores of all.   (I. i. 63)

Octavius' servant sees Caesar's body, and his eyes fill with tears:

> Thy heart is big, get thee apart and weep.
> Passion, I see, is catching; for mine eyes,
> Seeing those beads of sorrow stand in thine
> Began to water.   (III. i. 281)

Antony is proud of his tears:

> Had I as many eyes as thou hast wounds,
> Weeping as fast as they stream forth thy blood,
> It would become me better than to close
> In terms of friendship with thine enemies.   (III. i. 200)

Every one here is proud of such emotion. It is base to be hard of 'heart':

> You blocks, you stones, you worse than senseless things!
> O you hard hearts, you cruel men of Rome . . .
>   (I. i. 40)

Caesar was soft-hearted: 'When that the poor have cried, Caesar hath wept' (III. ii. 96). In his oration Brutus emphasizes his own emotion:

> As Caesar loved me, I weep for him . . . There is tears
> for his love . . .   (III. ii. 27–31)

So, too, Antony sheds tears during his oration, and has to stop his speech—'Poor soul, his eyes are red as fire with weeping' (III. ii. 120). He has to pause till his 'heart' come back to him from Caesar's coffin (III. ii. 111). 'If you have tears, prepare to shed them now' (III. ii. 173). Then the citizens weep too:

> O, now you weep, and I perceive, you feel
> The dint of pity: these are gracious drops. (III. ii. 197)

Softness of 'heart' is always a virtue in this play of emotions, especially love. 'O I could weep', says Cassius, 'my spirit from mine eyes' (iv. iii. 99). Brutus owes 'more tears' to the dead Cassius than those present shall see him 'pay' (v. iii. 101). At the last Brutus ends his long pilgrimage of honour in tears:

> Now is that noble vessel full of grief,
> That it runs over even at his eyes.　　(v. v. 13)

So rich is this play in emotion. It is suffused by a soft sympathy, an interflow of gentle love, sympathetic sorrow. It is well to observe how, in these 'weeping' passages, the emotion is associated with the words 'heart', 'spirit', 'fire', 'passion': all are important.

And so we have a play vividly and pictorially alive in point of bodily visualization, physical sympathy, and 'feasting'—a theme ever, as in *Timon*, *Antony and Cleopatra*, and Menenius (in *Coriolanus*), to be associated with generous love, life, and warmth of heart. The whole is suffused with a soft emotionalism. We might note the two curious 'school' references at i. ii. 300 and v. v. 26, the latter expressly sentimental. The emotional sympathy between person and person, just as the visual exactitude of their descriptions of each other and their attention to bodily facts and frailties generally, witness an especially erotic atmosphere—quite divorced from 'sex'—which, though not a readily observed surface-theme, is yet fundamental to our understanding. Life is here our theme. Life vivid, yet ailing, and yet again fiery and spirited, and yet again gentle, emotional. The vision is similar to the experience of love which looks through the physical and makes contact with the spirit. Thus we find many 'lovers' in the play. Even Brutus, who fights for 'honour' against love, shows love for Lucius, whom, as the tragic sequel of his choice tracks him down, he asks to play his instrument 'a strain or two'. 'Love' is everywhere important. Our vision has wider significances than those of physique: it sees through the body to the spirit. Our 'weeping' passages suggested the words

'heart', 'spirit', 'fire': to those I now pass, and to the theme
of the body (Caesar's, and, in a wider sense, Rome's) broken,
gashed, loosing streams of rich life-blood, fountains of life's
elixir. 'Blood', too, is here lovingly, almost erotically described: 'blood', and the 'heart' whose life it feeds, this
blending with 'passion' and 'emotion'.

There is an almost brutal enjoyment evident in our
imagery of slaughter, wounds, and blood: yet is it so flamed
with imagination's joy that there is no sense of disgust.
Consider the speech where Brutus advises against the more
'bloody' course of assassinating Antony—as though 'to
cut the head off and then hack the limbs'. Caesar must be
'dismember'd', must 'bleed': yet Brutus would 'carve him
as a dish' for the gods, not 'hew him as a carcass' for hounds.
He concludes that Antony

> can do no more than Caesar's arm
> When Caesar's head is off.   (II. i. 162–83)

Notice the 'blood'-thought, and the bold imagery of 'head',
'arm', 'limbs', 'dismember', 'hack', 'carve', 'hew'. It is
a remarkable speech. There is a vivid awareness of the act
in its physical appearance, sight of the broken, cut, bleeding
human frame. And yet much of it is almost unnecessary:
Caesar is not going to be carved into pieces, but stabbed.
But the centre act of the play is certainly a spilling of blood,
very vividly apprehended. Calpurnia has a dream wherein
she sees Caesar's statue

> Which, like a fountain with an hundred spouts,
> Did run pure blood; and many lusty Romans
> Came smiling, and did bathe their hands in it.
>   (II. ii. 77)

Decius interprets it:

> Your statue spouting blood in many pipes,
> In which so many smiling Romans bath'd,
> Signifies that from you great Rome shall suck
> Reviving blood, and that great men shall press
> For tinctures, stains, relics, and cognizance.   (II. ii. 85)

Blood is here finely expressed as a life-force. So the

shedding of it is, as it were, the spilling out of life. 'Life' and 'blood' may almost be equated. Hence the importance attached to 'blood' here. So Caesar is murdered, and falls at the base of Pompey's statue 'which all the while ran blood' (III. ii. 193). Then Brutus fulfils the dream-prophecy:

> Stoop, Romans, stoop,
> And let us bathe our hands in Caesar's blood
> Up to the elbows, and besmear our swords:
> Then walk we forth, even to the market-place,
> And, waving our red weapons o'er our heads,
> Let 's all cry, 'Peace, freedom, and liberty!'
>
> (III. i. 105)

Such is the 'lofty scene' (III. i. 112) of Caesar's death:

> How many times shall Caesar bleed in sport,
> That now on Pompey's basis lies along,
> No worthier than the dust!   (III. i. 114)

This imagery is lurid, startling, vivid—but not exactly gruesome, as in *Macbeth*. The most horrible effects are carried lightly. Antony greets the conspirators:

> I know not, gentlemen, what you intend,
> Who else must be let blood, who else is rank:
> If I myself, there is no hour so fit
> As Caesar's death's hour, nor no instrument
> Of half that worth as those your swords, made rich
> With the most noble blood of all this world.
> I do beseech ye, if you bear me hard,
> Now, whilst your purpled hands do reek and smoke,
> Fulfil your pleasure.   (III. i. 151)

'Rich', 'noble', 'purpled'. Brutus replies that though appearances show them 'bloody and cruel', yet Antony sees only their 'hands' and this 'bleeding business': but their 'hearts' are 'pitiful'. Then Antony asks that each render him his 'bloody' hand: but is moved to address Caesar's corpse:

> Had I as many eyes as thou hast wounds,
> Weeping as fast as they stream forth thy blood,
> It would become me better than to close
> In terms of friendship with thine enemies.   (III. i. 200)

—enemies 'sign'd in thy spoil and crimson'd in thy lethe'
(iii. i. 206). When the conspirators leave him alone with
the dead Caesar, he again expresses his grief in violent
blood-imagery:

> O pardon me, thou bleeding piece of earth,
> That I am meek and gentle with these butchers;
> Thou art the ruins of the noblest man
> That ever lived in the tide of times.
> Woe to the hand that shed this costly blood!
> Over thy wounds now do I prophesy,—
> Which, like dumb mouths, do ope their ruby lips,
> To beg the voice and utterance of my tongue—
> A curse shall light upon the limbs of men . . .   (iii. i. 254)

Civil war will rage in Italy, mothers but smile to see their
children 'quarter'd with the hands of war' (iii. i. 268);
which image of 'child' desecration is a normal Shakespearian image of essential life destruction, disorder, evil.
The impact of these speeches impresses on us one thing:
the 'costliness' of Caesar's blood. It is, as it were, a life-
stream of infinite value: hence the association of Caesar
with Olympus (iii. i. 74), the north star (iii. i. 60), and
music (i. ii. 16). It is thus recognized alike by Antony and
the conspirators who bathe in it as in a stream of life,
emblematic of fortune. Notice, too, the 'dumb mouths'
and 'ruby lips' of Caesar's wounds, the rich, almost joyous
visualization of physical detail: even the maimed and bleeding body is pictured with almost erotic perception. The
same exact attention recurs in Antony's description of
Caesar's 'mantle' in his oration. The mantle itself is endued
with a kind of personality, and each rent is noticed in turn:

> Through this the well-beloved Brutus stabb'd;
> And, as he pluck'd his cursed steel away,
> Mark how the blood of Caesar follow'd it . . .
>
>   (iii. ii. 180)

Again,

> I tell you that which you yourselves do know;
> Show you sweet Caesar's wounds, poor poor dumb mouths,
> And bid them speak for me . . .   (iii. ii. 228)

He would, if he had Brutus' eloquence, 'put a tongue in every wound of Caesar'. So strong the spirit of love works in our imagery here: it idealizes mantles, wounds, blood.

> Kind souls, what, weep you when you but behold
> Our Caesar's vesture wounded? Look you here,
> Here is himself, marr'd, as you see, with traitors.
>
> (III. ii. 199)

If the commons heard Caesar's will,

> they would go and kiss dead Caesar's wounds,
> And dip their napkins in his sacred blood,
> Yea, beg a hair of him for memory,

and bequeath it as 'a rich legacy' to their heirs (III. ii. 137). 'Sacred', 'rich', and the idea of 'kissing'. Something of exceeding richness and worth is desecrated in Caesar's assassination: a vital force, a stream of life, outflows at his death. And through all this imagery we notice a certain continuance of erotic perception, one with the details of bodily description and gentle emotionalism already observed. It is all visual, vivid. The actual stabbing of Caesar, the central act of the play, is vivid:

> Witness the hole you made in Caesar's heart... (v. i. 31)

Cassius talks of the sword 'that ran through Caesar's bowels'—it is to 'search this bosom' (v. iii. 42). Brutus, finding Cassius dead, says it is Caesar's spirit which 'turns our swords in our own proper entrails' (v. iii. 95). Stabbing is ever an important theme. Portia gives herself 'a voluntary wound, here in my side' (II. i. 300). 'If Caesar had stabbed their mothers', says Casca of the Citizens, they would have cheered him no less readily (I. ii. 276).

Caesar impresses one here as a weak, ailing, small man: yet his life-blood drenches the play. Herein is a strong contrast. Often, indeed, we are pointed to a body-spirit contrast. 'In the spirit of men there is no blood' (II. i. 168) —but in the blood of men there is a spirit: hence the power of Caesar's 'blood' throughout the play. 'Blood' is close, very close, to 'spirit':

> . . . every drop of blood
> That every Roman bears, and nobly bears,
> Is guilty of a several bastardy,
> If he do break the smallest particle
> Of any promise that hath passed from him.   (ii. i. 136)

'Rome, thou hast lost the breed of noble bloods' (i. ii. 151).
'Blood' may be closely equated with the spirit of honour, or
love:

> You are my true and honourable wife,
> As dear to me as are the ruddy drops
> That visit my sad heart.   (ii. i. 288)

Blood is 'vitality', the nearest physical thing to the spiritual.
'Young bloods look for a time of rest' (iv. iii. 262).
'Bloody' may often mean 'courageous' in Shakespeare.
'Blood' is thus associated with ideas of 'heart', and 'honour',
and riches. 'Riches' in Shakespeare are often close to the
heart's love: the association is stressed throughout *Timon*.
The emotionalism of this play is twined with the word
'heart'. Brutus had rather 'coin' his 'heart' and 'drop' his
'blood for drachmas' than incur the shame of bribery (iv.
iii. 72). So, too, Cassius' 'heart' is

> Dearer than Plutus' mine, richer than gold.
>   (iv. iii. 102)

He who denied Brutus 'gold' will give his 'heart' (iv. iii.
104), and asks Brutus to 'take it forth' with his own dagger.
'Heart' is a frequent word. Portia cries to 'constancy' to
set 'a huge mountain' between her 'heart and tongue' (ii.
iv. 7). 'Then burst his mighty heart'—Caesar's, at sight of
Brutus' ingratitude (iii. ii. 190). 'Heart' blends with the
emotionalism, eroticism of our play. The conspirators'
'hearts' are pitiful (iii. i. 169, 175). 'Brutus hath rived my
heart', cries Cassius (iv. iii. 84); his 'heart' is 'thirsty' for
Brutus' pledge of love (iv. iii. 160). 'Thy heart is big:
get thee apart and weep', says Antony to Octavius' servant
(iii. i. 281); Portia's 'bosom' will 'partake the secrets' of
Brutus' 'heart' (ii.i. 305); Brutus 'sits high in all the people's
hearts' (i. iii. 157); 'O my heart!' cries Titinius, on seeing

3

Cassius' body (v. iii. 58). See also 'bosom' at ii. i. 305 and
v. i. 7. 'Heart' is also something of fire and spirit: the
conspirators are 'the most boldest and best hearts of Rome'
(iii. i. 121); the evil spirit vanishes when Brutus has 'taken
heart' (iv. iii. 288); men may smile though they have
'mischief' in their 'hearts' (iv. i. 51). These suggestions
are everywhere, thickly scattered.

So in *Julius Caesar* our blood-imagery does not horrify.
It rather excites—it is a brilliant stream of rich life, sacri-
ficially poured out in a drama of vivid life, erotic perception,
dynamic and spiritualized humanity. All here is life,
emotion, 'heart', spirit: albeit the house of life, the body, is
frail, sickly, weak. The ailing flesh burns with an inner
vital flame. That flame may be all but equated with blood.
Antony talks both of the power of speech to 'stir men's blood'
(iii. ii. 227) and of being disposed to 'stir your hearts and
minds to mutiny and rage' (iii. ii. 126), which shows clearly
the close 'blood'-'heart' relation: so, too, Brutus suggests
that their 'hearts' should 'stir up' their limbs to an 'act of
rage' and after 'chide them' (ii. i. 176).

The contrast between 'body' and 'spirit', bridged by
'blood' and 'heart', is fundamental. Men are 'flesh and blood,
and apprehensive' (iii. i. 67; 'apprehensive' = finely
tuned, *Wheel of Fire*, App. B, 339). The persons are weak
in body: they are all strong in 'spirit'. Ligarius is an exact
instance:

> I am not sick if Brutus have in hand
> Any exploit worthy the name of honour. (ii. i. 316)

Again,

> By all the gods that Romans bow before,
> I here discard my sickness! Soul of Rome!
> Brave son, derived from honourable loins!
> Thou, like an exorcist, hast conjur'd up
> My mortified spirit. Now bid me run,
> And I will strive with things impossible;
> Yea, get the better of them.   (ii. i. 320)

So he follows Brutus with a strong 'spirit', a 'heart' 'new-
fired' (ii. i. 332). Portia, too, points the same contrast:

O constancy be strong! upon my side,
Set a huge mountain 'tween my heart and tongue;
I have a man's mind, but a woman's might.   (II. iv. 6)

The bodily weakness of Caesar is stressed by Cassius: on
what meat does he feed to make him so great? But the
strength of Caesar's 'blood' or 'spirit' dominates the drama:

We all stand up against the spirit of Caesar,
And in the spirit of men there is no blood.
O, that we then could come by Caesar's spirit,
And not dismember Caesar. But, alas,
Caesar must bleed for it . . .   (II. i. 167)

They do not 'come by Caesar's spirit'. They slay his
body, pour out his blood, but his 'spirit' wins. As an 'evil
spirit' he visits Brutus in Act IV and at Philippi. Again,

O Julius Caesar, thou art mighty yet
Thy spirit walks abroad and turns our swords
In our own proper entrails.   (v. iii. 94)

Caesar is revenged on Cassius with the sword that killed
him. This is the spirit-strength of Caesar out of all proportion to his ailing, puny body. His 'spirit' strides, a
Colossus, over the action. This contrast is stressed everywhere: hence the many illnesses, yet fiery strength, of all
our persons. All reinforce the central theme: Caesar's
personal weakness in body, even in mind; and his colossal
'spirit': the spirit of empire and order. 'Spirit' and 'fire'
are recurrent words. Besides those passages just observed,
I will now give some more instances, scattered over the
play.
     The conspirators, says Brutus, must undertake their
action 'with untired spirits' (II. i. 227); Cassius lacks some
part of Antony's 'quick spirit' (I. ii. 29). We are told that
he smiles as though he scorned his 'spirit' (I. ii. 206), at the
quarrel he could weep his 'spirit from his eyes' (IV. iii. 100),
and at the end he is 'fresh of spirit' (v. i. 91). No metallic
prison, says Cassius, 'can be retentive to the strength of spirit'
(I. iii. 95); again, 'we are governed with our mothers' spirits',
where spirit is contrasted with 'thews and limbs' (i. iii. 81–3).

'Spirit' may be compared with, or replaced by, the words 'metal' or 'mettle'. This blends with metal-imagery, especially swords and daggers observed above. Casca was 'quick mettle' at school (I. ii. 300); horses, 'hot at hand' make 'gallant show and promise of their mettle' (IV. ii. 24). 'Spirit' is often 'hot' or 'fiery'. Cassius refers to Brutus' 'honourable metal' (I. ii. 313), and Brutus to 'the insuppressive mettle of our spirits' (II. i. 134). 'See', says Flavius, 'whe'r their basest metal be not moved' (I. i. 66). To return to 'spirit': the name of Brutus will 'start a spirit' as soon as that of Caesar (I. ii. 147); but Lepidus is a 'barren-spirited' fellow (IV. i. 36), like Antony's horse, governed by Antony's 'spirit' (IV. i. 33). The 'melting spirits of women' need to be 'steeled with valour' (II. i. 122). The conspirators are 'the choice and master spirits of this age' (III. i. 163). Antony talks of 'ruffling up' the 'spirits' of the crowd (III. ii. 232). The idea is everywhere. All are obsessed with 'spirit'. And, as I have already noted, towering over the action is Caesar's 'spirit'. 'If then thy spirit look upon us now . . .', says Antony, after shaking hands with the conspirators (III. i. 195). And he prophesies that

> Caesar's spirit, ranging for revenge,
> With Ate by his side come hot from hell,
> Shall in these confines with a monarch's voice,
> Cry 'Havoc!' and let slip the dogs of war.　　(III. i. 270)

Hot from hell. Spirit is a thing of 'fire'.

The action of the play is 'most bloody, fiery, and most terrible' (I. iii. 130). Ligarius follows Brutus with 'a heart new-fired' (II. i. 332), his mortified spirit revivified. Brutus' arguments 'bear fire enough to kindle cowards' (II. i. 120). But sometimes the human will may pride itself in fighting against the fire of emotion. So Caesar tells Cimber that his prayers 'might fire the blood of ordinary men', but that Caesar does not bear 'such rebel blood that will be thawed from the true quality with that which melteth fools' (III. i. 40). The fire of passion may here 'melt' will-power. Hence the number of 'fire' or 'spirit' references and the constant suggestion of emotion and weeping. The play is full of the 'heart's' fire, the soft fire of emotion; which again is often the same as the fire of spirited action. 'Fire' is important as suggesting both action and emotion. Cassius is glad that his words have 'struck fire' from Brutus (I. ii. 177). Fire is spirit and so life itself. Casca is dull and lacks 'those sparks of life' which a Roman ought to possess (I. iii. 57). 'Fire' is also to be associated with 'pity' and 'weeping'. In Act I the Tribunes address the crowd:

> O you hard hearts, you cruel men of Rome
> Knew you not Pompey?   (I. i. 41)

The idea of 'hardness' is the reverse of passion's fire. The citizens' 'hearts' will not melt with pity: hence they are 'blocks', 'stones', 'worse than senseless things'. Antony repeats the idea with fire-imagery:

> You are not wood, you are not stones, but men;
> And, being men, hearing the will of Caesar,
> It will inflame you . . .   (III. ii. 147)

Antony's eyes are 'red as fire' (III. ii. 121)—a fine 'fire'-'weeping' association; so, too, Cicero's are ferret-like and 'fiery' from passion (I. ii. 186). Anger 'glows' on Caesar's cheek (I. ii. 183). Pity drives out pity as fire drives out fire (III. i. 171). Cassius is a 'hot friend cooling' (IV. ii. 19). Brutus 'carries anger as the flint bears fire', he shows a 'hasty spark' and is cool again (IV. iii. 111). So we have a clear train of ideas: man's body, visually, almost erotically, observed; thoughts of physical weakness and sickness; emotion, blood, the heart's passion—the life-forces encased in the body; finally, spirit, fire, the fine essence of vitality, the human spirit in all its resplendent power and beauty, housed as it may be in a frail tenement of flesh. Which flesh-frailty serves the more clearly to silhouette the fiery quality of 'spirit'.

This vision of man as body and spirit entwined is part of a wider scheme in which we may view the body and

spirit of a state. The sickly anarchy in Brutus' soul is a
reflection of that wider anarchy to be:

> ... the state of man,
> Like to a little kingdom, suffers then
> The nature of an insurrection.   (II. i. 67)

The individual-state association occurs elsewhere. Ligarius
asks Brutus what his enterprise may be:

> *Brutus.* A piece of work that will make sick men whole.
> *Ligarius.* But are not some whole that we must make sick?
> *Brutus.* That must we also ...   (II. i. 327)

That is, Rome is sick of Caesar's tyranny. Cassius said
as much before. Brutus remarks that Caesar 'hath the
falling-sickness':

> *Cassius.* No, Caesar hath it not; but you and I
> And honest Casca, we have the falling-sickness.
>
>   (I. ii. 257)

Rome itself is 'sick': neither wholly because of Caesar's
ambition, nor because of the conspirators' plot, but
because of both. There is disorder, an irruption. The
conspirators see Caesar as symbol of this disorder:

> Now could I, Casca, name to thee a man
> Most like this dreadful night,
> That thunders, lightens, opens graves, and roars
> As doth the lion in the Capitol,
> A man no mightier than thyself or me
> In personal action, yet prodigious grown
> And fearful as these strange eruptions are.   (I. iii. 72)

But Antony prophesies disorder as the result of Caesar's
murder:

> Over thy wounds now do I prophesy—
> Domestic fury and fierce civil strife
> Shall cumber all the parts of Italy ...   (III. i. 259)

Each side, as usual in Shakespeare, sees the other as the
cause of disorder: thus, absolutely, the disorder is one of
inharmonious relation only. But, just as Brutus sees his
own soul as disordered, so we have sight of the wider
disorder of Rome. And this disorder appears as a rough

unjointing of actuality, so that natural laws are suspended; and, beyond this, we see the spirit-world itself dissociated from any normal bodies of life, nakedly glaring its supernatural fires through Rome. We watch human 'bodies' and 'spirits' at work interlocking or severed from each other: but we also see not only the body of Rome but the spirit of Rome too severed from its body by the disorder of insurrection. The two modes, personal and political, are unified in the symbol of Caesar: he is both person and state, and so the pouring out of his life-blood is accompanied by the rending of that body which we call nature, and the disclosure of the fiery blood of a spirit-order which should normally be housed in the arterial veins of peaceful life:

> O world, thou wast the forest to this hart,
> And this, indeed, O world, the heart of thee.
>
> (III. i. 207)

Caesar is the 'heart' of the world. His death pours out the life-blood of communal life and order.

Caesar is the fiery symbol of Rome's spirit. He blazes in a fine majesty, supreme:

> Those that with haste will make a mighty fire
> Begin it with weak straws: what trash is Rome,
> What rubbish and what offal, when it serves
> For the base matter to illuminate
> So vile a thing as Caesar!   (I. iii. 107)

So speaks Cassius. But yet again we must observe the thought of 'fire'. And the spirit-world exposed is 'fiery'. I have elsewhere observed the 'tempest' and the numerous instances of disorder—men, birds, beasts, all behaving unnaturally, impossibly. Here I would emphasize that such disorder-symbols are related closely, in this play, to fire:

> But never till to-night, never till now
> Did I go through a tempest dropping fire.
> Either there is a civil strife in heaven,
> Or else the world, too saucy with the gods,
> Incenses them to send destruction.   (I. iii. 9)

There is 'civil strife' in the spiritual world, as in Brutus'
soul: or what appears to man as 'civil strife'. Anyway,
man has sight of unnatural, fearful, spirit-things: things
of fire, impossible and terrible:

> A common slave—you know him well by sight—
> Held up his left hand, which did flame and burn,
> Like twenty torches join'd, and yet his hand,
> Not sensible of fire, remain'd unscorch'd.   (I. iii. 15)

'Men all in fire walk up and down the streets' (I. iii. 25).
Cassius does not fear these portents. He walks about at
ease, baring his bosom to the thunderstone:

> And when the cross blue lightning seem'd to open
> The breast of heaven, I did present myself
> Even in the aim and very flash of it.   (I. iii. 50)

'All these fires, all these gliding ghosts' (I. iii. 63) are to
him but the evil which the slaying of Caesar will cure: so,
too, are they, from his view. Caesar is to Cassius a dire
thing of disorder. He and Antony are both right: either,
alone, is a force of order. Only Brutus, divided between
both sides, is to be directly associated with these disorder-
symbols. That I have shown elsewhere. So Cassius
presses on to action itself 'bloody, fiery, and most terrible'
(I. iii. 130) with a clear conscience. The night is truly
fearsome:

> Fierce fiery warriors fought upon the clouds,
> In ranks and squadrons and right form of war,
> Which drizzled blood upon the Capitol;
> The noise of battle hurtled in the air,
> Horses did neigh, and dying men did groan,
> And ghosts did shriek and squeal about the streets.
> O Caesar! these things are beyond all use,
> And I do fear them.   (II. ii. 19)

This spirit-blood blends the purely spiritual with life
forms, just as man's 'blood' is the nearest material substance to life or spirit. Now this spirit-reality strikes fear:
'I do fear them', 'now they fright me' (II. ii. 14, 26). Again

> You look pale and gaze,
> And put on fear and cast yourself in wonder. (I. iii. 59)

'It is the part of men', says Casca, 'to fear and tremble' when the gods send such portents (I. iii. 54). There is a heap of ghastly women 'transformed with their fear' (I. iii. 24). The divinity or spirituality of these appearances is stressed as well as their fearsomeness. There is 'civil strife in heaven' (I. iii. 11), 'nor heaven nor earth hath been at peace to-night' (II. ii. 1). Such spirit-forms are necessarily fear-inspiring to man. Here mankind has sight of abnormal, impossible events: ghosts walking from their graves, fires of all sorts in heaven and earth—pure spirit realities; again, in the natural world, distortion, abnormality—the slave with his burning hand, the lion in the Capitol, the night owl hooting all day, the beast without a 'heart' (II. ii. 40). 'Spirit' and 'matter' are, as it were, severed. That mating on which creation depends is suddenly cut apart, uncreated, chaos is come again. Neither spirit nor matter is now real, the fusion on which each depends is gone, each is derelict, meaningless, absurd. Matter uninfused with spirit is illogical: spirit naked is terrible. Hence man is afraid: afraid, as in *Macbeth*, of the alien and unknown; of spirit divorced from actuality, or actuality divorced from spirit. All this reflects the act opposed to creation and order: the slaying of Caesar, the shedding of his 'costly' spirit-blood. Though we must at times be prepared to adopt Cassius' view of Caesar as an evil, yet the balance of imaginative effects is stronger on the other side. In Shakespeare 'creation' is the result of blending elements, the divine and the earthly. These are mated. Here they are roughly unmated. And in this chaos, past, present, future are all jumbled together: dead men are alive, prophets and dreams and forebodings foretell the future. As the Weird Sisters prophesy things past, present, and to come —Glamis, Cawdor, and King—so these spirit-events range beyond the present. They are the timeless background, or rather the fiery life-blood, usually infused into the veins of time: but here they are not so infused, they are seen in themselves, chaotic. The fire of creation itself is spilt out

across the skies of Rome as a Caesar's blood is spilt on the
Capitol stones. Now fear is the note struck here and in
Macbeth where the 'spirit' is viewed naked. But love is the
response to the vision of spirit infusing matter. Here we
see spirit both alone and embodied in human life: hence
the play traverses psychic territories of fear and love.

I have called *Julius Caesar* erotic. The erotic perception indeed characterizes it throughout. And this erotic
nature of it is also one with its vivid apprehension of
'spirit'. Here there is an optimistic vision of spirit as
'fire'. In *Macbeth*, so close to *Julius Caesar* in its vision
of the soul's essence unmated to actuality, the spirit-
world is dark, formless, void. Here we have no such profound sight. The abysms of reality are not sounded. Spirit
is still 'fire', symbolic if you like, but yet 'fire', a thing of
life, a positive and known force, like 'blood'. Much of the
action, as in *Macbeth*, is in darkness: but that darkness is
ever lit by fire: you can read by light of 'the exhalations
whizzing in the air' (ii. i. 44). There is not the *Macbeth*-
murk, the *Macbeth*-negation. Here, on the ethical plane,
Brutus' act is a purposive one, a thing of fine honour and
spirit: spirit in turn is a thing of fire. Macbeth's act is
purposeless, unutterably negative and dark. With this
reservation, that the 'spirit' divorced from actuality is
bright in one and dark in the other—we may yet remember
the many glimmerings, as of Lady Macbeth's light, that
illume that murky hell—we can say that *Julius Caesar*
and *Macbeth* present similar visions. But the fiery quality
of *Julius Caesar* relates it also closely to *Antony and
Cleopatra*. 'Fire' and 'love' are close, since love is the
awareness and recognition of the spirit-flame in flesh.
Love is powerful throughout *Julius Caesar*; and there is
evil too. But in *Antony and Cleopatra* there is less actual
'fire', it is there housed in actuality, has no, or little,
autonomy. *Julius Caesar* forecasts both plays. In point
of 'evil' it resembles *Macbeth*, in point of 'fire' and love
Antony and Cleopatra: and these two themes must be
related to Brutus and Cassius respectively.

The *Julius Caesar* world is fiery-bright with a brilliant erotic vision, which sees a flaming spirit in history, in action, in man. The poet is in love with his story and its actors, and the general effect is one of optimism. Often in Shakespeare love is accompanied by the universal lights of heaven. They are apparent here. 'Stars' and 'sun' occur in magnificent passages.

> *Decius.* Here lies the east: doth not the day break here?
> *Casca.* No.
> *Cinna.* O pardon, Sir, it doth; and yon grey lines
>   That fret the clouds are messengers of day.
> *Casca.* You shall confess that you are both deceiv'd:
>   Here, as I point my sword, the sun arises,
>   Which is a great way growing on the south,
>   Weighing the youthful season of the year.
>   Some two months hence up higher toward the north
>   He first presents his fire; and the high east
>   Stands, as the Capitol, directly here.   (II. i. 101)

Brutus 'cannot by the progress of the stars give guess how near to day' (II. i. 2). There are Calpurnia's fine lines:

> When beggars die there are no comets seen,
> The heavens themselves blaze forth the death of princes.
>   (II. ii. 30)

Caesar compares himself to a star, his starry greatness a thing of steady light unquenchable, unshaken:

> But I am constant as the northern star,
> Of whose true-fix'd and resting quality
> There is no fellow in the firmament.
> The skies are painted with unnumber'd sparks,
> They are all fire and every one doth shine . . .   (III. i. 60)

Caesar is thus infinite as eternity itself, like the 'Bright Star' of Keats's sonnet. The play is brilliant with light and fire.

This fire-imagery is resplendent everywhere. Cassius rescued Caesar from Tiber as Aeneas carried Anchises 'from the flames of Troy' (I. ii. 113). It may be used in connexion with household articles—the taper burning in Brutus' closet (II. i. 35), the taper burning in his tent (IV. iii. 164, 275); in connexion with war—a 'torch light'

(v. v. 2); with suicide—Portia swallowed 'fire' (iv. iii. 156).
'Are those my tents where I perceive the fire?' asks Cassius
(v. iii. 13). The flaming passions of insurrection are a
fire. The citizens, inflamed by Antony, cry 'Burn!
Fire! Kill! Slay!' (iii. ii. 208):

> *4th Cit.*   Come, away, away!
>   We'll burn his body in the holy place,
>   And with the brands fire the traitors' houses. . . .
> *2nd Cit.* Go fetch fire.   (iii. ii. 258)

They will fetch 'fire-brands' (iii. iii. 41). Thus a disorderly act unlooses the 'fires' of spirited revenge. When
Brutus is dead his foes can but make a 'fire' of him (v. v.
55). The spirit-order, in man's passionate 'heart' or
behind the curtaining flux of time, is fire, like the 'fierce
fiery warriors' above Rome's Capitol. All here is fiery,
spiritual ardour, in love, honour, insurrection, revenge,
high intent of whatever kind. So the lights of heaven
burn down, sun and stars, dawn, 'exhalations', comets; all
take part in an action whose fiery spirit is worthy of their
company. Darkness shot with light characterizes this
play and *Macbeth*: but they change places—in *Macbeth*
the 'murk', here 'fire' predominates. The whole universe
of *Julius Caesar*—blood and fire blended in a fine act—is
crystallized at Cassius' death:

> O setting sun!
>   As in thy red rays thou dost sink to-night
>   So in his red blood Cassius' day is set;
>   The sun of Rome is set.   (v. iii. 60)

Caesar's blood spilt on the marble of 'Pompey's statua',
Cassius' on the plains of Philippi. The blaze of sunset
accompanies this final act as dawn-fire preluded Caesar's
murder.

This play is a play of love and fire. The human element
is emotional, erotic: that I analyse in my next essay. But
this love-theme is one with the fire-theme. Love is sight
of the material ablaze with spirit's fire. Here we often see
spirit naked, a naked flame and so, in a sense, unnatural,
fearful, evil. But it is presented romantically. Even

disorder, evil, fear is lurid, bright, romantic. The whole
play blazes with a fine vision of human excellence, a fiery
vision of life itself, that which feeds or slays the body of
man or the body of Rome: life as it appears outwardly,
also its vital spirit. So we find Mr. Masefield's epithet
to be justified. As he wrote it, Shakespeare saw life
'startlingly'. And this startling vision exposes the psychic
fires which feed human life, it shows the volcanic forces
behind the even tenour of existence. Roughly, the veil is
torn from the face of reality, and the spirit exposed naked:
something of vivid, startling, fiery strength.

But human life goes on. The fire of life is passed on from
one torch to another. Love conquers the disintegration
and disorder of the central acts. Friend still clasps the
hand of friend, love does not die, the wounds of Rome are
healed. No play of Shakespeare concentrates more on
'emotion', 'heart', 'love'. All the persons are 'lovers',
with a soft eroticism not quite 'passion', but powerful,
itself fiery. They all call each other 'noble'. These love-
strands are most important: they cast our thoughts back
to the vivid human visualization noted above, and forward
to the themes of my next essay. We thus watch the gashing of Rome, and the closing, healing of its wounds. We
watch the disjointed dereliction of 'spirit' and 'nature'
untuned, dislocated: but also the re-mating, the re-creation,
of love. Caesar himself was the lover of Rome. At the
opening, Caesar enters in resplendent power, his majesty
close-knitting Rome in concord and love. It is the feast
of Lupercal. And Caesar would have Antonius touch
Calpurnia in his course, so that she may shake off her
'sterile curse' (I. ii. 9). That is a vivid life-suggestion.[1]
His entry is heralded and accompanied by music:

> I hear a tongue shriller than all the music,
> Cry 'Caesar!' Speak; Caesar is turn'd to hear.   (I. ii. 16)

[1] This suggests Macbeth, who complains that

> Upon my head they plac'd a fruitless crown
> And put a barren sceptre in my gripe . . . (*Macbeth*, III. i. 61)

See my remarks in the essay entitled 'The Milk of Concord'.

So, with fanfare of music, holy feasting, thoughts of birth, opens the erotic brilliance of this Caesarean theme. It is a vivid life-vision. This harmony Brutus shatters; in Rome, in his own heart. At the end he would solace his tired soul with the music of his boy, Lucius. But the ghost of Caesar intervenes. Not till Brutus' death is Rome crowned again with peace. So the action first shows us love, friendship, imperial sway. This surface is rudely gashed by the daggers of revolt, torn open, and the naked flames exposed which feed the mechanisms of social order, life, and love. The wound heals, Antony's love for Caesar avenges his death, peace is restored. And love and friendship bring the only final peace to the souls of both Brutus and Cassius.

III

THE EROTICISM OF JULIUS CAESAR

THE human element in *Julius Caesar* is charged highly with a general eroticism. All the people are 'lovers'. This love is emotional, fiery, but not exactly sexual, not physically passionate: even Portia and Brutus love with a gentle companionship rather than any passion. Though the stage be set for an action 'most bloody, fiery, and most terrible', though the action be fine, spirited, and adventurous, and noble blood be magnificently spilt in the third act, yet the human element is often one of gentle sentiment, melting hearts, tears, and the soft fire of love. There are many major and minor love-themes. There is love expressed or suggested between Brutus and Cassius, Brutus and Caesar, and Antony and Caesar; Brutus and Portia, Brutus and Volumnius, Brutus and Lucius; Caesar and Decius, Cassius and Lucius Pella, Cassius and Titinius; Ligarius and Brutus, Artemidorus and Caesar. Probably there are other instances. The word 'lover' is strangely emphatic, sometimes meaning little more than 'friend', but always helping to build a general atmosphere of comradeship and affection. Love is here the regal, the conquering reality: the murder of Caesar is a gash in the body of Rome, and this gash is healed by love, so that the play's action emphasizes first the disjointing of 'spirit' from 'matter' which is evil, fear, anarchy; and then the remating of these two elements into the close fusion which is love, order, peace.

I shall note first the personal themes of Julius Caesar and Antony, and thereafter more closely observe the contrasted importance of Brutus and Cassius. The simplicity of *Julius Caesar* is a surface simplicity only. To close analysis it reveals subtleties and complexities which render interpretation difficult. Nor can I hope to avoid altogether obscurity and indecisiveness in the attempt to render the meaning of so involved a pattern. The play has, as it

were, four protagonists, each with a different view of the
action.

The figure of Julius Caesar stands out, brilliant. From
the start he is idealized in point of power, general respect,
glory. His failings must not receive our only attention: he
is endued dramatically with strength, importance, almost
divinity. He is a sublime figure-head, but, the general
acclamations at any time stilled, we see him as a man, weak,
egotistical, petulant. But his weakness must not prevent
our recognition of power behind such words as Cassius'

> Why, man, he doth bestride the narrow world
> Like a Colossus . . .   (I. ii. 135)

The Caesar-idea is accompanied by all the usual Shakespearian suggestions of world-glory and life-beauty. Here
they are raised to a high pitch. The men of Rome put on
their best 'attire' (I. i. 53) for his triumph, 'strew flowers
in his way' (I. i. 55). His images are robed and decked
with his 'trophies' and 'ceremonies' (I. i. 69–74). Every
one's attention hangs on his words:

> Peace, ho! Caesar speaks.   (I. ii. 1)

His entry is accompanied with music. He is associated with
images of infinity, the North Star and Olympus (III. i. 60,
74). He is, as it were, a frail man buoyed on the full flood
of success. He is conscious of his own triumphant destiny:

> . . . danger knows full well
> That Caesar is more dangerous than he:
> We are two lions litter'd in one day,
> And I the elder and more terrible.   (II. ii. 44)

The idea of Caesar is far greater here than Caesar the
man. It is so to Caesar himself. He has an almost superstitious respect for his own star, and is afraid of acting
unworthily of it: he persuades himself not to show fear,
since he is greater than danger itself. Often he has to
persuade himself in this fashion:

> Shall Caesar send a lie?
> Have I in conquest stretch'd mine arm so far,
> To be afeard to tell greybeards the truth?   (II. ii. 65)

This shortly follows his words, 'Mark Antony shall say I am not well' (II. ii. 55): either because now Decius is present, or purely due to his sudden attempt to live up to the Caesar-idea. He often vacillates like this. He tells Antony that Cassius is a danger, then pulls himself up sharply with, 'Always, I am Caesar' (I. ii. 212). We are, indeed, aware of two Caesars: the ailing and petulant old man, and the giant spirit standing colossal over the Roman Empire to be. There is an insubstantial, mirage-like uncertainty about this Caesar. How are we to see him? He is two incompatibles, shifting, interchanging. As the hour of his death draws near, this induces almost a sickening feeling, like a ship's rocking. This is the uncertainty, the unreal phantasma, of Brutus' mind, and, for a while, of ours. Caesar is himself, curiously, aware of both his selves: hence his rapid changes, his admixture of fine phrases resonant of imperial glory with trivialities, platitudes, absurdities. Confronted by Metellus Cimber's petition, he is intent, not on justice, but on preserving his own constancy. The North Star alone remains constant in the skies, and Caesar must be such a star to men:

> So in the world; 'tis furnish'd well with men,
> And men are flesh and blood, and apprehensive;
> Yet in the number I do know but one
> That unassailable holds on his rank,
> Unshak'd of motion: and that I am he,
> Let me a little show it, even in this,
> That I was constant Cimber should be banish'd,
> And constant do remain to keep him so.   (III. i. 66)

He wants primarily to 'show' his constancy: to the world, to himself. He must prove its existence. His egotism then knows no bounds. And yet his egotism is both compelling and ludicrous. The baffling coexistence of these elements in single speeches, single phrases even, is remarkable: there is nothing quite like it in Shakespeare. He can say with finality, 'Caesar doth not wrong' (III. i. 47). Petitions may 'fire the blood of ordinary men' but not Caesar's (III. i. 37). All this may seem a little foolish:

yet if we see only foolishness, we are wrong. We must observe both Caesars, keep both ever in mind: one physical and weak, the other all but supernatural in spiritual power, a power blazing in the fine hyperboles of his egocentricity. Cassius notes how superstitions now affect Caesar:

> For he is superstitious grown of late,
> Quite from the main opinion he held once
> Of fantasy, of dreams, and ceremonies.   (II. i. 195)

This is not surprising: it is a normal correlative to his superstitious respect for his idealized self. Nor, in this world, is superstition a fault: it is fully justified. Moreover Cassius himself (v. i. 77–9) and Calpurnia (II. ii. 13–14) express elsewhere an exactly similar change towards superstition. The Soothsayer's prophecy comes true. Dreams and auguries are justified by the event; portents are here faithful harbingers of destruction. Caesar's ghost appears twice to Brutus, and he knows his hour has come (v. v. 17–20). We are vividly conscious of the supernatural. So Caesar's superstition and his almost superstitious respect for his own importance are, in this universe, not irrational. Again, we are pointed to the root ideas here: physical weakness, spiritual energy, the supernatural. And this spiritual element burns fierce in the almost divine glory to which Caesar tries pathetically to adjust himself. Whatever it be, this Caesar-idea, it is more powerful than Caesar the man. It controls him while he lives, survives and avenges him after his death. 'The spirit of Caesar' is not reached by slaying Caesar's body: it rather gains strength thereafter. Therefore, whatever we may think of Caesar as a man, we must see him also as a symbol of something of vast import, resplendent majesty, and starry purpose.

Antony recognizes this fully. He loves Caesar. That is, he sees him as man and as hero and does not, like Brutus, distinguish between the two. Cassius despises him as a man, and therefore will not believe in him at all as a hero; Brutus loves him as a man but believes in him only too powerfully as a hero, and thinks him therefore dangerous. To Antony the two aspects are indistinguishable. This is equivalent to saying that Antony ardently, almost passionately, loves Caesar: for in such love—and only then—the spiritual and personal elements are blended. That is the function of love: in creation or recognition, it mates the spiritual with the material. Antony, the lover, can therefore unify our difficulties: in his words —and in his only, not in Caesar's—do we feel the dualism of Caesar's 'spirit' and physical being perfectly unified. In his words only we see the Caesar of history:

> O mighty Caesar! dost thou lie so low?
> Are all thy conquests, glories, triumphs, spoils,
> Shrunk to this little measure?   (III. i. 148)

We are suddenly at home here strangely: this is how we want to see Caesar, how we expect to see him, how we are never allowed to see him till he is dead. The conspirators' swords are 'rich with the most noble blood of all this world' (III. i. 155). Again,

> Thou art the ruins of the noblest man
> That ever lived in the tide of times.
> Woe to the hand that shed this costly blood!   (III. i. 256)

He sees him as a man he loved; also as a supremely noble man; and, still further, as a symbol of government and peace. Now that he is rashly slain, forces of disorder will rage unchecked:

> Domestic fury and fierce civil strife
> Shall cumber all the parts of Italy.   (III. i. 263)

Caesar's 'spirit' will have its revenge. In his oration he again stresses both Caesar's lovable personality and his importance as victor and national hero. His personal and national goodness are here entwined: to Antony Caesar is Rome's lover. Caesar hath 'wept' (III. ii. 96) for the poor of Rome, his captives' ransoms filled Rome's 'general coffers' (III. ii. 94). He is a national friend or lover over and beyond his love for Antony:

> He was my friend, faithful and just to me ... (III. ii. 90)

or his love for Brutus:

> For Brutus, as you know, was Caesar's angel:
> Judge, O you gods, how dearly Caesar lov'd him.
>
> (III. ii. 185)

So the people of Rome should 'mourn for him' (III. ii. 108)
as for a dear friend. Caesar is now shown as a general
lover. The common people, if they heard his will, would

> go and kiss dead Caesar's wounds,
> And dip their napkins in his sacred blood,
> Yea, beg a hair of him for memory,
> And, dying, mention it within their wills,
> Bequeathing it as a rich legacy
> Unto their issue.   (III. ii. 137)

Notice the strongly erotic emotion here. Throughout
Antony's speech, love—whether of Caesar for Brutus,
Antony or Rome, or of Antony or Rome for Caesar—is
stressed in contrast to the ever more sarcastically pro-
nounced suggestion of 'honour': 'honourable men whose
daggers have stabbed Caesar' (III. ii. 156). 'Love' is
pitted against 'honour'. Even Caesar's mantle is suffused
with emotion, almost sentimentality:

> If you have tears, prepare to shed them now.
> You all do know this mantle: I remember
> The first time ever Caesar put it on;
> 'Twas on a summer's evening, in his tent,
> That day he overcame the Nervii.   (III. ii. 173)

So personal can be Antony's appeal. At the other extreme
he sees Caesar's murder as a treason which plunges Rome
in disaster. When 'great Caesar fell', Rome fell too:

> O! what a fall was there, my countrymen;
> Then I, and you, and all of us fell down,
> Whilst bloody treason flourish'd over us.   (III. ii. 194)

Then Antony shows them Caesar's body itself:

> Kind souls, what! weep you when you but behold
> Our Caesar's vesture wounded? Look you here,
> Here is himself, marr'd, as you see, with traitors.
>
> (III. ii. 199)

Antony emphasizes the personal element throughout. But he is also aware of the political aspect. The idea of Caesar as an abstract principle of order is not, in his mind, divided from Caesar his friend, the lover of Rome, now a stricken lifeless body. He thinks of the wounds, the torn mantle that was Caesar's. Elsewhere he refers to Caesar's 'spirit': here, and usually, he sees Caesar as a lovable, noble, and great man whose murder is a senseless and wicked act. So close are the personal and public elements twined in his thoughts that he readily suggests that personal reasons must have urged the conspirators to their deed:

> What private griefs they have, alas, I know not,
> That made them do it . . .   (III. ii. 217)

Although Antony is, of course, ready to stress all that may suit his purpose, yet his attitude throughout his oration is exactly in line with his other thoughts and acts. He only has to be sincere to win over the citizens to his side:

> I am no orator, as Brutus is;
> But, as you know me all, a plain blunt man,
> That love my friend.   (III. ii. 221)

It is true: he does not need to act. He reads the will, Caesar's bequests to the Roman people. The citizens recognize Caesar now as 'royal'. He is 'most noble Caesar', and 'royal Caesar' (III. ii. 248, 249). The final effect is clinched in Antony's

> Here was a Caesar! When comes such another? (III. ii. 257)

Through making a division between Caesar the man and Caesar the national hero and dictator, Brutus, Cassius, and also Caesar himself, have all plunged Rome and themselves in disaster.

'Spirit' is continually felt as dissociated from 'body': 'We all stand up against the spirit of Caesar' (II. i. 167). This disjointing is at the root of the fiery portents, naked spirit unbodied in temporal and physical forms; the queer acts of beasts and men, bodies derelict of controlling, infusing 'spirit'. It is this division of thought that makes both Brutus and Cassius see Caesar as dangerous, though

Cassius himself suffers no inward division, since he does not see Caesar as powerfully evil, but rather as trivial, and blames not Caesar but Rome for the worship it accords him. He distinguishes only between Caesar the man—whom he sees singly—and the absurd idolatry of Rome. And, as we shall see, the disjointing of elements in man or state is to be related to Brutus rather than Cassius. Caesar, too, makes implicit distinction between himself as man and ruler. Now the central act, Caesar's assassination, is shown as a rough breaking of 'spirit' from 'body', whether of Caesar or Rome. Antony's love alone heals the dualism. Throughout he avoids this distinction. He unifies the dualism created by the poet in presenting Caesar as almost a dualized personality. It is the way of love. It unifies both the mind or soul of the subject, and the thing, person, or world that is loved, blending 'spirit' in 'body', seeing the physical afire with spirit-essence. So Antony alone knows the one Caesar better than Brutus and Cassius, better than Caesar himself, better than we who faithfully react to the impressions of the early scenes. Because he loves and is moved by love he sees things simplified, unified. His acts tend likewise to heal the gaping dualism of 'spirit' and 'matter' that has resulted from the gashing of Rome's civic body. Portents have blazed their terrors over Rome, the spirit of Rome being torn from its body; and supernatural portents, omens, ghosts continue after Caesar's death. Fierce civil chaos is threatened now, as Antony prophesies: the body of Rome disorganized, disjointed by lack of any controlling spirit. Antony speaks, acts, fights to heal Rome. The wounds of Rome, the separation of 'spirit' from 'body', are thus healed by a lover and his love. Caesar's 'spirit' is then at peace.

Caesar we must therefore be ready to regard as Antony sees him; and yet, as I have elsewhere shown, we are forced by the play's symbolic effects to see the action largely through the eyes of Brutus. That we may do this Caesar is also shown to us as he appears to Brutus: he is both man

and demi-god curiously interwoven. But it will be clear
that Brutus' failure to unify his knowledge of Caesar is a
failure properly to love him, love being the unifying
principle in all things, regularly opposed in Shakespeare
to disorder, treachery, evils of all kinds: this is the continual music-tempest contrast throughout the plays.
And Brutus' failure to love his friend, Caesar, is one with
his worship of abstract 'honour'. Therein we have the key
to his acts: he serves 'honour' always in preference to love.
Both his 'love' for Caesar and his 'honour' are given exact
expression. Cassius asks Brutus if he would not have
Caesar made king:

> I would not, Cassius; yet I love him well.
> But wherefore do you hold me here so long?
> What is it that you would impart to me?
> If it be aught toward the general good,
> Set honour in one eye and death i' the other,
> And I will look on both indifferently:
> For let the gods so speed me as I love
> The name of honour more than I fear death.   (I. ii. 82)

This love Brutus sacrifices to his 'honour'.

The rest of the play illustrates his attitude. Honour first,
love second. His anxieties have made him forget 'the
shows of love to other men' being 'himself at war' (I. ii.
46–7). Portia is distressed at his lack of kindliness. He
has risen 'ungently' from their bed; last night he 'suddenly arose' at supper, and paced the room 'musing and
sighing'. Questioned, he stared at her 'with ungentle
looks', stamped 'impatiently', and dismissed her 'with an
angry wafture' of his hand (II. i. 237–51). So she pits the
strength of love against his schemes of honour:

>   . . . and, upon my knees,
> I charm you, by my once-commended beauty,
> By all your vows of love and that great vow
> Which did incorporate and make us one,
> That you unfold to me, yourself, your half,
> Why are you heavy, and what men to-night
> Have had resort to you . . .   (II. i. 270)

She wins her fight—for the moment—and draws from him the deep emotion of:

> You are my true and honourable wife,
> As dear to me as are the ruddy drops
> That visit my sad heart.   (II. i. 288)

And she herself knows the meaning of honour and courage. She has given herself a 'voluntary wound' to prove her constancy. Brutus, hearing this, prays the gods to make him worthy of 'this noble wife' (II. i. 302). The Brutus-Portia relation is exquisitely drawn. It reminds us of Hotspur and Lady Percy. But Hotspur was stronger, more single in purpose, and, in a sense, more wary than Brutus: he gave away no secrets, whereas Brutus' surrender to Portia came near ruining the conspiracy. It is to be noted that 'honour' is so strong in Brutus that Portia knows she must play up to it, show herself courageous, possessing a sense of 'honour' like his. Brutus' obsession, almost to absurdity, with this thought is further evident from his long speech, prolixly expanding the idea that an oath is unnecessary to bind Romans to a noble enterprise:

> ... what other bond
> Than secret Romans, that have spoke the word,
> And will not palter? and what other oath
> Than honesty to honesty engag'd,
> That this shall be, or we will fall for it?   (II. i. 124)

Again, he nearly ruins his own cause: we may relate to this 'oath' speech the fact that some one has given away details of the conspiracy to Popilius Lena and Artemidorus. Brutus is always un-at-home with practical affairs, which is natural in a man so devoted to an ethical abstraction. He unwisely refuses to let Antony be slain; perhaps also unwisely objects to the inclusion of Cicero among the conspirators. He is, in fact, a disintegrating force in the conspiracy, just as he is a disintegrating force to Rome: without him, the conspiracy might well have been successful, and we should then give final sanction to

Cassius' rather than Antony's view of Caesar. Here we see the profound poetic necessity of Caesar's apparent weakness: it justifies Cassius' whole-hearted hostility. Cassius and Antony are both order-forces, love-forces in the play: Cassius' hate of Caesar is one with his love of his excellently arranged conspiracy, and his love of the conspiracy is a practical, efficient thing, as efficient as Antony's love of Caesar. Brutus loves primarily nothing but 'honour', but many things with secondary affection: Cassius, Portia, Caesar, the conspiracy. Brutus is thus divided in mind, in outlook. He is 'with himself at war' (I. ii. 46); in him

> the state of man,
> Like to a little kingdom, suffers then
> The nature of an insurrection.   (II. i. 67)

All the disorder-symbols in the play, all our ideas of disorder and disruption in reading it, our two-fold and indecisive vision of two Caesars—demi-god and dolt— are to be related closely to Brutus, rather than to Cassius or Antony. They enjoy a oneness of vision, a singularity of purpose: Brutus does not.

Brutus throughout continues his honourable course. He is aptly praised by Ligarius:

> Soul of Rome!
> Brave son, deriv'd from honourable loins!   (II. i. 321)

All the conspirators respect him for his 'honour'. He slays Caesar boldly, without wavering, in the cause of honour. Antony sends a message, asking to interview the conspirators:

> Brutus is noble, wise, valiant and honest,
> Caesar was mighty, bold, royal and loving:
> Say I love Brutus and I honour him;
> Say I fear'd Caesar, honour'd him and lov'd him.
>   (III. i. 126)

Brutus promises him safety by his 'honour' (III. i. 141); then assures him he can give him ample 'reasons' for Caesar's death. He thinks ever in terms of cold abstract processes of reason, and, unlike Antony and Cassius, ever fails in contact with the rich warm life of reality. So he always misjudges men: he lets Antony speak at Caesar's funeral. He is half-hearted: neither a good conspirator like Cassius nor a good lover like Antony. Next Brutus gives his 'public reasons' (III. ii. 7) for Caesar's death in his speech to the citizens. Again, he emphasizes 'honour':

> Romans, countrymen, and lovers! hear me for my cause, and be silent, that you may hear: believe me for mine honour, and have respect to mine honour, that you may believe: censure me in your wisdom, and awake your senses, that you may the better judge. If there be any in this assembly, any dear friend of Caesar's, to him I say, that Brutus' love to Caesar was no less than his. If then that friend demand why Brutus rose against Caesar, this is my answer:—Not that I loved Caesar less, but that I loved Rome more . . .
>
> (III. ii. 13)

This speech exactly exposes the love-honour dualism in Brutus' experience. Both before and after Caesar's death, we find Brutus' 'honour' conflicting with his loves: and always this failure to unify his experiences results in disorder, failure. He trusts to his abstractions pitifully: here he expects the citizens to be convinced by cold reasoning. One breath of Antony's passion, one sight of Caesar's mutilated body, will dispel that effect. So Antony's speech drives Brutus and Cassius from Rome.

Brutus shows himself cold in his quarrel with Cassius. The rights and wrongs of the matter are hard to decide and not important. Both appear faulty: Brutus has 'condemned' a friend of Cassius on a paltry charge, Cassius has refused money to Brutus, or so it seems. Brutus, however, can scarcely with any justice both blame Cassius for accepting bribes and for refusing himself money. His want is due to his own refusal to raise money 'by vile means' (IV. iii. 71), and to request a loan from Cassius is clearly to justify Cassius' use of bribery. However, the issue is vague. But a general truth emerges. Brutus is still hampering success by continued regard for his 'honour'. Cassius, less scrupu-

lous, shows, as always, more warmness of heart. Cassius is
always in touch with realities—of love, of conspiracy, of
war: Brutus is ever most at home with his ethical abstractions. He treasures to his heart the 'justice' of his cause:

> Remember March, the Ides of March remember:
> Did not great Julius bleed for justice' sake?
> What villain touch'd his body, that did stab,
> And not for justice? What, shall one of us,
> That struck the foremost man of all this world
> But for supporting robbers, shall we now
> Contaminate our fingers with base bribes,
> And sell the mighty space of our large honours
> For so much trash as may be grasped thus?
> I had rather be a dog, and bay the moon,
> Than such a Roman.   (IV. iii. 18)

The quarrel is exquisitely human and pathetic. As their
cause fails, these two 'noble' Romans—the word 'noble' is
frequent in the play—begin to wrangle over money.
Brutus starts by his noble apostrophe to 'justice': but soon
we feel his primary anxiety is a very practical one—lack of
gold:

> *Brutus.*   . . . I did send
>   To you for gold to pay my legions,
>   Which you denied me: was that done like Cassius?
>   Should I have answer'd Caius Cassius so?
>   When Marcus Brutus grows so covetous,
>   To lock such rascal counters from his friends,
>   Be ready, gods, with all your thunderbolts;
>   Dash him to pieces!
> *Cassius.*   I denied you not.
> *Brutus.* You did.
> *Cassius.* I did not: he was but a fool
>   That brought my answer back . . .   (IV. iii. 75)

We may observe, with reference to Brutus' self-idealisa-
tion here, that, if he did not deny Cassius gold, he certainly
ignored his letters on behalf of Lucius Pella. This quarrel
marks the failure of Brutus and Cassius. Their impending
joint failure is forecast in this inner dissension. Also it
suggests the failure of ideals unrelated to practical

expediency: Brutus' ship of 'honour' dashes on the hard rocks of finance. It is pathetic, human, and exactly true. At last their dissension is healed by Cassius' love. Brutus' coldness thaws. As with his wife earlier, a deeper loyalty replaces his frigid abstractions:

> Do what you will, dishonour shall be humour. (IV. iii. 109)

Next Brutus again reverts to abstractions: this time his prided stoic philosophy:

> *Cassius.* I did not think you could have been so angry.
> *Brutus.* O Cassius, I am sick of many griefs.
> *Cassius.* Of your philosophy you make no use,
>   If you give place to accidental evils.
> *Brutus.* No man bears sorrow better. Portia is dead.
>
> (IV. iii. 143)

Cassius is to 'speak no more of her' (IV. iii. 158). The news is corroborated by Messala. Brutus hears it a second time; there is no possibility of mistake. Again, he receives it dispassionately, to Cassius' wonder:

> I have as much of this in art as you,
> But yet my nature could not bear it so.   (IV. iii. 194)

'Art.' Brutus makes life a long process of 'art', almost 'fiction'. He aspires to impossibilities and unrealities, carries a great burden of 'honour' and 'nobility' through life: which honour is continually troubled by the deeps of emotion which he shares with Antony and Cassius. He is only outwardly cold. Throughout his story love is intermittent with the iron calls of honour. Caesar, Portia, Cassius (whose conspiracy he ruins, whose soldiership he hampers)—his love for all has been sacrificed to honour in one way or another. But that love itself need not be questioned. It is deep; its organ notes are pure:

> *Brutus.*   Noble, noble Cassius,
>   Good night, and good repose.
> *Cassius.*   O my dear brother!
>   This was an ill beginning of the night:
>   Never come such division 'tween our souls!
>   Let it not, Brutus.

Brutus.   Everything is well.
Cassius. Good night, my lord.
Brutus.   Good night, good brother.
                                    (IV. iii. 232)

'Brother' is emphasized. Notice how Cassius is always
ready to humble himself to Brutus—'my lord'. Their
practical failure is here clearly heralded: but a victory has
been realized in Brutus, a victory for love. Left alone, he
asks Lucius to play to him. Lucius' care-free purity of
youth always touches Brutus' heart to words which suggest
here—both in Act II and Act IV—a more spontaneous
love than any he shows to other people. He always speaks
gently to him: 'Bear with me, good boy, I am much
forgetful' (IV. iii. 255), and 'I trouble thee too much but
thou art willing' (IV. iii. 259). Lucius is sleepy. He knows
the dreamless sleep that holds no torment, unlike the
phantasma of Brutus' divided soul. He has already 'slept':

> *Brutus.* It was well done; and thou shalt sleep again;
>   I will not hold thee long: if I do live,
>   I will be good to thee.   (IV. iii. 263)

There is 'music and a song'. So music, with Brutus' love
for his boy, are blended here: music and love, healing,
unifying spells casting momentary peace on Brutus'
divided soul. The boy sleeps:

> If thou dost nod, thou break'st thy instrument;
> I'll take it from thee; and, good boy, good night.
>   (IV. iii. 271)

That is one extreme: extreme of peace, love and music,
realities Brutus has banished, repressed. He pays for his
momentary heaven. Swiftly its opposing hell returns.
The 'evil' in his soul accuses him:

> *Brutus.*   . . . Art thou any thing?
>   Art thou some god, some angel, or some devil,
>   That makest my blood cold and my hair to stare?
>   Speak to me what thou art.
> *Ghost.* Thy evil spirit, Brutus.   (IV. iii. 278)

There is no prolonged peace for Brutus. His life, in the

play, has been 'like a phantasma or a hideous dream'
(ii. i. 65), due, like nightmare, to a divided consciousness;
'evil' none the less potent for its deriving its existence from
the clash of two positive goods: 'honour' and 'love'.

Brutus is always obsessed with his 'honour'. Octavius
mocks Brutus and Cassius as 'traitors', saying he was not
born to die on Brutus' sword. To which Brutus replies:

> O, if thou wert the noblest of thy strain,
> Young man, thou couldst not die more honourable.
>
> (v. i. 59)

He often refers to himself in a strain which repels by its
egoism:

> . . . think not, thou noble Roman,
> That ever Brutus will go bound to Rome;
> He bears too great a mind.   (v. i. 111)

Curiously, this contradicts his words just spoken that
suicide is 'cowardly'. His life is one long contradiction,
one long abstraction.   This boast is of the same order as
his boast in the quarrel scene:

> There is no terror, Cassius, in your threats,
> For I am arm'd so strong in honesty
> That they pass by me as the idle wind,
> Which I respect not.   (iv. iii. 66)

He is so enwrapped in a sense of his own honour that others
can make no headway against his will.   The conspirators
always give way to him.   Cassius cannot resist his self-
haloed personality ever.   He submits to Brutus' judgement
as to coming down from the hills to meet Octavius and
Antony: the event is disaster.   Even in the fight 'Brutus
gave the word too early' (v. iii. 5).   Brutus is a continual
hindrance, usually exactly because of his exaggerated sense
of honour.   Yet he rouses our admiration by his con-
sistency, his steadiness of purpose in serving a figment of
his own mind.   Even when he finds Cassius dead, he shows
little emotion.   Yet we feel deep surges unspoken:

> I shall find time, Cassius, I shall find time. (v. iii. 103)

Strangely, though through his life he has banished the softer joys of love, when at the end he knows his enterprise to be an utter failure, Caesar's spirit victorious, he joys in the thought of friendship:

> The ghost of Caesar hath appear'd to me
> Two several times by night; at Sardis once,
> And, this last night, here in Philippi fields:
> I know my hour is come.   (v. v. 17)

Therefore—

>   Countrymen,
> My heart doth joy that yet in all my life
> I found no man but he was true to me.
> I shall have glory by this losing day
> More than Octavius and Mark Antony
> By this vile conquest shall attain unto.
> So fare you well at once; for Brutus' tongue
> Hath almost ended his life's history:
> Night hangs upon mine eyes; my bones would rest,
> That have but labour'd to attain this hour.   (v. v. 33)

Into the darkness of death he takes the simple joy that his followers have been true to him. There is resignation here, a knowledge of failure, an acceptance of tragedy. The things he valued have played him false. He has 'dismembered' Caesar, but has not 'come by' his 'spirit', partly because he himself from the first made that unreal mental division of Caesar the man and Caesar the imperial force in Rome. So Caesar's disembodied 'spirit', his ghost, Brutus' own creation, pursues Brutus to his death. And the long torment of division in Brutus' soul is closed, the wounding dualism healed in death, an easy 'rest'; and in thoughts of his friends' faith. Love, at the last, quietly takes him, honour-wearied, by the hand, into the darkness. But even in his dying he is anxious for 'honour'. 'Thy life hath had some smatch of honour in it' he says to Strato (v. v. 46), when asking him to hold his sword.

Antony speaks a noble eulogy over his body. Octavius will have it 'order'd honourably' (v. v. 79). Honour always. But Antony is right in saying Brutus slew Caesar 'in a

general honest thought' (v. v. 71), though he may be wrong
in attributing only 'envy' to the rest. Brutus is sincere
throughout. He unwaveringly pursues an ethical ideal
which appears somewhat bloodless in this play of imperial
glory, pulsing love, envy, ambition. Though bloodless, it yet
sheds blood. Brutus lets his abstraction loose in the world of
reality: he will not render Caesar what is Caesar's and offer
his ideal to God. He is the one properly 'ethical' force in
the play: the rest act by emotion. Yet this ethical cast
of thought itself creates division and disorder in his mind,
in his view of Caesar under the two aspects, man and
ruler:

> It must be by his death, and for my part
> I know no personal cause to spurn at him,
> But for the general.   (II. i. 10)

He is himself confused in this speech—as we, too, are
confused by the two Caesars, till Antony's strong love
creates the Caesar we know. Like Caesar himself, he is
anxious as to this tremendous power coming to the friend
he loves. What change may it work? All the disorder-
symbols of the play are to be related to Brutus' divided
allegiances. The vision of naked spirit flaming over Rome
is a projection of Brutus' own spirit-abstraction unharmonized with life. It cannot be too strongly emphasized
that the conspiracy without Brutus might have been a life-
force, a creating of order, not a destruction. So he ruins
first Caesar, then the cause of his own party. Antony wins
over the citizens by ringing the changes on Brutus'
favourite slogan, 'honour':

> So are they all, all honourable men.   (III. ii. 89)

Love's mockery of 'honour'. Over and over again he
drives it in: 'Brutus is an honourable man' (III. ii. 87 and
99), 'Sure, he is an honourable man' (III. ii. 104)—and
again at lines 129, 132, 216, 218. Again,

> I fear I wrong the honourable men
> Whose daggers have stabb'd Caesar; I do fear it. (III. ii. 156)

Brutus' honour pains and slays Portia, drives Cassius in

their quarrel almost to madness, while Brutus remains ice-cold, armed appallingly in 'honesty'. He shows little emotion at his dear ones' death. You can do nothing with him. He is so impossibly noble: and when we forget his nobility he becomes just 'impossible'. Thus when he would for once solace himself for a while with Lucius—his truest love—and Lucius' music, his 'evil spirit' denies his right to such relief. This incident corresponds exactly to the irruption of Banquo's ghost into Macbeth's feast. Macbeth especially desecrates hospitality, Brutus love. Neither may enjoy what they destroy. Brutus has put love from him. He rides roughshod over domestic happiness, like Macbeth. His acts disturb Portia, dislocate meals and sleep. So, too, Caesar and Calpurnia are roused from bed, and Caesar's hospitality desecrated. Cassius, on the contrary, invites people to dinner. The contrast is important. Such pursuit of an ethical ideal in and for itself, unrelated to the time and people around, is seen at the last to be perilous. It is a selfishness. His ethic is no ethic, rather a projection of himself. A phantasma of his own mind. Like Macbeth he projects his mental pain on his country. He alone bears what guilt there is in Caesar's end, since he alone among the conspirators sees—and so creates—its wrongfulness; he alone bears the burden of the conspiracy's failure. He only has a guilty conscience—anguished by an 'evil spirit'. But Cassius, at the last, is 'fresh of spirit' (v. i. 91). And yet, Brutus has glory by his losing day. He suffers, not because he is less than those around him but because he is, in a sense, far greater. He is the noblest Roman of them all. He suffers, and makes others suffer, for his virtue: but such virtue is not enough. Virtue, to Brutus, is a quality to be rigidly distinguished from love. Love regularly conflicts with it. He denies the greatest force in life and the only hope in death. He thus fails in life and dies sadly, pathetically searching at the end for some one 'honourable' enough to slay him. He has starved his love on earth: he thinks at the last of his faithful friends, would take what crumbs he can to solace him in the darkness.

4

Cassius is strongly contrasted with Brutus. He is described by Caesar:

> He reads much;
> He is a great observer and he looks
> Quite through the deeds of men; he loves no plays,
> As thou dost, Antony; he hears no music;
> Seldom he smiles, and smiles in such a sort
> As if he mock'd himself and scorn'd his spirit
> That could be mov'd to smile at any thing.
> Such men as he be never at heart's ease
> Whiles they behold a greater than themselves,
> And therefore are they very dangerous.   (I. ii. 201)

The description is not one to be ashamed of. Cassius has profound understanding, a rich personality. He is very sincere. He claims, rightly, to have nothing in him of the flatterer or scandalmonger: he is no 'common laugher' like Lucio (I. ii. 72–8). His seriousness makes him sombre, gloomy, ashamed of all trivialities. Smiles, plays, music—all are barred. Instead, we have knowledge of men, books, restlessness of temperament. He has something of the morbidity of the artistic temperament. He is a perfect artist in conspiracy. Caesar is afraid of Cassius, afraid of his insight, his depth of soul: afraid, primarily, of something he cannot understand. In point of profundity and earnestness Cassius is similar to the Duke in *Measure for Measure*. The Duke had 'ancient skill' in reading other's characters (IV. ii. 164). He contended especially 'to know himself' (III. ii. 253). As for pleasures, he was

> Rather rejoicing to see another merry, than merry at any thing which professed to make him rejoice: a gentleman of all temperance.   (*Measure for Measure*, III. ii. 255)

The Duke, too, was critical of music:

> . . . music oft hath such a charm
> To make bad good, and good provoke to harm.
> (*Measure for Measure*, IV. i. 14)

His utter sincerity—the sincerity which is at the heart of his ethic—is apparent in his distrust of display:

I love the people,
But do not like to stage me to their eyes:
Though it do well, I do not relish well
Their loud applause and Aves vehement;
Nor do I think the man of safe discretion
That does affect it.   (*Measure for Measure*, I. i. 68)

So, too, Cassius seems to suffer from a certain shy inward-
ness, hating shows and ceremonies. Cassius does not
'profess himself in banqueting to all the rout' (I. ii. 77);
but he invites Casca to a private supper, as I observe above.
And it is exactly this show and ceremony and music which
surrounds Caesar on his first entry: Cassius, like the Duke
of Vienna, instinctively distrusts it. Both are to be contrasted with Timon or Antony (in this play or *Antony and
Cleopatra*)—those more free-hearted heroes who love
feasting, music, display. These are both, in vastly different
ways, lovers, profound lovers, although the Duke may
appear, once, to deny love's power to grip his heart: in
them love is compressed, controlled, its essence not readily
apparent. Love is powerful in Cassius, but does not come
easily. He is too sincere to be happy. This comparison is
valuable since, though Cassius is in other respects vastly
different from the Duke, nevertheless, in point of this oneness yet richness of personality, the likeness is striking. For
Cassius has, like the Duke, a 'complete bosom' (*Measure
for Measure*, I. iii. 3). He is always, as it were, safe, invulnerable to chance, his own soul is a fortress:

I know where I will wear this dagger then;
Cassius from bondage will deliver Cassius:
Therein, ye gods, you make the weak most strong;
Therein, ye gods, you tyrants do defeat:
Nor stony tower, nor walls of beaten brass,
Nor airless dungeon, nor strong links of iron,
Can be retentive to the strength of spirit.   (I. iii. 89)

This assurance is born of a unity of soul. He is not divided,
like Brutus. It will at once be clear how Brutus stands to
Cassius much as Angelo to the Duke of Vienna. Angelo,
like Brutus, fails by his worship of abstract virtue: the

analogy there is immediately evident, and closer than the other. Now, however much we may dislike Cassius' acts —some have done so—it is clear that he possesses single-ness of purpose, and a sense of integrity which renders him fearless:

> Casca.   . . . Cassius, what night is this!
> Cassius. A very pleasing night to honest men.
> Casca. Who ever knew the heavens menace so?
> Cassius. Those that have known the earth so full of faults.
>
> (I. iii. 42)

He has taken deliberate pleasure in walking the streets 'unbraced', baring his 'bosom to the thunderstone':

> And when the cross blue lightning seem'd to open
> The breast of heaven, I did present myself
> Even in the aim and very flash of it.   (I. iii. 50)

So strongly is his integrity emphasized. Enduring no disorder in himself, he fears no outer disorder; knowing himself perfectly, he has no fears of the mysterious and unknown. He finds a place for these disorders. To him they reflect the terrors of Caesar's tyranny, a heaven-sent warning:

> . . . why, you shall find
> That heaven hath infus'd them with these spirits,
> To make them instruments of fear and warning
> Unto some monstrous state.   (I. iii. 68)

Caesar is fearful as these portents, himself like 'this dreadful night':

> A man no mightier than thyself or me
> In personal action, yet prodigious grown
> And fearful, as these strange eruptions are.   (I. iii. 76)

Cassius despises Caesar as a 'person'. Nor can he see him, as Brutus can, as a national hero. The adulation of Rome is absurd. He does not even blame Caesar at all. The fault is his countrymen's:

> And why should Caesar be a tyrant then?
> Poor man! I know he would not be a wolf,
> But that he sees the Romans are but sheep:
> He were no lion, were not Romans hinds.   (I. iii. 103)

Rome is 'rubbish' and 'offal' whose blaze illuminates 'so vile a thing as Caesar' (i. iii. 109). Cassius has nothing but contempt for Caesar, his glory is merely a madness in his admirers. He does not, like Brutus, see two Caesars: he sees only one—a frail, weak, contemptible man; and, next, the hero-worship of Rome. He, like Antony, knows his own mind. After the murder, we tend to see Caesar through Antony's eyes, but at the start of the play we often see him as Cassius sees him. In the middle action we see him with Brutus' indecisive vision. Marullus and Flavius set the note of hostility at the start. Throughout the first act we hear mainly Cassius' opinion, expressed at length to Brutus and Casca. Cassius' arguments to Brutus are clear and exact. Caesar is a weak man physically, a bad swimmer, subject to fever. Cassius is himself his equal, even his superior, if the swimming contest be admitted, and, after all, Caesar suggested it as a test of 'daring'.

> Ye gods, it doth amaze me
> A man of such a feeble temper should
> So get the start of the majestic world
> And bear the palm alone.   (i. ii. 128)

This frail man 'is now become a God' (i. ii. 116). Cassius must bow to him. Cassius' motive is clearly a sort of envy: but it is a fully conscious envy, which stands the test of his own reasoning. The Roman republican ideal is strong in him: he emphasizes it often. He will strike for Rome, for reason, for common sense. He sees Caesar's sudden access of power as a dangerous, fantastic, ludicrous thing: nor do Caesar's own acts and words—his fainting fits, his indecision, his pitiful attempts to be 'Caesar'—fail to bear out his view. Cassius is thus partially justified at the start. But there are other elements to be observed in him.

It is to be noted that he has little sense of abstract honour. To him the end justifies any means. He resembles Scott's 'Burley' in *Old Mortality*. The conspiracy is necessary. He wants Brutus. Therefore he will stoop to deception in the matter of the letters quite readily to

win him. Yet he can respect Brutus' 'nobility', without
understanding it:

> Well, Brutus, thou art noble; yet, I see,
> Thy honourable metal may be wrought
> From that it is dispos'd: therefore it is meet
> That noble minds keep ever with their likes;
> For who so firm that cannot be seduc'd?
> Caesar doth bear me hard; but he loves Brutus:
> If I were Brutus now and he were Cassius,
> He should not humour me.   (I. ii. 312)

This is a crucial and curious speech. I will attempt a
coherent paraphrase. Cassius honours Brutus for his high
ideals. Yet he sees that Brutus' 'honour' sense can readily
be 'wrought' from honourable loyalty to honourable conspiracy. It is a risky thing to be governed by. He is
baffled, as we are, and Brutus is, at the complex conflict in
Brutus' mind. Cassius, single in purpose, finds Brutus'
unsteadiness strange. Such noble men should therefore
keep, he says, not with other noble minds, but rather with
men of like opinions to their own. A man who worships
abstract honour can always and easily be reasoned into
pursuing almost any course in the name of that honour.
To Cassius such 'honour' is therefore a deceit and such
cold reasoning a dangerous thing: albeit it serves his
purpose here. He himself acts by instinct: instinctive
envy, a dark hatred of Caesar's absurd rise to power. He
observes, moreover, that Caesar dislikes him, but loves
Brutus. This is also at the root of his 'envy'. If Caesar
loved him, he says, no amount of reasoning would persuade him to the conspiracy. He himself could never
betray love. Cassius always follows personal emotions.
This argument silhouettes Cassius' personality vividly.
Cassius gives one the impression of loneliness, gloom,
disillusion: he has known the world 'full of faults'
(I. iii. 45). He is dark with thwarted ambition and
envy. But a certain golden star burns in his heart: a
great longing for love. At the start he is anxious for
Brutus' love:

Brutus, I do observe you now of late:
I have not from your eyes that gentleness
And show of love as I was wont to have:
You bear too stubborn and too strange a hand
Over your friend that loves you. (I. ii. 32)

Throughout the play Cassius' love of Brutus is emphasized. We find many emotions in him: envy, ardour, love. He possesses a certain spiritual loneliness and a sense of ultimate security, he is the captain of his soul. But he is not happy: rather given to gloom and foreboding. He is romantic, compact of poetry. Intellect is subsidiary with him, and he is more at home with realities than abstractions. He does not understand Brutus' ethical finesse. Yet respect for his friend causes him to give way to Brutus time after time, thereby ruining his own conspiracy. Frustrated in life, he appears regularly to expect the worst. He fears their 'purpose is discovered' (III. i. 17):

Brutus, what shall be done? If this be known,
Cassius or Caesar never shall turn back,
For I will slay myself. (III. i. 20)

And his foreboding is often justified. Brutus thinks they will have Antony 'well to friend', and he answers:

I wish we may: but yet have I a mind
That fears him much; and my misgiving still
Falls shrewdly to the purpose. (III. i. 144)

After Caesar's death he is maddened by Brutus' obsession with 'honour'. His complaint is typical. He interceded for a friend, Lucius Pella, whom Brutus subsequently punished for accepting bribes. Cassius champions personal emotions, personal fears and forebodings, antipathies and envies, personal love. Brutus upholds an intellectual ideal of 'honour'. They meet, one passionate and ardent, the other aloof, scornful, self-righteous:

Cassius. Most noble brother, you have done me wrong.
Brutus. Judge me, you gods! wrong I mine enemies?
  And, if not so, how should I wrong a brother?
Cassius. Brutus, this sober form of yours hides wrongs;
  And when you do them— (IV. ii. 37)

Throughout the quarrel Cassius is passionate in anger, grief, or love. Brutus is cold, aureoled in self-righteousness, unreachable, remote: but beneath emotion surges, too, in him. Cassius is the first to give way, to admit fault. Typically, he fights throughout, not, like Brutus, with reason, but with emotion. He is in this the more feminine of the two. First, anger; next, grief:

> Brutus hath riv'd my heart;
> A friend should bear his friend's infirmities,
> But Brutus makes mine greater than they are.
>
> (IV. iii. 85)

Brutus loves him not: a 'friendly eye' would not see such faults. Brutus' ethical scorn still lacerates him unmercifully. At last, he exposes the riches of his thwarted, longing, passion-soul:

> Come, Antony, and young Octavius, come,
> Revenge yourselves alone on Cassius,
> For Cassius is aweary of the world;
> Hated by one he loves; brav'd by his brother;
> Check'd like a bondman; all his faults observ'd,
> Set in a note-book, learn'd and conn'd by rote,
> To cast into my teeth. O, I could weep
> My spirit from mine eyes! There is my dagger,
> And here my naked breast; within, a heart
> Dearer than Plutus' mine, richer than gold:
> If that thou be'st a Roman, take it forth;
> I, that denied thee gold, will give my heart:
> Strike, as thou didst at Caesar; for, I know,
> When thou didst hate him worst, thou lovedst him better
> Than ever thou lovedst Cassius.   (IV. iii. 93)

Here Cassius challenges the rich worth of his emotional nature against the other integrity of Brutus. But what is there in Brutus that dare so boast its spiritual 'gold'? And Cassius wins, by power of love. They celebrate their new strength with a bowl of wine. His 'heart' is thirsty, he 'cannot drink too much of Brutus' love' (IV. iii. 162). Cassius is wrung with sorrow at Portia's death, and shows more grief than Brutus. And he gives way to Brutus on points of strategy. He is clearly the more experienced soldier:

> I am a soldier, I,
> Older in practice, abler than yourself
> To make conditions.   (IV. iii. 30)

Yet, as always, he gives way to Brutus. At this point he is, indeed, far more concerned with his and Brutus' love than any military expedients:

> O my dear brother!
> This was an ill beginning of the night:
> Never come such division 'tween our souls!
> Let it not, Brutus.   (IV. iii. 233)

Cassius' love thus saves the conspiracy from the final disgrace of 'division', enables it to meet its end intact.

But he himself appears to have passed beyond such interests. Although his temper flares for an instant at Antony's taunts, Antony who calls him a 'flatterer', the very thing he is not and would never be—'Now, Brutus, thank yourself . . .' (v. i. 45)—he appears to have found a new strength. Something in him is unloosed, freed, in the quarrel-scene: he has a strength and purpose independent of success. This 'something' is a kind of love. He still has forebodings. He tells Messala how 'ravens, crows, and kites' form a 'canopy most fatal' (v. i. 85–8) over their army. Like the others, Calpurnia, Caesar, Brutus, Cinna, he has begun to 'credit things that do presage' (v. i. 79). Yet he has always possessed a retreat, a lonely eyry of the spirit, which renders him fearless. Now, especially, he appears new in strength:

> I but believe it partly;
> For I am fresh of spirit and resolv'd
> To meet all perils very constantly.   (v. i. 90)

A visionary light settles on him, singles him now for the first time as protagonist. As ever, it is he who expects the worst, asks Brutus what he will do if the battle be lost:

> Let 's reason with the worst that may befall. (v. i. 97)

He parts from Brutus. There is no more noble parting in

Shakespeare. Next we see him in the flood of battle. Failure is imminent, his men fly:

> *Pindarus.* Fly further off, my lord, fly further off;
>   Mark Antony is in your tents, my lord:
>   Fly, therefore, noble Cassius, fly far off.
> *Cassius.* This hill is far enough. Look, look, Titinius;
>   Are those my tents where I perceive the fire?
> *Titinius.* They are, my lord.
> *Cassius.*   Titinius, if thou lovest me,
>   Mount thou my horse, and hide thy spurs in him,
>   Till he have brought thee up to yonder troops,
>   And here again; that I may rest assur'd
>   Whether yond troops are friend or enemy.   (v. iii. 9)

There is now a light-foot strength of spirit in Cassius: something fiery-strong, intangible, intractable to definition. He is yet strangely 'fresh of spirit' in disaster, in foreboding:

> Go, Pindarus, get higher on that hill;
> My sight was ever thick; regard Titinius,
> And tell me what thou notest about the field.
>   (v. iii. 20)

Pindarus leaves him:

> This day I breathed first: time is come round,
> And where I did begin, there shall I end;
> My life is run his compass.   (v. iii. 23)

Cleopatra-like, he thus celebrates his birthday under the shadow of impending tragedy. And yet, this birth-remembrance yet lights this death with a sudden expectancy, a birth—a death and birth:

> Come down, behold no more.
> O, coward that I am, to live so long,
> To see my best friend ta'en before my face!
>   (v. iii. 33)

A breathless expectancy keenly charges this scene. It is a positive, purposeful adventure, a stepping free, a death, like Cleopatra's, into love. Cassius the envious, the passionate, the lover, is now afloat on a love—Brutus

before, now Titinius. Names are but symbols through
which the spirit steps naked into the air and fire of love.
Cassius gives Pindarus his last charge, the air aquiver
with immortality. Like Antony, he bids his bondman
remember the condition by which the saving of his 'life'
has bound him to obedience:

> Come now, keep thine oath;
> Now be a freeman . . .   (v. iii. 40)

'Life', 'freeman': what are these associations? In my reading
of this scene I may be thought to tread a dangerous
precipice. For only by irrationalities are my statements
justified. But the associations here are powerful: the 'fire'
perceived by Cassius, the love of Titinius—'if thou lovedst
me'—'birth', 'shouts' of 'joy' (v. iii. 32), 'my best friend',
'saving of thy life', 'freeman': all this, together with the
event which proves indeed that victory has been mistaken
for failure, all stresses, not death, but life-in-death. The
sight of mortality is 'ever thick'. The associations here
contradict the logic: it is often the way of poetry. Cassius
all but accomplishes the fiery splendour and conscious
purpose of Cleopatra's death-in-love. His death is a death
of ecstasy and liberation. Pindarus will fly far 'where
never Roman shall take note of him' (v. iii. 50). Safe
and far, Pindarus or Cassius? Far from Rome. It is well
that the purest essence of this play's poetry be spilled over
his body:

> No, this was he, Messala,
> But Cassius is no more. O setting sun,
> As in thy red rays thou dost sink to-night,
> So in his red blood Cassius' day is set;
> The sun of Rome is set.   (v. iii. 59)

As the blood of the lover's heart streams out, the blood of
republican Rome is spilt on the plains of Philippi; and
the crimson of the great sun drops level to honour with
horizontal streams of fire the spirit of man victorious. This
is the Shakespearian sanction of love which has the

universe at its bidding. Cassius is now crowned with a wreath of victory: our final, most vivid, association:

> *Titinius.* Why didst thou send me forth, brave Cassius?
>   Did I not meet thy friends? And did not they
>   Put on my brows this wreath of victory,
>   And bid me give it thee? Didst thou not hear their shouts?
>   Alas, thou hast misconstrued every thing!
>   But, hold thee, take this garland on thy brow;
>   Thy Brutus bid me give it thee, and I
>   Will do his bidding. Brutus, come apace,
>   And see how I regarded Caius Cassius.
>   By your leave, gods:—this is a Roman's part:
>   Come, Cassius' sword, and find Titinius' heart.
>   (v. iii. 80)

'Heart' always in this play of fire and love. So Titinius crowns Cassius. 'Thy Brutus . . .'

> Shall it not grieve thee dearer than thy death
> To see thy Antony . . .   (iii. i. 197)

It is all one. This universe of kingly ambition, divided allegiances, envy, hostility, friendship—all is dominated and finally fused by love, the love and intimacy that beats here in imagery, incident, emotion, life, and death itself. So Titinius crowns Cassius, the lover, in death:

> Brave Titinius!
> Look, whether he have not crown'd dead Cassius!
>   (v. iii. 96)

Like Charmian over Cleopatra, he arranges the lover's crown, then hastens to follow his master. I have compared Cassius with the Duke in *Measure for Measure*; and now I relate his death to that of Cleopatra, to whom he is close in point of a certain romantic strength which solicits our respect apparently quite independently of any ethical judgement. What quality can we say binds these three? The Duke is the prince of ethical moralizers; Cleopatra, the Queen of Courtezans. Yet all three possess a certain unique richness of soul and range of feeling: and in this they conquer.

The imperial theme of mighty Caesar is thus the hub on which revolves a theme of wider scope, imperially crowned with fire of love's radiance. Human activity in all its ardour and positive splendour is set within an ever-present atmosphere of love. Man is vivid—in act and renown—all are 'noble'; his spirit-fire burns through physical weakness; the gashed body releases streams of red life. The slaying of Caesar is a grand, an historic act:

> How many ages hence
> Shall this our lofty scene be acted over
> In states unborn and accents yet unknown!
>
> (III. i. 111)

In assassination the conspirators are yet Caesar's 'friends' (III. i. 104). The power of Caesar has come on him un-prepared, he is himself embarrassed, fearful of the mighty sway of the world-empire to be trusted to his weakness. The fate of the western world trembles in the balance as he puts the crown aside, 'loath to lay his fingers off it' (I. ii. 243). He knows himself, as Cassius knows him, weak—as who would not be weak?—for such an Atlas burden; and he hates Cassius for knowing it. Till he is murdered, Cassius is right. But Brutus has offered us a dualized vision: Caesar, a man lovable, a friend—and Caesar potential, under stress of power become a danger, an enemy of Rome (II. i. 10–34). He, like Caesar himself, is uneasy. The division in his soul is, like our vision of the middle scenes, a rough tearing of 'body' from 'spirit', which dualism is at the root also of Caesar's fears—Caesar who knows himself a puny man, but must live up to a lion strength of spirit equal to Danger itself. Cassius, too, sees on the one side Caesar, the weakling, and, on the other, the adulation of Rome fit only for a god. All our early fears, doubts, insecurities of vision are related to this body-spirit dualism: hence our symbols of naked fire, spirit raging unfitted to the finite, and impossible events on earth, bodies uninfused with soul. Caesar dead, Antony's love at once—as never before—shows us Caesar as he was. Hitherto we saw him in terms of fear, in terms of what he might be; and the poet well stresses his weakness, which is, however, only weakness in comparison with the superhuman glory and power about to light upon his brows. Seeing him in terms of fear, we saw him unreal; unreal with the deathly unreality of time-thinking we meet in *Macbeth*. In Antony's vision the dualism is a unity. The Caesar of history swims into our ken in Antony's first words after the assassination. Love heals the severance of 'body' from 'spirit'. Perhaps Cassius was wrong. He was blind to Caesar's greatness. To see ahead and fear is evil and unreal: reality is now, and love. Cassius who ever looks ahead, foreboding ill, yet treasures also a spiritual fortress which has no fear, and finally falls back only on this soul-treasure in his breast. Caesar's spirit has proved his course of action wrong (v. iii. 45); but not his heart 'richer than gold'. As failure nears, his love is brighter, he steps free. Antony's victory is the conquest of love, love which saw only in Caesar a true friend and a great man, that made no 'god' comparisons nor foolishly stressed his physique, and, seeing the real Caesar, was content to trust him with Rome's fate. And Cassius' death, too, is a conquest of love. Time and again he sacrifices his conspiracy for Brutus. Brutus ruins an otherwise seaworthy plot. But Cassius drinks his fill of Brutus' love at the last, and dies 'fresh of spirit' in the cause of friendship. Brutus refuses love for honour. In incident after incident he brushes love aside. He alone is throughout wholly responsible for the dualism which wrenches 'spirit' from 'body', in Rome or in his own mind. True, I have said that Cassius' view of the Caesar problem is proved false by Antony. As the play stands, it is. But without Brutus and his 'honour' there would have been no Antony to redirect our vision. Then there would have been a straightforward assassination needing no disorder symbolism. During his life, Caesar fits Cassius' view well enough. There is nothing in him to show Cassius' fears unfounded, except in the sense, noted above, in which all 'fear' is evil. Again we see the exactitude of the poet's intuition in the variations he plays on the Caesar-idea. We realize how truly the poet has refused any one explicit statement[1] of the meaning of his symbolism:

> But men may construe things after their fashion,
> Clean from the purpose of the things themselves.
>
> (i. iii. 34)

These portents are different things to different people, and their meaning varies according to the event. But the Brutus-wavering, the Brutus-division is, in a final judgement, the only exact 'cause' of what disorder and evil there is in the play. Against him are set two lovers: the lover of the republican ideal, Cassius; the lover of Caesar, Antony. Both are positive forces. Brutus is negative, because his fine intellect sees equally with the vision of the other two.

But all these complexities are but threads woven on a cloth whose delicate texture is compact of love. All wounds are healed. Brutus and Cassius part nobly, lovers at the last. Aptly, our final words are 'this happy day' (v. v. 81). The baffling, maddening, phantasma of the two Caesars is over, and Caesar's 'spirit' is at rest. It no longer exists as a bodiless, homeless abstraction: perhaps it never did.

---

[1] In *Macbeth*, where the murder is so extreme an evil, its essential unnaturalness is emphasized for us. The meaning of the symbolisms is explicitly stated. See the choric dialogue in *Macbeth*, ii. iv.

IV

ROSE OF MAY: AN ESSAY ON LIFE-THEMES IN HAMLET

THERE are many themes in *Hamlet* which justify my present title. Usually they are contrasted, not associated, with the protagonist and his father's spirit. We see a surface-crust of life—trivial, dishonourable, sometimes beautiful—split open: within, breeding in the very heart of life, is a loathsome crime, a hideous death. Here I illustrate our contrast with especial regard to the life-themes; noting, however, the imaginative darkness which is the setting of the Ghost and, in the middle action especially, of Hamlet. Darkness and light are contrasted. Too often are these effects ignored and the difficulties of our complex vision consequently misunderstood. Such themes of life are apparent in Polonius, Laertes, Fortinbras, Ophelia. Elsewhere I have already indicated how clearly Claudius is drawn as a life-force in the early acts, directing attention to his feasting, his pleasant nature, his wisdom: 'an excellent diplomatist and king'. Here I shall observe in further detail his importance in point of courage and kingliness. Other life-colourings are evident in Ophelia's and Fortinbras' words about Hamlet as he was before the action—a soldier, a lover; in Osric, and the players. All these are to be contrasted with the Ghost, with death. Especially vivid and beautiful is Ophelia's flowery and watery end.

First, I shall consider Polonius, and here we must be ready always to see in the Polonius-Laertes relation a contrast or comparison with our main theme. There are three 'sons' in the play. For Mgr. Kolbe and Miss Campbell[1] have well observed that Fortinbras reflects a similar filial loss to that endured by Laertes and Hamlet. We

[1] In *Shakespeare's Way* and *Shakespeare's Tragic Heroes*.

must therefore observe carefully Fortinbras' ardour 、 recover lands lost by his father, as well as his uncle's attempts—here successful—to control him. Laertes' anger at Polonius' death bears an obvious significance: and we must notice too Polonius' paternal regard for Laertes' welfare at the start. Each theme shows us a studied picture of two generations in reciprocal activity. Especially clear is the personality of Polonius, and his attitude to life bears an important relation to the play as a whole. Polonius, a fussy old man, bids Laertes good-bye as he starts on his travels. He delivers his famous speech of 'precepts' (I. iii. 55–81). This speech, though acute, even profound, in parts, yet strikes a certain note throughout which may be called almost 'platitudinous', certainly 'perfunctory'. It is eminently practical. Polonius utters a commonplace, superficial wisdom. Laertes is to do nothing rash, is not to speak his own thoughts too readily; rather remain silent, and listen to others. He is to cement reliable friendships, avoid dangerous ones; to beware of quarrels, but carry through successfully any quarrel once started, as a precaution for the future. He is to dress carefully, because clothes make a powerful impression. He is not to lend or borrow money: borrowing hinders thrift, loan often loses 'both itself and friend'. Finally, he is to be true to himself—so that he may be true to others. Never the thing-in-itself, rather the appearance, appeals to Polonius; not the essence, but the surface. It is exactly this worldly reasoning, reasons given for every precept, which causes Polonius' speech to appear trivial and platitudinous. And this is important. We have here a typical attitude to life, typical paternal advice on the occasion of a typical problem: a young man's first adventures in life. We have, also, a certain tawdriness in Polonius' ethic: something superficial, not based on any profound convictions.

We find the same attitude in Polonius' conversation with Reynaldo. The old man sends his boy money; and would spy on his actions. Reynaldo is to find an acquaintance of Laertes' and suggest certain faults in his character in order to elicit the truth:

> . . . marry, none so rank
> As may dishonour him; take heed of that;
> But, sir, such wanton, wild and usual slips
> As are companions noted and most known
> To youth and liberty.   (ii. i. 20)

All the usual things. Sowing his wild oats. And throughout we observe Polonius' very superficial ethic: he has no idea of essential virtue or essential vice. Laertes must behave well on the whole, since good behaviour pays best. Vice must not hinder his success. But all faults habitually condoned may readily be passed over—'honour', the name and reputation, is everything: the essence, a mere nothing. Polonius has a liberal notion of 'honour', and his laxity disturbs Reynaldo:

> *Reynaldo.* My lord, that would dishonour him.
> *Polonius.* 'Faith, no . . .   (ii. i. 27)

Such is Polonius' morality, surface deep. But it has another side. It is tolerant. Polonius accepts the ordinary flux of human affairs, human conventions, without probing below the surface. He is worldly-wise, but no more. And these suggestions contrast vividly with Hamlet's agony: Hamlet, who mines into the essence, sees the ugliness beneath the fine superficies of life. There is a similarity besides a contrast. As Polonius inquires into Laertes' behaviour with paternal solicitude, as Fortinbras' uncle suppresses his nephew's high-spirited soldiership, so Claudius and the Queen would pluck out the dread secret of Hamlet. But Polonius and 'old Norway' are faced by typical problems: discretion controls youth, would direct 'the flash and outbreak of a fiery mind' (ii. i. 33). Whereas Claudius, and in part the Queen, are confronted by a grimmer task: the hiding of discretion's sin from the critical eyes of youth. This unnatural reversal it is that so tortures Hamlet and, itself utterly abnormal, wrenches him from all normal pursuits:

Yea, from the table of my memory
I'll wipe away all trivial fond records,
All saws of books, all forms, all pressures past,
That youth and observation copied there.   (I. v. 98)

So the gaping Death to which he swears fealty on the
battlements of Elsinore enthrones itself solitary king in
his soul. 'Trivial' things of everyday life, 'saws' (like
Polonius' 'precepts'), all life-'forms' imprinted on his
memory, none have relevance to this grave-revelation of
murder, disease, death, at the very heart of his home, his
country, his world. A formless death possesses him. It is
he who is old, he who must, ironic reversal, set himself
to tutor his elders in the ways of purity:

O shame! where is thy blush? Rebellious hell,
If thou canst mutine in a matron's bones,
To flaming youth let virtue be as wax,
And melt in her own fire: proclaim no shame
When the compulsive ardour gives the charge,
Since frost itself as actively doth burn
And reason panders will.   (III. iv. 82)

The time is out of joint and the age-youth sequence reversed. So trivial are Polonius' conventional anxieties by
this irremediable suffering in Hamlet.

The personification of Polonius vividly silhouettes the
nature of our main problem. Polonius is normal, in morality, in paternal solicitude: Hamlet, abnormal. Polonius is
insensitive to fine shades of virtue: Hamlet, hyper-
sensitive. Polonius suspects nothing of Claudius' crime.
He never sees deep. His folly has a certain practical
wisdom: it is easier not to see too deep. He accepts the
established order: in Claudius, in everything. He
blunders into Claudius' secret without knowing it:

Polonius. ... We are oft to blame in this,—
    'Tis too much prov'd—that with devotion' visage
    And pious action we do sugar o'er
    The devil himself.
King (aside).   O, 'tis too true!
    How smart a lash that speech doth give my conscience!

> The harlot's cheek, beautied with plastering art,
> Is not more ugly to the thing that helps it
> Than is my deed to my most painted word:
> O heavy burthen!   (III. i. 46)

He is always likely to be the last to find a profound truth: hence the humour of his pride in his policy:

> And thus do we of wisdom and of reach,
> With windlasses and with assays of bias,
> By indirections find directions out.   (II. i. 64)

He is, however, aware that his subtlety may lead him to dangerous mistakes—ironical, when we remember his end:

> . . . but, beshrew my jealousy!
> By heaven, it is as proper to our age
> To cast beyond ourselves in our opinions
> As it is common for the younger sort
> To lack discretion.   (II. i. 113)

Notice how he renders everything a little platitudinous and commonplace. Hamlet thinks him tedious, an old fool, scorns him. And eventually Polonius pays for his superficiality, his meddling in affairs too deep for one of his shallow understanding.

For the unique and mysterious reality respects not at all his intellectual meanderings and platitudinous generalizations:

> Thou wretched, rash, intruding fool, farewell!
> I took thee for thy better: take thy fortune;
> Thou findst to be too busy is some danger.   (III. iv. 31)

Polonius has been too readily content with the surface appearance, without suspecting the fires that seethe beneath. He fusses at Claudius' elbow, helping to discover Hamlet's secret: little guessing the horrible truth in terms of which alone the Hamlet-Claudius struggle is being fought out. So he hides behind curtains, thinking himself clever. He accepts his world: but he has never understood it. Hamlet, on the contrary, cannot accept it. He understands it too well. Events, natural and supernatural, give him little real chance. We may perhaps

tabulate three orders of reaction to the problem of existence: (i) an easy acceptance, often guilty of insincerity, a
refusal to see the unpleasant; (ii) rejection; and (iii)
profound acceptance, through sympathetic understanding.
Most of our people here must be placed in the first group;
Hamlet, for the greater part of the play, in the second—
he touches the third, perhaps, not very certainly or consistently, towards the end. Horatio represents the ideal.
He is,

> As one, in suffering all, that suffers nothing,
> A man that fortune's buffets and rewards
> Hast ta'en with equal thanks. (III. ii. 71)

He has inner unity—his 'blood' (emotion) and 'judgement'
are so well 'commingled' that he is 'not a pipe for fortune's finger to sound what stop she please' (III. ii. 75).
He unifies his vision of life. Now this Hamlet cannot
do. He sees death, not life: it is, at least, consistent, whereas
life has been shown unmeaning, self-contradictory, not
to the intellect only, but to the emotions too. Hamlet, in
his wholesale rejection of existence, sees all life as sullied,
smirched, all but unreal.

Hamlet is opposed not only to certain forms of life, but
even to life itself: Ophelia is rejected with Claudius.
Hamlet does not exactly suspect Ophelia of treachery—not
at first anyway: but he is a whole universe away from the
consciousness where love is possible. The poet has very
excellently shown us all varieties of innocence and guilt;
some, like Polonius and Gertrude, neither quite innocent
nor exactly guilty. There is a doubt. Hamlet's own words
on such 'doubt' are apposite. A man, he says, through
one single known blot in his nature

> Shall in the general censure take corruption
> From that particular fault: the dram of evil
> Doth all the noble substance of a doubt
> To his own scandal. (I. iv. 35)

The one evil permeates that which is doubtfully noble,
till all seems evil, and so is evil: there being 'nothing

either good or bad, but thinking makes it so' (ii. ii. 259).
So to Hamlet Denmark becomes a 'prison', or rather a
'ward' in that 'goodly' prison the world: but it is 'none' to
Rosencrantz and Guildenstern, who think differently.
There is a descending scale of evil from Claudius to
Ophelia who is quite guiltless. The 'dram of evil' infects
Hamlet's view of life. Thus, Death, in the form of the
Ghost, brings to birth a death in Hamlet's soul: his
father's life gave him birth, his father's ghost begets him
a second time in death. In this sense, he, and his vision,
contrast with our themes of life. So, though we always
see clearly the failings and falsities rampant in Hamlet's
world, we yet see with equal clarity that Hamlet is a dark
force in that world. In order the more clearly to silhouette
our life-themes I shall next notice the especial darkness
that distinguishes certain elements in the play.

The Ghost is a thing of darkness. It is 'this thing'
(i. i. 21), or 'this dreaded sight' (i. i. 25). It 'harrows' men
with 'fear and wonder' (i. i. 44). Though related in
appearance to a well-beloved king, its presence is a
'usurpation' of life by death:

> What art thou, that usurp'st this time of night,
> Together with that fair and warlike form
> In which the majesty of buried Denmark
> Did sometimes march? (i. i. 46)

Though endued with a certain royal sanctity, the apparition is also sombre and minatory:

> So frown'd he once, when, in an angry parle,
> He smote the sledded Polacks on the ice. (i. i. 62)

It is 'portentous' (i. i. 109) and clearly to be related to
such disorder-symbols as we find in *Macbeth* and *Julius
Caesar*, things which accompany disintegration in man or
state. The suggestion is exploited by Horatio, who refers
to the death of Julius Caesar (i. i. 114), when, among other
omens, there were 'disasters in the sun' (i. i. 118) and

> . . . the moist star
> Upon whose influence Neptune's empire stands
> Was sick almost to doomsday with eclipse. (i. i. 118)

The similarity to *Macbeth*, where the sun goes out, and the moon is 'down', is clear. The Ghost is a thing of dread import. It is forcefully contrasted with thoughts of divinity and grace, frequently associated with 'hell': again we see a similarity to the *Macbeth*-evil. Horatio knows that to give such a spirit rest, to free our world from its presence, will be an act of 'grace' (I. i. 131). It starts 'like a guilty thing' (I. i. 148) at the cock's crowing, herald of daylight and life. It is, true, 'majestical' (I. i. 143). But Marcellus also contrasts it with the holiest associations:

> It faded on the crowing of the cock.
> Some say that ever 'gainst that season comes
> Wherein our Saviour's birth is celebrated,
> The bird of dawning singeth all night long:
> And then, they say, no spirit dares stir abroad;
> The nights are wholesome; then no planets strike,
> No fairy takes, nor witch hath power to charm,
> So hallow'd and so gracious is the time. (I. i. 157)

'Gracious'. This speech is followed by Horatio's intensely beautiful lines on the dawn. The contrast is one of darkness and daylight: and the spirit of dark, walking 'in the dead vast and middle of the night' (I. ii. 198), is partly, at least, to be contrasted also with 'grace'.

When Hamlet hears that his father's spirit is abroad, he half knows that to converse with death is to risk the terrors of hell:

> If it assume my noble father's person,
> I'll speak to it, though hell itself should gape,
> And bid me hold my peace. (I. ii. 244)

Hamlet's address to the Ghost is a speech of piteous beauty and the yearning of love: it is also a speech of fear. Again, there is a 'grace' contrast:

> Angels and ministers of grace defend us!
> Be thou a spirit of health or goblin damn'd,
> Bring with thee airs from heaven or blasts from hell,
> Be thy intents wicked or charitable,
> Thou comest in such a questionable shape
> That I will speak to thee ... (I. iv. 39)

True, the spirit is, in a sense, Hamlet's father:

> I'll call thee Hamlet,
> King, father, royal Dane . . .   (i. iv. 44)

But the sepulchre where his 'canonized bones' were 'quietly inurned' has opened, and a 'dead corse' revisits 'the glimpses of the moon' and makes night 'hideous'. Hideous. That is our enigma. It is a portentous, unnatural thing, something mortality must reject: yet, at the same time, it is a loved father, an honoured king. Father and King: both are important. The ideals of love and kingship are at stake. But that father, that king, is dead. So, clearly, the Ghost is also Death. What is death? The spirit is indeed 'questionable'—in every sense. He certainly tells a tale which enlists our sympathy. He is morally justified by all laws of man. Yet, in being a ghost, he is outside the laws of man. Hence he is vividly shown as a thing of darkness. In this play the dark forces are given ethical sanction: but this alters not their darkness. Thus the Ghost must return to his prison-house at dawn: he may not, like Oberon, make sport with the morning's love. He is a spirit of another sort, stalking abroad 'in the dead vast and middle of the night'. What spaceless and soundless infinity reverberates in that line, what utter death . . . Is he devil or loved parent? Spirit of health or goblin damned? With exquisite aptness the poet has placed him, not in heaven or hell, but purgatory. Throughout our problem is unsolved for us. If we seek for a final answer we must say: the Ghost is neither 'right', nor 'wrong', but it is a thing of dark, not light; of Death, not Life.

The Ghost hints at the horrors of its death:

> I am thy father's spirit,
> Doom'd for a certain term to walk the night,
> And for the day confin'd to fast in fires,
> Till the foul crimes done in my days of nature
> Are burnt and purg'd away. But that I am forbid
> To tell the secrets of my prison-house,
> I could a tale unfold whose lightest word
> Would harrow up thy soul, freeze thy young blood,

Make thy two eyes, like stars, start from their spheres,
Thy knotted and combined locks to part,
And each particular hair to stand on end,
Like quills upon the fretful porpentine:
But this eternal blazon must not be
To ears of flesh and blood.   (I. v. 9)

In truth, no radiant spirit. This is but the eschatological
equivalent for the bodily horror of physical death, ever in
this play most vividly contrasted with life. The poison by
which this death was accomplished was one whose effect

Holds such an enmity with blood of man
That swift as quicksilver it courses through
The natural gates and alleys of the body,
And with a sudden vigour it doth posset
And curd, like eager droppings into milk,
The thin and wholesome blood: so did it mine;
And a most instant tetter bark'd about,
Most lazar-like, with vile and loathsome crust,
All my smooth body.   (I. v. 65)

He is cut off 'even in the blossoms of my sin' (I. v. 76).
We find here a statement of absolute death. On the plane
of nature, hideous, 'loathsome'; on the plane of eschatology, horrible beyond words, a purgatory which sounds
indeed far more like hell. Essential death is hell: what is
heaven but absolute life? Such is the true meaning and
reality of our Ghost. And this is the father Hamlet loved:
a goodly king, the imperial strength of Denmark. Every
loving son tends to regard his parent as existing almost
beyond the breath of evil. Hamlet finds his thus suddenly
cast up from death, a thing of hideous spiritual nakedness,
tormented for his 'foul crimes'. Absolute death, absolute
evil, disease and horror, and all life now but a tale told by
a ghost . . . this is Hamlet's vision. He has seen the
utmost horror of evil and death at the heart of life. The
Ghost's words blacken both time and eternity. It is to
be observed that in his most famous soliloquy and his
graveyard meditations Hamlet's thoughts range over the
whole of life: the particular situation is to him part of a

universal problem. The 'royal bed' of Denmark is unclean, Hamlet's kingly father is a loathsome death. And
from this height of hideous knowledge Hamlet strides as
a man among Lilliputians, an eminence which is a sickly,
dizzying state. Horatio limns Hamlet's fate fairly true:

> What if it tempt you toward the flood, my lord,
> Or to the dreadful summit of the cliff
> That beetles o'er his base into the sea,
> And there assume some other horrible form,
> Which might deprive your sovereignty of reason
> And draw you into madness? think of it:
> The very place puts toys of desperation,
> Without more motive, into every brain
> That looks so many fathoms to the sea
> And hears it roar beneath. (I. iv. 69)

So the very place of Hamlet's knowledge does later put
toys of desperation in his mind.[1] It is really impossible
to regard the Ghost as a purely 'good' apparition: to
regard it so is to ignore all imaginative colourings. It is

[1] I refer to his 'To be or not to be . . .' soliloquy. I am aware that
Mr. Middleton Murry considers that he has shown the opening of this
soliloquy to refer, not to suicide, but to Claudius' assassination: he reads
it as 'to act or not to act'. It is not my desire, here or elsewhere, to
attack other critics' interpretations, but merely to present my own. But,
since Mr. Murry has adduced his essay against my reading, I would
observe: (i) That Mr. Murry himself realizes that the play provides no
coherent data for his paraphrase:

> The question *why* Hamlet is certain that any attempt to kill the King
> will involve his own death is interesting. Shakespeare seems to have
> taken it for granted, for the necessity is not apparent in the play as we
> have it. (*Things to Come*, p. 232.)

(ii) That this drives him back on the 'old play which very probably lies
behind our *Hamlet*': an argument which casts suspicion on his interpretation. (iii) That the soliloquy is throughout a perfect unit as a piece of
suicide-thought, the 'sea of troubles', of course, being—it is a usual
Shakespearian figure—the turmoil of Hamlet's soul: and Hamlet's words
are 'to be', not 'to act'. (iv) That such suicide-thought blends beautifully
with the death-theme throughout the play. Hamlet, as Mr. Murry notes,
elsewhere meditates on suicide. So that this, Hamlet's most famous
soliloquy, becomes a perfect microcosm of the Hamlet-idea.

1954: But see '*Hamlet* Reconsidered', *The Wheel of Fire*, 1949.

neither 'good' nor 'bad'. True, its effects are mostly evil; it is also actually the effect of an evil—Claudius' crime; it is thus related to evil on every side. Itself it is only, what, indeed, is evident enough, a thing of essential death which is dangerous to life.

Throughout the early action subsequent to the ghost-scenes Hamlet is shown as enduring intense soul-sickness and melancholia. That sickness I have elsewhere analysed. He is, too, inactive, since his mental pain paralyses him. Rosencrantz and Guildenstern for a moment or two bring back the Hamlet of courtesy and friendship: but he soon finds them to be tools of the King. The players more vividly outline his melancholia. He envies the actor's artistic passion: he, to whom every passion is now meaningless and absurd. When given rein, his own passion turns in on itself, a spiritual masturbation, futile, self-hating:

> Why, what an ass am I! This is most brave,
> That I, the son of a dear father murder'd,
> Prompted to my revenge by heaven and hell,
> Must, like a whore, unpack my heart with words,
> And fall a-cursing like a very drab,
> A scullion! (II. ii. 619)

But he catches an element of the player's force, and turns it at last to action. With the play he gives his melancholia a purpose. Here there is ceremony, a 'Danish march', we see the King and Queen in happy state festivity: but the evil in Claudius' conscience, through the medium of Hamlet, explodes this festive joy. Hamlet is wildly exultant, like a boy who has let off a gunpowder charge. He is shattering the surface lies which cause him such disgust. At last, he has done something. He is now awake again, calls for music. We begin to see his negative consciousness as something which has its own purposive and positive aspect: and then at once he becomes very like Macbeth, who also symbolizes a dark consciousness in a succession of actions. Summoned to his mother, he speaks thus:

'Tis now the very witching time of night,
When churchyards yawn and hell itself breathes out
Contagion to this world: now could I drink hot blood,
And do such bitter business as the day
Would quake to look on. Soft! now to my mother.
O heart, lose not thy nature; let not ever
The soul of Nero enter this firm bosom:
Let me be cruel, not unnatural:
I will speak daggers to her, but use none;
My tongue and soul in this be hypocrites;
How in my words soever she be shent,
To give them seals never, my soul, consent!   (III. ii. 413)

Compare Macbeth's:

        Now o'er the one half-world
Nature seems dead and wicked dreams abuse
The curtain'd sleep: witchcraft celebrates
Pale Hecate's offerings, and wither'd murder,
Alarum'd by his sentinel, the wolf,
Whose howl 's his watch, thus with his stealthy pace,
With Tarquin's ravishing strides, towards his design
Moves like a ghost. Thou sure and firm-set earth,
Hear not my steps, which way they walk, for fear
Thy very stones prate of my whereabout,
And take the present horror from the time,
Which now suits with it. Whiles I threat, he lives;
Words to the heat of deeds too cold breath gives.
                              (*Macbeth*, II. i. 49)

Hamlet's 'intentions' are different from Macbeth's: their
states of soul—poetically conveyed as much by imagery
as by logic and action, by the impressions of 'murder',
'night' and 'witchcraft', and the contrasted ones of 'day'
and 'earth'—are similar. To fail to recognize this
similarity is to trust in intellectual abstractions, to refuse
the poetic and imaginative impression. Here Hamlet
fears his state of soul may lead him to murder his own
mother: he prays to be saved from the rising devil within.
Coming next on Claudius he again expresses his negative
state of soul. He shows himself eager, not merely to right
the wrong in Denmark, which would be a thinking in

terms of life, a seeing of things from the life-aspect—just what he cannot do—but to torment Claudius through eternity as he has recently tormented him at the play:

Up, sword; and know thou a more horrid hent:
When he is drunk asleep, or in his rage,
Or in the incestuous pleasure of his bed;
At gaming, swearing, or about some act
That has no relish of salvation in 't;
Then trip him, that his heels may kick at heaven,
And that his soul may be as damn'd and black
As hell, whereto it goes.   (III. iii. 88)

He must plunge Claudius in death, death absolute and eternal: which is hell. Then only will Hamlet's revenge be commensurate with the hell he himself endures. He thinks always in terms of death. So death-consciousness, as with Macbeth, causes Hamlet to blind himself to the serene reason of life. He is now making people pay for his own suffering. His mother's 'incest' has nauseated him: therefore he will be utterly cruel, it is his intention to wring her heart. First he slays Polonius, and seems to hope he may have caught the King at an evil moment. And yet this thought cannot have been his true motive but merely his explanation after. He has just left the King praying. Like Macbeth's, it is a motiveless act. His mother weeps.

A bloody deed! Almost as bad, good mother,
As kill a king, and marry with his brother. (III. iv. 28)

So unjustly does Hamlet's vision darken fact. It was so with Ophelia earlier. Now he prosecutes his purpose of cruelty relentlessly, until his mother implores him to desist his catalogue of abuses, which turn her thoughts to her own past weakness. Wilder, still wilder, he exults in her pain, till the Ghost itself interrupts:

Save me, and hover o'er me with your wings,
You heavenly guards! What would your gracious figure?
                                                    (III. iv. 103)

The Ghost, to Hamlet, is, of course, 'gracious': and for

that very reason the whole of life is hell. This apparition may most easily be interpreted in terms of conscience. Something in Hamlet warns him he ought not to have spared the king, ought not to have so cruelly wrung his mother's heart. This 'conscience' aptly comes as his father's ghost. For that spirit, from the first, urged Hamlet to avenge his own death more for the sake of Denmark's life than for his own satisfaction: he made no stipulations as regards Claudius' damnation; and he expressly warned Hamlet against the death-consciousness and consequent cruelty to his mother:

> If thou hast nature in thee, bear it not;
> Let not the royal bed of Denmark be
> A couch for luxury and damned incest.
> But, howsoever thou pursuest this act,
> Taint not thy mind, nor let thy soul contrive
> Against thy mother aught: leave her to heaven,
> And to those thorns that in her bosom lodge,
> To prick and sting her.   (I. v. 81)

That is, he warns Hamlet against including others beyond Claudius in his condemnation; urges him to one act, one act only. The imperial honour of Denmark's throne is primary in the Ghost's command, but becomes secondary in Hamlet's mind. So now:

> Do not forget: this visitation
> Is but to whet thy almost blunted purpose.
> But, look, amazement on thy mother sits:
> O, step between her and her fighting soul:
> Conceit in weakest bodies strongest works:
> Speak to her, Hamlet.   (III. iv. 110)

Thenafter Hamlet is kinder to his mother. He implores her to be truer to his own ideals. He even asks her forgiveness:

> Forgive me this my virtue;
> For in the fatness of these pursy times
> Virtue itself of vice must pardon beg,
> Yea, curb and woo for leave to do him good.
>   (III. iv. 152)

But again, he breaks out in a long speech of cruel sarcasm —this time, however, directed mainly against the King. As for Polonius, Hamlet is once repentant, more often callous:

I'll lug the guts into the neighbour room. (III. iv. 212)

He is horribly jocular about Polonius' body and its worms in conversation with the King. In all these scenes subsequent to the play we see the highest arc in the curve of Hamlet's death-activity. For these exulting hours his consciousness relieves itself in action: the cruel sparing of Claudius, the slaying of Polonius, brutality to his mother.

Hamlet has thus been exposed suddenly as a dark and dangerous force: which force is related (i) to the ghost scenes and (ii) to his passive melancholia of the second act. Now he has started to put 'melancholia' into action. Therefore, before he leaves the court, he has begun to appear as a danger, the rest to demand our sympathy if only in the cause of law and order, of life. So, juxtaposed with these extreme examples of Hamlet's death-activity, we find equally extreme instances of life-values asserting themselves boldly. Hamlet meets Fortinbras' forces. They go

> . . . to gain a little patch of ground
> That hath in it no profit but the name. (IV. iv. 18)

'The name'—the usual Shakespearian emphasis on the abstract nature of 'honour'. But this 'honour' is a powerful, positive force. Hamlet contrasts it with his own negative purposes:

> Witness this army of such mass and charge
> Led by a delicate and tender prince,
> Whose spirit with divine ambition puff'd
> Makes mouths at the invisible event,
> Exposing what is mortal and unsure
> To all that fortune, death and danger dare,
> Even for an egg-shell. Rightly to be great
> Is not to stir without great argument,
> But greatly to find quarrel in a straw
> When honour 's at the stake. How stand I then,
> That have a father kill'd, a mother stain'd,

> Excitements of my reason and my blood,
> And let all sleep? While, to my shame, I see
> The imminent death of twenty thousand men,
> That, for a fantasy and trick of fame,
> Go to their graves like beds, fight for a plot
> Whereon the numbers cannot try the cause,
> Which is not tomb enough and continent
> To hide the slain? O, from this time forth,
> My thoughts be bloody, or be nothing worth! (IV. iv. 47)

'Bloody' meaning not merely 'murderous', but 'passion-ate'. The Shakespearian life-value of warrior-honour is here endued with almost 'divine' sanction: abstract, unreason-able, absurd, a 'fantasy'—but noble, purposive, creative.

Kingship is another ideal, powerful through Shake-speare. The King is the symbol of order, acting by the divine right of his office. This is often important. Now Claudius, criminal though he be, is finely drawn as a politic, wise, and gentle king in all the early scenes. He shows a genuine anguish at Polonius' death and Ophelia's madness. His words are those, not of a Shakespearian vil-lain, but of a kind-hearted and good king. Having gained his throne and queen by the blackest of crimes, he now passionately and genuinely longs for peace and order and all the harmonious decencies of life. And this is not at all impossible. But now Laertes is returned. Laertes comes as a revolutionary, a disorder force, against Claudius, the King, symbol of order:

> Save yourself, my lord:
> The ocean, overpeering of his list,
> Eats not the flats with more impetuous haste
> Than young Laertes, in a riotous head,
> O'erbears your officers. The rabble call him lord:
> And, as the world were now but to begin,
> Antiquity forgot, custom not known,
> The ratifiers and props of every word,
> They cry 'Choose we: Laertes shall be King':
> Caps, hands, and tongues, applaud it to the clouds:
> 'Laertes shall be king, Laertes king!'   (IV. v. 98)

Laertes and the King confront each other and their

meeting has a fine dignity, which dignity derives from their passionate faith in themselves, their love or office. They meet on equal terms, unlike Hamlet and Claudius. Those are 'mighty opposites' of 'life' and 'death' which form no contact; these, both creatures of 'life', speak the same language, in word or act. Their dialogue thus silhouettes the Hamlet-theme by a vivid contrast. And we must note the clear stressing of the usual Shakespearian thought, kingship and 'order' opposed to violence and revolution:

> *Laertes.*   ... O thou vile king,
>   Give me my father!
> *Queen.*   Calmly, good Laertes.
> *Laertes.* That drop of blood that 's calm proclaims me bastard,
>   Cries cuckold to my father, brands the harlot
>   Even here, between the chaste unsmirched brow
>   Of my true mother.
> *King.*   What is the cause, Laertes,
>   That thy rebellion looks so giant-like?
>   Let him go, Gertrude; do not fear our person:
>   There 's such divinity doth hedge a king,
>   That treason can but peep to what it would,
>   Acts little of its will. Tell me, Laertes,
>   Why thou art thus incens'd. Let him go, Gertrude.
>   Speak, man.
> *Laertes.* Where is my father?
> *King.*   Dead.
> *Queen.*   But not by him.
> *King.* Let him demand his fill.
> *Laertes.* How came he dead? I'll not be juggled with:
>   To hell, allegiance! vows, to the blackest devil!
>   Conscience and grace, to the profoundest pit!
>   I dare damnation. To this point I stand,
>   That both the worlds I give to negligence,
>   Let come what comes; only I'll be reveng'd
>   Most throughly for my father.   (IV. V. 115)

Notice the tense thrust and parry of this dialogue; its nervous force, its reciprocity of will. Claudius and Laertes meet as two expert fencers who understand their

5

art. Notice, too, the stress on 'rebellion', 'treason', 'allegiance', 'vows'. Claudius stands up bold in his kingly office: an office which, if we have regard to the text, he has so far fulfilled admirably. Here is the 'king' ideal potent enough and quite as independent of Claudius' original crime as is the Priest's sacred office when celebrating Mass independent of his private life. This Laertes opposes with his love. That love would dare 'hell', 'the blackest devil', 'damnation'—the dark forces that have sullied the life of Hamlet, and left him unable to act, like Laertes, with purposive valour. But the evil of Claudius' crime, which through the Ghost infects Hamlet and his actions, now infects Laertes. He eventually descends to treachery. The evil propagates itself, disintegrating life.

I have noted two scenes in this act stressing life-values: but there is more to observe. There is Ophelia. Throughout Ophelia is innocent, sweet, loving. She suggests an absolute ideal of innocence and purity. But she has at first no active, assertive power. She is a reflection of Hamlet's own potentiality for romance: something circumstance has crushed. So, too, she is later crushed by the Hamlet-world. Throughout she has reminded us of Hamlet's old self, Hamlet the lover:

> He hath, my lord, of late made many tenders
> Of his affection to me.   (I. iii. 99)

Elsewhere she speaks a lovely description of Hamlet's old perfection. But now, in her madness, she becomes an active force. Her presence now stresses the pathos of innocent beauty suffering unjustly, but irrevocably. Her broken songs and speeches express two elements of pain: her father's death and Hamlet's rejection of her love. Both are suggested by her words, reminiscent of love and death; and there is a flowery innocence and fresh beauty in Ophelia here. She talks or sings of 'flowers' much:

> . . . Larded with sweet flowers;
> Which bewept to the grave did go
> With true-love showers.   (IV. v. 37)

Her snatches recollect the plaintive love-lyricism of
Feste's songs. She gives out flowers to those present:
rosemary, pansies, fennel, rue; and talks of violets.
Laertes' description of her is apt:

> O rose of May!
> Dear maid, kind sister, sweet Ophelia!   (IV. v. 157)

She is all sweetness, flowery prettiness, in her madness.
Her 'nothing' of madness is more than 'matter' (IV. v. 174).

> Thought and affliction, passion, hell itself,
> She turns to favour and to prettiness.   (IV. v. 188)

In the same way her death, by its beauty, is more than
life. Both her madness and her death must be contrasted
with the melancholia and death in Hamlet's mind. Life's
sweetest creation in the play is thus brought to death. To
Laertes it is senseless, meaningless. Why should Ophelia
suffer?

> O heavens! is 't possible a young maid's wits
> Should be as mortal as an old man's life?
> Nature is fine in love, and where 'tis fine
> It sends some precious instance of itself
> After the thing it loves.   (IV. v. 159)

That is, Nature herself loves her creations: and sacrifices
her own choicest flowers of humanity to deck the bier of
her love's death. This is true of Polonius and also of
King Hamlet. Nature ruins Hamlet's life in the cause of
his father's death, Ophelia in the cause of Polonius. The
impact of this scene is one of flowery pathos, love's purity
conquering by its very frailty and distress. Like other 'life'-
scenes, here in the fourth act all so close-knit, it contrasts vividly with the sombre deed that caused her grief.

Then there is the description of Ophelia's death. Again,
there is an emphasis on 'flowers':

> There is a willow grows aslant a brook,
> That shows his hoar leaves in the glassy stream;
> There with fantastic garlands did she come
> Of crow-flowers, nettles, daisies, and long purples . . .
> (IV. vii. 167)

This insistently reminds us of *Lear*, in those latter scenes where love is for a while victorious, where nature's sweets, music, and love blend to build a heaven in that bleak world. Mr. Edmund Blunden has observed how nature becomes a sweet and kindly rather than a bitter force towards the end of *Lear*. And we must recognize that this sense of nature beautiful is to be referred to Lear's awaking into love and self-knowledge: nature is, for a while, fulfilled: in Lear, in his setting. Ophelia's watery death is vividly described:

> Her clothes spread wide;
> And, mermaid-like, awhile they bore her up:
> Which time she chanted snatches of old tunes,
> As one incapable of her own distress,
> Or like a creature native and indued
> Unto that element: but long it could not be
> Till that her garments, heavy with their drink,
> Pull'd the poor wretch from her melodious lay
> To muddy death.   (IV. vii. 176)

Ophelia's death is here endued with a strange, unearthly beauty. Flowers, 'mermaid-like', a 'creature' native to the 'element' of water—all mingling with flowers and music, 'snatches of old tunes' which remind us of *Twelfth Night*. All this clearly touches *Antony and Cleopatra* in its flowers, its music, its thoughts of beauty blended with 'mermaids', creatures of 'element' unnatural to man. Love here is a theme of flowery sweetness, a fine blossom of the soul too cruelly crushed by tragedy. Death by water is, in Shakespeare, a constantly recurring suggestion with strong relevance to love: love eternal lost, or apparently lost, in the floods of time, or love victoriously blending with the water that would engulf it to make another beauty 'rich and strange' more lovely in death than life. So Ophelia's death has an immortal loveliness that itself slays death. This scene grows out of our death-atmosphere, a thing of life, a vision translucent of an essence unconquerable by all the ghosts of hell and their whining messages of revenge. Ophelia touches a life-beauty in death just as Hamlet touches a death-beauty in life. 'Death' itself, in this play of death-horror, 'she turns to favour and to prettiness'. She dies crowned with flowers. This again touches the Lear-vision, where the purgatorial crown of Lear's flower-madness blends with a Cordelia's love. Still more vividly it touches *Antony and Cleopatra*. Ophelia clambering on 'pendent boughs' with her 'coronet weeds' forecasts, with a difference, Cleopatra and her diadem of love. Only at this point does the slow pain of *Hamlet* form any contact with the radiance of *Antony and Cleopatra*. Flowers, music, water-life, love: all blend in Ophelia.

Now Ophelia's burial again presents a contrast between her flowery sweetness and the harshness of her tragedy, here curiously incarnated in the priest. This is a contrast between creation's flower-delight of girlhood and the professional expert on theology and eschatology. It is the same life-death contrast apparent throughout. Cruelly, the priest speaks over her body:

>   . . . for charitable prayers,
> Shards, flints, and pebbles should be thrown on her:
> Yet here she is allow'd her virgin crants,
> Her maiden strewments and the bringing home
> Of bell and burial.   (v. i. 253)

Again,

> We should profane the service of the dead
> To sing a requiem, and such rest to her
> As to peace-parted souls.   (v. i. 259)

Why is orthodoxy so harsh in this play? Why is death ever hell or, at the best, purgatory, in the Ghost's terrible revelation, Hamlet's meditations, and here? Heaven is no death. This play is a play throughout of death: and death, essential and absolute death, is hell, not heaven. Heaven can only be expressed aptly in a life-vision of sorts: even Dante needs Beatrice in his Paradiso, and Gretchen calls Faust to the empyreal life. The priest here suggests the horror of death with all the hideous torments sanctioned

by his Church. In the Shakespearian metaphysic pure
spirituality is sombre: life is 'spirit' mated to 'body'. So
now the voice of love, that is, of life, counters the priest's
words:

> *Laertes.*   Lay her i' the earth:
>   And from her fair and unpolluted flesh
>   May violets spring!   (v. i. 261)

Flowers again. So, too, the Queen scatters flowers on her
grave:

> *Queen.* Sweets to the sweet: farewell!
>   I hoped thou should'st have been my Hamlet's wife;
>   I thought thy bride-bed to have deck'd, sweet maid,
>   And not have strew'd thy grave.
> *Laertes.*   O, treble woe
>   Fall ten times treble on that cursed head,
>   Whose wicked deed thy most ingenious sense
>   Depriv'd thee of! Hold off the earth awhile,
>   Till I have caught her once more in mine arms:
>   Now pile your dust upon the quick and dead,
>   Till of this flat a mountain you have made,
>   To o'ertop old Pelion, or the skyish head
>   Of blue Olympus.
> *Hamlet.*   What is he whose grief
>   Bears such an emphasis? whose phrase of sorrow
>   Conjures the wandering stars, and makes them stand
>   Like wonder-wounded hearers? This is I,
>   Hamlet the Dane.   (v. i. 266)

Notice here (i) the Queen's stressing of the Hamlet-
Ophelia relation, with all its suggestions of life unenjoyed,
unfulfilled; (ii) Laertes' strong love, love expressed in
mountain-imagery suggestive of infinity, as in *Coriolanus*;
and (iii) Hamlet's challenging presence, continuing the
infinity idea—here 'stars' (compare II, ii, 116–7)—and
asserting his right to confront Laertes unashamed.

Indeed, he has that right. From his depth of agony he
can claim his love to be not less but greater than Laertes'
—he, from whom a pitiless fate has wrenched all love's
integrity for ever. Remember Ophelia's description of

his visit to her just after he had seen the Ghost. Remember
the sickly pain of his dialogue with her—'I loved you not'
—wrung from him when the universe itself was tottering.
Now

> I loved Ophelia: forty thousand brothers
> Could not, with all their quantity of love,
> Make up my sum.   (v. i. 292)

It is true. Agonizingly true. Throughout he has repressed, not admitted, this love, he has not allowed it in
his mind, has never talked of her in his soliloquies. Now
it breaks out sincere. But next he jeers at Laertes' passionate grief. Was not his own of equal passionate strength
till its own power rendered grief itself meaningless, and
love became slowly inverted first to melancholia, then
exultant cruelty? But if love is to dress itself in the finery
of words, then Hamlet, too, can voice the Shakespearian
'infinity' as well as others:

> And, if thou prate of mountains, let them throw
> Millions of acres on us, till our ground,
> Singeing his pate against the burning zone,
> Make Ossa like a wart! Nay, an thou'lt mouth,
> I'll rant as well as thou.   (v. i. 303)

Rant. All rant. Did not his mother profess just such love
for his father? We are arrant knaves all, believe none of
us. So Hamlet returns, after his sea-adventure, after our
sight of the noble things in the life he despises. All these
life-themes, culminating in Ophelia's life-in-death, contrast vividly with Hamlet.

Hamlet has met death-adventures on the high seas.
He has risked death twice: from the King's sealed orders,
and the pirates. He alone boards the pirate's ship. He
bears, like Macbeth, a 'charmed life'. Whilst Ophelia
drowns at home, Hamlet, himself living in thoughts only
of death, is invulnerable to the sea-death threatened by his
captors. Death, in fact, will not have him: his time is not
yet. He is to do 'a good turn for them' (iv. vi. 22), they
spare his life. Hamlet has been far, in soul as in body, on

the infinite waters of death. We see him again first in the
graveyard. Here Hamlet surveys the whole range of life:
the politician, the courtier, the lawyer, 'a great buyer of
land'; all nothing more than food for death. Life's triviality is stressed, as in the early Polonius scenes:

> *Hamlet.* . . . This might be my lord such-a-one, that praised
> my lord such-a-one's horse, when he meant to beg it; might
> it not?
> *Horatio.* Ay, my lord.
> *Hamlet.* Why, e'en so: and now my Lady Worm's; chapless,
> and knocked about the mazzard with a sexton's spade:
> here's fine revolution, an we had the trick to see 't.
>
> (v. i. 92)

And Yorick:

> . . . Here hung those lips that I have kissed I know.not
> how oft. Where be your gibes now? your gambols? your
> songs? your flashes of merriment, that were wont to set the
> table on a roar? Not one now, to mock your own grinning?
> quite chap-fallen? Now get you to my lady's chamber, and
> tell her, let her paint an inch thick, to this favour she must
> come; make her laugh at that. (v. i. 207)

So it goes on, the mellow beauty of this resigned philosophy of death. All life is but this, Yorick's skull the
emblem and symbol of human destiny. In this scene
Hamlet thinks of all human life. His personal problem is
ever a universal one: it was the same in his 'To be or not
to be . . .' soliloquy. There, too, all forms of life, all pains
that flesh is heir to, were contrasted with death. We are
reminded of *Timon*, where the same universalizing grows
from the particular pain. So, after surveying the pro-
fessions, Yorick, whom he loved, 'my lady' in her chamber,
finally Hamlet observes, too, the greatest names of history,
classical names of imperial splendour, as always the summit of the great secondary Shakespearian value of world-
glory:

> . . . Why may not imagination trace the noble dust of
> Alexander, till he find it stopping a bung-hole? (v. i. 224)

And,

> Imperious Caesar, dead and turn'd to clay,
> Might stop a hole to keep the wind away.   (v. i. 236)

So clearly in this scene is the universality of Hamlet's death-thinking apparent: all life, to him, is but dust. But through all these thoughts there is a peace: a resignation, an absence of bitterness. Intermittent though it be, we find it again in Hamlet's good-humoured jests with Yorick. In the graveyard scene Hamlet's imaginary 'politician' recalls Polonius, the 'courtier' Rosencrantz and Guildenstern, the lady in her chamber, painting an inch thick, Ophelia: 'I have heard of your paintings too, well enough; God has given you one face, and you make yourselves another . . .' (III.i.148). Now the 'buyer of land' comes before us in Osric:

> . . . He hath much land, and fertile: let a beast be lord of beasts, and his crib shall stand at the king's mess: 'tis a chough; but, as I say, spacious in the possession of dirt. (v. ii. 86)

Bitter enough. But his jests afterwards are not all unkind. And his words to Horatio before the end witness a profound acceptance of death:

> Not a whit, we defy augury: there's a special providence in the fall of a sparrow. If it be now, 'tis not to come; if it be not to come, it will be now; if it be not now, yet it will come; the readiness is all: since no man has aught of what he leaves, what is't to leave betimes? Let be.   (v. ii. 230)

Here Hamlet is at peace, at last: at peace with death. Like Macbeth, he emerges safe, just before the close: next, each submits to the necessity whither his fate has been driving him. Hamlet slays Claudius; Macbeth, in effect, submits himself to justice. Which two are correspondent acts, just as Hamlet's sparing of Claudius' life is equivalent to Macbeth's murder of Duncan.

The dark forces of the play loosed by Claudius' crime are seen conflicting with life-forces. In the person of Claudius, his past murder conflicts with his present desire for peace and happy life. He is the apparent origin of the death-force: through Hamlet, the fact is brought home

to him that he has a 'bosom black as death' (iii. iii. 67).
In Hamlet himself, knowledge of evil disintegrates his
life-beauty:

> O, what a noble mind is here o'erthrown!
> The courtier's, soldier's, scholar's, eye, tongue, sword;
> The expectancy and rose of the fair state,
> The glass of fashion and the mould of form,
> The observ'd of all observers, quite, quite down!
> And I, of ladies most deject and wretched,
> That suck'd the honey of his music vows,
> Now see that noble and most sovereign reason,
> Like sweet bells jangled, out of tune and harsh:
> That unmatch'd form and feature of blown youth
> Blasted with ecstasy: O, woe is me,
> To have seen what I have seen, see what I see!   (iii. i. 158)

Notice the universal scope of Ophelia's words, all excellence of human life is her theme, and was, too, Hamlet's
heritage. The death-forces are devastating. They—or
Hamlet, their instrument—commend the ingredients of
the King's poisoned chalice to his own lips at the end: but
first they slay indiscriminately, innocent and guilty alike.
The whole problem converges on Hamlet. His position is,
from the start, quite intolerable, his loss of values inevitable. He has had a sight of so loathsome an evil. For
we may call Claudius' crime, although it is past, yet a
present evil in the eyes of Hamlet. But we must remember
that 'evil' is a surface concept only, 'death' and 'life' being
the profounder antagonism. 'Evil', in fact, might be itself
defined as the 'human conception of a death-activity
invading life'. 'Evil' implies human desires, human dislike. It is the form 'death' and 'death-forces' usually take
in men's eyes. Death itself, however, is absolute: it is
beyond 'good' and 'evil'. Now there is one only solution
to the enigma of evil close twined, as here, with love:
absolute acceptance. From that acceptance will be born
creative action. Yet here it is as though the poet has
expressed the profoundest of problems: an instance where
there can be no acceptance, given a subject with a noble

and sensitive mind. For that reason the life-forces shown to have a hideous evil at their source, the body ᴏ Denmark has an internal sore, running, poisoning, nauseating. This is Hamlet's problem. This forces his death-philosophy and cynic pain. Not Denmark, not merely values of love, honour, kingship are at stake: rather life itself, creation. They are seen to be rotten, and if an Ophelia or Polonius suffers with a once-loved mother, that mother with her criminal lord, what is that, in a world where such cankerous evil gnaws? Besides, Hamlet actually sees this evil now in his mother, in Ophelia: they are more in his mind, his mother especially, than is Claudius. In this dramatic statement of the baffling problem of sight-blasting evil seen in the bosom of love and at the very heart of life, the poet has well shown that original evil, Claudius' crime, to be all but unforgivable. He has also shown that life to be absolutely, in the present, a good thing, a beautiful thing, not an evil. The middle action stresses the enigma well. Hamlet, the hero, evil-obsessed, has become a death-force, like Macbeth. Close after, all the Shakespearian 'values' jostle each other for our notice, the chief villain holding an honourable place, the whole reaching a climax in the beauty of Ophelia's death, which touches *Antony and Cleopatra* just as Hamlet's death-activity touches *Macbeth*: which points the utter contrast clearly. Therefore, having regard to this complex interaction and incompatibility of 'right' and 'wrong', 'death' and 'life', we shall see *Hamlet* as either one of the profoundest statements concerning the problem of 'evil' ever set on paper, or, observing this most dangerous sublimation of our adverse forces at the moment when the hero has, to say the least, strained our sympathies, we must see in the middle action one of the most blundering examples of technical infelicity ever honoured with the title of poetic drama.[1]

[1] There is a third possibility. We could fall back on the 'old play'. But where the new one offers us a profound vision, there seems little wisdom in that.

The *Hamlet*-enigma drives us to the gospel ethic as our only perfect solution. Jesus' God is a God of the living, not of the dead. The old order of revenge, 'an eye for an eye, a tooth for a tooth', must give way to the new order of acceptance: 'resist not evil'. The paradoxical nature of these statements is baffling. Yet *Hamlet* shows the other, the 'common-sense' ethic, to be, in truth, self-contradictory. The profundity of the *Hamlet*-problem necessitates an equally profound positive solution. But it would, I think, be a great error to credit Hamlet himself with any promptings toward such an ethic. His delay is not a matter of conscience. He shows a negative, but not a positive idealism. Throughout, he evinces little sign of any forgiveness. He is true to his father's ghost. And human nature endorses his faithfulness. But another authority has told us to 'let the dead bury their dead'. That thought, perhaps, provides the best solution to the enigma of *Hamlet*.

Hamlet ends, however, on a note of pure tragedy. A sense of tragic expiation concludes our baffling and indecisive vision. Hamlet and Laertes, death-consciousness and life-ardour, oppose each other. The fight is arranged by Claudius, who here stands poised between the two realities: the blackest of murderers, yet a king—and a good one. He pits his present grace (Laertes) against his past crime (Hamlet). Hence arises our feeling of universal issues at stake in this fight. It, too, is indecisive. Each side wins, and loses. But at the last Laertes and Hamlet exchange forgiveness. 'The king 's to blame' (v. ii. 331), and flights of angels, perhaps, sing Hamlet to the rest his father's spirit has not found. And Fortinbras brings peace and order to Denmark.

Additional Note: For my final interpretation of *Hamlet* see my essay '*Hamlet* Reconsidered', *The Wheel of Fire*, enlarged edition, 1949.

V

THE MILK OF CONCORD: AN ESSAY ON LIFE-THEMES IN MACBETH

... Thy will be done, in earth as it is in heaven; give us this day our daily bread, and forgive us our trespasses as we forgive them that trespass against us; and lead us not into temptation but deliver us from evil.

THE opposition of life and death forces is strong in *Macbeth*. Here we find the dark and evil negation endued with a positive strength, successfully opposing things of health and life. Elsewhere I have discussed the evil: here I give a primary attention to the life-themes it opposes. They are: (i) Warrior-honour, (ii) Imperial magnificence, (iii) Sleep and Feasting, and (iv) Ideas of creation and nature's innocence. These are typical Shakespearian themes. In *Hamlet* we find the same opposition. There it is often baffling. Here life-forces are vividly and very clearly contrasted with evil, with forces of death and ill-omen, darkness and disorder. Especially, creation is opposed by destruction.

Throughout the main action of *Macbeth* we are confronted by fear. The word occurs ubiquitously. Fear is at the heart of this play. Now, if we consider the beginning and ending too, we find a very clear rhythm of courage, fear, and courage. The play ends on a note of courage. Macbeth is from the first a courageous soldier. His warrior-honour is emphasized. He is 'brave Macbeth' (I. ii. 16), 'valour's minion' (I. ii. 19), 'Bellona's bridegroom' (I. ii. 54), 'noble Macbeth' (I. ii. 67). Duncan exclaims:

> O valiant cousin! worthy gentleman!   (I. ii. 24)

He is 'a peerless kinsman' (I. iv. 58)—the Duncan-Macbeth relationship is always stressed. Courage in war is a thing of 'honour' (I. ii. 44). So Macbeth is rewarded for his valour by a title, earnest of an even greater 'honour' (I. iii. 104). At the start Macbeth's honourable

valour is firmly contrasted with the traitor's ignoble
revolt. There is no honour in absolute courage: it must
be a service, or it is worthless. Macbeth knows this.
Duncan lavishes praises on him and he replies:

> The service and the loyalty I owe,
> In doing it, pays itself. Your highness' part
> Is to receive our duties; and our duties
> Are to your throne and state, children and servants,
> Which do but what they should, by doing everything
> Safe toward your love and honour.   (I. iv. 22)

'Honour' again: the word occurs throughout, strongly
emphasized. Notice the 'family' suggestion. Throughout
thoughts of the family (especially childhood), clan, or
nation are associated here. All are units of peace, concord,
life. All are twined with 'honour'. So the subject is bound
to his lord by love and honour. The value of warriorship
may not be dissociated from allegiance: it is one with the
ideal of kingship and imperial power. But against this
bond the evil is urging Macbeth. The evil in him hates to
hear Duncan proclaiming princely honours on Malcolm,
despite the promise of more distinctions for such as
himself:

> Sons, kinsmen, thanes,
> And you whose places are the nearest, know
> We will establish our estate upon
> Our eldest, Malcolm, whom we name hereafter
> The Prince of Cumberland; which honour must
> Not unaccompanied invest him only,
> But signs of nobleness, like stars, shall shine
> On all deservers.   (I. iv. 35)

Here we should observe the suggestion of harmony and
order. Sons, kinsmen, thanes—all are bound close
together. Scotland is a family, Duncan its head. A natural
law binds all degrees in proper place and allegiance. Only
in terms of this allegiance is courage an honourable ideal.
Observe, too, how the king's 'honours' are compared
to 'stars', the king's gentle rule of love thus blending with
the universal lights. But the evil that grips Macbeth

must hide from such things of brilliance and universal beauty:

> Stars, hide your fires;
> Let not light see my black and deep desires:
> The eye wink at the hand; yet let that be,
> Which the eye fears, when it is done, to see. (I. iv. 50)

Throughout the evil in Macbeth is opposed to such order, to all family and national peace, and is alien to sun, moon, or star, blotting their radiance from man (II. iv. 7; II. i. 2: II.i. 4–5). Now Macbeth, having accomplished so much, strikes next at the very roots of his own new-bright honour:

> We will proceed no further in this business:
> He hath honour'd me of late; and I have bought
> Golden opinions from all sorts of people,
> Which would be worn now in their newest gloss,
> Not cast aside so soon. (I. vii. 31)

By such a deed of dishonour no substantial honour may be won. The valour of such an act is itself shameful:

> Prithee, peace:
> I dare do all that may become a man;
> Who dares do more is none. (I. vii. 45)

Yet Lady Macbeth wins largely by appealing to Macbeth's 'valour' (I. vii. 40). If he now fails in courage, she will henceforth despise equally his courage and his love (I. vii. 39): warriorship and love being ever close in Shakespeare, either in contrast or association. And Macbeth really gives way all along from fear: from fear of fear. He has fought for the King, exulting wildly in absolute courage. Next there is an extreme reaction to absolute fear. Now the evil finds the only thing he fears: dishonour. He suffers at his first temptation from abstract fear, which fixes itself to a ghastly act so that it may form some contact with the real. That act is one of essential dishonour. He has been terrified ever since the evil first gripped him, ever since he muttered 'present fears are less than horrible imaginings' (I. iii. 137). The same contrast is expressed by him when fronting Banquo's ghost (III. iv. 99–107).

He fears no hostile actuality, only the unreal evil, the abstract and absolute fear. This evil he dare not face from the start, so flies from it to actuality, expresses it there. He lacks spiritual courage to meet it on its own spiritual terms, and hence projects his disordered soul into action and murders Duncan. Undue horror and fear of the deed drives him to it: in the same way his fearful conscience will not let him rest there, and he commits more murders. He is all the time flying from evil instead of facing it. But at the end he emerges fearless. And this is not only a warrior's valour when opposed by Malcolm's army. By his murderous acts he has at last actually conquered his fear of evil, that is, his fear of fear:

> I have supp'd full with horrors;
> Direness, familiar to my slaughterous thoughts,
> Cannot once start me.   (v. v. 13)

He sees himself a criminal: sees the evil in himself. Not daring to see his own potential criminality, he became a criminal. But now, seeing his own evil, he becomes fearless. From the beginning there was no possible antagonist for the supernatural evil but an equivalently supernatural good. The evil was never properly actualized: to fight it there must be a good also set beyond the actual. Hence the birth of our religions; hence, too, the constant opposition of 'grace' and thoughts of divinity in *Macbeth* set against the things of dark and evil.[1] Macbeth at the last, by self-knowledge, attains grace. He knows that he must forfeit 'honour' and all things of concord and life:

> . . . that which should accompany old age,
> As honour, love, obedience, troops of friends,
> I must not look to have; but, in their stead,
> Curses, not loud but deep, mouth-honour, breath,
> Which the poor heart would fain deny, and dare not.
>   (v. iii. 24)

[1] This opposition of 'grace' and 'evil' I have already observed in *The Wheel of Fire*. It has also been recently stressed by Mgr. Kolbe, who notes that phrases or words suggestive of a 'sin'-'grace' contrast occur more than four hundred times in *Macbeth*.

These are the social realities he has desecrated by his
fearsome rule. A rule of fear. Fear is here our dominant
emotion. Not only Macbeth—all are paralysed by fear
during the middle action. At the start, we saw courage,
unity, honour, under the gracious rule of Duncan. But
the valour of Scotland is temporarily smothered by evil.
When at the end security and peace return, the contrast
is marked by Siward's words on his son, who 'has paid a
soldier's debt' (v. vii. 68), and died 'like a man' (v. vii.
72):

> *Siward.*   Had he his hurts before?
> *Ross.* Ay, on the front.
> *Siward.*   Why then, God's soldier be he!
>   Had I as many sons as I have hairs,
>   I would not wish them to a fairer death.   (v. vii. 75)

So we see courage desecrated by evil and fear, then at the end
courage—in Macbeth or young Siward—victorious. This
is how the *Macbeth*-negation hits into, destroys for a while,
the positive ideals of honour and warriorship, so that not
only Macbeth but Banquo, Macduff, Malcolm, Ross—all
suffer fear, all for a while are powerless under the evil. The
matter of young Siward's death marks the restoration of
nobility and courage, accompanying Malcolm's restoration to his rightful kingship.

This warrior-theme is closely twined with our next
positive value: imperial magnificence. On the ethical—
as opposed to the metaphysical—plane, Macbeth fails
through trying to advance from deserved honour as a
noble thane to the higher kingly honour to which he has no
rights. This kingship he attains, yet never really possesses it.
He is never properly king: his regality is a mockery. Now,
through the murk which envelops the action, there are
yet glimpses of this sensuous glory which Macbeth desires
but which ever eludes his grasp. Such suggestions stare
out, dully glowing, solid things of world-power. This
sensuous glory is always undermined, blurred, by the dark,
the abysmal negation, the evil. The *Macbeth*-world is
insubstantial, an emptiness, its bottom knocked out of it;

a hideous nightmare falling, like Satan dropping in his flight through chaos. Solidity, reality, are grasped in vain by the falling soul. Macbeth and his wife reach out for power and glory: the sense-forms correspondent are crowns and sceptres. The glint of these burns grimly and sullenly through the murk.

Lady Macbeth would drive from her lord

> All that impedes thee from the golden round,
> Which fate and metaphysical aid doth seem
> To have thee crown'd withal.   (I. v. 29)

The 'golden round': solid, glorious gold to bind the brow with royalty. The same glinting solidity burns in the phraseology, especially the final word, of:

> Which shall to all our nights and days to come
> Give solely sovereign sway and masterdom. (I. v. 70)

These things are, as it were, the finest flower of world-honour, the sweetest prizes of life. They are glorious things of life. So she presses him on to win the 'ornament of life' (I. vii. 42), though Macbeth objects to this absurd grasping of additional royalty by a man royally honoured already. He would wear his 'golden opinions' in 'their newest gloss' rather than risk losing them so soon (I. vii. 32). So Macbeth sees clearly that the gold of evil desire will add nothing to his real honour: yet he cannot resist. Miss Spurgeon has observed that 'dresses' and dress-metaphors occur frequently in *Macbeth*. Often, as in this passage, these may be considered to blend with our 'crowns' and 'sceptres' to build a vague background of royal splendour. But all are vague. Their solidity is rendered dubious, is blurred, by the evil, the dark, the insubstantiality. They are things of noble reality dreamed in hell; unenjoyed by the guilty soul, to whom nightmare is reality and all sense-splendour an unattainable dream. Outward royalty is, by itself, a nothing in comparison with nature's kingliness:

> Our fears in Banquo
> Stick deep; and in his royalty of nature
> Reigns that which would be fear'd . . .   (III. i. 49)

So he fears, envies, hates Banquo who has the reality of honour whereas he has but a mockery, a ghoulish dream of royalty. He envies Banquo's posterity their royal destiny won in terms of nature, not in terms of crime; and is maddened at the insecure mockery of his own kingship:

Upon my head they plac'd a fruitless crown,
And put a barren sceptre in my gripe . . .   (III. i. 61)

He has grasped these gold power-symbols to himself: and they are utterly 'barren' in every sense; barren of joy and content, barren of posterity. So falsely has Macbeth made himself the centre and end of all things: a 'fruitless' philosophy. To this the evil has tricked him. He and his wife are without 'content' (III. ii. 5). When he visits the Weird Sisters in their cavern he sees an apparition with a crown. Again, the glint of royal metal shines through the dark:

What is this,
That rises like the issue of a king,
And wears upon his baby-brow the round
And top of sovereignty?   (IV. i. 86)

Notice the vivid suggestion of babyhood: I return to it later. Again, in his vision of future Scottish kings, these same sense-forms are emphasized and their maddening effect on him redoubled:

Thou art too like the spirit of Banquo; down!
Thy crown does sear mine eyeballs. And thy hair,
Thou other gold-bound brow, is like the first.
A third is like the former . . .   (IV. i. 112)

As though this were not enough sensuous blaze of kingship, there is the eighth figure with a glass reflecting more kings, with exaggerated symbols of glory and power:

. . . and some I see
That two-fold balls and treble sceptres carry:
Horrible sight! Now, I see, 'tis true;
For the blood-bolter'd Banquo smiles upon me,
And points at them for his.   (IV. i. 120)

Macbeth's agony is not properly understood till we realize his utter failure to receive any positive joy from the

imperial magnificence to which he aspired. Hence his
violent jealousy when he sees Banquo's crowned and
sceptred posterity. He lives a life of death, in darkness,
reft of all sense-grandeur and solid joy. He cannot
conquer the evil in his soul and rest in the acclamations
and honour of his land: rather spreads his own spiritual
darkness over Scotland. His robes are ridiculous on him:

> . . . now does he feel his title,
> Hang loose about him, like a giant's robe
> Upon a dwarfish thief.   (v. ii. 20)

He is a 'tyrant bloody-scepter'd' (iv. iii. 104). His life
reads as an absurd lust for the impossible. Malcolm, in his
pretence of Macbeth-villainy, stresses two vices: lust and
avarice. Macbeth's crime, on this level, is almost an inverted, an introverted, lust or love; a self-desire, expressed by an action which aims at grasping glory-forms
to itself. So Malcolm pretends he would

> . . . cut off the nobles for their lands,
> Desire his jewels and this other's house.   (iv. iii. 79)

Such riches-references are valuable. They serve to relate
the utter negation of *Macbeth* with love-themes in Shakespeare. Macbeth's evil is a kind of lust, like Malcolm's
supposed iniquity:

> . . your wives, your daughters,
> Your matrons and your maids, could not fill up
> The cistern of my lust . .   (iv. iii. 61)

An introverted, selfish 'lust'. Malcolm's confession must
be exactly related to Macbeth, suggestive of Macbeth's
lust and avarice. Macbeth's awareness of 'spirit' naked,
divorced from the actual, is thus seen to take the shape of
avarice, self-love, greed: an absolute introversion expressed
in action. Though the evil itself is more ultimate than
'ambition' or 'greed', yet such ideas help us to understand
the imaginative value of what sensuous splendour we find
dully glowing in this insubstantial, insensible, world of
negation. The 'riches' thought is, moreover, vivid in
Macduff's

> I would not be the villain that thou think'st
> For the whole space that's in the tyrant's grasp,
> And the rich East to boot.   (IV. iii. 35)

'The rich East'; and Malcolm mentioned 'jewels'. Both are frequent in Shakespeare's love-imagery. The gracious Duncan distributed 'largesse' and a diamond (II. i. 14-15) to his hosts. Moreover, the nearest imaginative correspondence to *Macbeth* in all Shakespeare is to be found in *Lucrece*. There is the same abysmal evil, the same guilt-horror, the same darkness, the same fear. *Lucrece* is a valuable and necessary commentary on *Macbeth*: much that is implicit in *Macbeth* is explicitly and prolixly stressed there. So Macbeth compares himself to Tarquin (II. i. 55). Macbeth's evil is a lust, like unruly love; a centring of reality in the self. A turning-inward of the mind and its purposes, an obsession with the solitary self unharmonized with wider considerations. So he sells his 'eternal jewel' (III. i. 68) for the riches and glory of unrighteous kingship. 'Jewels' may thus suggest spiritual or earthly riches here, as elsewhere in Shakespeare. That is why the gracious Duncan gives largesse and diamonds, why the Holy King of England heals 'the Evil' with 'a golden stamp, put on with holy prayers' (IV. iii. 153-4). Imperial magnificence is continually being suggested, only to be blurred by the dark and evil effects. The evil is opposed to the supreme glory of kingship. In blood-imagery, the two curiously blend: sensuous glory with horror. The evil smear of dull red becomes twice a brilliant gold:

> I'll gild the faces of the grooms withal;
> For it must seem their guilt.   (II. ii. 56)

and,

> Here lay Duncan,
> His silver skin lac'd with his golden blood,
> And his gash'd stabs looked like a breach in nature
> For ruin's wasteful entrance.   (II. iii. 117)

The gold-blood association is vivid again in 'an untitled tyrant bloody-scepter'd' (IV. iii. 104), noted above.

So much for Macbeth's insecure tenure of imperial magnificence. Now I pass to the even more fundamental ideas of 'sleep', 'feasting', and 'nature'. Sleep and feasting are important. Peaceful sleep is often disturbed by nightmare; this I have observed elsewhere. Here we may observe how closely 'sleep' is twined with 'feasting'. Both are creative, restorative, forces of nature. So Macbeth and his Queen are reft of both during the play's action. Feasting and sleep are twin life-givers:

> Methought I heard a voice cry, 'Sleep no more!
> Macbeth does murder sleep', the innocent sleep,
> Sleep that knits up the ravell'd sleave of care,
> The death of each day's life, sore labour's bath,
> Balm of hurt minds, great nature's second course,
> Chief nourisher in life's feast—   (II. ii. 36)

The retributive suffering is apt. Macbeth murdered Duncan in sleep, after feasting him. It was a blow delivered at 'innocent sleep'; sleep, like death in *Antony and Cleopatra*, the gentle nurse of life. Macbeth does more than murder a living being: he murders life itself. Because he murdered hospitality and sleep, therefore his punishment is a living death, without peaceful sleep or peaceful feeding:

> But let the frame of things disjoint, both the worlds suffer,
> Ere we will eat our meal in fear, and sleep
> In the affliction of these terrible dreams
> That shake us nightly . . .   (III. ii. 16)

So Lennox prays for the time when Scotland

>   may again
> Give to our tables meat, sleep to our nights,
> Free from our feasts and banquets bloody knives,
> Do faithful homage and receive free honours . . .
>   (III. vi. 33)

'Homage' and 'honours'. The thought is ever—as I have noted above—of a society, or family, built into a unity by mutual respect, place and degree, in which alone 'honour' can exist: so Macbeth's crime is a kind of parricide—

hence the suggestions of parricide in II. iv. and III. vi.
Such suggestions, untrue to fact, hold yet an imaginative
truth. And this society is a life-force blending with 'sleep'
and 'feasts'.

Now the evil-feasting opposition is powerful here. Duncan compares his joy in Macbeth's success to a banquet:

> True, worthy Banquo; he is full so valiant;
> And in his commendations I am fed;
> It is a banquet to me. (I. iv. 54)

Macbeth's honourable prowess is a life-bringing food
to Duncan, to Scotland. Lady Macbeth's hospitality to
Duncan is emphasized: she is his 'honoured hostess' (I. vi.
10), his 'fair and noble hostess' (I. vi. 24). She and
Macbeth entertain him with a fine feast:

> *Hautboys and torches. Enter a Sewer, and divers Servants
> with dishes and service, and pass over the stage.* (I. vii)

Feasting and music: a usual grouping of effects, as in
Timon, Coriolanus, and *Antony and Cleopatra.* Lady Macbeth
plots murder whilst Duncan is feasting:

> He has almost supp'd: why have you left the chamber?
> (I. vii. 29)

Duncan, wearied by 'his day's hard journey' (I. vii. 62), goes
to his chamber to sleep 'soundly' (I. vii. 63), after having
distributed his bounty to his hosts: he is 'in unusual
pleasure' and 'shut up in measureless content' (II. i. 13–17),
the 'content' that his murderers never achieve (III. ii. 5).
So Lady Macbeth is again called 'most kind hostess' (II. i.
16). Next 'wine and wassail' (I. vii. 64) is put to the
dastardly use of drugging Duncan's grooms. They
are made 'the slaves of drink and thralls of sleep' (III.
vi. 13). Lady Macbeth steels herself by the same means
(II. ii. 1). There is the grim irony of the bell which 'invites'
Macbeth to the murder:

> Go, bid thy mistress, when my drink is ready
> She strike upon the bell. (II. i. 31)

The domestic and feminine note jars hideously with the

horror beneath. 'Drink' is often suggested. There is the porter whose drunken festivities are used to heighten our awareness that hellish evil is stalking the earth: here again, evil conquers the innocent festivity. Through all these effects we see the same opposition: feasting, a life-force, especially the hospitality wherewith the sacred Duncan is greeted by his 'kinsman' and 'subject'; and against this, the hideous murder. It is at once, as Macbeth observes (I. vii. 12–16), a desecration of a 'double trust': hospitality, social order, allegiance, life itself: 'the wine of life' (II. iii. 100) is drawn.

After the murder, feasting is again emphasized. It is shown how

> . . . this even-handed justice
> Commends the ingredients of our poisoned chalice
> To our own lips.   (I. vii. 10)

Macbeth finds he has 'put rancours in the vessel of' his 'peace' (III. i. 67). He may not feast with his lords in peace and harmony.[1] Banquo's ghost breaks into the attempted festivity, disperses it, throws it into disorder. At the start, hospitality, conviviality, 'welcome' and 'degree' are emphasized: the very things Macbeth has so brutally desecrated.

> *Macbeth.* You know your own degrees; sit down: at first
> And last the hearty welcome.
> *Lords.*   Thanks to your majesty.
> *Macbeth.* Ourself will mingle with society,
> And play the humble host.
> Our hostess keeps her state, but in best time
> We will require her welcome.

---

[1] We may compare the Greek legend of King Phineus and the Harpies. Indeed, my attention was first drawn to the 'feasting' in *Macbeth* by looking for something in the tragedies to correspond with the Harpies and Banquet incident of *The Tempest*, which, according to my interpretation as given in *Myth and Miracle*, reflects the whole 'Shakespeare Progress'. Mr. Colin Still's remarkable analysis of *The Tempest* first drew my attention to the extreme importance of the 'Banquet' there, which he relates, with other themes, to ancient myth and ritual. See *Shakespeare's Mystery Play: a study of 'The Tempest'* (1921; see p. vii above).

Lady Macbeth. Pronounce it for me, sir, to all our friends;
  For my heart speaks they are welcome.
Macbeth. See, they encounter thee with their hearts' thanks.
  Both sides are even: here I'll sit i' the midst:
  Be large in mirth; anon we'll drink a measure
  The table round. (III. iv. 1)

Hospitality is bounteous. Every phrase there is important.
The murderer withdraws Macbeth's attention and Lady
Macbeth again stresses the thought of welcome:

Lady Macbeth.   My royal lord,
  You do not give the cheer: the feast is sold
  That is not often vouch'd, while 'tis a-making,
  'Tis given with welcome: to feed were best at home;
  From thence the sauce to meat is ceremony;
  Meeting were bare without it.
Macbeth.   Sweet remembrancer!
  Now, good digestion wait on appetite,
  And health on both! (III. iv. 33)

'Digestion', 'health', 'sauce', 'meat'. Against this life-
force of feasting, conviviality, social friendliness and order,
comes a death, a ghost, smashing life-forms with phantasms
of evil and guilt: an unreality, a 'nothing', like the air-
drawn dagger, creating chaos of order and reality, dispersing the social unit. It is the conquest of the real and
the life-giving by the unreal and deathly. It corresponds
to the murderous deed whose 'hideous trumpet' (II. iii. 87)
waked the 'downy sleep' (II. iii. 81) of Macbeth's guests at
Inverness, raising them to walk like 'sprites' (II. iii. 84) from
death, like Hamlet's father, shattering at that dead hour all
natural peace and rest. After the Ghost's disappearance
Macbeth recovers, again speaks words of 'love', 'health',
and friendly communion:

          Come, love and health to all;
  Then I'll sit down. Give me some wine; fill full.
  I drink to the general joy o' the whole table,
  And to our dear friend Banquo, whom we miss;
  Would he were here! to all, and him, we thirst,
  And all to all. (III. iv. 87)

The Ghost reappears. It is, like the phantasmal dagger, a 'horrible shadow', an 'unreal mockery' (III. iv. 106), and it opposes the natural joys of feasting and 'health', life-forms, life-forces, just as Macbeth's original 'horrible imaginings', the 'horrid image' of the proposed murder, unfixed his hair and made his heart beat wildly 'against the use of nature', shook his 'state of man' and smothered 'function' in 'surmise' (I. iii. 140–1). So the evil makes of unity, 'love', feasting and social order a chaos, dispersing and disintegrating the society. The disorder-thought is important, running throughout Shakespeare and vividly apparent here: order is the natural grouping of life-forms, disorder is evil—Macbeth's crime was essentially an act of disorder, a desecration of the ties of hospitality, blood-relationship, and allegiance.

> *Lady Macbeth.* You have displac'd the mirth, broke the good
>   meeting,
>   With most admir'd disorder.   (III. iv. 109)

The guests are to 'stand not upon the order' of their 'going' (III. iv. 119)—phrase contrasting vividly with Macbeth's opening words: 'You know your own degrees'. Macbeth and Lady Macbeth dwell in but 'doubtful joy' after their act of 'destruction' (III. ii. 7). Death, destruction, chaos—these are the forms of evil opposed to the life-joys of feast and friendship, and all social concord.

The three outstanding scenes of the middle action all illustrate the evil-feasting opposition. First there is Duncan's murder in sleep and after elaborate feasting by his host, kinsman, and subject: all concepts which stress Macbeth's ruthless desecration of social units of human life. Next, we find Banquo's ghost violently forbidding that Macbeth enjoy that hospitality and feasting which he has desecrated. Our third scene is that with the Weird Sisters in their cavern. The contrast with the banquet scene is vivid. Here we watch a devils'-banqueting, the Weird Women with their cauldron and its holocaust of hideous ingredients. The banquet-idea has been inverted.

Instead of suggesting health, this one is brewed to cause 'toil and trouble'. The ingredients are absurd bits of life like those of Othello's ravings (*Othello* IV. i. 42), now jumbled together to 'boil and bake' in the cauldron: 'eye of newt', 'toe of frog', a dog's tongue, a lizard's leg, and so on. Mgr. Kolbe has well called them 'chaotic incongruities'. But not only are there animal-pieces: we have a Jew's liver, a Turk's nose, a Tartar's lips, the 'finger of birth-strangled babe'. Though the bodies from which these are torn are often themselves, by association, evil, yet we must note the additional sense of chaos, bodily desecration, and irrationality in the use of these absurd derelict members, things like the 'pilot's thumb' (I. iii. 28) mentioned earlier. The ingredients suggest an absolute indigestibility. It is a parody of banqueting, a death-banquet, a 'hell-broth' (IV. i. 19). It is all quite meaningless, nameless, negative, utterly black:

> *Macbeth.* How now, you secret, black and midnight hags!
>   What is 't you do?
> *The Weird Women.* A deed without a name. (IV. i. 48)

Formerly an 'unreal mockery', a death-phantom, shattered a life-giving banquet. Here, by inversion, a death-banquet produces from its hideous 'gruel' (IV. i. 32) not bodily sustenance, but more phantoms. The one is a life reality disorganized by a spirit suggesting life that is past (Banquo's ghost); the other is a feast of death and essential disorder (because of the disjointed ingredients) giving birth to spirits suggesting life that is to come (the Apparitions and their prophecies). The evil disorder in the cauldron produces forms of futurity, futurity being essentially a disorder-force until it is bodied into the life-forms of the present. Thus the spirits, whether of life past or life to come, are equally inimical to Macbeth's peace. This hell-broth is a death-food, though it is not meant to be eaten: eating is good, in the cause of life. It brings forth spirits, that is evil, not earthly, things: spirit uninfused in bodies being, in the phraseology of my interpretations, purely evil. Equally evil are the correspondent bodies disorganized (bodies of nature, state, family, or man): for bodies disorganized are formless, and, if formless, soulless, 'soul' and 'form' being naturally equated. Therefore here and elsewhere, all disorder symbols may readily be equated with 'naked spirit'. So here the disordered ingredients produce correlevant spirits, apparitions rise from the deathly cauldron and its chaotic contents. Though in this sense, and in their effect, evil, these spirits yet accomplish their purpose by suggesting life-forces: the Bloody Child and the Child crowned with a Tree in his hand. But to Macbeth they bring evil. On them Macbeth's derelict soul feeds its fill, feeds on death-food—'I have supp'd full with horrors' (v. v. 13). He drinks down the ghostly future. He feeds his starved soul with hope, thinks that

> Our high-plac'd Macbeth
> Shall live the lease of nature, pay his breath
> To time and mortal custom.   (iv. i. 98)

He is readily convinced by the Apparitions' assurances in terms of 'nature'—Birnam wood, childbirth. As I observe later, he fails to understand the real significance of these Apparitions. His spiritual sustenance feeds him with hope—not, as it pretends and he thinks, in terms of natural law, but only in terms of itself, that is, unreality, meaningless essences abstracted from the future; things which do not exist, and, when they do, will be different from their present blurred appearance as received by him. It is all a death-banquet and its spiritual food, to him, a poison. Hence it at once leads Macbeth to a deed of family destruction. He murders Lady Macduff, her children, Macduff's household, all that 'trace him in his line' (iv. i. 153); again, a chaotic blow against a life-force, a family unit.

The Cauldron Scene, with its disjected members of animal and human bodies, and also its prophecies relating to 'nature', suggests a yet wider view of the opposition active throughout *Macbeth*. The *Macbeth*-evil attacks honour and imperial magnificence, life-forms of feeding, health, society: it also decisively attacks 'nature'. Nature in its purity is clearly another 'life' theme, only one degree removed from 'feasting'. But nature is seldom apparent here in purity and grace: when it is, that appearance is important. Nature-references blend with human themes, especially in point of procreation and childhood. First, I shall review the images of nature's purity, many of them blending with thoughts of human birth: birth and childhood are here our outstanding life-themes. After this I shall pass to the more fantastical effects of unreality and supernature.

We do not find here quite the close human-nature association of *Lear*. Natural effects are nevertheless numerous. We are confronted usually by a nature-distortion, a reality essentially unnatural, all but unreal. Most of the nature here is therefore an impossible, an unnatural nature. There are, however, a few suggestions of nature in her native integrity and beauty. Like our numerous thoughts of divine 'grace' and angels, these contrast with the evil. So the gracious Duncan regards Macbeth as a flower nurtured by himself:

> I have begun to plant thee, and will labour
> To make thee full of growing.   (I. iv. 28)

His 'plenteous joys' are 'wanton in fulness' (I. iv. 33). Lady Macbeth counsels her lord to

> look like the innocent flower,
> But be the serpent under 't.   (I. v. 66)

A characteristic Shakespearian thought of nature's 'innocence', the only aspect of nature which is, curiously, truly 'natural' to mankind. Nature's creative beauty is remarked by Banquo:

> *Duncan.* This castle hath a pleasant seat; the air
>   Nimbly and sweetly recommends itself
>   Unto our gentle senses.
> *Banquo.*   This guest of summer,
>   The temple-haunting martlet, does approve,
>   By his loved mansionry, that the heaven's breath
>   Smells wooingly here: no jutty, frieze,

> Buttress, nor coign of vantage, but this bird
> Hath made his pendent bed and procreant cradle:
> Where they most breed and haunt, I have observ'd,
> The air is delicate.   (I. vi. 1.)

Notice the strong emphasis on 'senses', 'wooing', and 'delicate' air; and the 'procreant cradle', the thought of 'breeding': the passage has a vivid similarity to *Antony and Cleopatra*. Notice, too, the word 'guest', and touches of divine suggestion, 'temple', 'heaven', which blend with other such throughout *Macbeth*. The dialogue gives us a perfect contrast in microcosm to the *Macbeth*-evil. Macbeth's crime is a blow against nature's unity and peace, a hideous desecration of all creative, family, and social duties, all union and concord: this is the bond he breaks, the 'great bond' that keeps him 'pale' (III. ii. 49). Now that 'humane statute' has 'purged the general weal' (III. iv. 76) it is natural to mankind to live in peace and love. But Macbeth breaks all fetters of restraining humanity. He ruthlessly destroys Macduff's family. Lady Macduff thus compares her lord to a parent bird in a passage which closely corresponds to the dialogue just quoted. Macduff, mysteriously conquered by the evil, or, rather, in order to oppose it (both are fundamentally the same) has deserted his family:

> He loves us not;
> He wants the natural touch: for the poor wren,
> The most diminutive of birds, will fight,
> Her young ones in her nest, against the owl.   (IV. ii. 8)

She urges that Macduff's flight was dictated by 'fear', not 'love' or 'wisdom'. It is partly true: fear grips every one whilst the evil rages in Scotland. Macduff is forced to sacrifice the bond of family love—'those precious motives, those strong knots of love' (IV. iii. 27). He leaves them to their death:

> What, all my pretty chickens and their dam
> At one fell swoop?   (IV. iii. 218)

An unnatural act, necessitated by the unnatural evil.

All is chaos, turbulence, disorder—to be contrasted with family or national peace, humanity's natural concord.

Nature's food of 'milk' is often mentioned in this connexion. Lady Macbeth fears her lord's 'nature': he is 'too full o' the milk of human kindness' (I. v. 17–18). She invokes spirits of evil to take her own 'milk for gall' (I. v. 49). Then, boasting of her conquest over natural pity, she speaks the terrible lines:

> . . . I have given suck, and know
> How tender 'tis to love the babe that milks me:
> I would, while it was smiling in my face,
> Have pluck'd my nipple from his boneless gums,
> And dash'd the brains out, had I so sworn as you
> Have done to this.   (I. vii. 54)

The child-thought is frequent. There is the unnatural horror of the 'birth-strangled babe' (IV. i. 30), and the matter of Macduff's mysterious birth. Again:

> And pity, like a naked new-born babe,
> Striding the blast, or heaven's cherubin, hors'd
> Upon the sightless couriers of the air . . .   (I. vii. 21)

Unsullied nature's fresh innocence here blends with the angelic hosts—'heaven's cherubin'—of supernatural grace. Babyhood and 'milk' are vividly suggested. There is another milk-reference. Malcolm, pretending to be another Macbeth, would

> Pour the sweet milk of concord into hell,
> Uproar the universal peace, confound
> All unity on earth.   (IV. iii. 98)

Notice the close association of childhood's innocency ('milk') with 'concord'.[1] This evil is antagonistic not only

---

[1] Compare *Richard II*, I. iii. 129:
> And for we think the eagle-winged pride
> Of sky-aspiring and ambitious thoughts,
> With rival-hating envy, set on you
> To wake our peace, which in our country's cradle
> Draws the sweet infant breath of gentle sleep.

to man but to the universe, a blow at all 'unity', at nature, creation, and the 'universal peace', so terrible that the sun is blackened and heaven's thunder reverberates the desolation of human families:

> ... each new morn
> New widows howl, new orphans cry, new sorrows
> Strike heaven on the face, that it resounds
> As if it felt with Scotland and yell'd out
> Like syllable of dolour.   (IV. iii. 4)

Innocent nature is in agony. Twice Macbeth is contrasted with a lamb (IV. iii. 16—'a weak poor innocent lamb'; and IV. iii. 54). Evil fear is contrasted with 'a summer's cloud' (III. iv. 111) and 'good men's lives' die like 'flowers' (IV. iii. 171). So nature will rise to avenge Macduff whose slaughtered wife and children demand redress:

> ... your eye in Scotland
> Would create soldiers, make our women fight,
> To doff their dire distresses.   (IV. iii. 186)

Nature would 'create' soldiers to avenge Macduff's children, make 'women' fight to avenge his wife. 'Creation' is an important idea in the play. Toward the close, nature's assistance is vividly apparent. Macbeth is 'ripe for shaking' (IV. iii. 238). He himself knows it:

> I have lived long enough: my way of life
> Is fall'n into the sear, the yellow leaf ...   (V. iii. 22)

But the avenging forces are mostly young and fresh, to avenge the desecration of nature's childlike peace:

> there is Siward's son,
> And many unrough youths that even now
> Protest their first of manhood.   (V. ii. 9)

Malcolm himself is compared to a flower dew-sprinkled: the Scottish lords would 'dew the sovereign flower and drown the weeds' (V. ii. 30). So sweet a nature-image again suggests nature's assistance: which thought is even more clearly apparent in the matter of Birnam wood. Not a

human arm, only attacks Dunsinane. The very trees rise
against Macbeth, league with his enemies. That is
creative nature accusing, asserting her strength after her
long torment of destruction. So Birnam wood marches
against Macbeth.

For nature is here tormented. I have observed some normal
nature references. There are many more abnormal ones.
Our vision here presents an experience of utter negation
which wrenches all life-forms into distorted and ghoulish
impossibilities. Many such images I have discussed elsewhere. But there are a few more points to observe. The
Weird Sisters from the start are presented as in essence
unnatural.[1] They 'look not like the inhabitants o' the earth,
and yet are on't' (I. iii. 41). Banquo wonders whether they
are 'fantastical' or that which 'outwardly' they 'show', that
is, whether they are real life-forms (I. iii. 53). Their other-
ness to all natural laws is emphasized by their power to
vanish, to become, what they are, a pure nothing, death-
symbols:

> *Banquo.* The earth hath bubbles, as the water has,
>   And these are of them. Whither are they vanish'd?
> *Macbeth.* Into the air; and what seem'd corporal, melted
>   As breath into the wind. Would they had stay'd!
> *Banquo.* Were such things here as we do speak about?
>   Or have we eaten on the insane root
>   That takes the reason prisoner?   (I. iii. 79)

Their unnaturalness and unreality are powerfully stressed.
They are outside nature and the reflection of nature in
the mind, 'reason'. They are things of insanity, related
to that abortion of nature's vegetation—the 'insane root'.
The *Macbeth*-evil is so clearly opposed to nature that
Lady Macbeth, who fears her own as well as Macbeth's (I. v. 17) nature, prays to be 'unsexed'. She continues:

---

[1] I omit the Hecate scenes and speeches. They do not seem to me to
blend with the whole play. Even so, they may be Shakespearian, added
at some later date than the original composition: which would account for
their inclusion in the Folio. See *The Shakespearian Tempest*, App. B.

> . . . make thick my blood,
> Stop up the access and passage to remorse,
> That no compunctious visitings of nature
> Shake my fell purpose, nor keep peace between
> The effect and it! Come to my woman's breasts,
> And take my milk for gall, you murdering ministers,
> Wherever in your sightless substances
> You wait on nature's mischief!   (I. v. 44)

Twice here 'nature' is stressed. This is a play of things outside nature, of 'sightless substances'. She goes on to pray that 'thick night' and hell-smoke may hide her deed from the eye. That is our usual contrast: blackness, nothingness, and life-forms of nature, of sense. The evil torments nature. Its nightmare is a nature-distortion—'the cursed thoughts that nature gives way to in repose' (II. i. 8). In this world 'nature seems dead' and 'wicked dreams' are active (II. i. 50). So the 'present horror' of deadest night must not be interrupted by any sense-forms of sight or sound. The deed of murder is one which must not be looked on—Caroline Spurgeon has shown that this is often emphasized. Nor must it be heard:

> Thou sure and firm-set earth
> Hear not my steps, which way they walk, for fear
> Thy very stones prate of my whereabout,
> And take the present horror from the time,
> Which now suits with it.   (II. i. 56)

Macduff's knocking aptly strikes avenging sounds after this act of silence and darkness. Death is, indeed, the exact opposite of nature and all natural effects:

> death and nature do contend about them,
> Whether they live or die.   (II. ii. 7.)

Our whole world is unnatural, beyond physical laws, 'metaphysical' (I. v. 30). All sense-forms and natural phenomena are attacked. There is a powerful sense-nothing opposition: in which *Macbeth* is directly analogous to *Timon*. Timon moves towards a death-philosophy and attains the 'nothing' of death. It is exactly this 'nothing', this death-negation, that is here projected into action and attacks our life-forms. And, in respect of this negation opposed to creation, we may note a similarity to *Othello*. There 'values' are attacked; love, warriorship. Here not only values, but all life-forces and forms. This opposition is most vivid in the air-drawn dagger scene. 'Sense' here contrasts with the 'delicate senses' of the martlet passage. The dagger is a nothing, to be contrasted with ordinary sense-forms:

> Art thou not, fatal vision, sensible
> To feeling as to sight? or art thou but
> A dagger of the mind, a false creation
> Proceeding from the heat-oppressed brain? (II. i. 36)

Again,

> Mine eyes are made the fools o' the other senses,
> Or else worth all the rest . . . (II. i. 44)

That incident is typical of the whole play: evil is opposed to all natural processes; that is, a pervading death opposes life. The *Macbeth* 'nothing' pits its 'fantastical' (I. iii. 139) realities or unrealities against sense-forms and life-forces, against 'nature': the weird behaviour of sun, tempest, falcon and owl, Duncan's horses—all is 'unnatural, even like the deed that 's done' (II. iv. 10), all has 'turn'd wild in nature' (II. iv. 16), all is ' 'gainst nature still' (II. iv. 27). All this is one with a murder which gashed 'a breach in nature' (II. iii. 119), a murder against nature's outward form of life, the body, 'nature's copy' (III. ii. 38); and against sleep, 'great nature's second course' (II. ii. 39), the 'season of all natures' (III. iv. 141). As Macbeth's course becomes more reckless, the evil forces him to imprecate wholesale tempest and disorder on the universe. He would have the 'winds' untied, fighting against 'churches', swallowing up 'navigation,' blowing down 'corn' and 'trees'; castles, palaces, pyramids, let all fall; he would let 'the treasure of nature's germens tumble all together' till destruction itself 'sicken' (IV. i. 52–60). Notice here the suggestions of (i) the *Macbeth* 'grace' (churches), (ii) imperial sway ('palaces'[1]), and (iii) nature: against all these the evil fights. So the torment goes on: essential disorder, essential destruction—Timon's curses put into violent action. Lady Macbeth's sleep-walking is 'a great perturbation in nature' (v. i. 10), for

> unnatural deeds
> Do breed unnatural troubles ...   (v. i. 79)

It is a fitting culmination to this theme of dark and nightmare, evil which is set beyond any natural law of sense-contact:

> *Doctor.* You see, her eyes are open.
> *Gentlewoman.* Ay, but their sense is shut.   (v. i. 28)

So she walks, her body present but her consciousness beyond the imaginable universe pacing the lonely corridors of agonized remembrance in the other world of sleep. The play's action has been all along a waking nightmare: here nightmare usurps the powers allowed to waking life. It is Death's supreme conquest over 'nature'. But the death-evil itself is outside nature, beyond it. This is suggested by the Doctor's words to Macbeth, who asks if he can minister to his wife's spiritual disease:

> Therein the patient
> Must minister to himself.   (v. iii. 45)

Either that—or call in some supernatural 'grace'. The Doctor suggested as much before:

> More needs she the divine than the physician.
> God, God forgive us all!   (v. i. 82)

The mighty forces of 'grace' and 'evil' must finally decide the issue for Macbeth. That is another profound

---

[1] And, we might add, 'pyramids'. That these have imperial significance in Shakespeare is apparent from *Antony and Cleopatra*:

> ... rather make
> My country's high pyramides my gibbet ...   (v. ii. 60)

So minute are the effects of *Macbeth*. It is the same with the Porter's speech: nature's 'plenty', irrational action, equivocation, hell and heaven, thoughts of dress—all are typical *Macbeth*-ideas.

opposition. An equivalent abstraction—one might almost say 'unreality'—must be 'solicited' (IV. iii. 149) to counter-act the abstraction and unreality which is evil. But, under the banner of divine grace ('the most pious Edward'), all our forces are embattled for Scotland's weal: imperial right (Malcolm); warrior-honour, Siward and his son; nature itself (Birnam wood); and, finally, even disorder and deathly abnormality, turning against itself: Macduff, child of unnatural birth.

I have regarded the evil in relation to life-forces. These may be divided as follows: (i) Human values, Warrior-honour and Imperial Sway; (ii) Human nature, sleep and feasting; (iii) Pure nature—animals, birds, winds, sun, and stars. Most important of all, we must observe the emergence of child-references. The negation here opposes all values, health, and nature: the creative process. Destruction is set against creation: hence our many references to mother's 'milk', the martlet's and wren's nest and young, to 'chickens', 'lambs', the strange use of 'egg' and 'fry' (IV. ii. 84–5), and the child-themes: the phrase, 'child of integrity' (IV. iii. 115), Lady Macbeth's baby at her breast, the baby-spirit of Pity astride the winds of heaven, the two child apparitions—the Bloody Child, and the Child whose 'baby-brow' is crowned with gold: Banquo's descendants, Malcolm, Donalbain, Fleance,[1] the scene of Macduff's son, his 'babes' (IV. i. 152), crying 'orphans' (IV. iii. 5), the birth-strangled babe (IV. i. 30), young Siward, who 'only lived but till he was a man' (V. vii. 69), and the other 'unrough youths' (V. ii. 10). Subjects are 'children' (I. iv. 25) of the king, Scotland the 'mother' of its people now turned to a 'grave', a vivid birth-death contrast (IV. iii. 166); Scotland's peace is those people's 'birthdom' (IV. iii. 4), the throne Malcolm's 'due of birth' (III. vi. 25), the Queen that 'bore' him a saintly mother (IV. iii. 109). The 'nothing' of death-atmosphere, here active and pervasive, silhouettes these 'birth' and 'child'

[1] Compare the escape of the Holy Child in the Massacre of the Innocents; and *Henry V*, III. iii. 38–41.

themes which struggle to assert themselves, struggle to be born from death into life. At the end youth comes armed against Macbeth. Birth opposes death. 'Issue' is an important word. Youth and babyhood oppose our evil. Macbeth murdered aged innocence and purity linked to the 'great office' (I. vii. 18) of kingship. Child innocence with all heaven, all imperial sovereignty, and all nature on its side, tree-sceptred, confronts the murderer:

> What is this
> That rises like the issue of a king,
> And wears upon his baby-brow the round
> And top of sovereignty?   (IV. i. 86)

Macbeth, himself destruction, is to be destroyed: he is a symbol of time itself from its death-aspect. In so far as you see time as destruction, you see it itself continually destroyed: in so far as a man becomes destructive, he is himself destroyed. The time-concept is very clearly woven with Macbeth's tale; contrasting with the eternity of *Antony and Cleopatra*. The Weird Women first met Macbeth as voices of past, present, and future, with their prophecies about Glamis, Cawdor, and Kingship. They suggest absolute time. Macbeth's crime is, however, an attempt to dislocate time, to wrench the future into the present, just as it is a crime against order and degree, a wild vaulting ambition to attain unrightful 'honour'. He wants all time to be his, and so gets none of it. He would 'ravin up' his 'own life's means' (II. iv. 28). He wrongs the majestic and unhurrying pace of time. What is time but a succession of deaths, minute by minute? And yet again it is a succession of births. Macbeth would expedite the death-aspect of time, and so catch the 'future in the instant' (I. v. 59), would destroy the present, Duncan. But in the Cauldron Scene we see time as creation. There is a vivid destruction-birth sequence. The Armed Head, recalling Macdonwald's head 'fixed' on the 'battlements' (I. ii. 23), blends with the 'chaos' and 'disorder' thought throughout, the torn animal and human limbs that

constitute the cauldron's ingredients, and moreover
suggests both the iron force of evil and also its final
destruction. This is followed by the Bloody Child and the
'Child, crowned, with a Tree in his hand'; observe how the
crowned contrasts with the severed head, and how its
victory is directly associated with nature. The order is
important. Violent destruction, itself to be destroyed; the
blood-agony of birth that travails to wrench into existence
a force to right the sickening evil; the future birth splendid
in crowned and accomplished royalty. It suggests the
creative process in all its miraculous strength and power to
pursue its purpose. Ironically, these apparitions give to
Macbeth, who regards their words whilst remaining blind
to themselves, not despair, but hope. He, who has placed
his trust in chaos, hopes himself to 'live the lease of nature'
(iv. i. 99). But this joy is short-lived. For we may note
again how powerfully our positive, creative essences are next
suggested by the 'show of eight Kings'. They are rich in
imperial glory. But they are more. They, too, suggest, in a
wide sense, the creative process itself, the process Macbeth
would annihilate, would cut off at the present root. He
too readily grasped his own future to himself: but would
annihilate the future of others. He would have time
disjointed to serve his ends. But Banquo is to have all the
wealth of posterity, all that creative joy in which alone
human happiness consists. Too late he learns that to get
kings is more blessed than to be king, creation more
blessed than possession. For possession divorced from
creation melts in the grasping hand: like flowers 'dying
or ere they sicken' (iv. iii. 173). So here, a right kingly
creation in all its inevitable splendour and future integrity
passes before his eyes; and its imperial strength and
unending glory, its line stretching even to 'the crack of
doom' (iv. i. 117), confronts his own brief-living destructive self, doomed to end, his 'eternal jewel' (iii. i. 68)
lost, with the end of his own agony. This is shown him
by the Weird Women, the 'instruments of darkness'
(i. iii. 124) and evil; and they thus league against him,

know and show the limitations imposed on evil, for Macbeth is childless, with a fruitless crown and barren sceptre, as evil is ever childless, unproductive. So he knows the process of life to hold no hope for him. It is merely a cruel catalogue of deaths strung together in time:

> To-morrow, and to-morrow, and to-morrow,
> Creeps in this petty pace from day to day
> To the last syllable of recorded time,
> And all our yesterdays have lighted fools
> The way to dusty death. Out, out, brief candle!
> Life 's but a walking shadow, a poor player
> That struts and frets his hour upon the stage
> And then is heard no more: it is a tale
> Told by an idiot, full of sound and fury,
> Signifying nothing.   (v. v. 19)

He sees all life from the death-aspect of time. And he is now himself reconciled to the 'nothing', the negation of evil and death. He finds peace in the profundities of his own nihilistic death-experience: death and 'nothing' are realities: life has no meaning. The evil has worked its way with him, and left him with no hope in life. Even so, there is yet death. Like the earlier Cawdor, he dies well.

The Weird Women, I have said, are not themselves from every aspect opposed to creation and life. They know evil to be futile, they know their own futility. They are unreal, and know it, know their existence and purposes to be self-contradictory. So, of their two main prophecies in the Cauldron Scene, those relating to Birnam Wood and Macduff's birth, the one is fulfilled in terms of natural law, the other in terms of an event itself so abnormal as to be all but unnatural:

> And let the angel whom thou still hast serv'd
> Tell thee, Macduff was from his mother's womb
> Untimely ripp'd.   (v. vii. 43)

If, as has been sometimes suggested, Macduff means that his mother died before his birth, the suggestion is pregnant to our interpretation: life born out of death. But, in whatever sense we take its meaning, we see that disorder itself turns on disorder. So, too, the death-concept ever contradicts itself and becomes life to any intense contemplation. Absolute disorder prohibits self-consistency: it helps to slay itself. Death gives birth to life. Not nature alone, but 'both the worlds' (III. ii. 16), natural and unnatural, life and death, come against Macbeth. And here we may observe an important effect in the Cauldron Scene. The three apparitions suggesting the conflict of death and birth rise from the hell-broth in the cauldron to 'thunder'. The Weird Sisters instinctively fear Macbeth's demand about Banquo's descendants— 'Seek to know no more' (IV. i. 103). Even the Apparitions, being reflections of human reality, were their 'masters' (IV. i. 63). Now, threatened by Macbeth's 'eternal curse' (IV. i. 105) they reluctantly expose their own impermanency, the eternal unreality of evil. The cauldron vanishes (IV. i. 106), and the line of future kings passes to the music of 'hautboys' (IV. i. 106).

In a final judgement the whole play may be writ down as a wrestling of destruction with creation: with sickening shock the phantasmagoria of death and evil are violently loosed on earth, and for a while the agony endures, destructive; there is a wrenching of new birth, itself disorderly and unnatural in this disordered world, and then creation's more firm-set sequent concord replaces chaos. The baby-peace is crowned.

Additional Note, 1965: This essay has proved fertile. In 1933 Professor L. C. Knights, who had previously reviewed *The Imperial Theme* in *The Criterion*, explained at length its influence on his own *Macbeth* analyses (*How Many Children had Lady Macbeth?*, 1933; Note B, p. 70). Since then Professor Cleanth Brooks' 'The Naked Babe' (*The Well Wrought Urn*, 1949) has redeveloped parts of its argument. Mr. Roy Walker's *The Time is Free* (1949) is an important full-length study upon similarly imaginative lines, which I hope soon to see again in circulation.

VI

THE ROYAL OCCUPATION: AN ESSAY ON CORIOLANUS

I TAKE my title from Antony's words to Cleopatra:

> Oh, love,
> That thou could'st see my wars to-day, and knew'st
> The royal occupation! thou shouldst see
> A workman in 't.   (*Antony and Cleopatra*, IV. iv. 15)

In *Antony and Cleopatra*, the two values, War and Love, oppose each other: the same contrast is at the core of *Coriolanus*. War is, in both plays, shown as the cruder ideal: here, where only the positive values survive, all cynic and fearful negations rejected, a certain limitation in the War-value emerges distinct. In a wide sense, this value represents nobility, practical efficiency, power and ambition: it includes nearly all positive life-qualities but love. Yet such are but moderately good: their immoderate pursuit leads to isolation and pride. Antony is haloed with warrior-nobility beyond any protagonist in Shakespeare. But there is a short scene in his story that suggests the poison hearted in such success. Ventidius explains that he has not followed up his victory over the Parthians lest too great a success displease his master:

> Who does i' the wars more than his captain can
> Becomes his captain's captain: and ambition
> The soldier's virtue, rather makes choice of loss,
> Than gain which darkens him.
> I could do more to do Antonius good,
> But 'twould offend him.

Instead,

> I'll humbly signify what in his name,
> That magical word of war, we have effected.
>   (*Antony and Cleopatra*, III. i. 21–31.)

Ambition is here 'the soldier's virtue'. So, too, in *Othello* we hear of the wars 'that make ambition virtue'. But this ambition leads to a pride which is seen to limit the very success on which it would thrive. It is self-contradictory, self-poisoned, this value of warrior ambition. So, in a wide understanding, is there intrinsic fault in any ambition, or indeed any value, which is not a multiple of love. This is the theme developed in *Coriolanus*.

The play's style is bare. It holds little of the undulating, heaving swell of *Othello's* music, the fireworks of *Julius Caesar*, the fine frenzies of *Lear* or *Macbeth*; it usually refuses the deeps of passion's threnody that toll the pilgrimage of *Timon*. Rather there is here a swift channeling, an eddying, twisting, and forthward-flowing stream; ice-cold, intellectual, cold as a mountain torrent and holding something of its iron taste. We are in a world of hard weapons, battle's clanging contacts, civic brawls about 'grain' and 'corn'; a town-life somewhat limited and provincial, varied with the sickening crashes of war. There is little brilliance, little colour. Some lovely natural images stand out, but they scarcely build any dominant delight till the last act, for which, however, they serve to prepare us. Here even fishes may have metallic fins:

> He that depends
> Upon your favours swims with fins of lead
> And hews down oak with rushes. (I. i. 183)

The imagery is often metallic—such as 'leaden pounds' (III. i. 314), or 'manacles' (I. ix. 57) or 'leaden spoons, irons of a doit' (I. v. 5), or as when Coriolanus' harshness forces his mother to kneel 'with no softer cushion than the flint' (v. iii. 53). This metal suggestion blends naturally elsewhere with the town setting. There is frequent mention of buildings. We hear of 'hunger' breaking 'stone walls' (I. i. 210), of 'unroofing' the city (I. i. 222), of 'the spire and top of praises' (I. ix. 24). There is reference to 'Publius and Quintus' who 'our best water brought by conduits hither' (II. iii. 250). Antium is praised for its fine buildings:

> A goodly city is this Antium. City,
> 'Tis I that made thy widows: many an heir
> Of these fair edifices 'fore my wars
> Have I heard groan and drop . . .   (iv. iv. 1)

—a grim boast. The plebeians short-sightedly have helped to 'melt the city leads' upon their own 'pates' (iv. vi. 82), their 'temples' will be 'burned in their cement' (iv. vi. 85). The fire-metal association is reflected rather differently in:

> One fire drives out one fire, one nail one nail.
>   (iv. vii. 54)

Such references often derive from the essentially 'civic' setting. And the present civilization is clearly a hard one —a matter of brick and mortar, metals and stones. This is not the world of *Antony and Cleopatra*. There human civilization catches a divine fire and blazes back to the sun and moon something of their universal glory. Consider how Antony describes the rich ooze of Nile, sun-fecundated and pregnant of harvest riches (*Antony and Cleopatra*, ii. vii.) Then turn to *Coriolanus*:

> The Volsces have much corn; take these rats thither
> To gnaw their garners.   (i. i. 254)

We hear of 'one poor grain or two' from 'a pile of noisome musty chaff' (v. i. 26–7). Here 'store-houses' are 'crammed with grain' (i. i. 83), the belly is 'the store-house and the shop' (i. i. 137) of the body. ' 'Tis south the city mills' is a natural phrase (i. x. 31). The difference from the wide universalism in *Antony and Cleopatra* is vivid. We are limited by city walls. And cities are here metallic, our world constricted, bound in by hard walls: and this constriction, this suggestion of hardness, is rooted deep in our theme. The persons of *Antony and Cleopatra* continually show a tendency to cohere, to make friends with each other. Hostile cities are here ringed as with the iron walls of war, inimical, deadly to each other, self-contained. Our city-imagery blends with our war-imagery, which is also hard and metallic; and that itself is fused with the theme of Coriolanus' iron-hearted pride. The whole association is bound closely in a speech of Menenius, in which a building is emblematic of Coriolanus' hardness of soul in warring against his native town:

> *Menenius.* See you yond coign o' the Capitol, yond corner-stone?
> *Sicinius.* Why, what of that?
> *Menenius.* If it be possible for you to displace it with your little
> finger, there is some hope the ladies of Rome, especially his
> mother, may prevail with him.   (v. iv. 1)

And even when the iron of pride is vanquished, the ladies deserve 'to have a temple built them' (v. iii. 207).

War is here violent, metallic, impactuous. It does not exactly attain the sunset glow of Othello's romance, his 'pride, pomp, and circumstance of glorious war'. Nor is it so grimly portentous and horror-burdened as the warring of Macbeth and Banquo with the rebel chiefs. Yet it is very much a thing of blood and harshness, and, especially, metal. Coriolanus' wars are terrible in their ringing, iron blows; in the breaking through city walls; in the clamorous concomitant of sounding 'alarums'. Weapons are scattered throughout the play—they even invade the purely civic themes. Here 'wives with splits and boys with stones' may rise against Coriolanus in Antium (IV. iv. 5). Again,

> But make you ready your stiff bats and clubs:
> Rome and her rats are at the point of battle:
> The one side must have bale.   (I. i. 165)

The epithet 'stiff' is as typical of this play as 'soft' is of *Antony and Cleopatra*. Coriolanus is 'a rod' to Rome's friends (II. iii. 99). War is hard here. The 'casque' is contrasted with the 'cushion' (IV. vii. 43), and the same contrast appears in:

> When steel grows soft as is the parasite's silk
> Let him be made a coverture for the wars!   (I. ix. 45)

Again,

> . . . This peace is nothing, but to rust iron, increase tailors,
> and breed ballad-makers.   (IV. v. 233)

Numerous weapons—it is unnecessary to observe them in

detail—are mentioned throughout, as when we hear of
soldiers 'filling the air with swords advanced and darts'
(I. vi. 61), or of the patricians as 'the helms of the state'
(I. i. 79). Individual combats are things of sickening
impact, force opposed to force, violent, hard, metallic.
Coriolanus' soldiers may bear against Aufidius 'a shield
as hard as his' (I. vi. 80). Aufidius, thinking of Coriolanus,
tells how he

> . . . thought to crush him in an equal force,
> True sword to sword . . .   (I. x. 14)

Coriolanus was 'wont to thwack' Aufidius (IV. v. 188); he
'scotched him and notched him like a carbonado' (IV. v.
198). Such violent suggestions are powerful in Aufidius'
greeting to Coriolanus:

> Let me twine
> Mine arms about that body, where against
> My grained ash an hundred times hath broke,
> And scarr'd the moon with splinters: here I clip
> The anvil of my sword . . .   (IV. v. 112)

Notice the 'moon' infinity-suggestion. We have here an
infinite, but harsh, warrior-strength. 'Anvil' is suggestive:
so, also, Coriolanus would 'forge' a name for himself from
burning Rome (v. i. 14). 'What his breast forges, that his
tongue must vent' (III. i. 258). Aufidius dreams of violent
contests with Coriolanus:

> We have been down together in my sleep,
> Unbuckling helms, fisting each other's throat,
> And wak'd half dead with nothing.   (IV. v. 130)

He hoped 'once more to hew' Coriolanus' 'target from his
brawn' (IV. v. 126). Menenius tells the citizens that the
state will keep its course

> cracking ten thousand curbs
> Of more strong link asunder than can ever
> Appear in your impediment.   (I. i. 72)

The play starts with a crowd of citizens eager to avenge
their wrongs with 'pikes' (I. i. 24); 'trail your steel pikes'
(v. vi. 152) is a fitting conclusion.

These violent crashes of contest are things of blood. 'Blood' is emphasized. Volumnia, stern mother of a warrior son, loves to picture Coriolanus painted in such glory:

> . . . his bloody brow
> With his mail'd hand then wiping, forth he goes . . .
>
> (I. iii. 37)

Virgilia is terrified at the thought:

> His bloody brow! O Jupiter, no blood!

And Volumnia answers:

> Away, you fool! it more becomes a man
> Than gilt his trophy: the breasts of Hecuba,
> When she did suckle Hector, look'd not lovelier
> Than Hector's forehead when it spit forth blood
> At Grecian sword, contemning.   (I. iii. 42)

Notice the desecration of the idea of 'birth' in this passage, comparable with *Macbeth*. Cominius, in the battle, sees Coriolanus thus spattered with gore:

> Who's yonder,
> That does appear as he were flay'd? O gods!
> He has the stamp of Marcius; and I have
> Before-time seen him thus.   (I. vi. 21)

We have a warfare of crashing blows and spurting blood. Its violence is emphasized throughout. Here human ambition attains its height by splitting an opponent's body, the final signature of honour is the robe and reeking caparison of blood. Now all our imagery of clanging contest, iron blows, blood, ambition, and warrior-honour —it is heavy throughout, and strikes a note of harshness peculiar to this play—centres on Coriolanus. He enters 'cursing' (I. iv. 29), and 'bleeding' (I. iv. 61). He is not lit with the blaze of chivalry that aureoles Antony: he is a man of iron, mail-fisted. I will next show the especial relevance of this quality to Coriolanus. Here he is in his bloody pride, and iron fortitude:

> . . . his sword, death's stamp,
> Where it did mark, it took; from face to foot
> He was a thing of blood, whose every motion

> Was tim'd with dying cries: alone he enter'd
> The mortal gate of the city, which he painted
> With shunless destiny: aidless came off,
> And with a sudden re-inforcement struck
> Corioli like a planet: now all 's his:
> When, by and by, the din of war gan pierce
> His ready sense; then straight his doubled spirit
> Re-quicken'd what in flesh was fatigate,
> And to the battle came he; where he did
> Run reeking o'er the lives of men, as if
> 'Twere a perpetual spoil: and till we call'd
> Both field and city ours, he never stood
> To ease his breast with panting.   (ii. ii. 111)

Notice the metallic suggestion: the city 'gate', 'din' which 'pierces' his sense, the fine hyperbole of Coriolanus 'striking' the whole town with planetary impact. All this is blended with 'blood'—he is 'a thing of blood', 'painting' Corioli with its people's blood, himself 'reeking'. There is, too, 'death'. His sword is 'death's stamp', he runs over 'the lives of men', and 'dying cries' punctuate his advance. Iron, blood, death. There is something terrible in this description. He is indeed ruthless as death himself, a 'shunless destiny'.[1] This is our grim protagonist. So he charges through the action like a steel-headed spear a-wing in the air of battle, destructive. So, at the end, we are not surprised to find him turning into a blind mechanism of self-centred pride:

> . . . when he walks, he moves like an engine, and the ground shrinks before his treading: he is able to pierce a corslet with his eye; talks like a knell, and his hum is a battery.
> (v. iv. 19)

This is the price of his excessive and exclusive virtue. Grim as he is in his warring and pride, we must observe, too, his essential virtue. He is a thing complete, a rounded perfection. We can no more blame him for his ruthless valour than we blame the hurtling spear for finding its

---

[1] Compare *Othello*, iii. iii. 275:
    'Tis destiny unshunnable, like death.

mark. And yet Coriolanus has no mark: that is his tragedy. Compact of nobility and strength, he pursues his course. But he is too perfect a pure unit, an isolated force: no deep love of country is his. His wars are not for Rome: they are an end in themselves. Therefore his renegade attack on Rome is not strange. His course obeys no direction but its own: he is a power used in the service of power. The spear turns out, in mid flight, to be a boomerang, and hurtles back on the hand that loosed it. So he whirls like a planet in the dark chaos of pride, pursuing his self-bound orbit: a blind mechanic, metallic thing of pride and pride's destiny.

Throughout the play we are aware of his 'grim looks' (I. iv. 58) and, as Titus Lartius aptly phrases it:

> The thunder-like percussion of thy sounds.   (I. iv. 59)

That line is typical of a curious twist of style here. Continually we find, in prose or poetry, a violent and startling polysyllable set amid humble companions, often monosyllables. I quote a few to suggest their quality: 'Here is the steed, we the caparison' (I. ix. 12); 'Make good this ostentation and you shall' (I. vi. 86); 'But now 'tis odds beyond arithmetic' (III. i. 245); 'Like interrupted waters and o'erbear . . .' (III. i. 249); 'That love the fundamental part of state' (III. i. 151); 'For we are peremptory to dispatch' (III. i. 286); 'In peril of precipitation' (III. iii. 102). That last recalls another fine phrase:

> That the precipitation might down stretch
> Below the beam of sight.   (III. ii. 4)

Often there are two such lines successive:

> Unseparable, shall within this hour,
> On a dissension of a doit, break out.   (IV. iv. 16)

or,

> This is a poor epitome of yours,
> Which by the interpretation of full time . . . (V. iii. 68)

Sometimes we find two thunderous words in one line, as

when the rabble is forgotten and a Coriolanus and
Aufidius are left in single combat:

> In acclamations hyperbolical;   (I. ix. 51)

and,

> Than violentest contrariety;   (IV. vi. 73)

or,

> Murdering impossibility, to make
> What cannot be, slight work.   (V. iii. 61)

The name 'Coriolanus' itself fits well and aptly into this
pattern:

> To his surname Coriolanus 'longs more pride
> Than pity to our prayers;   (V. iii. 170)

And,

> Coriolanus in Corioli.   (V. v. 90)

In prose, there is a sprinkling of strange polysyllables
outstanding from plainer speech: microcosm (II. i. 69),
conspectuities (II. i. 71), empiricutic (II. i. 128), cicatrices
(II. i. 163), carbonado (IV. v. 199), directitude (IV. v. 221),
factionary (V. ii. 29). Many of these cause blank amaze-
ment among the rabble, or Volscian menials: and are
thus related to the main idea of the aristocrat contrasted
with commoners. So, in our line units, there is, as it were,
an aristocrat among a crowd of plebeian words, and often
that protagonist word falls with a hammer-blow that
again reminds us of metal:

> 'Tis fond to wail inevitable strokes.   (IV. i. 26)

Again, with implicit reference to 'harshness', there is the
clanging note of:

> A name unmusical to the Volscians' ears
> And harsh in sound to thine.   (IV. v. 64)

Such protagonist words apply aptly to our protagonist's
actions:

> That would depopulate the city, and
> Be every man himself.   (III. i. 264)

and,

> . . . to wind
> Yourself into a power tyrannical.   (III. iii. 64)

But, whether directly or indirectly related to Coriolanus,

each anvil-blow of such lines as these reminds us of 'the thunder-like percussion of his sounds'; and each seems to strike another rivet in his iron armoury of pride. Each line reflects the whole play, where Coriolanus strides gigantic, thunderously reverberating his aristocracy above the multitude.

Nature-images point us to the same thought. They both contrast with our metallic images, preparing us for the love-victory later, and point the natural excellence of our hero. He is rather like a finely-modelled motor-cycle, flashing in bright paint and steel, every line suggesting power and speed, standing among a row of pedal-bicycles. We therefore find a continual contrast between strong and weak things in nature, usually animals, which contrast is directly or indirectly related to the Coriolanus-plebeian opposition. Animals, and other nature references, go in pairs. We have lions and hares, foxes and geese (I. i. 175–6); oaks and rushes (I. i. 185); a bear scattering children (I. iii. 34); a boy and a butterfly (I. iii. 63–71); men and geese (I. iv. 34); the cat and the mouse (I. vi. 44); a hare being hunted (I. viii. 7); weeds before a vessel's keel (II. ii. 109); eagles and crows (III. i. 139); boys and butterflies again, butchers and flies (IV. vi. 94–5); Hercules shaking down ripe fruit (IV. vi. 99); a 'harvest-man' mowing corn (I. iii. 39); the shepherd and the wolf (IV. vi. 110). Such imagery continually suggests the inborn inequality of men. Coriolanus is endued from birth with nature's aristocracy. He exceeds Romans and Volscians alike—scattering his enemies like leaves before a wind, despising his own countrymen like vermin. Aufidius, indeed, is a 'lion' he is 'proud to hunt' (I. i. 239); but to him the Roman citizens are 'camels' or 'mules' (II. i. 270, 266), or 'dogs' to be beaten for barking (II. iii. 224), their tribune an 'old goat' (III. i. 177). The Volscians are suggested to be no better:

> . . . when they shall see, sir, his crest up again, and the man in blood, they will out of their burrows, like conies after rain, and revel all with him.   (IV. v. 223)

Such phraseology continually points us to a certain essential triviality in those who make up the crowds of Romans or Volscians. The Roman plebeians are as 'a beast with many heads' which 'butts' Coriolanus from Rome (IV. i. I). He is of a different stock from such animals. Even the patricians feel his inborn superiority:

> . . . the nobles bended
> As to Jove's statue, and the commons made
> A shower and thunder with their caps and shouts.
>
> (II. i. 281)

'Jove', and 'thunder': Coriolanus is often imaged grim as a wrathful God. Elsewhere his 'thunder' is contrasted with the 'tabor' (I. vi. 25). He fights 'dragon-like' (IV. vii. 23). Again:

> *Sicinius.* Is 't possible that so short a time can alter the condition of a man?
> *Menenius.* There is differency between a grub and a butterfly; yet your butterfly was a grub. This Marcius is grown from man to dragon: he has wings; he 's more than a creeping thing.   (V. iv. 9)

Again a vivid contrast, this time between Coriolanus superficially at least as a man among men and Coriolanus that ogre of self-nursed anger and unrelenting iron into which he develops. But his ugliness is but an excessive, because self-limited, beauty: the beauty of natural excellence, unbending to any law but its own. He is born into a sovereignty of strength and conscious superiority:

> I think he'll be to Rome
> As is the osprey to the fish, who takes it
> By sovereignty of nature.   (IV. vii. 33)

The same contrast rings out in his final boast:

> If you have writ your annals true, 'tis there,
> That, like an eagle in a dove-cote, I
> Flutter'd your Volscians in Corioli:
> Alone I did it.   (V. v. 114)

Yet a mightier power beats down his pride. At the climax love disarms his vengeance. When Volumnia pits his filial love against his pride, this new antagonism again

finds noble expression in natural—or rather universal—
imagery more powerful than that already observed. To
Coriolanus, 'the rock, the oak not to be wind-shaken'
(v. ii. 118), his mother comes, strong in her weakness,
comes to the iron giant of her own moulding:

> My mother bows;
> As if Olympus to a molehill should
> In supplication nod.   (v. iii. 29)

Now it is he who is weak as a 'gosling' (v. iii. 35). His
mother kneels:

> What is this?
> Your knees to me? to your corrected son?
> Then let the pebbles on the hungry beach
> Fillip the stars; then let the mutinous winds
> Strike the proud cedars 'gainst the fiery sun;
> Murdering impossibility, to make
> What cannot be, slight work.   (v. iii. 56)

Here, then, we have our Coriolanus-idea: something of
iron strength and natural excellence which sticks

> i' the wars
> Like a great sea-mark, standing every flaw,
> And saving those that eye thee!   (v. iii. 73)

But great as is this contrast, there is a greater. The simple
power of love is endued with a dignity and universal
sanction comparable only with 'Olympus', the 'stars', the
'fiery sun'. In that comparison men and lions and all
brave beasts are levelled with 'molehills', and 'pebbles'.
Our style and imagery, whether of metals, of protagonist
words, or of natural reference, point clearly the direction
of our analysis.

From the first we know Coriolanus' nobility to be
poisoned by pride. The citizens consider him chief 'enemy
to the people' (i. i. 8) and would proceed 'against him first'
(i. i. 28):

> *Second Citizen.* Consider you what services he has done for
> his country?
> *First Citizen.* Very well; and could be content to give him
> good report for 't, but that he pays himself with being proud.

Second Citizen. Nay, but speak not maliciously.

First Citizen. I say unto you, what he hath done famously, he did it to that end: though soft-conscienced men can be content to say it was for his country, he did it to please his mother, and to be partly proud; which he is, even to the altitude of his virtue.

Second Citizen. What he cannot help in his nature, you account a vice in him. You must in no way say he is covetous.

First Citizen. If I must not, I need not be barren of accusations; he hath faults, with surplus, to tire in repetition.

(I. i. 30)

This is a fairly just estimate. Coriolanus' 'pride' and 'virtue' are shown not as two distinct attributes, but rather as a single quality twined in the pattern of his 'nature'. Each is curiously intrinsic to the other. Throughout we must observe this. He continually 'pays himself' for his virtue by being aware of it—if we consider primarily his virtue; or, if we first regard his pride, then his services are done 'to please his mother' and to be 'partly proud' (i.e. perhaps, 'pertly' or 'proud of his parts, or natural qualities'). But neither is primary. His pride and virtue are aspects of the single Coriolanus: and that Coriolanus is dedicated to one thing: honour, considered as an end in itself. Coleridge's remark on Macbeth suits better Coriolanus: he desires 'a temporal end in itself'. And 'honour', though elsewhere it is considered 'infinite', must here be regarded as a temporal 'end' in comparison with love. He does no real service for Rome, but rather wars for war's sake, gathers honour for honour's sake. This is how his honour is dissociated from love. His nobility is always living on capital, and quickly goes bankrupt.

Coriolanus' scorn of his inferiors knows no limit. So he addresses the citizens:

> What's the matter, you dissentious rogues,
> That, rubbing the poor itch of your opinion,
> Make yourselves scabs?
> (I. i. 168)

They are 'curs', 'rats': he continually speaks his scorn broadcast. In the wars he drives them on by curses:

> All the contagion of the south light on you,
> You shames of Rome! you herd of—Boils and plagues
> Plaster you o'er, that you may be abhorr'd
> Further than seen and one infect another
> Against the wind a mile!   (I. iv. 30)

Such despisal is ugly: it is the obverse of his pride. Even his soldiering is a thing beyond 'strokes', a demonic energy, in word or look, as described by Titus Lartius:

> Thou art left, Marcius:
> A carbuncle entire, as big as thou art,
> Were not so rich a jewel. Thou wast a soldier
> Even to Cato's wish, not fierce and terrible
> Only in strokes; but, with thy grim looks and
> The thunder-like percussion of thy sounds,
> Thou madest thine enemies shake, as if the world
> Were feverous and did tremble.   (I. iv. 54)

His warrior-strength and violent invective are thus intertwined, and both related to pride and his ceaseless quest of honour. Coriolanus' wars are things of hate, violence, blood, and death:

> There is the man of my soul's hate, Aufidius,
> Piercing our Romans . . .   (I. v. 11)

So he fights till he appears 'as he were flay'd' (I. vi. 22), and needs a 'gentle bath' and 'balms' (I. vi. 63–4). But he is drunk with battle's ecstasy and loves

> this painting
> Wherein you see me smear'd.   (I. vi. 68)

Though he more usually employs curses, he can, at a moment of war-intoxication, turn out platitudes to his followers about his 'country', but whenever he talks so, we can detect a certain triteness in his patriotic phrases. They ring a little hollow and come out too pat and glib:

> . . . if any fear
> Lesser his person than an ill report;
> If any think brave death outweighs bad life,
> And that his country's dearer than himself;

> Let him alone, or so many so minded,
> Wave thus, to express his disposition,
> And follow Marcius.   (i. vi. 69)

The action of the play will show how Coriolanus' egotism
later contradicts his words: he is to himself then far dearer
than his country.   But the soldiers acclaim this speech
with cheers, lift him on their shoulders.   He feels a wave
of real comradeship:

> O, me alone! make you a sword of me?
> If these shows be not outward, which of you
> But is four Volsces? none of you but is
> Able to bear against the great Aufidius
> A shield as hard as his.   (i. vi. 76)

Notice the equating of Coriolanus with a 'sword': it is
suggestive.   He is almost an automaton in fight, a slaying-
machine of mechanic excellence.   This breath of sympathy
with his men is exceptional and does not last.   He appears
in a truer light when he meets Aufidius, and they join
combat in terms of 'hate' and 'fame':

> *Marcius.* I'll fight with none but thee; for I do hate thee
>   Worse than a promise-breaker.
> *Aufidius.*   We hate alike:
>   Not Afric owns a serpent I abhor
>   More than thy fame and envy.   (i. viii. 1)

So it is ever.   Coriolanus' fighting is given no glamour of
romance, like Antony's.   It is something at whose report

>   ladies shall be frighted,
> And, gladly quak'd, hear more . . .   (i. ix. 5)

But, whether or not it is done in true patriotism, it is
valuable to Rome:

>   . . . the dull tribunes
> That, with the fusty plebeians, hate thine honours,
> Shall say against their hearts, 'We thank the gods
> Our Rome hath such a soldier'.   (i. ix. 6)

He is useful—for a while.   Such strength, however, is
valuable only whilst it acknowledges its provisional virtue.
   Coriolanus' fault lies in his pursuing honour as an end in

itself. He does not even like praise and thanks. This, too,
is a kind of pride. He instinctively rejects thanks. Partly,
perhaps, because he knows his deeds are not done for Rome,
or, if he does not yet know it, fears he may be forced to
know it and would rather turn his mind from the matter;
and, partly, because the giving and receiving of praises is
a kind of payment, a levelling of differences, a mingling
with inferior beings who cannot have anything to give
him worth his attention. He would stand alone, unpaid,
self-praised only: he 'pays himself by being proud' (I. i.
33). No one but his mother is worthy to praise him:

> Pray now, no more; my mother
> Who has a charter to extol her blood,
> When she does praise me, grieves me. I have done
> As you have done; that's what I can; induc'd
> As you have been; that's for my country:
> He that has but effected his good will
> Hath overta'en mine act.   (I. ix. 13)

Here he jerks out platitudes again. They are not sincere.
He does not believe any one has overtaken his acts. He
is irritated by these praises and offers of reward. His
wounds 'smart to hear themselves remember'd' (I. ix. 28).
The army 'profanes' its drums and trumpets by flourishing
his honour, he would not be shouted forth 'in acclamations
hyperbolical' (I. ix. 41, 51). He is embarrassed, un-
generous, in receipt of tangible honours. And this
ungenerosity, at root, springs from one fact: his pursuit of
honour as an end in itself. He would not have it desecrated
idolatrously by gifts and praises: it is to him the divine
reality. Superficially a fine attitude, it yet secretes its own
insidious poison. Tangible rewards and praises ought
rather to meet a gracious response, thus restoring that
balance between individual merit and the community
which pride wills to disturb. Only the most abstract, and
enduring, of honours calls forth any delight in him: the
title 'Coriolanus'. It is honour he loves, not gold nor
human gratitude, just abstract, bloodless, profitless
honour: and no more perfect abstraction exists than a

name. At this summit of attainment, he abruptly changes
our theme:

> The gods begin to mock me. I, that now
> Refus'd most princely gifts, am bound to beg
> Of my lord general.   (I. ix. 78)

This is his request:

> I sometime lay here in Corioli
> At a poor man's house; he used me kindly:
> He cried to me; I saw him prisoner;
> But then Aufidius was within my view,
> And wrath o'erwhelm'd my pity.   (I. ix. 82)

Here is a new quality: like a rivulet subterranean, waters
of love below the hard crust of his iron pride. Once again
it is to be apparent, then gushing its fountains over the
dry waste. Then 'the gods' are to 'laugh at' him, as here
they 'mock' him. This is the deep prompting of love, in
whatever form, which mocks the desert Elysium of Pride.
Here it is weak. 'Wrath' was more powerful than 'pity',
as later love treads down his wrath. Cominius praises
him for his generosity—was there even a touch of self-
approbation in the request itself?

> *Cominius.*   . . . Deliver him, Titus.
> *Lartius.* Marcius, his name?
> *Coriolanus.*   By Jupiter! forgot.
>   I am weary; yea, my memory is tir'd.
>   Have we no wine here?   (I. ix. 89)

These waters are deep-buried, apparent for an instant,
soon 'forgot'.

Coriolanus has been spoilt by his mother. We are
frequently reminded of her past ideals in bringing up her
boy. She is obsessed with love of her son's success. She
rebukes Virgilia for her weakness in sorrowing whilst her
husband is at the war. She describes her own love:

> . . . When yet he was but tender-bodied and the only son of
> my womb, when youth with comeliness plucked all gaze his
> way, when for a day of kings' entreaties a mother should not
> sell him an hour from her beholding, I, considering how

honour would become such a person, that it was no better
than picture-like to hang by the wall, if renown made it not
stir, was pleased to let him seek danger where he was like to
find fame. To a cruel war I sent him; from whence he
returned, his brows bound with oak. I tell thee, daughter,
I sprang not more in joy at first hearing he was a man-child
than now in first seeing he had proved himself a man.

(I. iii. 6)

Such an instinct is natural, but Volumnia is no ordinary mother. She loves to picture him, gowned in blood,
urging on his men with the clarion voice of scorn.
His violence, his embattled pride, his ruthless scorn of
inferiors, all feed her proud love. Valeria talks of his little
boy:

> O' my word, the father's son: I'll swear, 'tis a very pretty
> boy. O' my troth, I looked upon him o' Wednesday half an
> hour together: has such a confirmed countenance. I saw him
> run after a gilded butterfly; and when he caught it, he let it
> go again; and after it again; and over and over he comes,
> and up again; catched it again; or whether his fall enraged
> him, or how 'twas, he did so set his teeth and tear it; O, I
> warrant, how he mammocked it! (I. iii. 62)

On which this iron mother comments with a grim
approval: 'One on 's father's moods'. It is so. This little
incident reflects well Coriolanus' merciless power, his
unpitying condemnation of the weak, his violent self-will:
above all, his quality of strength misused. Here even
war's nobility is always a matter of violence, blood,
cruelty, bought at the expense of others' misery:

> A goodly city is this Antium. City,
> 'Tis I that made thy widows: many an heir
> Of these fair edifices 'fore my wars
> Have I heard groan and drop. (IV. iv. 1)

So, too, we are shortly to observe how he has bought his
title 'Coriolanus' at the expense of 'widows in Corioli' and
'mothers that lack sons'. His course is throughout one
of destruction: any ideal not geared to love whirls on
destructively, ungoverned, undirected, murderous. Such

warrior-strength dissociated from patriotism is here painted grim indeed: this incident of Coriolanus' boy and the butterfly is a true indication to our understanding of the protagonist.

Volumnia is the iron mother of an iron son. She has no interest, no sympathy, no understanding, save in one direction: her son's honour. She scorns Virgilia, who does not seem to fit in with this glory-quest, this ceaseless pursuit of a phantom. To Virgilia, Coriolanus is a man, not a machine to grind out fresh-made honours from the rough material of slain enemies. She fears for his wounds, his life, his success, and her anxieties meet scorn from the older woman. But Coriolanus comes home safe and garlanded, the mother's dreams are made true to the height of her extremest hopes. At the news she is all eagerness, violent in her snatching, possessive desire for fresh money-bags to swell their treasury of honour:

> Honourable Menenius, my boy Marcius approaches; for the
> love of Juno, let's go. (II. i. 110)

Letters have come from him:

> Look, here's a letter from him: the state hath another, his
> wife another; and, I think, there's one at home for you.
> (II. i. 118)

'At home'—it is infinitely pathetic, so is all this distorted ambition. Like her son's pride it is a fine thing poisoned only by its mis-concentrated isolation. As she waits her words come out breathlessly—he has come 'the third time home with the oaken garland' (II. i. 137). The general 'gives my son the whole name of the war' (II. i. 148). She is irritated at Virgilia's doubts as to the truth of these bright tidings—'True! pow, pow'; she thanks the gods that he is wounded (II. i. 133), and catalogues his scars. He is hurt

> I' the shoulder and i' the left arm: there will be large cicatrices
> to show the people, when he shall stand for his place. He
> received in the repulse of Tarquin seven hurts i' the body.
> (II. i. 162)

She counts them as a miser his coins. It is absurd, this counting of wounds, these statistics of honour:

> He had, before this last expedition, twenty-five wounds upon him. (II. i. 169)

Trumpets sound, a shout proclaims her son's approach. Her exultation is uncontrollable:

> These are the ushers of Marcius: before him he carries noise, and behind him he leaves tears:
> Death, that dark spirit, in 's nervy arm doth lie;
> Which, being advanc'd, declines, and then men die. (II. i. 174)

Again emphasis on Coriolanus' 'sounds', the clanging percussions of his prided course; again, emphasis on 'death', the 'dark spirit' on which he and she would build a positive life-joy, his and his mother's isolated love-pride. So she exults in others' 'tears'. Her joy is already twined with 'death', and that grim death-dealer, her son, will later let her know it. That 'dark spirit' already hovers above the son that triumphs, and the mother who treats too lightly Corioli-tears will herself take league with that death against her son. This is a play not alone of iron, but of irony. The climax casts its shadow back, as before when the gods 'mocked' Coriolanus: now as he kneels to his mother at the hour of his honourable triumph we may remember how she is fated to kneel to him in the dark hour of his triumphant ignominy. Volumnia is pathetic in her fierce, instinctive, maternal joy: so sweet a reality bears so deadly a poison. When she speaks to him, however, her tremulous passion holds no meanness. Its accents are those of love alone:

> *Volumnia.*   Nay, my good soldier, up;
> My gentle Marcius, worthy Caius, and
> By deed-achieving honour newly nam'd,—
> What is it?—Coriolanus must I call thee?—
> But, O, thy wife!
> *Coriolanus.*   My gracious silence, hail!
> Would'st thou have laugh'd had I come coffin'd home,
> That weep'st to see me triumph? Ah, my dear,

> Such eyes the widows in Corioli wear,
> And mothers that lack sons.
> *Menenius.*   Now, the gods crown thee!
> *Coriolanus.* And live you yet? (*To Valeria*) O my sweet lady,
>   pardon.
> *Volumnia.* I know not where to turn: O, welcome home:
>   And welcome, general; and ye're welcome all.
>
> (ɪɪ. i. 188)

No word from Virgilia. But her silent tears, counterpoint to this radiant triumphing, speak more than many volumes. The mother's heart is brimful of joy:

> *Volumnia.*   I have liv'd
>   To see inherited my very wishes
>   And the buildings of my fancy: only
>   There's one thing wanting, which I doubt not but
>   Our Rome will cast upon thee.
> *Coriolanus.*   Know, good mother,
>   I had rather be their servant in my way
>   Than sway with them in theirs.   (ɪɪ. i. 214)

He would prefer to continue as he is than to unbend in order to receive higher honours. He will not, cannot, mix harmoniously with lesser men. Essential aristocracy drives out his citizenship.

So the Roman populace hate Coriolanus. His pride makes him a fit symbol of their discontent. But the people are too lacking in intellect to force any issue themselves. They are shown as stupid, blocks of wood. Their tribunes, however, are subtle, and their subtlety uses Coriolanus' pride to work his ruin. They hate him for his superiority, his essential aristocracy: which hate is itself but another pride in themselves. Menenius tells them so:

> . . you blame Marcius for being proud?   (ɪɪ. i. 36)

After a rigmarole of his wry humour, he tells them they are

> . . . a brace of unmeriting, proud, violent, testy magistrates,
>   alias fools, as any in Rome.   (ɪɪ. i. 46)

He is right. To fear and concentrate on another's pride is itself a kind of pride. We have a triple set of proud forces here: (i) Coriolanus and his mother, (ii) Aufidius, and (iii) the Tribunes. The latter parties are, as it were, stimulated to opposition by the Coriolanus-pride. Proudness begets proudness, multiplying its poison. By those two parties Coriolanus and his mother are later dragged apart, Coriolanus himself shot from one to the other. This is how his pride turns back on itself, self-slaughterous, creating its own antagonists. We observe how Coriolanus' excellence itself antagonizes the tribunes, thus splitting Rome into two parties. The patricians and plebeians here are not dangerously inimical: only the protagonist representatives of each stir up strife. Menenius throughout holds a fairly just balance. Both sides like him. His humorous speeches are an apt commentary on the action. He can see the dangers that are brewing, and throughout urges both sides toward reason and harmony. He observes and rebukes the cunning and rash schemings of the tribunes, and is equally ready to persuade Coriolanus to bear himself graciously in the matter of his election.

Coriolanus again shows his distaste of praise when his deeds are formally rehearsed to the senate, and retires from the room. He is further disgusted at having to wear the 'gown of humility', parading his valorous deeds before the people, showing them his naked wounds, in order to solicit their votes for the Consulship. He owes the senate 'his life and services' (II. ii. 138). Yet he cannot feel a servant to the community as a whole. He hates this formality:

> I do beseech you,
> Let me o'erleap that custom, for I cannot
> Put on the gown, stand naked and entreat them,
> For my wounds' sake, to give their suffrage: please you
> That I may pass this doing.   (II. ii. 139)

It is a part he will 'blush in acting' (II. ii. 149). At last he submits. Menenius leaves him alone with his disgust to meet the citizens, muttering

> Bid them wash their faces
> And keep their teeth clean.   (II. iii. 66)

He goes through it in a stiff, self-mocking, almost humorous manner, carries it off somehow to the people's content:

> Pray you now, if it may stand with the tune of your voices
> that I may be consul, I have here the customary gown.
>
> (II. iii. 91)

All they want is that he shall 'ask it kindly' (II. iii. 81): exactly what he cannot do. Coriolanus is now sincere, terribly sincere. He knows his 'own desert' (II. iii. 71) alone has brought him here. He hates the lie of pretending a petitionary humbleness to his inferiors, craving reward for his services:

> Better it is to die, better to starve,
> Than crave the hire which first we do deserve.
>
> (II. iii. 120)

In so doing he is false to his highest intuition: that of his own worth. He is merely nobility and human excellence supreme and supremely conscious of itself, diluted with no drop of allaying humility. Humility is hypocrisy, a hateful lie to his soul. So deep is 'pride' rooted in his 'nature', as the citizens early remarked. But he satisfies the citizens. Yet the tribunes, hearing of his insolent manner, persuade them to revoke their election. Their pride, answering Coriolanus' insolence, now splits Rome into two antagonist parties, undermines the peace and health of communal life.

This quarrel is a gaping sore in the body of Rome. The thought is emphasized often. Metaphors from bodily disease occur throughout.[1] Accordingly in the first scene Menenius tells the citizens that their rebellion is as irrational as that of rebel limbs turning against the body's

---

[1] Miss Spurgeon has already called attention to the 'disease' metaphors here and in *Hamlet*. I acknowledge a debt to her essay. We must observe the similarity in the use of these metaphors in the two plays. Each side sees the other as a 'disease'. Ultimately, we must consider the disease not localized in a person at all, but rather as a disjointed *relation* between a unit and its environment. The same happens with the 'disease' images in *Macbeth* and *Julius Caesar*.

stomach. His fable points the absurdity of any one party
in an organic state expecting to stand alone. The belly,
accused of grasping all the food for itself, answers:

'True is it, my incorporate friends', quoth he,
'That I receive the general food at first,
Which you do live upon; and fit it is,
Because I am the store-house and the shop
Of the whole body: but, if you do remember,
I send it through the rivers of your blood,
Even to the court, the heart, to the seat o' the brain;
And through the cranks and offices of man,
The strongest nerves and small inferior veins
From me receive that natural competency
Whereby they live . . .
                    . . . Though all at once cannot
See what I do deliver out to each,
Yet I can make my audit up, that all
From me do back receive the flour of all,
And leave me but the bran'.   (I. i. 134)

The state of Rome is a 'body'. The dissensions in Act I
are concerned with 'corn' and 'grain'. This is important.
From start to finish the health of the state, its food, its very
life, is involved. 'Pride' is early contrasted with 'food'.
Now Coriolanus'—and his mother's—isolated aristocracy
of pride in the cause of that honour to which both are
devoted is a poison. Coriolanus' worth is debilitated by
its incapability of feeding the body of Rome. Though
there is love between mother and son, yet this love exists
not to rule, but in the cause of ambition. Coriolanus'
love is largely a love of his mother's admiration. Volumnia's is likewise impure in its desire of her son's honour as
an end in itself: it is partial, selfish, proud. The tribunes,
during the later action, continually refer to Coriolanus'
pride as a disease. Nor is the image unjust. Coriolanus is
noble; he is far superior to his community; he is an exquisite piece of humanity. Yet, merely by his failing in any
way to mix with his setting, he is dangerous as a microbe,
itself no doubt worthy enough, in an organism to which it

7

is by nature alien. He wields an isolated and inimical virtue, a poisoning, disintegrating force, creating other prides around him, furthering civil strife.

'Body' metaphors or 'disease' metaphors are percurrent, twined in this way with the concept of political 'order'. The first citizen is the 'great toe' of the assembly (i. i. 159). So Coriolanus himself addresses the tribunes:

> Are these your herd?
> Must these have voices, that can yield them now
> And straight disclaim their tongues? What are your offices?
> You being their mouths, why rule you not their teeth?
> Have you not set them on?   (iii. i. 33)

Again, he refers to their insurrection as a 'measles':

> *Coriolanus.*   . . . so shall my lungs
> Coin words till their decay against those measles,
> Which we disdain should tetter us, yet sought
> The very way to catch them.
> *Brutus.*   You speak o' the people,
> As if you were a god to punish, not
> A man of their infirmity.   (iii. i. 77)

Here the 'disease' metaphor can be applied by Coriolanus. We can consider the application just by regarding the tribunes as themselves partly at fault. A despot is not evil while he is tolerated: often he may be good. Order is the aim of government. Without the tribunes Coriolanus would not have been a danger: pride can only exist whilst it is denied by another pride: it thrives on dynamic opposition. This opposition between the tribunes and Coriolanus results in an insecure equilibrium, poor substitute for organic harmony. Each party may deserve the label of 'measles', since either alone would be harmless. The fault is that of dual authority:

> By Jove himself!
> It makes the consuls base: and my soul aches
> To know, when two authorities are up,
> Neither supreme, how soon confusion
> May enter 'twixt the gap of both and take
> The one by the other.   (iii. i. 107)

Such 'order' thought is to be directly related to our 'body' images. Coriolanus says that the common people would not press to war 'even when the navel of the state was touch'd' (III. i. 123). The state is an organism: any forgetfulness of that fact leads to sickness. So Coriolanus urges (III. i. 150–60) that the tribunes be quelled, being a poison to the state's body. He would attempt to cure the body 'with a dangerous physic'—the risk involved in opposing the tribunes—since the state is 'sure of death without it'. He would 'pluck out the multitudinous tongue' (the tribunes), and urges those who 'love the fundamental part of state' to follow him. The people's advance to power shows them to 'lick the sweet which is their poison', and the state is 'bereav'd of that integrity which should become 't'. Throughout the idea of the organic whole, integrity, the body of the state is emphasized. In terms of this metaphor we must analyse Coriolanus' own pride: it all applies equally to him. From the reverse view it is he who is 'a foe to the public weal' (III. i. 176). He ever loathed the people, their cowardice, uncertainty, stupidity, uncleanness. His despisal, certainly, is shown at every turn to be justified. But, justifiable or not, it is a poison. And it is, moreover, itself ugly as a hideous sore:

> Hence, rotten thing! or I shall shake thy bones
> Out of thy garments. (III. i. 179)

The intense aristocracy of his nature leads him to extremes, and he becomes the subject of dangerous insurrection. Cominius tries to pacify the tribunes:

> That is the way to lay the city flat;
> To bring the roof to the foundation,
> And bury all, which yet distinctly ranges,
> In heaps and piles of ruin. (III. i. 204)

To the plebeians, Coriolanus is a truly dangerous disease:

> Sir, those cold ways,
> That seem like prudent helps, are very poisonous
> Where the disease is violent. (III. i. 220)

The quarrel develops into a fight. Menenius does all he can for peace. It is, indeed, noticeable how mild are the patricians—all of them but Coriolanus—and how gullible the plebeians. The play does not emphasize directly the conflicting of parties, but rather the birth of conflicting individual prides dragging parties asunder.[1] The tribunes repay Coriolanus' insolence by words that ring true enough. They well stress the irrational unsociability of his attitude:

> Where is this viper
> That would depopulate the city and
> Be every man himself?   (III. i. 263)

There is more 'disease' imagery. Menenius repudiates the foolishness of Rome eating her own child, 'like an unnatural dam' (III. i. 293):

> *Sicinius.* He's a disease that must be cut away.
> *Menenius.* O, he's a limb that has but a disease;
>   Mortal, to cut it off; to cure it, easy.   (III. i. 295)

He urges Coriolanus' past service, admitting his present faults:

> *Menenius.*   The service of the foot
>   Being once gangren'd, is not then respected
>   For what before it was.
> *Brutus.*   We'll hear no more.
>   Pursue him to his house, and pluck him thence;
>   Lest his infection, being of catching nature,
>   Spread further.   (III. i. 306)

So it is now urged on Coriolanus that he should apologize for his rashness:

> There's no remedy;
> Unless, by not so doing, our good city
> Cleave in the midst, and perish.   (III. ii. 26)

Again, 'the violent fit o' the time craves it as physic for the whole state' (III. ii. 33). This 'disease' imagery is insistent. Coriolanus is a poisonous agent in the political organism. He is a thing of death, always ominous of death: and the danger is not over till he himself dies.

[1] We might compare Mr. John Galsworthy's *Strife*.

For however excellent and noble he is in himself, as a unit, yet this very unitary excellence, self-bound and radiating no natural warmth from its plated cuisses of pride, is automatically a poison. By no inconsistency we yet admire his unswerving course:

> His nature is too noble for the world:
> He would not flatter Neptune for his trident,
> Or Jove for 's power to thunder. His heart 's his mouth:
> What his breast forges, that his tongue must vent;
> And, being angry, does forget that ever
> He heard the name of death.   (III. i. 255)

Noble: but a truly dangerous nobility, preferring itself now before his party who vainly implore his consideration, later before his country. He acts as a cancerous threat, a death-force. Here a positive value, warrior-honour, yet secretes a death. Coriolanus is drawn as a man of death throughout. His virtue is the virtue of destruction: so is any world-value divorced from love, when raised to its extreme, a destruction, a death-phantom masquerading as life. In war a man of death, in peace he is a social poison. His extreme worship of a secondary value in and for itself forces him to run on his own tragedy and death. This play, though far from *Hamlet*, has many 'death' references. Like *Hamlet*, it ends with a dead march.

But Coriolanus' rashness is one with his integrity and sincerity. Pathetically, he cannot understand his mother's sudden disapproval:

> I muse my mother
> Does not approve me further, who was wont
> To call them woollen vassals, things created
> To buy and sell with groats, to show bare heads
> In congregations, to yawn, be still and wonder,
> When one but of my ordinance stood up
> To speak of peace or war.   (III. ii. 7)

This is illuminating. It directly refers Coriolanus' pride to his mother's teaching. She has made him what he is. But she now finds she has created something beyond her control. She has filled him from birth with scorn of his inferiors, and this scorn she sanctions until she sees its danger. Now the logical result of her teaching is apparent: regardless of danger, her son presses on toward his fate in the name of that pride she instilled in him, projection of her own love. Now she wishes he

>   had not show'd them how ye were dispos'd
> Ere they lack'd power to cross you.   (III. ii. 22)

His friends and his mother implore him to repent. To which he answers:

> For them! I cannot do it to the gods;
> Must I then do 't to them?   (III. ii. 38)

He is, as his mother says, 'too absolute' (III. ii. 39):

> I prithee now, sweet son, as thou hast said
> My praises made thee first a soldier, so,
> To have my praise for this, perform a part
> Thou hast not done before.   (III. ii. 107)

At last he gives way to her entreaties. Then, in a rebound of disgust, he again refuses. Volumnia for the first time speaks harshly to him:

>   At thy choice, then:
> To beg of thee, it is my more dishonour
> Than thou of them. Come all to ruin; let
> Thy mother rather feel thy pride than fear
> Thy dangerous stoutness, for I mock at death
> With as big heart as thou. Do as thou list.
> Thy valiantness was mine, thou suck'dst it from me,
> But owe thy pride thyself.   (III. ii. 123)

Her scorn conquers him immediately. As again later, he cannot withstand that. But Volumnia is not so blameless as she imagines. She may not be herself proud as he is: but that pride of his is the exact projection of her own limited love.

The tribunes easily succeed in angering him, so that he breaks out again. His mask of meekness is torn aside and he flames at the word 'traitor'. Banished, he flings back the most virulent scorn, clothed in hideous metaphors of unhealth. Which almost neurotic vision is, like Hamlet's, the measure of his own spiritual disease:

You common cry of curs! whose breath I hate
As reek o' the rotten fens, whose loves I prize
As the dead carcasses of unburied men
That do corrupt my air, I banish you;
And here remain with your uncertainty!
Let every feeble rumour shake your hearts!
Your enemies, with nodding of their plumes,
Fan you into despair! Have the power still
To banish your defenders; till at length
Your ignorance, which finds not till it feels,
Making not reservation of yourselves,
Still your own foes, deliver you as most
Abated captives to some nation
That won you without blows! Despising,
For you, the city, thus I turn my back:
There is a world elsewhere.   (III. iii. 120)

His parting with his mother is noble and restrained. He
has been true to his nature and does not repine. His pride
satisfied, the next dearest thing in his heart, his love, rings
nobly in this hour of sorrow:

Nay, mother,
Where is your ancient courage? you were used
To say extremity was the trier of spirits;
That common chances common men could bear;
That when the sea was calm all boats alike
Show'd mastership in floating; fortune's blows,
When most struck home, being gentle wounded, craves
A noble cunning: you were used to load me
With precepts that would make invincible
The heart that conn'd them.   (IV. i. 2)

All this to his mother: hardly a word to his wife. At this
extreme trial, we again observe how violent is this mother's
love, how it alone calls forth any response from Coriolanus.
Yet even this is close-twined with his pride: he loves her
in part for her idolization of him, and cannot forget himself and his deeds at any moment:

My mother, you wot well
My hazards still have been your solace . . .   (IV. i. 27)

So, in all gentleness and nobility, Coriolanus parts from

his family and friends. We cannot deny the aptness of Volumnia's scorn addressed to the tribunes when he is gone:

> *Volumnia.*   . . . Hadst thou foxship
>   To banish him that struck more blows for Rome
>   Than thou hast spoken words?
> *Sicinius.*   O blessed heavens!
> *Volumnia.* More noble blows than ever thou wise words;
>   And for Rome's good. I'll tell thee what; yet go:
>   Nay, but thou shalt stay too: I would my son
>   Were in Arabia, and thy tribe before him,
>   His good sword in his hand.   (iv. ii. 18)

Again:

>   'Twas you incensed the rabble:
>   Cats, that can judge as fitly of his worth
>   As I can of those mysteries which heaven
>   Will not have earth to know.   (iv. ii. 33)

Which is true enough. Coriolanus is shown as infinitely superior to the tribunes in all noble qualities, in all exquisite strength. He is proud as a lion might be proud among jackals. But that is no reason why jackals should tolerate a lion in their midst. The Coriolanus-pride is proved empirically unsound: relying on itself, abstracted from the nurturing earth of society, it can only blossom in decay. Volumnia speaks well of her anger:

>   Anger's my meat; I sup upon myself,
>   And so shall starve with feeding.   (iv. ii. 50)

Like Coriolanus, Volumnia feeds on herself. So any such exclusive pride or love will be found eventually to destroy itself in order to prolong its own life. It is, as the play shows, self-contradictory. Soon Volumnia's ceaseless quest of honour for her son will lead her to oppose him as a traitor to his country.

From the start he had seeds of treachery in his pride, unsubdued as it was to love of country or kin. Always, it came first. Now the note of treachery is struck by a short scene between a Volscian and a renegade Roman. Following it, we have Coriolanus' approach, grim figure of isolated wrath, to Antium his native city's foe. He enters Aufidius' house, feeding, like his mother, on the anger tearing at his own breast. As a grim harbinger of thunder and death, he interrupts the Volscian feasting, their conviviality and music. He swears friendship with Aufidius.

But, in the wider issues of communal life, the loss of Coriolanus to Rome is slight. No man is indispensable. Coriolanus away, the tribunes no longer jealous, Rome is at peace. Either he, or they, had to go. The great cause of natural order cares no whit who or what is sacrificed. It is no respecter of persons.

> *Sicinius.* We hear not of him, neither need we fear him;
>   His remedies are tame i' the present peace
>   And quietness of the people, which before
>   Were in wild hurry. Here do we make his friends
>   Blush that the world goes well, who rather had,
>   Though they themselves did suffer by 't, behold
>   Dissentious numbers pestering streets, than see
>   Our tradesmen singing in their shops and going
>   About their functions friendly.   (IV. vi. 1)

Menenius realizes the truth of it. Coriolanus' mind outstepped his civic powers and rights, and he is better away. Menenius has 'grown most kind of late' (IV. vi. 11) to the tribunes:

> *Sicinius.*   Your Coriolanus
>   Is not much miss'd, but with his friends:
>   The commonwealth doth stand, and so would do,
>   Were he more angry at it.
> *Menenius.* All's well; and might have been much better, if
>   He could have temporiz'd.   (IV. vi. 12)

For now the tribunes are loved by their citizens who greet them with prayers and salutations. Patricians and plebeians are in harmony again. All is peace and good-will:

> *Sicinius.* This is a happier and more comely time
>   Than when these fellows ran about the streets,
>   Crying confusion.

Brutus.   Caius Marcius was
     A worthy officer i' the war; but insolent,
     O'ercome with pride, ambitious past all thinking,
     Self-loving—
Sicinius.   And affecting one sole throne,
     Without assistance.
Menenius.   I think not so.
Sicinius. We should by this, to all our lamentation,
     If he had gone forth consul, found it so.   (IV. vi. 27)

On top of this comes the news of Coriolanus' threatening
advance. Quickly all is fear. Now have the tribunes
helped to ravish their own daughters, to melt the city on
their own heads (IV. vi. 81). Coriolanus comes as a super-
man, a thing divine and grim, a black wrath impending
terrific judgement on the city that has scorned him. He is
inhuman of stature, outdistancing lesser men who wronged
divinity itself in wronging him:

     He is their god: he leads them like a thing
     Made by some other deity than nature,
     That shapes man better; and they follow him,
     Against us brats, with no less confidence
     Than boys pursuing summer butterflies,
     Or butchers killing flies.   (IV. vi. 90)

He is again shown us as essentially superior, of a higher
order than others. Autocratic as ever, he marches now on
his native city:

                   Tullus Aufidius
     The second name of men, obeys his points
     As if he were his officer.   (IV. vi. 124)

Menenius presents a sudden change of attitude: now he
reminds the tribunes of their ill-done work, reproaches
them with this result. All is chaotic fear in Rome. Coriolanus in truth comes as no weakling in revenge:

                   . . . I will fight
     Against my canker'd country with the spleen
     Of all the under fiends.   (IV. v. 96)

To him, Rome is 'canker'd', diseased. And he, who has
'drawn tuns of blood' from the 'breast' of Corioli (IV. v.

105), will cure his native city by the same ruinous prescription.

He wields an uncanny power over the Volscian army. Aufidius' lieutenant marvels at it:

> *Lieutenant.* I do not know what witchcraft's in him, but
>   Your soldiers use him as the grace 'fore meat,
>   Their talk at table, and their thanks at end;
>   And you are darken'd in this action, sir,
>   Even by your own.
> *Aufidius.*   I cannot help it now,
>   Unless, by using means, I lame the foot
>   Of our design. He bears himself more proudlier,
>   Even to my person, than I thought he would
>   When first I did embrace him: yet his nature
>   In that's no changeling; and I must excuse
>   What cannot be amended.   (iv. vii. 2)

Notice again, Coriolanus' natural excellence commanding a magic respect; the theme of Aufidius' own pride, put by for the moment so as not to wound the 'foot' of a communal enterprise—again a 'body' metaphor; the emphasis on Coriolanus' 'natural' pride, which, unlike that of the tribunes or Aufidius, cannot bend to any ignominious scheming or insincerity. This passage clearly silhouettes the pride of Coriolanus: the more noble in its regardless course, its deep rootings in his 'nature'. And yet, that 'nature' is to conflict soon with the other natural promptings of love. Here Coriolanus passes from one insecurity to another. Such excellence joined to pride creates enemies. He never bends to expediency. Though Aufidius admires him, and knows he will be to Rome

> As is the osprey to the fish, who takes it
> By sovereignty of nature,   (iv. vii. 34)

he yet waits his chance to rise on his rival's fall. Well he sees Coriolanus' essential weakness:

>   First he was
> A noble servant to them; but he could not
> Carry his honours even.   (iv. vii. 35)

That is, he could not remain a 'servant'; which is true.

His 'power', excellent in itself, contains the seeds of its own swift death:

> So our virtues
> Lie in the interpretation of the time:
> And power, unto itself most commendable,
> Hath not a tomb so evident as a cheer[1]
> To extol what it hath done.   (iv. vii. 49)

Aufidius sees clearly. His incisive criticisms are just. Finest of all, is his remark:

> When, Caius, Rome is thine,
> Thou art poor'st of all; then shortly art thou mine.
>
>   (iv. vii. 56)

Poor, indeed, if that had been the event.

Rome supplicates his mercy, but he is iron to her prayers. He will not hear Cominius:

> Yet one time he did call me by my name:
> I urg'd our old acquaintance, and the drops
> That we have bled together. Coriolanus
> He would not answer to; forbad all names;
> He was a kind of nothing, titleless,
> Till he had forg'd himself a name o' the fire
> Of burning Rome.   (v. i. 9)

Dr. Bradley has noted how references to Rome's 'burning' cluster towards the close of this play:

> I tell you, he does sit in gold, his eye
> Red as 'twould burn Rome; and his injury
> The gaoler to his pity.   (v. i. 63)

He awaits his revenge, a sword to slay, not for a cause but for the sword's own senseless sake, wrapping himself in folds of bitter remembrance. Menenius will try next. He cannot have dined when Cominius was rejected:

> He was not taken well; he had not dined:
> The veins unfill'd, our blood is cold, and then
> We pout upon the morning, are unapt
> To give or to forgive; but when we have stuff'd

---

[1] The generally accepted reading of this crux is 'chair'. 'Cheer' appears to me to make better sense (1954).

These pipes and these conveyances of our blood
With wine and feeding, we have suppler souls
Than in our priest-like fasts . . .   (v. i. 50)

Notice the 'mechanic' and 'city' imagery, here, as often
elsewhere in the play, blended with 'body' imagery. The
'body' and 'state' or 'city' are ever reciprocally metaphoric.
As in this speech, Menenius' epicureanism and humour
are strongly contrasted with Coriolanus' steely pride.
Menenius who loves 'a cup of hot wine with not a drop
of allaying Tiber in't' (II. i. 52) vainly thinks the iron of
Coriolanus' heart can be so readily melted. Menenius
shares with Timon and Antony this strain of conviviality
and warm-hearted freedom of spirit in feasting. Which are
just the qualities Coriolanus lacks: with him there is no
surrendering of individuality to feasting or amusement or
love. All is dominated by the one pride which knits his
faculties to a steely centre of self-consciousness sharp as a
pin-point; and as small and brittle. So Menenius fails to
move him:

> *Menenius.* See you yond coign o' the Capitol, yond corner-stone?
> *Sicinius.* Why, what of that?
> *Menenius.* If it be possible for you to displace it with your little
> finger, there is some hope the ladies of Rome, especially his
> mother, may prevail with him.   (v. iv. 1)

He tells how Marcius 'is grown from man to dragon' (v.
iv. 13). He is now all metal, an iron-jointed mechanism.
Any love he may have known is now frozen—witness
Cominius' words:

> I offer'd to awaken his regard
> For 's private friends: his answer to me was,
> He could not stay to pick them in a pile
> Of noisome musty chaff: he said 'twas folly,
> For one poor grain or two, to leave unburnt,
> And still to nose the offence.   (v. i. 23)

As Menenius notices, his mother, wife, child are among
that 'one poor grain or two'. So strongly has his pride

fettered, endungeoned, and doubly portcullised his love. He is now all iron—or tin:

> *Menenius.* . . . he no more remembers his mother now than an eight-year-old horse. The tartness of his face sours ripe grapes: when he walks, he moves like an engine, and the ground shrinks before his treading: he is able to pierce a corslet with his eye; talks like a knell, and his hum is a battery. He sits in his state, as a thing made for Alexander. What he bids be done is finished with his bidding. He wants nothing of a god but eternity and a heaven to throne in.
>
> *Sicinius.* Yes, mercy, if you report him truly.
>
> *Menenius.* I paint him in the character. Mark what mercy his mother shall bring from him: there is no more mercy in him than there is milk in a male tiger.   (v. iv. 16)

He is a god but for 'mercy'. Put without hyperbole, he is, like Brutus in *Julius Caesar*, an excellent man but for love.

We here watch human excellence, power, valour, even virtue, abstracted from love, or, at the least, overruling love, raised to a high pitch, and pursuing its logical course. That is our hero in his loveless pride. He has never shown love. For love too, whether it be love of mother, wife, friend, or community, is itself a regal mistress: its delicate tyranny tolerates no precedent value. Love subject to any quality quite loveless—pride, ambition, self-concentration of any sort—is not yet love: conversely, 'honour' which is not servanted to some quality which is a function of love, becomes rapidly pride, ambition, vainglory. Thus Coriolanus has not yet shown love for his mother. Similarly, she has shown love for his glory, not for him. She loved him as a box to be crammed with honours. She would have him bloody-streaked, dismembered, dead, in winning honour: then his 'good report' would be her son (I. iii. 22). She strangely objectifies his honour and glory as a thing to love beyond himself, and thus, though herself at least loving after a fashion, she finds she has created a thing apparently loveless, an idiot robot, a creaking clockwork giant; a stone Colossus whose tread will be heavy on his com-

patriot's bodies, a son trying to warm his ice-bound heart
at the blaze of a mother's home. The poison hearted in
this family pride from the start works swift and
sure. They thought to love honour first, next love itself.
Therefore Love, who is a jealous god, has wedged open
their supposed love, thrown them asunder. They may
not think to love each other on their own exclusive terms
of pride, despising all around them, haloed in their own
nobility. No two can love each other without loving the
community. Love, not its object, is the ultimate reality:
and they loved not even an object, but a phantom, 'honour'.
Falstaff spoke true enough. Antony, who does not love
Cleopatra, but rather is 'in love with' her, both through
the other blended with a mighty principle transcending
both, is generous, like Timon, to all men, a universal
bounty burning from both as from the sun whose unlimited life-gold down-burns in love with earth. So, to
Cleopatra, Antony is himself the universe, its sun and
moon, its earth and seas. But these two, Volumnia and
Coriolanus, have loved parochially, provincially, among
the grey slated roofs, the pipes and conduits, the stony
roads and walls, of this metallic, urban, exclusive
setting. They, too, have been exclusive, iron-fenced from
contact with their unhonoured inferiors. So their love has
come second to pride, with the result that at the last son
and mother oppose each other, face to face inimical, one
for Rome, one for Corioli. They were, indeed, rather 'in
pride with each other' making honour the universal reality,
letting it usurp the imperial diadem of love. That exclusive
union has wedged them apart: their very isolation in love,
which is pride, has now put leagues between them. In
exactly the same way Macbeth and his queen are 'in
crime with one another': and as that, because of its
hostility to their environment, drives them to ruin, so
surely pride drives on these two. Volumnia, proud scorner
of the plebeians, through that very scorn she has in-
culcated in her boy, now sides with Rome's 'mechanics'
against the son she taught to loath and despise them. He,

who arrayed himself all glistering in tinsel honour 'to
please his mother', now finds the sequel of his barren
quest demands he now gild himself in that mother's
blood. No Shakespearian play drives its protagonists to
so bitterly ironic a climax.

Coriolanus' love is to be pitted against his pride. When
the two were indistinguishable, the poison was not
apparent. But now his vengeance is thrown up as a
jagged rock against love's furnace skies. As his mother,
wife, and child come to him, that other 'nature' which his
pride has desecrated proves stronger than he thought:

> My wife comes foremost; then the honour'd mould
> Wherein this trunk was framed, and in her hand
> The grandchild to her blood. But, out, affection!
> All bond and privilege of nature, break!
> Let it be virtuous to be obstinate.
> What is that curt'sy worth? or those doves' eyes,
> Which can make gods forsworn? I melt, and am not
> Of stronger earth than others. My mother bows;
> As if Olympus to a molehill should
> In supplication nod: and my young boy
> Hath an aspect of intercession, which
> Great nature cries, 'Deny not'. Let the Volsces
> Plough Rome, and harrow Italy: I'll never
> Be such a gosling to obey instinct, but stand,
> As if a man were author of himself
> And knew no other kin.   (v. iii. 22)

Again we can observe the strange metallism blending
with 'body' images—the 'honour'd mould'; and the
stress on 'nature' is important. Throughout Coriolanus
has fought for honour against nature's simple joys. His
pride, like Macbeth's crime, is—in a less violent fashion
—a defacing of 'nature'. For he would commit the
absurdity of considering a man 'author of himself', a
solitary excellence not rooted in nature's creative process.
So they stand before him, speak to him.

> Like a dull actor now,
> I have forgot my part, and I am out,
> Even to a full disgrace.   (v. iii. 40)

He speaks to Virgilia lovingly. But his mother, as always, calls forth his deepest notes of affection. He strangely breaks off his greeting to his wife:

> You gods! I prate,
> And the most noble mother of the world
> Leave unsaluted: sink, my knee, i' the earth;
> Of thy deep duty more impression show
> Than that of common sons.   (v. iii. 48)

In truth, no common son: and for that very reason he now unnaturally opposes his mother. She kneels, on the hard 'flint' (v. iii. 53) of earth before his flinty heart.

> What is this?
> Your knees to me? to your corrected son?
> Then let the pebbles on the hungry beach
> Fillip the stars; then let the mutinous winds
> Strike the proud cedars 'gainst the fiery sun;
> Murdering impossibility, to make
> What cannot be, slight work.   (v. iii. 56)

Notice the 'star' and 'sun' imagery, continually used in Shakespeare with relation to love's infinity, its universal sanction. To which his mother answers:

> Thou art my warrior;
> I holp to frame thee. Do you know this lady?
>   (v. iii. 62)

So he turns to Valeria with a lovely phrase:

> The noble sister of Publicola,
> The moon of Rome, chaste as the icicle
> That 's curdied by the frost from purest snow
> And hangs on Dian's temple: dear Valeria!   (v. iii. 64)

A fine instance of the important lyric imagery with which the sheeted iron of this play glints from time to time—as when Coriolanus refers to himself in battle as

> In ᵢ   ːs sound as when I woo'd, in heart
> As merry as when our nuptial day was done,
> ᵼ ¹ tapers burn'd to bedward.   (i. vi. 30)

This is the soft love which would dissolve the metal of his fierceness, and such sweeter images suggest the fundamental contrast. They remind us of a buried love in this giant of death and war whose wounds are 'like graves i' the holy churchyard' (III. iii. 51), who ever outwardly shows 'a grim appearance' (IV. v. 66). He has been called a 'flower' (I. vi. 32), a 'jewel' (I. iv. 56). We are delicately prepared for the close by such phrases. Now Coriolanus' pride is opposed by the three forms of feminine beauty: motherhood, wifehood, maidenhood. Hence his lovely words to Valeria. Coriolanus blesses his boy in terms of that iron nobility which is his solitary pride. But he tells the ladies not to slay his honour, not to tell him wherein he is 'unnatural'. Volumnia urges their sorrow, that they who should joy at his approach, dread it. He would make

> the mother, wife and child to see
> The son, the husband and the father tearing
> His country's bowels out.   (v. iii. 101)

They know not how to forge their prayers; his ruin and theirs are alternative, and they know no petition that does not violate their hopes. They must lose their 'dear nurse', their country, or him. Too late Volumnia learns that the community makes first demand on her, and so she must now at this hour reject her own son. Her dreams have come all too true. He is before her, victorious pride and vindicated honour his sole gods. She rises to wrath now: if he will sack Rome, he must enter over his mother's womb. She implores him to negotiate peace, to earn blessings rather than curses. If he conquer Rome,

> the benefit
> Which thou shalt thereby reap is such a name,
> Whose repetition will be dogg'd with curses.   (v. iii. 142)

To that his love of 'honour' has brought him. He has

> affected the fine strains of honour,
> To imitate the graces of the gods . . . .   (v. iii. 149)

Can he not use his strength with godlike mercy, riving but an oak with his thunder? We are pointed again to the futility of power divorced from mercy, honour not rooted in love. Nor is it honourable, she tells him, so to

cherish wrongs. Yet this travesty of honour and farce of
love, hashed medley of conflicting loyalties, is but the
logical result of their old mutual isolation in pride. Now
she lances all her mother's devotion against the plated
armoury of his will:

> There's no man in the world
> More bound to 's mother; yet here he lets me prate
> Like one i' the stocks. Thou hast never in thy life
> Show'd thy dear mother any courtesy,
> When she, poor hen, fond of no second brood,
> Has cluck'd thee to the wars and safely home,
> Loaden with honour.   (v. iii. 158)

Which lovely image throws back light on years of devotion,
pathetic unwisdom of all-too-natural mother-love. Faulty
though it has been, it was love, albeit seconded to 'honour'.
She tries if its strength can now right a lifetime of misuse.
She speaks now to her 'great son' (v. iii. 140) only 'what
to a mother's part belongs' (v. iii. 168). Still he is silent.

> He turns away:
> Down, ladies; let us shame him with our knees.
> To his surname Coriolanus 'longs more pride
> Than pity to our prayers. Down: an end;
> This is the last: so we will home to Rome,
> And die among our neighbours.   (v. iii. 168)

But love is a subtle as well as a potent antagonist. She
finally appeals to him through his very pride. She now
uses that mysterious pride-love—neither quite love nor
pride—which has been their dominant emotion through
their life, to deflect his purpose, trying if his set intent can
withstand the flame of a mother's scorn:

> Come, let us go:
> This fellow had a Volscian to his mother;
> His wife is in Corioli and his child
> Like him by chance. Yet give us our dispatch:
> I am hush'd until our city be afire,
> And then I'll speak a little.   (v. iii. 177)

Once before her scorn succeeded where prayers had
failed. Here again its victory is simple and immediate.

Instead of burning Rome, melting the 'city leads' (IV. vi.
82) on Rome's 'mechanics', at this moment Coriolanus
finds he has only melted the iron of his own lifelong pride
in love's filial fire. In face of Volumnia's scorn it is found
to be but a function of that love, itself intrinsically a
nothing. He holds her hand in silence:

> O, mother, mother!
> What have you done? Behold, the heavens do ope,
> The gods look down, and this unnatural scene
> They laugh at. O my mother, mother! O!
> You have won a happy victory to Rome;
> But, for your son,—believe it, O, believe it,
> Most dangerously you have with him prevail'd,
> If not most mortal to him.   (v. iii. 182)

The heavens do truly open, as for the first time he realizes
love's intolerant autonomy within his own breast. Here
that love, beating equally in a gosling's 'instinct' (v. iii. 35)
and a Coriolanus' pride, itself more iron-strong than
any antagonist, turns delicately back the sword of pride
on the hand that wields it. Love, after all, rules this
metallic world. Coriolanus' eyes 'sweat compassion':

> Ladies, you deserve
> To have a temple built you: all the swords
> In Italy, and her confederate arms,
> Could not have made this peace.   (v. iii. 206)

Love has proved more strong than 'swords'. Now all the
past scattered nature poetry of the play springs to our
memory, newly-bright. And Volumnia's and Coriolanus'
exclusive pride is justified: justified by failure. It has, in
each, bowed to a greater than itself. Each for the first
time loves purely, but at the cost of lasting severance.
So, throughout the Roman plays, the great Shakespearian
value of warrior-honour is found to exist only in lieutenantry to the imperial throne of Love.

Now Rome rejoices. Music celebrates love's victory in
the Roman streets that have hitherto reverberated only
the brawls of civic strife or the harsh alarums of Coriolanus'
triumph. We remember Volumnia's hideous boast:

These are the ushers of Marcius: before him he carries noise, and behind him he leaves tears:

> Death, that dark spirit, in 's nervy arm doth lie;
> Which, being advanc'd, declines, and then men die.
> (II. i. 179)

A strange memory after the scene we have just witnessed. But now a different music celebrates the victory of love:

> The trumpets, sackbuts, psalteries and fifes,
> Tabors and cymbals and the shouting Romans,
> Make the sun dance.   (v. iv. 52)

So glorious an image breaks over the urban provincialism of the play: the universe itself responds and thrills to love's victory. It goes on and on—'music still, with shouts'. In this iron universe of war, ladies have won with love where iron walls and weapons and the more iron plates of pride have so long made but improper racketings:

> *First Senator.* Behold our patroness, the life of Rome!
> Call all your tribes together, praise the gods,
> And make triumphant fires; strew flowers before them:
> Unshout the noise that banish'd Marcius,
> Repeal him with the welcome of his mother;
> Cry 'Welcome, ladies, welcome!'   (v. iv. 67)

'Life', 'fires', 'flowers', 'sun' and 'music'; and before, 'drink' (v. iii. 203): all blend with 'gods' and 'ladies.' We are in a new world—the world of *Antony and Cleopatra*.

Coriolanus returns to his death at Antium. He goes, rightly, to meet the death which is the wage of his long pride. First a traitor to Rome, now he is a traitor to the Volscians. So surely his 'honour' has landed him among contradictions. He is accordingly sacrificed that communities may remain in health. But he is now purified. All may be forgiven to one who loves greatly, who enthrones a love above all other values. Moreover, by bowing to love, every other value is mysteriously itself enriched and enlarged. Coriolanus first sought nobility in itself, unrooted in the soil of communal life. He has tried to live on capital, which was soon exhausted, and left him only a renegade and treacherous pride: that too spent itself swiftly, and became bankrupt; for any loveless value pursued for itself must shortly prove penniless, unless rooted in a love, fading as a cut flower. But love draws on an infinite exchequer. Therefore Coriolanus now, as never before, enlists our sympathy, and can fling out his boast for the first time with a reckless joy and a new strength of pride which holds a magnificent finality. So he reminds the conspirators how he once scattered their Volscians in battle. His pride has bowed to love. It is as though love has now lent his pride its own easy grace and splendour, something of its own infinity. That infinity now aureoles our protagonist at the end:

> The man is noble and his fame folds-in
> This orb o' the earth.   (v. v. 125)

Because he sacrificed his iron 'honour' to love, love blazons his honour with a phrase worthy of the flashing universe of *Antony and Cleopatra* itself.

This is no easy play to enjoy. It has no rich colourings, no luxuriant emotions, no easy melodies of diction: or, if any, but little and widely scattered. But we work through the metallism of its imagery, the sickening crash and iron clangour of its contests, its grimness and its sounds of death, to so exquisite a consummation, in which the whole is suddenly aglow with heating love, that I doubt if there is any more concentrated emotion in Shakespeare than in those lines where Coriolanus' love for his mother dissolves his pride, or whether any speech gives a more exquisite thrill of delight than his final cry of triumph at the hour of his death. Like *Hamlet*, this play of death ends with a dead march. But long after that there rings yet Coriolanus' final cry, a note of triumph never struck in *Hamlet*, the cry of a mighty value, vanquished indeed by a mightier, yet itself a thing of royal integrity and splendour:

> If you have writ your annals true, 'tis there,
> That, like an eagle in a dove-cote, I
> Flutter'd your Volscians in Corioli:
> Alone I did it.

VII

THE TRANSCENDENTAL HUMANISM OF
ANTONY AND CLEOPATRA

There be three things which are too wonderful for me, yea, four which I know not:
The way of an eagle in the air; the way of a serpent upon a rock; the way of a ship in the midst of the sea; and the way of a man with a maid.

I

IN the early acts of *Timon of Athens* we knew a world especially finite, sensuous, convivial, and brilliant; and this was reversed to an infinite solitude, gloom, and death. In *Antony and Cleopatra* those brighter elements maintain throughout, and serve even to diffuse a glory over death. Here finite and infinite are to be blended. Throughout we have a new vital complexity surpassing other plays; a wider horizon, a richer content. It is probably the subtlest and greatest play in Shakespeare, or, at least, paragoned only by *The Tempest*. The action compasses the Mediterranean and its citied shores; the Roman empire is revivified at its climacteric of grandeur and shown as something of so boundless and rich a magnificence that the princes who sway its destiny appear comparable only to heroes of myth, or divine beings. Yet the persons here are human enough too, and the events sharply realized. Although the play presents, as a whole, a visionary and idealistic optimism, there is no absence of realistic, and, indeed, coarse essences, or of tragic pathos. In this essay I note mainly those effects which contribute to the prevailing optimism. In my next, I observe more exactly the elements of negation. All evil is, however, resolved in the whole. In *Lear* we have a copious realism within a pessimistic and limited vision; here we have a similar wealth within a correspondingly optimistic and unlimited vision. *Lear* extends a view eminently naturalistic, its scope is bounded by 'nature' and our world. *Antony and*

Cleopatra discloses a vision rather 'universalistic': nature itself is here transfigured, and our view is directed not to the material alone, nor to the earth alone, but rather to the universal elements of earth, water, air, fire, and music, and beyond these to the all-transcending visionary humanism which endows man with a supernatural glory. The vision is eminently a life-vision and a love-vision: and our love-theme ranges from purely sensuous delights to the rarefied heights—as in *Timon* it falls to the gloomy deeps —of intense spiritual contemplation. But throughout, all is subdued to a single rare poetic quality of an especial kind. The sensuous is not presented sensuously; the poet's medium purifies all it touches, as though all were thinned yet clarified from a new visionary height. Since this quality is most important for our general understanding I shall first offer some remarks on the play's style: and afterwards pass to a comprehensive analysis of the varying imaginative themes, the interweaving colours of its design.

This poetry is both metaphysical and emotional: but the emotion is ever thrice-distilled, like Troilus' love, a 'thrice-repured nectar'; so finely wrought in delicate yet vividly dynamic phrase or word that we find a maximum of power within a minimum of sense-appeal, either visual or aural. There are sense-effects, and they are powerful: but they are always so refined, visually and aurally, that we must recognize them to possess only a secondary delight. We do not find those floods of emotion that surge in *Othello* and *Timon*, nor the violent impactuous image or passion that strikes wonder in *Macbeth* and *Lear*. Here the most tremendous image is thrown off carelessly, or dreamily: an accessory, but not an essential. Yet there is a certain sharpness, keenness in these poetic effects, like the biting air on a mountain height; thence we have a panoramic view not blurred by clouds of sense or passion, nor twilit in any sunset emotion, but clean, crystal-clear, in a medium washed by bright sunlight, where phrases are sharp and brittle as icicles gleaming.

There is a pre-eminence of thin or feminine vowel-sounds, 'e' and 'i'; and a certain lightness and under-emphasis of passion, which yet robs it of no intrinsic power; a refusal of the resonant and reverberating stress, an absence of any direct or prolonged sensuous pleasure in phrase, word, or syllable. It is not easy to speak it: nothing short of intensest intellectual and imaginative concentration can do its delicate subtleties justice. Its quick changes keep the intellect awake; to speak it is to think it as well as feel it, for there is no easy overriding the intellectual content, while leaving all to the emotional cadence. Tragic poetry is rather like a tidal river. The river of logic is lost in the opposing passionate tide: it is often enough to remember and submit to the passion. Here the tide ebbs; intellect and emotion flow together. Nor is that all: there are dotted islets dividing the stream into diverging and rejoining channels, and a light wind ruffles aslant the surface, stirring it into a myriad criss-cross ripples which sparkle in the sun above the moving deeps.

This insistence on thin vowels, especially 'i's, this reluctance to luxuriate in the emotional and colourous phrase, as in *Othello*, or to loose any violent flood of passion, as in *Lear* and *Timon*, is evident throughout. Here are some typical phrases: 'by the fire that quickens Nilus' slime . . .' (I. iii. 68); 'her infinite variety' (II. ii. 241); 'that great medicine hath with his tinct gilded thee' (I. v. 36); 'O heavenly mingle!' (I. v. 59); 'trimming up the diadem' (V. ii. 345);'quicken with kissing' (IV. xiii. 39). This small movement has an illustrative second line:

> That which is now a horse, even with a thought
> The rack dislimns, and makes it indistinct,
> As water is in water.   (IV. xii. 9)

'Dislimns', 'indistinct'—there is an ethereality about these vowel sounds which reflects a primary quality in our vision here. Other such words are 'riveted trim' (IV. iv. 22), 'riggish' (II. ii. 245), 'dragonish' (IV. xii. 2), 'diminutives'

(IV. x. 50), 'discandying' (III. xi. 165), 'tremblingly' (V. ii. 346). Here is a fine line of the kind:

> Make mingle with our rattling tabourines. (IV. viii. 37)

Again:

> With thy sharp teeth this knot intrinsicate
> Of life at once untie. (V. ii. 307)

'The night is shiny' (IV. ix. 3). This recurrent 'i'-sound will be found an important strand in the vowel-patterning throughout. There is something feminine in it—in its subtlety, its apparent weakness, yet intense buried energy. There are no organ notes here, rather a strange birdlike trilling, which yet compasses the finest tragic passion in exquisite melody:

> Alack, our terrene moon
> Is now eclipsed . . . (III. xi. 153)

The feminine word 'terrene' is set against the rich, yet elongated, vowel-sound of 'moon', fights against it, blends with it. Fruity, luscious vowel-sounds are not allowed their own way. Thin sounds are set against richer cadences:

> O sun,
> Burn the great sphere thou movest in! darkling stand
> The varying shore o' the world. (IV. xiii. 9)

The light endings, 'in', 'darkling', 'varying', are pitted against the masculine vowels, 'sun', 'burn', 'world'. The result is a certain lilting, rippling melody curiously countering the tragic passion beneath. We get this lilt again in the rhythm of: 'O thou day o' the world . . .' (IV. viii. 13), or 'a lass unparallel'd' (V. ii. 319), or 'I wore his sword Philippan' (II. v. 23). Again:

> . . . there is nothing left remarkable
> Beneath the visiting moon. (IV. xiii. 67)

Effects are often gained by the apparently unmusical ending '-ing'. I have noticed 'kissing', 'discandying' and 'tremblingly'; we have also met 'rattling', 'varying', 'darkling', 'nothing', 'visiting'. 'Lackeying the varying tide' occurs elsewhere (I. iv. 46); and a passionate movement ends with 'triumphing' (IV. viii. 16). I have selected typical examples. But throughout there is a certain tenuousness and ethereality in the phraseology and rhythms of which these 'i'-sounds are single instances. The effects are vastly different from Othello's throbbing, pulsing floods of emotion: in Othello's language, in Timon's, there is blood in its veins, coursing, throbbing. Cleopatra's is veined with a more tenuous and fiery elixir. There is no sonority, nor, in fact, any deep notes at all in the play. Tragedy is taken lightly, almost playfully: yet this lilting merriment of diction holds, strangely, a more intense fire than the solemn cadences or curbless passions of the sombre plays. All feeling here is more subtle: pure emotion but one strand twisted in a more complex pattern. Hence it is not an easy style. The inner power is of poetry's finest gold-dust, unmixed with baser elements: but it has to be sifted in our understanding from its bedding of brown sand and lucid stream, where it sparkles, myriad spots of solid fire. Thus the poetry is a little arduous of appreciation, its essences elusive. Yet, once found and owned, it makes certain more facile favourite Shakespeare passages seem like brass in comparison. In despising all normal emotional and sensuous associations, working outside the organ cadences of ordinary tragedy, this poetry yet catches the most evanescent tragic essence on the wing:

> O infinite virtue, comest thou smiling from
> The world's great snare uncaught? (IV. viii. 17)

The 'snare' image is at first sight strangely inapposite: the completed association miraculous. Again:

> Here 's sport indeed! How heavy weighs my lord!
> Our strength is all gone into heaviness. (IV. xiii. 32)

This is rare music. Often the soaring tragic emotion is, paradoxically, closely pinned to earth: witness the sharp realism in:

> No more, but e'en a woman, and commanded
> By such poor passion as the maid that milks
> And does the meanest chares. (IV. xiii. 73)

The most powerful phrases are often colourless. Antony is a 'workman' in the 'royal occupation' of fighting (IV. iv. 17). A world of meaning is compressed in the simplest phrase: 'a Roman thought hath struck him' (I. ii. 87). Where else in our literature could the commonplace word 'husband' unfurl such starry wells of light as in Cleopatra's simple phrase:

> . . . Husband, I come.   (V. ii. 290)

Then, when it chooses, this style, like some diaphanous-winged and shimmering dragon-fly of the spirit, outsoars the more 'emotional' kinds, outdistances them with a fine ease. Though despising the sensuous and the sentimental, it yet dares and accomplishes so sweeping a miracle as:

> His face was as the heavens: and therein stuck
> A sun and moon, which kept their course, and lighted
> The little O, the earth.   (V. ii. 79)

However 'unemotional' it may have appeared, it yet holds in it a more dynamic and intense power, and emotion, than any other: words and phrases here are as atoms compressing an infinite force and energy. This emotional fibre may be tenuous: but it is tough as wire. The style of *Othello* is like a large glowing coal; that of *Macbeth* like the sparks from an anvil; *Lear*, like a rocket; *Timon*, like phosphorus churned to flame in a tropic ocean. That of *Antony and Cleopatra* is like a thin, blazing, electric filament, steadily instinct with keenest fire.

We have here a strangely keen yet somewhat unemotional vision. Whatever our elements—whether of feasting and drinking, passionate lust, or military splendour—they are transformed by this peculiar alchemy into essences intensely spiritual, rarefied. This is the process of all poetry: but here it is carried farther. Here, where our subject is one very largely sensuous, our medium is peculiarly desensualized. But the subject-matter is itself various: it ranges from the material and sensuous, through the grand and magnificent, to the more purely spiritual. There is an ascending scale. The style,

the poetic vision of the whole, endorses this movement: it
views its world as one rising from matter to spirit, and
hence, seeing all things in terms not of their immediate
appeal, but rather their potential significance, we find that
all here is from the first finely gilded with the tinct of
spiritual apprehension. I shall now attempt an analysis of
this ascending scale. There are a variety of themes to be
noticed, and I shall deliberately stress the more optimistic
and glorious effects: there are others, but they are subsidiary. In selecting certain veins of imagery, suggestion,
and symbol for special analysis I do not limit their significance to any one immediate meaning. And we must
realize that my 'ascending scale' is a purely intellectual
arrangement of imaginative essences, its only justification
being its purpose to enrich our imaginative vision of a
complex whole. The complexity is amazing. One image
may serve numerous purposes. Antony and Cleopatra,
we are told, were publicly enthroned in chairs of gold.
Now this gold-reference has a varied content. It angers
Caesar and precipitates the action; it emphasizes the
riotous extravagance of Antony's nature; it illustrates the
world-power of our protagonists, their imperial eminence;
and it shows them symbolically throned in a rich setting
worthy of their opulent and infinite love. Empire-imagery
throughout serves at least a dual purpose: suggesting both
the material magnificence which Antony loses, and
shadowing symbolically the finer spiritual magnificence
of love for which he sacrifices it. 'Crowns' occur in both
connexions. Hence certain repetitions are unavoidable:
and any exact definition of symbolic content is, as always,
impossible. The mass-effect is somewhat like a bird's
glistening plumage, glinting variously as you change your
viewpoint. The imagery is ever-shifting, dazzling,
iridescent. But a purposive attention to these varied,
interrelated strands in the play's texture will help us to
rise to the height of its theme and understand its peculiarly
transcendental realism. In my middle sections I shall
note: first, themes of imperial magnificence, the imperial

power and warrior-honour Antony sacrifices for love; second, the more physical and sensuous love-themes and love-imagery in dialogue and suggestion; third, the natural and elemental symbolisms, in their suggestion of the mating of elements, and also, in their varying ascent from the material to the ethereal, reflecting and blending with our love-theme; and, finally, the more spiritual and transcendental elements in this love-theme itself.

II

The geographical and historical setting lends itself to rich names and glittering catalogues:

> Labienus—
> This is stiff news—hath, with his Parthian force,
> Extended Asia from Euphrates;
> His conquering banner shook from Syria
> To Lydia and Ionia. (I. ii. 107)

Again:

> Great Media, Parthia, and Armenia,
> He gave to Alexander; to Ptolemy he assign'd
> Syria, Cilicia, and Phoenicia . . . (III. vi. 14)

And

> . . . he hath assembled
> Bocchus, the king of Libya; Archelaus,
> Of Cappadocia; Philadelphos, king
> Of Paphlagonia; the Thracian king, Adallas;
> King Malchus of Arabia; King of Pont;
> Herod of Jewry; Mithridates, king
> Of Comagene; Polemon and Amyntas,
> The kings of Mede and Lycaonia,
> With a more larger list of sceptres. (III. vi. 68)

We might observe a fair sprinkling of 'feminine' vowels in these names. The action strides across the empire. Scenes occur at Rome, Messina, Misenum, Syria, Athens, and Actium. And we never forget for long that hub of the circling action: Cleopatra's palace at Alexandria. We have an impression of wide empire and vast issues at stake in the wars waged by sea and land. Continued reference to the sea helps to vitalize this effect. Like so many images here it serves a complex purpose: it enlarges, varies, and enriches our geographical vision; adds light to glisten with other more concrete symbols of scintillating brilliance; and, finally, with other elements—earth, air, fire— it stresses the play's peculiarly universal scope.

We hear that Sextus Pompeius 'commands the empire of the sea' (I. ii. 197), and 'is strong at sea' (I. iv. 36). Pompey will 'rid all the sea of pirates' (II. vi. 37). Such phrases as these are common:

> And that is it
> Hath made me rig my navy; at whose burthen
> The anger'd ocean foams.   (II. vi. 19)

Again: 'the people love me, and the sea is mine' (II. i. 9).

> Thou canst not fear us, Pompey, with thy sails;
> We'll speak with thee at sea: at land, thou know'st
> How much we do o'er-count thee.   (II. vi. 24)

'Sea' and 'land' are often juxtaposed like this. Again, of Pompey, we heard earlier:

> *Antony.* What is his strength by land?
> *Caesar.* Great and increasing: but by sea
> He is an absolute master.   (II. ii. 167)

Again we hear of 'sea and land' at I. iv. 78. Nautical terms recur often: such as the 'harbour' (III. ix. 11), where there is 'a ship laden with gold' (III. ix. 4); Antony's sails, referred to as his 'sea-wing', (III. viii. 29); the 'rudder' of Cleopatra's ship (III. ix. 57); her ship's 'flags' (III. xi. 11); the 'sea-side' (III. ix. 20); we hear of a 'great navy rigg'd' (III. v. 20); of 'quick-sands' (II. vii. 65). There is the 'noise of a sea-fight' heard off the stage in III. viii. and again at IV. x. The final catastrophe depends largely on Antony's decision to meet Caesar by sea rather than land: during the fighting there are numerous sea-references (III. vii, viii, ix, xi). There is the drinking-scene on board Pompey's galley (II. vii); the drinkers bid farewell to 'Neptune' at the end of it. One of Antony's speeches is vivid:

> Is it not strange, Canidius,
> That from Tarentum and Brundusium
> He could so quickly cut the Ionian sea,
> And take in Toryne? (III. vii. 21)

Enobarbus, too, vividly describes Antony's flight at Actium:

> I can behold no longer:
> The Antoniad, the Egyptian admiral,
> With all their sixty, fly and turn the rudder:
> To see 't mine eyes are blasted. (III. viii. 11)

Octavia, says Caesar, should have been met on her return from Athens with ceremony 'by sea and land' (III. vi. 54). This sea-imagery heightens our sense of imperial magnificence and limitless power:

> I, that with my sword
> Quarter'd the world, and o'er green Neptune's back
> With ships made cities— (IV. xii. 57)

Again:

> Thou art, if thou darest be, the earthly Jove:
> Whate'er the ocean pales, or sky inclips,
> Is thine, if thou wilt ha 't. (II. vii. 73)

But, though extending our material vision, it has, too, a more subtle suggestion. It is part of the glistening, elemental, ethereal suggestion throughout: it suggests the quicksilver sheen of the Mediterranean, dotted with islands, coasted with cities, a bright expanse breaking the hard crust of solid earth, interlacing the material with something more elusive, fluid, and brilliant. To this other suggestion I shall return later, where I relate it to more imagery of rivers, cloud, and air.

This 'sea' and 'land' imagery blends with a wider 'world' imagery, as in my last quotation. Miss Spurgeon has observed that the word 'world' or 'earth' recurs continually, usually in relation to the main persons, themselves drawn to heroic proportions. Thus Antony is

> The triple pillar of the world transform'd
> Into a strumpet's fool. (I. i. 12)

Pompey endangers 'the sides of the world' (I. ii. 205); the 'third o' the world' belongs to Lepidus (II. ii. 67); 'the world' and Antony's 'great office' divides Antony from Octavia (II. iii. 1); Menas asks Pompey if he will be 'lord of all the world' (II. vii. 66); the triumvirs are 'world-sharers' (II. vii. 76), Lepidus 'a third part of the world' (II. vii. 97). Says Caesar:

> Yet, if I knew
> What hoop should hold us staunch, from edge to edge
> O' the world I would pursue it.   (II. ii. 120)

And Octavia:

> Wars 'twixt you twain would be
> As if the world should cleave, and that slain men
> Should solder up the rift.   (III. iv. 30)

Antony and Cleopatra levy 'the kings o' the earth for war' (III. vi. 67). We hear of 'half the bulk o' the world' (III. ix. 64), 'half to half the world opposed' (III. xi. 9), of Caesar as 'the universal landlord' (III. xi. 72). After the war there is to be 'universal peace' and the 'three-nook'd world shall bear the olive freely' (IV. vi. 5). These references point to the protagonists' almost superhuman power and nobility. Such images are used without any restraint: here mankind is all but deified. In Antony's countenance 'the worship of the whole world lies' (IV. xii. 85), he is 'the greatest prince o' the world' (IV. xiii. 54), the 'crown o' the earth' (IV. xiii. 63), and 'this dull world' in his absence, 'no better than a sty' (IV. xiii. 61). Caesar hears of Antony's death:

> The breaking of so great a thing should make
> A greater crack: the round world
> Should have shook lions into civil streets
> And citizens to their dens: the death of Antony
> Is not a single doom; in the name lay
> A moiety of the world.   (V. i. 14)

Caesar is now 'sole sir o' the world' (V. ii. 120)—he and Antony 'could not stall together in the whole world'
8

(v. i. 39); now is there one only left from the three 'senators of this great world' (ii. vi. 9).

These thick-scattered 'world' references all suggest imperial magnificence and human grandeur—of the men, Antony in particular is idealized beyond all natural limits. In this play human nature is given no limited framework, as in *Lear*. The imperial setting is brilliant, strongly idealized, a world resplendent and magnificent. Human excellence in all its potential beauty and excelling power rides proudly here. Naturalism is transcended. The earth itself, with its sea and land, is a little thing, a bauble in comparison with such heroes. The setting is not, in fact, our little world at all: it is either (i) the Mediterranean empire idealized beyond all rational limits; or (ii) the universe. A new 'universalism', to coin the term, replaces the *Lear*-naturalism: the latter views man in relation to his 'natural' setting, the former sees man as he is transfigured under the intense ray of love and keenest poetic vision. Here 'the gods' of orthodox paganism—like those in *Lear*, conceived but faintly— are insignificant beside the human drama. The imagery and suggestion throughout point the transcendental, not the natural, qualities in man, or even in 'nature'. We are subdued by them not to the ethnologist's, but rather to the lover's apprehension. Now this general elevation of humanity is related to two main streams of imagery: those of (i) War, and (ii) Love: which may be said to correspond to our two settings just observed. These two Shakespearian values are vividly present. The first is twined with the empire-theme: the second rises from out that theme, is both blended and contrasted with it. The brilliant love-vision rises from this magnificent dream of imperial Roman splendour. Though these two values clash in the play's action, yet the differing victories of each point the other's peculiar essence: Antony sells a warrior's honour and an emperor's sway for the Imperial Theme which is Cleopatra's love. Each theme wins a victory; one spiritual, the other material. I shall note

next those stressed and highly-coloured phrases which
continually emphasize Antony's nobility in war; and afterwards pass from 'war' to 'love'.

Antony's prowess is praised by Philo at the start:

> . . . those his goodly eyes,
> That o'er the files and musters of the war
> Have glow'd like plated Mars, now bend, now turn,
> The office and devotion of their view
> Upon a tawny front: his captain's heart,
> Which in the scuffles of great fights hath burst
> The buckles on his breast, reneges all temper,
> And is become the bellows and the fan
> To cool a gipsy's lust.   (I. i. 2)

There is Cleopatra's lovely phrase:

> Look, prithee, Charmian,
> How this Herculean Roman does become
> The carriage of his chafe.   (I. iii. 83)

Also her fine farewell:

> Your honour calls you hence;
> Therefore be deaf to my unpitied folly,
> And all the gods go with you! upon your sword
> Sit laurel victory! and smooth success
> Be strew'd before your feet!   (I. iii. 97)

War 'drums' Antony from his 'sport' (I. iv. 29). Caesar
speaks a fine apostrophe in Antony's praise, outlining the
'honour' that Antony has thrown to the winds:

> When thou once
> Wast beaten from Modena, where thou slew'st
> Hirtius and Pansa, consuls, at thy heel
> Did famine follow; whom thou fought'st against,
> Though daintily brought up, with patience more
> Than savages could suffer: thou didst drink
> The stale of horses, and the gilded puddle
> Which beasts would cough at: thy palate then did deign
> The roughest berry on the rudest hedge;
> Yea, like the stag, when snow the pasture sheets,
> The barks of trees thou browsed'st; on the Alps
> It is reported thou didst eat strange flesh,

Which some did die to look on: and all this—
It wounds thine honour that I speak it now—
Was borne so like a soldier, that thy cheek
So much as lank'd not.   (I. iv. 56)

Notice the usual Shakespearian reference to 'honour' in our last passages. Here there is a 'horse' reference scarcely typical of such references throughout: they are numerous and usually to be related more directly and picturesquely to war-strength and chivalrous excellence. Cleopatra thinks about her Antony when she is alone:

O Charmian,
Where think'st thou he is now? Stands he, or sits he?
Or does he walk? or is he on his horse?
O happy horse, to bear the weight of Antony!
Do bravely, horse! for wot'st thou whom thou movest?
The demi-Atlas of this earth, the arm
And burgonet of men.   (I. v. 18)

She hears from the messenger that he

soberly did mount an arm-gaunt steed,
Who neigh'd so high, that what I would have spoke
Was beastly dumb'd by him.   (I. v. 48)

It has not always so vivid and pictorial a significance: sometimes it is negative enough as when Antony refers to the cloud-figures which change their form:

That which is now a horse, even with a thought,
The rack dislimns . . .   (IV. xii. 9)

Cleopatra is 'yon ribaudred nag of Egypt' (III. viii. 20). To Enobarbus the image comes readily, because he is essentially a soldier by temperament: if Caesar 'has a cloud in 's face' he remarks bluntly:

He were the worse for that, were he a horse;
So is he, being a man.   (III. ii. 52)

And again, when Cleopatra insists on taking active part in the war, he murmurs:

If we should serve with horse and mares together,
The horse were merely lost; the mares would bear
A soldier and his horse.   (III. vii. 8)

—a delightful miniature of the whole play, which turns on the opposition of warriorship, or empire, and love. The same is true of another passage where the horse assumes tremendous proportions in a sweeping association:

> The third o' the world is yours; which with a snaffle
> You may pace easy, but not such a wife.   (II. ii. 67)

The metaphoric exaggeration is typical here: the horse only submits to the same process as his master—becoming a Colossus in the poet's imagination. The warrior and his war-horse are raised to proportions commensurate with their romantic valour. The play is impregnated with an idealized militarism. Once Antony and Caesar are thought of as two mighty war-horses who could not 'stall together' in the whole world (V. i. 39). We hear of cavalry often—of 'twelve thousand horse' (III. vii. 60), 'my legions and my horse' (III. viii. 43), 'the ne'er yet beaten horse of Parthia' (III. i. 33). Our world is one of military opulence by sea and land, navies cutting the blue sea into foam, wheeling squadrons raising clouds of dust, vast armies but pawns in the play of the protagonists, themselves Titans of imperial power. The full value of such suggestions is apparent in this passage:

> You come not
> Like Caesar's sister: the wife of Antony
> Should have an army for an usher, and
> The neighs of horse to tell of her approach
> Long ere she did appear; the trees by the way
> Should have borne men; and expectation fainted,
> Longing for what it had not; nay, the dust
> Should have ascended to the roof of heaven,
> Raised by your populous troops . . .   (III. vi. 42)

These 'horse' references are very significant: they heighten and intensify our feeling for military magnificence. But they do not clash with the prevailing and pervading glow of beauty. The horse in Shakespeare is elsewhere clearly idealized, as a beautiful animal—especially in *Venus and Adonis* (265–324). It is often strongly idealized as a war

symbol.[1] The two main elements of this play's vision—
War, or Empire, and Love—though they are opposed in
the action, are not always opposed imaginatively. Every
fine effect of each contributes to the total splendour and
unity within and from which each in turn draws imaginative sustenance. Each and all is heavily gilded, glorified.
The final result is that the love-theme rises high in
splendour on the structure of imperial and military
magnificence. The process is, in fact, curiously implied
by an unobtrusive image:

> . . . much is breeding,
> Which, like the courser's hair, hath yet but life,
> And not a serpent's poison.   (I. ii. 205)

A horse's hair, placed in water, was believed to grow into
a serpent. So Antony's soldiership, in the waters of his
passion, breeds in him and Cleopatra, the Serpent of Old
Nile, a Love which endangers the Empire. This appears a
straining of symbolic suggestion, no doubt: but the ideas
of 'breeding', of 'water', the 'serpent', and the 'courser'
are all important, and recurrent: especially the thought of
element 'mingling'—a word I notice later—with element
in order to 'breed'.

To return to Antony's soldiership. It is 'twice the other
twain' (II. i. 34); his name a 'magical word of war' (III. i.
31); he is a 'grand captain' (III. i. 9). Antony, like Othello,
recalls in tragedy his hour of military pride:

> . . . he at Philippi kept
> His sword e'en like a dancer; while I struck
> The lean and wrinkled Cassius; and 'twas I

---

[1] Notably at *Henry V*, III. vii. 1–110: from which I select the following:
. . . It is a beast for Perseus: he is pure air and fire; and the dull elements
of earth and water never appear in him, but only in patient stillness while
his rider mounts him.' Again, '. . . it is a theme as fluent as the sea: turn
the sands into eloquent tongues, and my horse is argument for them all:
'tis a subject for a sovereign to reason on, and for a sovereign's sovereign
to ride on . . .'. The Dauphin's horse is his 'mistress'. The relevance of
these passages to *Antony and Cleopatra* is clear. See also the description of
Prince Henry, *1 Henry IV*, IV. i. 97–110, quoted in my opening essay.

That the mad Brutus ended: he alone
Dealt on lieutenantry, and no practice had
In the brave squares of war: yet now—No matter.
(III. ix. 35)

Cleopatra buckles on his armour, and he replies:

O love,

That thou could'st see my wars to-day, and knew'st
The royal occupation! thou should'st see
A workman in 't.   (IV. iv. 15)

Cleopatra (IV. iv. 36), Antony (III. xi. 22–28), and Caesar
(IV. i. 5) all seem to feel that, were it a question of
individual prowess, Antony would achieve the victory. He
goes to the battle 'a man of steel' (IV. iv 33), and, when
defeat is certain, he yet prides himself on his old superiority:

... this pine is bark'd

That overtopp'd them all.   (IV. x. 36)

Thinking Cleopatra to be dead, he discards his armour:

... bruised pieces, go;

You have been nobly borne.   (IV. xii. 42)

He 'quarter'd the world' with his sword (IV. xii. 58).
He is 'the greatest prince o' the world, the noblest' (IV.
xiii. 54), the 'garland of the war' and 'soldier's pole' (IV. xiii.
64). Caesar speaks a noble eulogy at his death:

... thou, my brother, my competitor

In top of all design, my mate in empire,
Friend and companion in the front of war ... (V. i. 42)

Antony's warrior nobility is thus reiterated through the
play: we are never suffered to forget it. But humanity is
doubly idealized: in war and in love. Antony in both is
supreme—his peerless activity in the front of action shows
him noble: his love shows him divine. This imperial and
war-like setting is apt for our theme—love's proud and
flaming trajectory into the unknown, its aristocratic
disregard of the baser element, imperial splendour, from
which it rises colossal.

   The pomp and glitter of this Mediterranean empire
is vivid throughout. The world is our protagonists'

empire and kings their slaves. They map out the fate of nations as a householder the paths of his back-garden. Antony sends message to Cleopatra:

> ... I will piece
> Her opulent throne with kingdoms; all the east,
> Say thou, shall call her mistress. (I. v. 45)

Such references are scattered over the whole play. Antony makes casual reference to having feasted 'three kings' (II. ii. 80); 'six kings' show Canidius the way of yielding (III. viii. 43); Caesar will shower 'principalities' on Cleopatra if Antony be betrayed (III. xi. 19); Caesar can order Antony to 'take in that kingdom and enfranchise that' (I. i. 23); 'kings' have trembled to kiss Cleopatra's hand (II. v. 29)—have been 'fellows' to Antony's servants (IV. ii. 13). Antony and Cleopatra levy the 'kings o' the earth for war' (III. vi. 68); Cleopatra will give Scarus a gold suit of armour—'it was a king's' (IV. viii. 27). Antony had 'superfluous kings for messengers' (III. x. 5). So, too, Julius Caesar 'mused of taking kingdoms in' while he kissed Cleopatra (III. xi. 83). Antony, Octavius Caesar, Cleopatra—all are imperial to a world of 'kings'; their subject empire vast, rich, magnificent. This splendour Antony barters for love. Every imprint that this imperial suggestion and imagery leaves outlined in our imagination increases our sense of glorious love. World-empire and love are variously correlative and contrasted: their inter-significance is here crucial and dynamic. Throughout we are reminded that Antony wilfully throws away kingdoms for his Cleopatra. For her even great Caesar 'lay'd his sword to bed' (II. ii. 232). Antony's reckless course is emphasized:

> Cleopatra
> Hath nodded him to her. He hath given his empire
> Up to a whore ... (III. vi. 65)

Again:

> The greater cantle of the world is lost
> With very ignorance; we have kiss'd away
> Kingdoms and provinces. (III. viii. 16)

That is one aspect. It is necessary to know it, however love's integrity may force us rather to another. Here is the other:

> Let Rome in Tiber melt, and the wide arch
> Of the rang'd empire fall! Here is my space.
> Kingdoms are clay: our dungy earth alike
> Feeds beast as man: the nobleness of life
> Is to do thus . . .   (i. i. 33)

That is our final vision here: man is transfigured by love's orient fire. Without it he is, as the beasts, mere product of 'dungy earth'. Love here translineates man to divine likeness—it is the only 'nobleness of life'. This is the finely petalled design transcending its birth as the flower's intellectual and patterned markings transcend the manure which gives it sustenance. Man is lit with this visionary light; the whole play engoldened with love's sun. 'Gold' references are frequent. They are integral to the richly-caparisoned structure of the play. Like so much else, they serve both as symbols of material wealth and suggestions of the glory for which it is exchanged. I shall next note some of these references, afterwards passing to those strands of imagery which outlimn for us the quality of Antony's and Cleopatra's love.

Riches and gold are percurrently suggested. Antony sends Cleopatra a precious stone—'this orient pearl' (I. v. 41):

> Say, the firm Roman to great Egypt sends
> This treasure of an oyster.   (I. v. 43)

He kissed the jewel before parting with it, it is an ambassador of love: so, too, precious metals and jewels are consistently symbols in Shakespeare of love's riches, as in *Timon*, whether by association or contrast. The association is pointed in a lovely phrase—Antony's messenger, says Cleopatra, is 'gilded with his tinct' (I. v. 37). Cleopatra promises another messenger 'gold' if he brings good news (II. v. 28): she continues:

> Why, there's more gold.
> But, sirrah, mark, we use
> To say the dead are well: bring it to that,
> The gold I give thee will I melt and pour
> Down thy ill-uttering throat. (II. v. 32)

Again, if his news is good:

> I'll set thee in a shower of gold, and hail
> Rich pearls upon thee. (II. v. 45)

Later she gives him gold (III. iii. 34). There are other images of wealth. There is the picture of Antony and Cleopatra in 'chairs of gold', and 'on a tribunal silver'd' (III. vi. 3). There is the ship 'laden with gold' (III. ix. 4) which Antony offers to his followers. Antony sends Enobarbus' 'treasure' after him, and the messenger unloads his mules of it (IV. vi. 21). He adds more to it, his bounty 'crowns' turpitude with gold (IV. vi. 34). There is the gold armour Cleopatra promises to Scarus (IV. viii. 27) and Antony's rejoinder:

> He has deserved it, were it carbuncled
> Like holy Phoebus' car. (IV. viii. 28)

Cleopatra gives Caesar a list of her 'money, plate, and jewels' (V. ii. 138). All this wealth-imagery—there is more, in the passages quoted at the end of my essay—refers not only to material magnificence, but is part of the general intoxication whereby we form some contact with our protagonists' costly love. The symbolic value is clear: this world was heaven to Cleopatra till the gods stole her 'jewel'—Antony (IV. xiii. 78).

III

I have outlined something of the impregnating atmosphere of wealth, power, military strength, and material magnificence. Now I pass to the purely erotic suggestions. These I shall treat in an ascending scale, starting from the sensuous and material, and, noting in my following section the animal and elemental symbolism, shall pass on finally to those images which tune our senses to appreciate the more purely spiritual essences in the play.

Antony's passion is variously depicted as lust and high spiritual love. Both aspects are stressed, but not equally: the passion theme as a whole is clearly raised above mere animal desire, though that desire is yet closely inwoven with it. First, we must note this 'lower' element of physical passion and physical indulgence generally. Feasting is constantly referred to. Antony's life with Cleopatra is composed chiefly of love and feasting. And feasting, we must remember, is in Shakespeare not only a matter of sensuous pleasure, but a life-force. Its relevance in a play of sexual love is clear. Early Enobarbus cries:

> Bring in the banquet quickly; wine enough
> Cleopatra's health to drink.   (I. ii. 11)

Charmian talks of heating her liver with drinking (I. ii. 23). Says Enobarbus: 'Mine, and most of our fortunes, to-night, shall be—drunk to bed' (I. ii. 45). We hear that Antony

> fishes, drinks, and wastes
> The lamps of night in revel.   (I. iv. 4)

Antony's feasting is freely criticized. So was Timon's. Yet it is a powerful theme here. Again:

> . . . to sit
> And keep the turn of tippling with a slave;
> To reel the streets at noon, and stand the buffet
> With knaves that smell of sweat.   (I. iv. 18)

Antony is engaged in 'lascivious wassails' (I. iv. 56). Pompey prays that Cleopatra may keep Antony from the wars:

> Tie up the libertine in a field of feasts,
> Keep his brain fuming; Epicurean cooks
> Sharpen with cloyless sauce his appetite;
> That sleep and feeding may prorogue his honour
> Even till a Lethe'd dulness!   (II. i. 23)

The 'lower' aspect of our feasting theme is vividly suggested. Antony is an 'amorous surfeiter' (II. i. 33). He excuses his laxity to Caesar on the score of having 'newly

feasted' six kings—he 'did want what he was i' the morning' (II. ii. 80). Those were 'poisoned hours' that bound
him up from knowledge of himself (II. ii. 94). Maecenas
questions Enobarbus on Antony's riotous life in Alexandria:

> *Enobarbus.*   . . . we did sleep day out of countenance, and
> made the night light with drinking.
> *Maecenas.* Eight wild boars roasted whole at a breakfast, and
> but twelve persons there; is this true?   (II. ii. 181)

In this life-vision of infinity the life-force, feasting, is
itself infinite. When he first meets Cleopatra Antony asks
her to 'supper' (II. ii. 228), and is in return asked to be her
guest. So he,

> Being barber'd ten times o'er, goes to the feast,
> And for his ordinary pays his heart
> For what his eyes eat only.   (II. ii. 229)

She 'drunk him to his bed' on another occasion (II. v. 21).
There is the feasting between Antony, Caesar, and Pompey:

> *Pompey.*   . . . but, first
> Or last, your fine Egyptian cookery
> Shall have the fame. I have heard that Julius Caesar
> Grew fat with feasting there.   (II. vi. 63)

Now 'four feasts are toward' (II. vi. 74); Cleopatra is
Antony's 'Egyptian dish' (II. vi. 134); says Enobarbus,
'we have used our throats in Egypt' (II. vi. 143). There
is the actual feast scene on Pompey's galley:

> *Music plays. Enter two or three Servants with a banquet.*

This scene, set on board ship, with music sounding,
as it grows more and more riotous in humour, conviviality,
and song, is a fine compression of many of the most typical
and important subsidiary elements in the play:

> *Pompey.* This is not yet an Alexandrian feast.
> *Antony.* It ripens towards it.   (II. vii. 102)

Again:

> *Enobarbus.*   Ha, my brave emperor! [*To Antony.*
> Shall we dance now the Egyptian Bacchanals,
> And celebrate our drink?

Pompey.   Let 's ha 't, good soldier.
Antony. Come, let 's all take hands,
    Till that the conquering wine hath steep'd our sense
    In soft and delicate Lethe.
Enobarbus.   All take hands.
    Make battery to our ears with the loud music:
    The while I'll place you: then the boy shall sing;
    The holding every man shall bear as loud
    As his strong sides can volley.
                    [*Music plays. Enobarbus places them hand in hand.*
                                      (II. vii. 109)

There follows the song to Bacchus, 'monarch of the vine'.
Here Antony's free-hearted and thriftless pleasures win
a victory over Caesar's icy policy. Caesar alone demurs
from this excessive drinking, and it is he who calls the
feast to a conclusion. But, whilst it lasts, Antony is to us,
as to Enobarbus, 'my brave Emperor': they all want to
hear of his Egyptian experiences, his Egyptian revelry.
His royal entertainment and rich experience there make
him, not Caesar, the hero of the day. Nor must this sensuous element be blurred by any too strict an ethic. It is
presented in two-fold guise, like Antony's love: as riotous
waste—criticism is levelled against Antony for his reckless revelry; but also—and this is most important—as
something of princely and royal magnificence; and, like
Timon's, of a marvellous and inexhaustible bounty. And
we must remember its power as a 'life' symbol. So this
drinking scene ends with a flourish of trumpets and a
farewell to 'Neptune':

    These drums! these trumpets, flutes! what!
    Let Neptune hear we bid a loud farewell
    To these great fellows; sound and be hang'd, sound out!
                    [*Sound a flourish, with drums.*
                                      (II. vii. 138)

The reiteration of music, the accompaniment of song, in
this scene is also noteworthy: music being an important
element in the play. To conclude our feasting references
—at the end, when fortune is deserting Antony, he

suddenly summons courage and confidence, and recapturing his old merriment, cries to Cleopatra:

> Come,
> Let's have one other gaudy night: call to me
> All my sad captains; fill our bowls once more;
> Let's mock the midnight bell.   (III. xi. 182)

Now he 'is Antony again', she 'will be Cleopatra' (III. xi. 187). Antony will 'force the wine peep through' his captains' scars (III. xi. 191). So they go to 'drown consideration' (IV. ii. 45), to be 'bounteous' at their meal (IV. ii. 10). This element of feasting is stressed throughout. Cleopatra knows the Roman stage will parody their love, emphasizing its more material forms:

> . . . the quick comedians,
> Extemporally will stage us, and present
> Our Alexandrian revels; Antony
> Shall be brought drunken forth, and I shall see
> Some squeaking Cleopatra boy my greatness
> I' the posture of a whore.   (V. ii. 216)

The love theme is closely welded with all this. The more spiritual reality grows, flames from this sensuous and living bounty: the two are not separate, rather twin aspects of a single reality. So, too, the transcendental humanism is everywhere but a development from a vital realism. Next I shall note, before passing to the more spiritual, volatile, and paradisal suggestions, those references which further stress a purely physical eroticism.

This love is often referred to as 'lust'. At the start we hear of Antony cooling 'a gipsy's lust' (I. i. 10). Pompey uses the word twice in reference to Antony (II. i. 22 and 38). Maecenas talks of 'the adulterous Antony' (III. vi. 93). When tragedy overtakes him, Antony abuses Cleopatra for her impurity:

> You were half blasted ere I knew you: ha!
> Have I my pillow left unpress'd in Rome,
> Forborne the getting of a lawful race,
> And by a gem of women, to be abus'd
> By one that looks on feeders?   (III. xi. 105)

His love is 'filth'. The gods, he says,

> In our own filth drop our clear judgements; make us
> Adore our errors; laugh at 's, while we strut
> To our confusion.   (III. xi. 112)

Again:

> I found you as a morsel cold upon
> Dead Caesar's trencher; nay, you were a fragment
> Of Cneius Pompey's; besides what hotter hours,
> Unregister'd in vulgar fame, you have
> Luxuriously pick'd out: for, I am sure,
> Though you can guess what temperance should be,
> You know not what it is.   (III. xi. 116)

At this point love's vision is questioned. Physical alone, without faith or constancy, it is unclean, stupid, a madness. In the story our view alternates. We see both aspects, physical and spiritual—so Cleopatra is 'this foul Egyptian' (IV. x. 23), 'triple-turn'd whore' (IV. x. 26). Enobarbus earlier called her Antony's 'Egyptian dish' (II. vi. 134). Lust is clearly emphasized: though the preponderance is heavy enough on the other side, we cannot for long forget this blending of spiritual fire with material pleasures. Thus we have a developing scale of sensuous and erotic suggestion, layer on layer, leading from feasting and drinking and all riotous bodily excess, to the towering vision of transfigured man, godlike and immortal, in empire or, as I shall show, in love, which is this play's final statement. But there is more purely physical love-suggestion to be observed. Sex is discussed freely by Charmian and Iras in their talk with the Soothsayer:

> *Charmian.* Then belike my children shall have no names:
>   prithee, how many boys and wenches must I have?
> *Soothsayer.* If every of your wishes had a womb,
>   And fertile every wish, a million.
> *Charmian.* Out, fool! I forgive thee for a witch.
> *Alexas.* You think none but your sheets are privy to your
>   wishes.   (I. ii. 35)

Cleopatra's ladies are devotees to a very physical love. 'Fertile' is important. Such talk is usual in Cleopatra's household. We have her conversation with Mardian, the eunuch:

Cleopatra.   . . . I take no pleasure
　　In aught an eunuch has: 'tis well for thee,
　　That, being unseminar'd, thy freer thoughts
　　May not fly forth of Egypt. Hast thou affections?
Mardian. Yes, gracious madam.
Cleopatra. Indeed!
Mardian. Not in deed, madam; for I can do nothing
　　But what indeed is honest to be done:
　　Yet have I fierce affections, and think
　　What Venus did with Mars.   (I. v. 9)

Cleopatra's palace, with its oriental setting, the languorous beauties of Cleopatra herself, the sinuous nakedness of her slaves, all has a certain serpentine and ungodly attraction —something of hot unchastity, and this is reflected in such dialogues. It is part of the play and not to be neglected: important, to the whole complex vision. This sex theme is conceived with a freedom blending naturally with those instances of nature's fruitfulness and the mixing of elements to be noticed later. Another theme might be adduced, in this context of lust and sex-talk: the sadistic one of torture, in Cleopatra's and Antony's threats. Cleopatra addresses the messenger:

　　　　　　　　　　Hence,
　　Horrible villain! or I'll spurn thine eyes
　　Like balls before me; I'll unhair thy head:
　　Thou shalt be whipp'd with wire, and stew'd in brine,
　　Smarting in lingering pickle.   (II. v. 63)

Antony has Thyreus whipped:

　　　　　　　　Whip him, fellows,
　　Till, like a boy, you see him cringe his face,
　　And whine aloud for mercy.   (III. xi. 99)

The love-realism of the play is far from tenuous. It is a human analogue to the continual suggestion of earth's fruitfulness—such as the sun breeding creatures and crops from the ooze of Nile (II. vii. 20–31). All these elements are strongly physical, yet levelled everywhere by the tight intellectual patterning and technique of the play as a whole and its language in particular. The poetry itself always escapes direct sensuous appeal, nor does the wider technique in scene arrangement and dialogue allow any one sensuous suggestion to develop far enough to give delight unchecked. The sensuous element is always part of a patterning itself far from sensuous. We are given a view of physical delights and passions from the poetic height of a rarefied vision, missing nothing, over-emphasizing nothing, aware of all significances and relations, mapped out below, juxtaposed, understood. The vision is too crystal-clear to under-emphasize the physical, yet also too spiritually and keenly awake to allow itself to become subdued to what it works in. It is a chaste vision of unchastity: we feel the poet's mind alive before us, as, in exquisite purity and profound insight, it delights in its creation of love and lust intrinsicate. The clear avoidance of direct sensuous delight may be illustrated simply enough. I quote a few lines from *Romeo and Juliet*:

> Spread thy close curtain, love-performing night,
> That runaway's eyes may wink, and Romeo
> Leap to these arms, untalk'd of and unseen.
> Lovers can see to do their amorous rites
> By their own beauties; or, if love be blind,
> It best agrees with night. Come, civil night,
> Thou sober-suited matron, all in black,
> And learn me how to lose a winning match,
> Play'd for a pair of stainless maidenhoods:
> Hood my unmann'd blood, bating in my cheeks,
> With thy black mantle; till strange love, grown bold,
> Think true love acted simple modesty.   (III. ii. 5)

There is nothing like that about *Antony and Cleopatra*. The sensuously beautiful is never developed for its own sake: it is a necessary accompaniment to a spiritual love—but that love itself, at its finest moments, so far transcends the sensuous that all sensuous suggestion melts, like morning mist, to nothingness in its sun. Set beside Juliet's words Cleopatra's:

> By Isis, I will give thee bloody teeth,
> If thou with Caesar paragon again
> My man of men. (I. v. 70)

So far from being couched in a luxurious bedding of soft
undulating emotions, our last phrase here stands next to
that first violent petulancy, 'bloody teeth', and all our
emotion is compressed into that gem of love poetry, 'my
man of men': phrase hard as a little piece of grit, as colourless, as ordinary—yet alive with a universe of electronic
passions.

There is another strand in the eroticism here, similar to
that in *Julius Caesar*: recurrent references to personal and
physical, and especially facial, details. Cleopatra inquires
the colour of Octavia's hair, her height, the shape of her
face (II. v. 114; III. iii). Her detailed queries and comments are delightful. Of Antony we hear:

> those his goodly eyes
> That o'er the files and musters of the war
> Have glow'd like plated Mars, now bend, now turn,
> The office and devotion of their view
> Upon a tawny front. (I. i. 2)

Antony's hair is often noticed. He himself says:

> My very hairs do mutiny; for the white
> Reprove the brown for rashness, and they them
> For fear and doting. (III. ix. 13)

Again he refers to his 'grizzled head' (III. xi. 17), and
Cleopatra to 'the curled Antony' (v. ii. 304). 'Thou
blushest', she says to him, 'and that blood of thine is
Caesar's homager' (I. i. 30). Antony tells Eros to 'put
colour in his cheek' (IV. xii. 69). We hear of wine
'peeping through' scars (III. xi. 191); of Cleopatra's
'bluest veins' (II. v. 29), and 'downy windows', her eyes
(v. ii. 319). Cleopatra would look Caesar 'i' the face' (v.
ii. 32). Caesar 'has a cloud in's face' (III. ii. 51). Eternity
is in the 'lips', 'eyes', and 'brows' bent' of the lovers (I. iii.
36). All this concrete and visual eroticism—there is
more— is close-woven, naturally, in such a play: part of
the rich interplay here of body and spirit. Our vision

here shows us a sheen of purest light playing on a rugged land of matter, touching its crags with startling fire, lighting those lakes that interlace it till they burn themselves refulgent as the heavenly origin itself. To this point I shall now direct my analysis, where the imagery advances beyond the solid and sensuous to suggestions more elemental and ethereal: the imagery of water, air, fire. Then, returning to the love-theme, I shall finally notice in that connexion the themes of music, and stress again the peculiarly transcendental humanism of the play. So we may advance to an understanding of why and in what sense this play is not merely a story of a soldier's fall, but rather a spelled land of romance achieved and victorious: a paradisal vision expressed in terms of humanity's quest of love.

IV

As in *Julius Caesar*, *Macbeth*, and *Lear*, it is important to observe the animal references scattered through the play. There is no direct symbolism: animal images are always implicit in their context, serving a direct purpose apart from their cumulative suggestion. This is true throughout: there is little straining after symbolic effects—all tends to be implicit, probable, realistic, and yet instinct with visionary fire. There are certain animals indeterminate in suggestion: mules, the ass, the cow, the dog, hares, the lion, the boar, the bear, the stag, the 'horned herd'. On the whole, they form a fairly picturesque assemblage: some are fierce, but animal fierceness is not emphasized here—this is, of course, necessary in a play so divergent from the *Macbeth* and *Lear* modes. But there are others more significant. 'Serpents' and 'snakes' are often mentioned. This image suggests sinuous grace and fascination joined to danger: its aptitude in connexion with Cleopatra is evident. Cleopatra is the 'Serpent of old Nile'. But again, that phrase points us to another significance: one suggesting life in an element less material than earth. This play stresses particularly two kinds of life: aquatic and aerial.

First, there is the Serpent, often associated with the Nile. This river is often here in our imaginations. The name 'Nile', with its tenuous soft vowel-sound, brims with the very emotional colour of the river itself sinuously winding through the rich desert ooze, and both suggest the serpent to which it gives birth, the 'serpent of old Nile' (I. v. 25), the 'pretty worm of Nilus' (v. ii. 243). 'Snakes' occur at II. v. 40, and II. v. 95; 'serpents' at II. v. 79, and IV. xiii. 25. There is, too, the 'dragonish' shape of the cloud at IV. xii. 2; and the 'crocodile' and 'serpent of Egypt', both bred out of the Nile mud (II. vii. 29–31). I return to this Nile-imagery later. Here are other examples of water-life: 'tawny-finn'd fishes' (II. v. 12), a 'salt-fish' (II. v. 17), the oyster (I. v. 44), the dolphin (v. ii. 89), mermaids (II. ii. 212), nereids (II. ii. 211), and—if I may include him— Cleopatra's 'diver' (II. v. 16). Hence 'swimming' is a natural image here:

> Our fortune on the sea is out of breath
> And sinks most lamentably.   (III. viii. 34)

Water-flies and sea-birds occur, the aquatic blending with the aerial suggestion. We hear of 'flies and gnats of Nile' (III. xi. 166), 'the swan's down-feather' on the tide (III. ii. 48), of going 'a-ducking' (III. vii. 65), of Antony 'like a doting mallard', clapping on 'his sea wing' (III. viii. 29). We also have many examples of pure aerial life: the 'fly' (II. ii. 186), the 'breese' (III. viii. 24), the beetle (III. ii. 20); and there is a fine list of birds—the dove (III. xi. 197), the cuckoo (II. vi. 28), the 'estridge' (III. xi. 197), the 'Arabian bird' (III. ii. 12), the nightingale (IV. viii. 18), swallows building their nests in Cleopatra's sails (IV. x. 16), the eagle (II. ii. 186), the kite (III. xi. 89), quails (II. iii. 37), cocks (II. iii. 36). The image occurs naturally in Dolabella's remark on Antony:

> An argument that he is pluck'd, when hither
> He sends so poor a pinion of his wing.   (III. x. 3)

Cleopatra will catch Seleucus' eyes 'though they had wings' (v. ii. 156). There is a clear and significant newness about this animal-imagery: it helps to define the watery and ethereal quality which interpenetrates our vision. There is continued suggestion of immaterial life-modes, beautiful and volatile, swimming free in ocean or air, to be contrasted with the ominous and loathsome effects in *Macbeth* —which yet, as I remark elsewhere, has many 'bird' references—and the rough and tousled creatures in *Lear*. Here, there is always something strangely beautiful, a rarefied yet vivid life-apprehension. Though ethereal, our life-images are to be related to our erotic theme. They are physical and ethereal at once. In this play nature is ever at work, blending, mingling, dissolving element in element, to produce new strangeness, new beauty. The natural imagery here reflects our love-theme: the blending of elements reflects the blending of sexes in love. Hence our earth is here fruitful, and many references to life-processes occur, throwing the sex-talk of Cleopatra's girls into a new light: for human and physical love is, to a pure vision, itself pure as the dissolving of clouds in rain. I shall next observe such references.

There is imagery of trees, flowers, fruits; the benison of earth's foison, harvest fruitfulness, picturesque cultivation, and flowery joy. Nature is kindly and productive: the mating of sun and earth is an apt setting for the mating of our protagonists. In our animals, we found creatures picturesque through legendary association: the Arabian bird, mermaids, dolphins, the dragon. Here flowers and evergreens are present in association with human happiness and glory:

> Prove this a prosperous day, the three-nook'd world
> Shall bear the olive freely. (IV. vi. 6)

Again:

> . . . upon your sword
> Sit laurel victory! and smooth success
> Be strew'd before your feet! (I. iii. 99)

We hear of 'the morn-dew on the myrtle-leaf' (III. x. 9). Caesar 'wears the rose of youth upon him' (III. xi. 20)—

in contrast to Cleopatra and Antony when fortune leaves them:

> Against the blown rose may they stop their nose
> That kneel'd unto the buds. (III. xi. 39)

Antony's followers desert to 'blossoming Caesar', which blends into a tree-image:

> . . . and this pine is bark'd,
> That overtopp'd them all. (IV. x. 36)

Antony, without his honour, is 'branchless' (III. iv. 24). We have 'barks of trees' (I. iv. 66). Antony speaks of the changing forms taken by his imaginary cloud, and outlines a

> blue promontory
> With trees upon 't . . . (IV. xii. 5)

We hear of plants 'ill-rooted' (II. vii. 2), of 'trees' bearing 'men' (III. vi. 46); treasons are 'planted' (I. iii. 26), human strength is 'sap' (III. xi. 191). Our last 'flower' reference is the most lovely of all:

> Where souls do couch on flowers, we'll hand in hand,
> And with our sprightly port make the ghosts gaze.
> (IV. xii. 51)

Other vegetable-life suggests earth's bounty. We have the onion (I. ii. 181; IV. ii. 35), salad (I. v. 73); 'the roughest berry on the rudest hedge' (I. iv. 64); the 'pasture' sheeted with snow (I. iv. 65). The clown brings Cleopatra figs:

> This is an aspic's trail: and these fig-leaves
> Have slime upon them, such as the aspic leaves
> Upon the caves of Nile. (V. ii. 353)

Which in the fifth act quaintly casts back its shadow on Charmian's words in the second scene:

> *Soothsayer.* You shall outlive the lady whom you serve.
> *Charmian.* O excellent! I love long life better than figs.
> (I. ii. 31)

There are grapes:

> Come, thou monarch of the vine,
> Plumpy Bacchus with pink eyne!
> In thy fats our cares be drown'd,
> With thy grapes our hairs be crown'd. (II. vii. 120)

Cleopatra, in her last speech, says

> Now no more
> The juice of Egypt's grape shall moist this lip.
>
> (v. ii. 284)

The earth's fruitfulness is often stressed. We have a reference to the mild, fruitful seasons of spring and autumn:

> Like to the time o' the year between the extremes
> Of hot and cold, he was nor sad nor merry.   (i. v. 51)

We have mention also of wheat (ii. vi. 38), of reapers (iii. vii. 36), of 'death' as a 'scythe' (iii. xi. 194). 'Grace' is to 'grow' where tears fall (iv. ii. 38). Again,

> O, then we bring forth weeds,
> When our quick minds lie still; and our ills told us
> Is as our earing.   (i. ii. 118)

There is Antony's fine description of the Nile's fertility:

> *Antony (To Caesar).* Thus do they, sir: they take the flow o'
>   the Nile
> By certain scales i' the pyramid; they know
> By the height, the lowness, or the mean, if dearth
> Or foison follow: the higher Nilus swells,
> The more it promises: as it ebbs, the seedsman
> Upon the slime and ooze scatters his grain,
> And shortly comes to harvest.
> *Lepidus.* You've strange serpents there.
> *Antony.* Ay, Lepidus.
> *Lepidus.* Your serpent of Egypt is bred now of your mud by the
>   operation of your sun: so is your crocodile.
> *Antony.* They are so.   (ii. vii. 20)

Notice the rich watery suggestion—land and water blended in 'slime and ooze'. Elsewhere we hear of 'the fire that quickens Nilus' slime' (i. iii. 68), and of 'the o'erflowing Nilus' humorously suggested to 'presage famine' (i. ii. 50). The fitness of this 'fruitfulness' imagery in a play whose theme is one of vivid life and love may be seen from Agrippa's words on Cleopatra:

> Royal wench!
> She made great Caesar lay his sword to bed:
> He plough'd her, and she cropp'd.   (ii. ii. 231)

Such 'nature' as I have noted, earth's fecundity and
flowery delight, the swift forms of sea and air life, inter-
penetrates our theme of human splendour, human love.
The magnificence and glory of human love is set within a
picturesque and fruitful universe: it is all, like the fruitful
season 'between the extremes of hot and cold' a 'heavenly
mingle' (I. v. 59). Earth and sun are mated to produce
rich harvests, and this blends with the richer harvest of
our protagonists' love, and, finally, the mating of life and
death, where, in passion's ecstasy, the 'strength' of 'death'
is 'entangled' with the 'force' of life (IV. xiv. 48). I shall
now pass to the actual elements of water and air apart from
that life they breed.

There is a certain liquidity, a 'melting' and 'dissolving'
of element in element throughout the play. It is finely
apparent in the passage just quoted of the Nile basin, the
river ebbing to leave rich tracts of 'slime and ooze'. It is
one form of the mating-theme apparent throughout.
Another characteristic image occurs a little later, in
Antony's mock-description of the crocodile to satisfy the
drunken Lepidus:

> *Lepidus.* What manner o' thing is your crocodile?
> *Antony.* It is shaped, sir, like itself; and it is as broad as it hath
> breadth: it is just so high as it is, and moves with it own
> organs: it lives by that which nourisheth it; and the elements
> once out of it, it transmigrates.
> *Lepidus.* What colour is it of?
> *Antony.* Of it own colour too.
> *Lepidus.* 'Tis a strange serpent.
> *Antony.* 'Tis so. And the tears of it are wet. (II. vii. 46)

An amusing image: the 'strange' beast, creature of water
and land, pictorially dropping its liquid tears into the ooze
and slime of Nile. A typical suggestion of 'strange' life
and liquidity. Throughout we are reminded of 'strange'
life-forms. Antony is reported to have eaten 'strange
flesh which some did die to look on' (I. iv. 68): hence our
aerial and aquatic animals, creatures of element strange to
man, and the frequent serpents; serpents of all being the

most remote from human understanding, so vividly
peculiar and picturesquely dangerous that their very
strangeness and sinuous unreality strikes more fear than
the strength of lions.

Water-imagery occurs continually. We are often reminded of the Nile. We also continually meet the ideas
of 'sea' and 'land' in juxtaposition. I have already noticed
in some detail this wide 'sea' and 'land' suggestion and
the numerous nautical terms in reference to the empire-
theme. Such 'water', 'land', and 'ship' suggestion applies
equally to our analysis at this point. It is brought in
almost gratuitously in a dialogue between Enobarbus
and Menas:

Menas. . . . You and I have known, sir.
Enobarbus. At sea, I think.
Menas. We have, sir.
Enobarbus. You have done well by water.
Menas. And you by land.
Enobarbus. I will praise any man that will praise me; though it
    cannot be denied what I have done by land.
Menas. Nor what I have done by water.
Enobarbus. Yes, something you can deny for your own safety:
    you have been a great thief by sea.
Menas. And you by land.   (II. vi. 86)

The association and contrast of land and sea are emphatic.
There are many water-references. There is that curious
metaphor of 'the vagabond flag upon the stream lackeying the varying tide' (I. iv. 45): an image of stillness
within, or upon, motion—far different from the *Timon*-
stream which 'flies each bound it chafes'. We hear similarly of

                the swan's down-feather
    That stands upon the swell at full of tide,
    And neither way inclines.   (III. ii. 48)

Again, an image of a calm, full tide, a swelling flood, deeps
placid, falling and lifting in a soft undulation. Sea-
imagery here is not used tempestuously as so often in
Shakespeare: the sea is rather static, often the playground

of warring navies, navies that threaten 'most sea-like' (iii. xi. 171), but itself not hostile. Hence a ship here may be 'leaky' to suggest human tragedy (iii. xi. 63), but not, as in *Macbeth*, 'tempest-toss'd'. There is a certain stillness interpenetrating the drama's activity throughout: and water-imagery blends with this effect. It is as a still sheen of level quicksilver interlacing and interpenetrating earth's surface: ocean surrounding islands and touching coasts, rivers cutting the land. A fine nautical metaphor is applied to Antony:

> A rarer spirit never
> Did steer humanity.   (v. i. 31)

'Rare', blending with 'strange', is a typical word, applied also to Cleopatra (ii. ii. 210). There is a lovely description of Cleopatra's river-fishing at Alexandria where she awaits Antony's return:

> Give me mine angle; we'll to the river: there,
> My music playing far off, I will betray
> Tawny-finn'd fishes; my bended hook shall pierce
> Their slimy jaws; and, as I draw them up,
> I'll think them every one an Antony,
> And say, 'Ah, ha! you're caught'.   (ii. v. 10)[1]

There is the fine picture of Cleopatra in her barge (ii. ii) to which I return later: there again there is tranquillity, stillness.

Now the suggestion of 'water' juxtaposed with 'land' is important. The two are frequently associated and

---

[1] 'Fishing' may be a love-thought in Shakespeare. Compare *Much Ado*, iii. i. 26–8:

> The pleasant'st angling is to see the fish
> Cut with her golden oars the silver stream,
> And greedily devour the treacherous bait:
> So angle we for Beatrice.

In that scene the lyric note is emphasized by this image, the 'lapwing', and the 'pleached bower' with 'honeysuckles ripen'd by the sun'. Its nature-imagery is closely correspondent to that of *Antony and Cleopatra*. 'Bird' imagery is continually used in Shakespeare in association with love and thoughts of innocence. Thus Macduff's son will live 'as birds do' (*Macbeth* iv. ii. 32).

contrasted. 'Water' appears to suggest something more free and unfettered than earth's solidity: its presence is apt to this peculiar vision. Antony fights beside Cleopatra by sea, strongly as he is warned against it: it thus becomes almost a symbol of his love, opposing the solid prudence of his soldiership. The suggestion cannot be formalized, however: there is no allegory. Yet we might observe that it is further suggested by a soldier's speech to Antony:

> Let the Egyptians
> And the Phoenicians go a-ducking: we
> Have used to conquer, standing on the earth,
> And fighting foot to foot.   (III. vii. 64)

The sea is associated clearly with femininity, softness, and the East as opposed to manly strength. Shakespeare's love-imagery often takes him East. And his supreme love-vision takes here the form of West conflicting with East. But throughout we notice a certain diffusing of one element over the other, or interspacing it. We are reminded of the Mediterranean, its islands, the shore and its rivers gleaming through the land and flooding out their tenuous silver in the glistening expanse. Sometimes the two elements are imaged as at war, the finer one victorious: again, reflecting the vast theme of East and West, or Love and Empire, opposed:

> Let Rome in Tiber melt, and the wide arch
> Of the rang'd empire fall!

cries Antony (I. i. 33); and Cleopatra echoes the thought:

> Sink Rome, and their tongues rot
> That speak against us!   (III. vii. 16)

Cleopatra is fond of the image. She cries:

> Melt Egypt into Nile! and kindly creatures
> Turn all to serpents!   (II. v. 78)

and again:

> . . . O, I would thou didst,
> So half my Egypt were submerg'd and made
> A cistern for scal'd snakes!   (II. v. 93)

These 'melting' images obviously blend with the detailed description of the Nile in flood, the 'ooze and slime' of its bed. The 'melting' idea is frequent. I notice more uses of 'melt' later: the word occurs in two out of these four quotations, and the suggestion is present in all of them. Element 'melts' in element. Thus metal may 'melt' in fire: and Cleopatra uses the image when she threatens to 'melt' the gold she gave the messenger and pour it down his 'ill-uttering throat' (II. v. 34). Authority 'melts' from Antony (III. xi. 90). But more usually we have a blending of earth and water, or water and air. We hear of 'quick-sands'—again, as in our Nile descriptions, an image of earth melted into liquid:

> These quick-sands, Lepidus,
> Keep off them, for you sink.   (II. vii. 65)

The poet equally stresses the union of water and air. It is finely present in one very concrete image:

> Swallows have built
> In Cleopatra's sails their nests.   (IV. x. 16)

Or it may be presented in terms of weather, and I shall next notice this weather-suggestion: everywhere we should observe especially the idea of 'melting', 'dissolving'—it is a crucial theme in the play. For the blending of elements is similar to that blending of the sexes in love which is our main story: and from that we pass, even farther, to a blending of life and death. Often we find the word 'mingle', as well as 'melt'. Gray and brown 'mingle' in Antony's hair (IV. viii. 20); his disposition, 'nor sad nor merry', is a 'heavenly mingle' (I. v. 59); and Antony tells his followers to 'make mingle' with their 'rattling tabour-ines' (IV. viii. 37). The word can apply to love as well as music: Cleopatra 'loved' Antony and 'her fortunes mingled' with his 'entirely', even to death (IV. xii. 24). I have al-ready observed how earth and water, and elsewhere earth and sun, fecundate, in this play's imagery, the Nile basin, so that it brings forth crops and strange creatures. Now, in our weather-imagery, we shall again find a suggestion

of earth's fruitfulness very often: 'showers' or 'dew', for
instance, expressed as symbols of refreshing moisture.
But there is also reference to other elemental forms, hail,
snow, clouds, wind. All these are important, suggesting
both ethereality and a blending of element with element
to produce new beauty.

There is little violent storm-suggestion: *Antony and
Cleopatra* here diverges clearly from *Macbeth, Lear,* or *Julius
Caesar.* Air-imagery is here peaceful. Even Cleopatra's
passion, though its 'tempestuous' nature is once—and only
once—suggested, is yet also likened to gentle 'showers':

> *Antony.* She is cunning past man's thought.
> *Enobarbus.* Alack, sir, no; her passions are made of nothing
>> but the finest part of pure love: we cannot call her winds and
>> waters sighs and tears; they are greater storms and tempests
>> than almanacs can report: this cannot be cunning in her;
>> if it be, she makes a shower of rain as well as Jove.
>>
>> (I. ii. 155)

'Shower' is typical—again:

> *Caesar.* Farewell, my dearest sister, fare thee well:
>> The elements be kind to thee, and make
>> Thy spirits all of comfort! fare thee well.
> *Octavia.* My noble brother!
> *Antony.* The April's in her eyes: it is love's spring,
>> And these the showers to bring it on. Be cheerful.
>>
>> (III. ii. 39)

We have mention of varied elemental mixtures. We hear
of 'when snow the pasture sheets' (I. iv. 65). Here is a
delightful mingling of weather-imagery and gold-imagery:

> I'll set thee in a shower of gold, and hail
> Rich pearls upon thee.   (II. v. 45)

Julius Caesar 'bestowed his lips' on Cleopatra's hand 'as
it rain'd kisses' (III. xiii. 84). Cleopatra has a speech developing this theme more fully:

> *Antony.* Cold-hearted toward me?
> *Cleopatra.*   Ah, dear, if I be so,
>> From my cold heart let heaven engender hail,
>> And poison it in the source; and the first stone

> Drop in my neck: as it determines, so
> Dissolve my life! The next Caesarion smite!
> Till by degrees the memory of my womb,
> Together with my brave Egyptians all,
> By the discandying of this pelleted storm,
> Lie graveless, till the flies and gnats of Nile
> Have buried them for prey!   (III. xi. 158)

'Life' here is thought of as 'dissolving': a thought we shall meet again. So, too, the pelleted storm 'discandies', that is, melts or thaws. The word recurs elsewhere:

>   The hearts
> That spaniel'd me at heels, to whom I gave
> Their wishes, do discandy, melt their sweets
> On blossoming Caesar.   (IV. x. 33)

A beautiful image of dissolving rain on flowers. Notice again the frequent word 'melt'. There is another fine image of dew:

> I was of late as petty to his ends
> As is the morn-dew on the myrtle-leaf
> To his grand sea.   (III. x. 8)

These are images of water and air, the water forming or dissolving. There are also references to pure air, 'wind':

> Some o' their plants are ill-rooted already; the least wind i'
> the world will blow them down.   (II. vii. 1)

'The least wind i' the world': a pointed contrast to *Macbeth*. Enobarbus' reason 'sits in the wind' against him (III. viii. 45). Antony's affairs come to Caesar 'on the wind' (III. vi. 63). Cleopatra, at her death, is 'fire and air' (V. ii. 292), and almost her last words are:

> As sweet as balm, as soft as air, as gentle . . .   (V. ii. 314)

Her death is imaged as a dissolution, a melting from bodily existence into some more fiery and spiritual mode; and we remember her earlier cry—'dissolve my life' (III. xiii. 162). Hence, too, Charmian's choric utterance at Cleopatra's dying:

> Dissolve, thick cloud, and rain; that I may say,
> The gods themselves do weep!   (V. ii. 303)

The 'soft' and 'gentle' of Cleopatra's speech are typical words. Cleopatra wonders that Iras 'and nature can so gently part' in death. Antony's life with Cleopatra is 'soft': 'the beds i' the east are soft', says Antony (II. vi. 51). Antony and Cleopatra live 'for the love of Love and her soft hours' (I. i. 44). Wine 'steeps the sense in soft and delicate Lethe' (II. vii. 113). Death is here soft as 'a lover's bed' (IV. xii. 101), sweet as 'a lover's pinch' (V. ii. 298). Contrast these paradisal 'sleep' and 'bed' suggestions with the feverish nightmare sleep of *Macbeth*. Cleopatra's dying is a soft melting, a dissolving, a blending of essence with essence. Also at Antony's death Cleopatra cries: 'The crown o' the earth doth melt' (IV. xiii. 63). Hence, too, Antony's dialogue with Eros:

Antony. Eros, thou yet behold'st me?
Eros.   Ay, noble lord.
Antony. Sometime we see a cloud that 's dragonish;
   A vapour sometime like a bear or lion,
   A tower'd citadel, a pendent rock,
   A forked mountain, or blue promontory
   With trees upon 't, that nod unto the world,
   And mock our eyes with air: thou hast seen these signs;
   They are black vesper's pageants.
Eros.   Ay, my lord.
Antony. That which is now a horse, even with a thought
   The rack dislimns, and makes it indistinct,
   As water is in water.
Eros.   It does, my lord.
Antony. My good knave Eros, now thy captain is
   Even such a body: here I am Antony;
   Yet cannot hold this visible shape, my knave.   (IV. xii. 1)

Death is thus a change of mode, a melting, a dissolving and, perhaps, a reforming in some newer fashion of this 'visible shape': an indistinct union, as of 'water in water'. Enobarbus prays likewise that the moon may 'the poisonous damp of night dispunge' upon him (IV. ix. 13). We may observe how all our massed 'air' and 'water' imagery bears relevance to the death-theme in this vision. Death is a soft, changeful dissolution: like the crocodile, the elements once out, man 'transmigrates' (II. vii. 51). There is a unity-suggestion, quite different from the earlier dualism of life and death in *Hamlet* or *Timon*, where death was hideous or a 'nothing'. The positive element in Antony's death is repeated and further developed, in Cleopatra's: where, as I have noted, death is a casting-off of 'baser elements', an entry into modes 'as sweet as balm, as soft as air'.

We now ascend from water and air to air and fire. I shall next note the fire-imagery, which includes 'sun' and 'moon' references, and may also be related to that glittering brilliance of gold and other precious metals already noticed. In *Othello* and *Timon* this imagery replaces human love: the loved one lost, the hero's yearning cries to the heavenly lamps, to sun, moon, or star. *Lear*, earth-bound in its naturalism, shows no such vivid imagery: the 'travelling lamp' is strangled in *Macbeth*. Here heaven's fire drops benediction from its empyrean: love is blended with the universe. It is as though the great God absorbs human emotions as the sun drinks the sea, to shower them down afresh in newer life. In this happy vision all dark negations but serve to emphasize a positive brilliance: 'the spots of heaven, more fiery by night's blackness' (I. iv. 12). Already we have noticed the serpent bred 'by the operation of your sun' on Nile's mud (II. vii. 30). Sun and earth are finely mated in this passage: the whole theme of our play is a mating of element with element. There is a clinging mesh of cohering elements, blended in love, to frame our picture of man blending with woman in love, of life dissolved in the other element of death. The mating of sun and Nile is here important. The sun-lover woos Cleopatra herself: she is 'with Phoebus' amorous pinches black' (I. v. 28); a phrase recalling that wherein 'the stroke of death' is 'as a lover's pinch'—a passionate mating of life with death, life surrendered to death's mastering passion (v. ii. 298); so, too, Antony runs to death 'as to a lover's bed' (IV. xii. 101). But there are other passages, where such images are contrasted

with love. 'Moon and stars!' cries Antony, when he
finds Cleopatra false (III. xi. 95). He will 'lodge Lichas
on the horns o' the moon' (IV. x. 58). Enobarbus recognizes his iniquitous fall from loyalty's faith. The night is
'shiny': in bitterness of his own love's failure, like
Othello, he cries out to the moon, heaven's bending eye
whose lovelight keeps eternal faith with earth:

> Be witness to me, O thou blessed moon,
> When men revolted shall upon record
> Bear hateful memory, poor Enobarbus did
> Before thy face repent!   (IV. ix. 7)

Antony, knowing he must shortly die, speaks farewell to
the sun:

> O sun, thy uprise shall I see no more:
> Fortune and Antony part here; even here
> Do we shake hands.   (IV. x. 31)

In these, whatever direct relation they bear to the theme
of prosperous love is one of contrast: man, in his tragic
pain, cries out to sun or moon, who know no failure, whose
station is firm based and faith unfaltering; like Keats's
'Bright Star', whose steadfast gaze bends unwavering its
frosty beam on phosphor sea or snow-masked earth, till
darkness itself becomes but an element of light. Elsewhere sun, moon, or star are themselves but love-symbols:
they burn or fade as love's torch flickers uncertain. Stars
are the vestal priestesses to idealized humanity:

> Let all the number of the stars give light
> To thy fair way!   (III. ii. 65)

Then the universe itself depends for its life and light on
love's victorious integrity. Cleopatra is faithless: therefore,

> . . . my good stars, that were my former guides,
> Have empty left their orbs, and shot their fires
> Into the abysm of hell.   (III. xi. 145)

Again, referring to Cleopatra's treachery:

> Alack, our terrene moon
> Is now eclips'd; and it portends alone
> The fall of Antony!   (III. xi. 153)

9

Cleopatra is 'thou day o' the world' (iv. viii. 13). As
Antony is brought dying to Cleopatra, she cries:

> O sun,
> Burn the great sphere thou movest in! darkling stand
> The varying shore o' the world.   (iv. xiii. 9)

Now love is itself the sun and moon and stars; itself the
universe. Cleopatra's death is to Antony as a light
extinguished:

> Since the torch is out,
> Lie down, and stray no farther.   (iv. xii. 46)

So is his death to her:

> Ah, women, women, look,
> Our lamp is spent, it's out!   (iv. xiii. 84)

Now

> there is nothing left remarkable
> Beneath the visiting moon.   (iv. xiii. 67)

The world is unlighted, a barren promontory, without
love: or, if lit at all, then by a wan moon, bending its idle
gaze on profitless things. So 'the bright day is done',
and Cleopatra and her girls are 'for the dark' (v. ii. 193);
Cleopatra is now more constant than 'the fleeting moon'
(v. ii. 240). 'O eastern star', cries Charmian at her
death (v. ii. 310), and

> . . . golden Phoebus, never be beheld
> Of eyes again so royal!   (v. ii. 320)

At Antony's death, 'the star is fall'n' and 'time is at his
period'(iv. xii. 106). This 'sun', 'moon', and 'star' imagery
elevates the love-theme to universal stature: it lights the
whole play with a glitter and a brilliance, merging with
the gold-imagery and the watery sheen already observed,
so that the vision is seen as through a dropping shower of
fire; and it adds the fourth empyreal element to our
ascending scale—earth, water, air.

There is, however, darkness in the play: darkness by which
these lights are the richer, a soft velvet darkness, from which
the lamps of heaven burn brilliant, 'the spots of heaven more
fiery by night's blackness' (i. iv. 12). Or again, a darkness lit

byrevelryandfeast. 'Wemadethenightlightwithdrinking'
(II. ii. 182) says Enobarbus, and, at the end, Antony
would 'have one other gaudy night' (III. xi. 183). He
would 'burn this night with torches' (IV. ii. 41). Nights
here are rich, gaudy, with an Orient fire beautiful as day.
The lovers wander through the streets of Alexandria by
night (I. i. 53). Fire is also to be related, as in *Julius
Caesar*, to man's 'spirit'. Spirit is fiery. This fire-imagery
is one with that erotic brilliance and spiritual fire of love
which 'gilds' Antony's messenger 'with his tinct' (I. v. 37).
All 'spirit' and all fine ardour are instinct with 'fire'.
Octavia's sighs will 'blow the fire up in Caesar'(II.vi.135).
Lepidus entreats Enobarbus to let his speech 'stir no
embers up' (II. ii. 13). 'I will show the cinders of my
spirit', says Cleopatra, 'through the ashes of my chance'
(v. ii. 173). At his death Antony's body is a case, 'cold', reft
of his 'huge spirit' (IV. xiii. 89). Spirit is fire, and love in
Shakespeare 'a spirit all compact of fire' (*Venus and
Adonis*, 149). Therefore, dying into love, crowned with
its aureole blaze, Cleopatra knows:

> I am fire and air; my other elements
> I give to baser life.   (v. ii. 292)

Our spiralling and visionary ascent demands no paltry
earth alone, no limited naturalism, but rather a universal
stage. Such images are recurrent:

> To be called into a huge sphere, and not to be seen to move
> in 't, are the holes where eyes should be, which pitifully
> disaster the cheeks.   (II. vii. 16)

The wide universe is our stage, all elements our actors.
'The elements be kind to thee' (III. ii. 40) prays Caesar.
The quadruple elemental system is stressed here:

Antony. Their preparation is to-day by sea;
  We please them not by land.
Scarus.   For both, my lord.
Antony. I would they 'ld fight i' the fire or i' the air;
  We 'ld fight there too.   (IV. x. 1)

Yet higher, beyond all material and visual symbols, like the lark's ascending flight, ever higher, to blend his song with the sun's blaze of fire, we leave the 'elements' and notice, finally, our highest love-accompaniment: music.

V

I now return more directly to our theme of human love. Music is ever 'the food of love' and its accompaniment (*Twelfth Night*, I. i. 1) in Shakespeare, as light is its visual symbol.[1] Starting from empire-imagery, feasts, and physical love; next passing to nature, to the 'water' and 'cloud' suggestion and thoughts of earth's bounteous harvest, the ethereal nature-magic of volatile or shimmering sea life; we now pass beyond all material and visual symbols, and, leaving those elements, earth, water, air and fire, approach the higher aether and more vivid incandescence of human art. Music sounds often in the play. At the start of the banquet on Pompey's galley, 'music plays' (II. vii). It recurs again for the Bacchic song:

Enobarbus.   All take hands.
  Make battery to our ears with the loud music.

(II. vii. 114)

'Trumpets' and 'flutes' bid 'a loud farewell' to Neptune at the end (II. vii. 138). Here, as often, the action takes place at night: but it is a 'gaudy night' (III. xi. 182). This is riotous music, a clash and blare of sensuous enjoyment. So, too, is that which Antony calls for later to celebrate his victorious entry into Alexandria:

Trumpeters,

  With brazen din blast you the city's ear;
  Make mingle with our rattling tabourines;
  That heaven and earth may strike their sounds together,
  Applauding our approach.   (IV. viii. 35)

[1] Miss Spurgeon has observed numerous 'light' effects in *Romeo and Juliet*. This has been a help to me. Compare my reference to 'lightning' as a love-symbol in a letter to *The Times Literary Supplement*, ' Shakespeare and Bergson', 17 Jan. 1929. See p. 332.

But there is other music: more soft, more finely tuned to the highest vision which this play discloses from beyond its melting clouds. Cleopatra, like Orsino, assuages her love-loneliness with music. Mardian 'sings' to her (I. v. 9). Again:

Cleopatra. Give me some music; music, moody food
Of us that trade in love.
Attendant.   The music, ho!   (II. v. 1)

Cleopatra describes how she will fish, her 'music playing far off' (II. v. 11). So, too, in Enobarbus' description of Cleopatra in her barge, which I notice in detail later, we hear that 'flutes' sounded to the strokes of the oars (II. ii. 200). Finally, there is the fine symbolic effect where mysterious music from beneath 'the earth' or 'i' the air' sounds an ethereal prelude to the final love-sacrifice; our protagonists' fall, or rise, from earthly splendour, their ascent to love's empyrean. The stage direction is: 'Music of the hautboys as under the stage'.

Fourth Soldier. Peace! what noise?
First Soldier.   List, list!
Second Soldier. Hark!
First Soldier.   Music i' the air.
Third Soldier.   Under the earth.
Fourth Soldier. It signs well, does it not?
Third Soldier.   No.
First Soldier.   Peace, I say!
    What should this mean?
Second Soldier. 'Tis the god Hercules, whom Antony lov'd,
    Now leaves him.
First Soldier. Walk; let 's see if other watchmen
    Do hear what we do.   (IV. iii. 12)

Even earth vibrates in this transcendent play, its myriad whirling atoms alive, burning, dancing, quiring the immortal theme. The world glows with love's fire. Here the disparity between matter and spirit, the human and divine, is always mingled, blended, melted into unity: so the little earth itself 'makes mingle' (IV. viii. 37) with its orchestra of elements, responds in magic harmony to that spheral music wherein a human death and life and love strike together one single chord in the melodic silences of the Divine.

The wide magnificence and suffusing and spirited glory that this play bodies forth are as laurel-leaves to cluster the brows of our human protagonists: a divine humanism is here. Our main persons are often compared to gods and heroes. Scarus fights 'as if a god, in hate of mankind, had destroy'd in such a shape' (iv. viii. 25); he deserves his gold armour 'were it carbuncled like holy Phoebus' car' (iv. viii. 28). Antony's soldiers have shown 'all Hectors' (iv. viii. 7). Caesar is 'a god' (iii. xi. 60), and Pompey nearly becomes one:

> Thou art, if thou darest be, the earthly Jove:
> Whate'er the ocean pales or sky inclips,
> Is thine, if thou wilt ha 't. (ii. vii. 73)

Most such comparisons are used to engild Antony. He cries to Alcides, his 'ancestor' (iv. x. 57); he compares his armour to the 'seven-fold shield of Ajax' (iv. xii. 38). We hear that he 'loved' the god Hercules (iv. iii. 16). Our human-divine association is necessarily to be related to love. We are told that Lepidus 'loves Caesar' and 'adores Mark Antony' (iii. ii. 7–8): and they are accordingly the 'Jupiter of men' and 'the god of Jupiter' (iii. ii. 9–10). Antony is 'the demi-Atlas of this earth' (i. v. 23), he 'continues still a Jove' (iv. vi. 29), he is entreated to 'look over Caesar's head and speak as loud as Mars' (ii. ii. 5); 'his goodly eyes have glowed like plated Mars' (i. i. 4); though 'he be painted one way like a Gorgon' to Cleopatra, yet 'the other way's a Mars' (ii. v. 116). 'The worship of the whole world' lies in Antony's 'countenance' (iv. xii. 86). Here even a servant is associated with 'Narcissus' (ii. v. 96). The 'god' or 'hero' association is continual. Cleopatra lifts up the dying Antony:

> . . . had I great Juno's power,
> The strong-wing'd Mercury should fetch thee up,
> And set thee by Jove's side. (iv. xiii. 34)

Mankind is endued with supernatural glory. Cleopatra is credited with supernatural power, too—sometimes in an evil sense. In her 'witchcraft joins with beauty' (II. i. 22) —she fascinates mysteriously though her lip is 'waned' by years. Her age is again suggested: she is 'with Phoebus' amorous pinches black, and wrinkled deep in time' (I. v. 28). In spite of that, she holds Antony and others. She is his 'charm' (IV. x. 29 and 38); she is a 'witch' (IV. x. 60), a 'spell' (IV. x. 43), a 'great fairy' (IV. viii. 12). She is 'my Thetis' (III. vii. 61), she makes a shower 'as well as Jove' (I. ii. 161). Her mysterious magic and fascination are suggested and emphasized: so, too, is her regal dignity. Though the 'witch' references alone might detract something from her human splendour, yet her royalty is strong. She is 'Sovereign of Egypt' (I. v. 34); 'Royal Egypt, Empress' (IV. xiii. 70); 'most noble Empress' (V. ii. 71). She would 'rail so high' as to make Fortune 'break her wheel' (IV. xiii. 43), she would 'throw her sceptre at the injurious gods' (IV. xiii. 75). Her death is

> fitting for a princess
> Descended of so many royal kings. (V. ii. 329)

'Being royal', says Caesar, she 'took her own way' (V. ii. 339). Her 'majesty' is stressed by Charmian (III. iii. 46), and Alexas:

> Good majesty,
> Herod of Jewry dare not look upon you
> But when you are well pleas'd. (III. iii. 2)

Cleopatra's personality radiates royalty and magic; Antony's, warriorship and Herculean heroism. The value of these suggestions is most evident in a fine passage remarkably enclosing Antony and Cleopatra, emperor and empress of an Oriental kingdom of love, in an imaginative setting, opulent, regal, divine:

> *Caesar.* Contemning Rome, he has done all this, and more,
> In Alexandria: here 's the manner of 't:
> I' the market-place, on a tribunal silver'd,
> Cleopatra and himself in chairs of gold

> Were publicly enthron'd: at the feet sat
> Caesarion, whom they call my father's son,
> And all the unlawful issue that their lust
> Since then hath made between them. Unto her
> He gave the stablishment of Egypt; made her
> Of lower Syria, Cyprus, Lydia,
> Absolute queen.
> *Maecenas.*   This in the public eye?
> *Caesar.* I' the common show-place, where they exercise.
> His sons he there proclaimed the kings of kings:
> Great Media, Parthia, and Armenia,
> He gave to Alexander; to Ptolemy he assign'd
> Syria, Cilicia, and Phoenicia: she
> In the habiliments of the goddess Isis
> That day appear'd; and oft before gave audience,
> As 'tis reported, so.   (III. vi. 1)

Notice the life-theme of birth (cp. III. xi. 162–3), heavily exaggerated, like feasting and all our other effects: the natural is expanded to its farthest limits and beyond, to infinity itself. The exaggeration here is the measure of its implicit artistic importance: we have our vision continually thus directed to some strange transfiguration of man. There is lust and showiness in this picture: but they are overweighted by love's resplendence, love's fruitfulness. So, throughout the play, far-flung kingdoms, gold and silver, power and pomp and vainglory, all are but too unworthy caparisons to a love more strangely gold, which encompasses not alone earth's tinsel royalties; to which death is but a purifying flame; and which, Phoenix-like, can rise with pinions that outsoar the empyrean. To that imperial theme our imperial magnificence directs our gaze. Antony and Cleopatra are here symbolically enthroned in love's regality: which blending of earthly and spiritual royalty, of West and East, of empire and love, is throughout the core and heart of our vision. The protagonists change a crown of gold for the more sparkling and ethereal diadem of love.

'Crown' references are very widely scattered. The word is beating in the poet's mind: for humanity is

everywhere crowned as with an aureole blaze. 'Garlands'
are mentioned by Charmian jesting (i. ii. 6). Grief is
'crowned' with consolation (i. ii. 179); the messenger whose
news breaks the heart of love should come 'like a Fury
crown'd with snakes' (ii. v. 40). There is that line in the
Bacchic song—'with thy grapes our hairs be crown'd' (ii.
vii. 123); we hear of 'laurel' victory (i. iii. 100) and the
'myrtle-leaf' (iii. x. 9), phrases which suggest such
crowns as Antony, lord of victory, dispenses to his officers:

> So thy grand captain Antony
> Shall set thee on triumphant chariots and
> Put garlands on thy head.   (iii. i. 9)

So, too, Antony 'crowns' Enobarbus' 'turpitude' with gold
(iv. vi. 34). The bosom of love is his 'crownet', his 'chief end'
(iv. x. 40). He is himself the crowning glory of creation,
'the crown o' the earth' (iv. xiii. 63). Cleopatra, in her
apostasy from love, once offered to lay her 'crown' at
Caesar's feet (iii. xi. 76). But at her death, she is 'again
for Cydnus' (v. ii. 228) to meet her Antony, and so Charmian must 'bring our crown and all' (v. ii. 232). Here life
is crowned with immortality:

> Give me my robe, put on my crown; I have
> Immortal longings in me.   (v. ii. 282)

Therefore in death Charmian knows that that crown must
be inviolate, meticulously exact on the still brow pale with
eternity: Your crown 's awry;
> I'll mend it, and then play.   (v. ii. 321)

'I found her', says the guard of Charmian, 'trimming up
the diadem' (v. ii. 345): the diadem of love, and Crown of
Life.

Humanity is in truth 'crowned' here by potency of
love's vision transfiguring mortality. Man's lineaments
are lit divine, and 'death' itself proud to take such persons
(iv. xiii. 88). So earth and its empires are but toys in
comparison with love's infinity:

> . . . Here is my space.
> Kingdoms are clay: our dungy earth alike

> Feeds beast as man: the nobleness of life
> Is to do thus; when such a mutual pair
> And such a twain can do 't, in which I bind
> On pain of punishment, the world to weet
> We stand up peerless.   (I. i. 34)

Earth, in this diaphanous vision whereby life-forms are dissolved into love-forms new and strange, is but 'dungy'; imperial splendour but 'clay'. So, at the end, Cleopatra refers to that 'thing' which appears to be our life's negation, that 'thing' (v. ii. 5) termed 'death', and says that it 'never palates more the dung'[1] (v. ii. 7): the dung of the kingdoms of the earth, of temporal existence, fertilizing the rich arable lands of the infinite, and its harvest fruits of love. The world is well lost for love. Without love it is futile, unclean, a 'sty':

> Noblest of men, woo 't die?
> Hast thou no care of me? Shall I abide
> In this dull world, which in thy absence is
> No better than a sty?   (IV. xiii. 59)

Thus Iras' gentle death tells the world 'it is not worth leave-taking' (v. ii. 301). The world is nothing unless translineated by love's eyes, engilded by its fire. Then it was truly divine:

> It were for me
> To throw my sceptre at the injurious gods;
> To tell them that this world did equal theirs
> Till they had stol'n our jewel.   (IV. xiii. 74)

---

[1] If we follow the Folio reading. There can be no certainty. I defended the emendation 'dug' in a letter to *The Times Literary Supplement*, 23 Dec. 1926. We might compare *2 Henry VI*, III. ii. 388:

> If I depart from thee, I cannot live;
> And in thy sight to die, what were it else
> But like a pleasant slumber in thy lap?
> Here could I breathe my soul into the air,
> As mild and gentle as the cradle-babe,
> Dying with mother's dug between its lips.

The 'baby' is frequent as suggesting peace of consciousness or community, often associated directly with love. See *Richard II*, I. iii. 132–3; *Troilus*, I. i. 12; III. ii. 176–7; IV. ii. 4–6; *Venus and Adonis*, 974; *Titus Andronicus*, II. iii. 25–9.

Such love, whose light plays on earthly contours, is itself infinite, unbounded by those limits:

Cleopatra. If it be love indeed, tell me how much.
Antony. There's beggary in the love that can be reckon'd.
Cleopatra. I'll set a bourn how far to be belov'd.
Antony. Then must thou needs find out new heaven, new earth.
(I. i. 14)

Antony is 'infinite virtue' (IV. viii. 17); Cleopatra, 'infinite variety' (II. ii. 241). The swift glamour and integrity of love has brought to blossom in this 'dungy' world a flower all petalled in fire, born of time's earth, yet lifting its bright fruitage to the airs of eternity:

Eternity was in our lips and eyes,
Bliss in our brows' bent; none our parts so poor,
But was a race of heaven. (I. iii. 35)

'A race of heaven': such is our transcendent humanism. Love has properties of eternal worth: Cleopatra, Queen of Love, would be 'eternal' in Caesar's triumph (V. i. 66). This blending of the finite and the infinite forbids any limited naturalism, such as we find in *Lear*. That vision stands to this exactly as the ordinary human contemplation of humanity stands to that incandescent radiance and electric vitality exposed and released when love unfurls its multifoliate star. Therefore here 'nature' embraces not earth and tempest, as in *Lear*, but rather earth, water, air, and fire: it is the universal, not the earthly, nature—hence our creatures of translucent water and diaphanous air, images of melting cloud and heaven's fire.

Earthly 'nature' here is often subsidiary to man: 'the trees by the way should have borne men' to welcome Octavia's approach (III. vi. 46). Many of our fruit-references are picturesque with human association: the laurel, myrtle, grape, olive, rose: so, too, our animal-imagery blends with life-forms coloured by mythology: the Arabian bird, the dolphin, mermaids. 'Nature', in its limited sense 'earth-nature,' has no autonomous rights here, except to heighten our sense of the universal marriage of

element with element. It is one square on the chess-board
of the infinite, and that is mysterious, a thing far beyond
man's intellect. The smaller 'nature' is thus either
romantically picturesque or quite civilized—even the
cloud-forms limn sky-pictures of 'dragons' or 'towered
citadels': and earth itself dissolves in music, a string
vibrating to the wide sweep of love. 'Nature' is infinite
and mysterious. All here is tinged with strangeness: the
crocodile is 'a strange serpent', says Lepidus, after drinking
in Antony's keen analysis, a model of lucid scientific
research, from that knowledge of nature's infinity which
mocks the little systems of our varying science:

> It is shaped, sir, like itself; and it is as broad as it hath breadth...
>
> (II. vii. 47)

A standing model for the metaphysician. The unique
reality cannot be transliterated by intellect: and every
scientist who departs one jot from Antony's biology steps
into necessary error. The universe is infinitely and
beautifully mysterious. The soothsayer knows it:

> In nature's infinite book of secrecy
> A little I can read. (I. ii. 9)

This is not the *Lear*-nature: but a wider, more universal
nature. So here love itself is a mystery, that words cannot
enclose:

> Sir, you and I must part, but that 's not it:
> Sir, you and I have lov'd, but there 's not it;
> That you know well: something it is I would,—
> O, my oblivion is a very Antony,
> And I am all forgotten. (I. iii. 87)

Prophecies are rightly enough interwoven in this vision,
'natural' laws being here only surface deep, mysteries
hidden within. And they are not, as in *Macbeth*, half-
right. half-wrong: they are true forecasts, as far as they go,
of material events. This applies to both the Soothsayers,
who prophesy respectively to Cleopatra's girls (I. ii) and
Antony (II. iii).

But no temporal events are here of primary importance, except as symbols of a deeper significance than surface failure or success. Mgr. Kolbe has noticed that 'fortune' is a recurrent word. That is valuable: but it only indirectly points us to the central idea of our vision. I cannot agree with Mgr. Kolbe's deductions. The play shows us more than 'a great gamble'. Caesar's 'fortune' is often mentioned: that is, temporal fortune. Antony says Caesar beats him at games of chance (II. iii. 32–8); his personality crushes Antony's in any temporal engagement. But all such success is clearly here quite secondary. 'The false housewife, fortune' (IV. xiii. 44) is, merely, but a trivial, untrustworthy goddess. At the end Caesar is not 'Fortune', only 'Fortune's knave' (V. ii. 3): death 'shackles accidents and bolts up change' (V. ii. 6); time is dissolved, and eternity's star burns solitary-bright in the dark. We watch, at the close, no temporal sequence, but rather the shadows cast in time by the progress of purposes infinite and eternal: which eternal significance makes the battling of empires but a child's game in comparison.

This is why great matters appear so lightly handled, almost as a game. Humour is throughout inwoven here, whether it be Cleopatra's 'riggishness' (II. ii. 245), hopping 'forty paces through the public street' (II. ii. 234), or her playing of tricks on Antony:

Charmian.   'Twas merry when
    You wager'd on your angling; when your diver
    Did hang a salt-fish on his hook, which he
    With fervency drew up.
Cleopatra.   That time—O times!—
    I laugh'd him out of patience; and that night
    I laugh'd him into patience: and next morn,
    Ere the ninth hour, I drunk him to his bed;
    Then put my tires and mantles on him, whilst
    I wore his sword Philippan.   (II. v. 15)

The words 'merry' (I. v. 52) and 'mirth' (I. iii. 4) are apt here. Antony gives a kingdom for a 'mirth' (I. iv. 18).

Lepidus is a continual theme of mirth, whether in the banquet scene, or later, when his eulogies of Antony and Caesar are mocked in III. iii. 'What sport to-night?' cries Antony (I. i. 47). War 'drums' Antony from his 'sport' (I. iv. 29): sportiveness is often present. Antony is a merry lover, 'disposed to mirth' (I. ii. 90). Scarus, during the battle, cries:

> Let us score their backs,
> And snatch 'em up, as we take hares, behind:
> 'Tis sport to maul a runner. (IV. vii. 12)

'Here's sport indeed', says Cleopatra, lifting up the wounded Antony (IV. xiii. 32). Games and 'sports' (II. iii. 34) are mentioned: cards (IV. xii. 19), cock-fighting (II. iii. 36), quails (II. iii. 37), dice (II. iii. 33)—the last three in Antony's speech about Caesar's superiority in fortune; fishing (II. v. 10–18), and billiards (II. v. 3). At the end Cleopatra gives Charmian leave to 'play till doomsday' (v. ii. 232), and Charmian repeats the phrase after Cleopatra's death:

> Your crown's awry;
> I'll mend it, and then play. (v. ii. 321)

Antony and Cleopatra are both essentially sportive. There is, indeed, sometimes a delicate, sometimes a boisterous humour running throughout. The spirit of the romantic comedies is here blended with tragedy. A certain sportive spirit stirs the play's surface into ripples of shimmering laughter. The worst vices are but boyish 'sports': tragedy is a game. Life is all 'chance and hazard' (III. vii. 48) and men 'laugh away their fortunes' (II. vi. 109). Again, we touch that peculiar quality, whereby the elements of this drama are transformed by a clear yet altering medium, a vision which sees its subject all levelled under a strange optimism, in which Antony's sensuousness is pure as a boy's pranks, the tragic agony of Cleopatra cleansed by girlish merriment.

VI

I have analysed certain varied skeins from the more colourous silks in our pattern, unthreading and re-weaving them, making a design at once simpler to understand and yet far more frayed, inexact, and untidy than the original. But such analysis is necessary. We cannot regard the purely human and narrative element as all-important, with our imaginative design as a pleasant but inessential subsidiary vaguely realized in twilight consciousness; least of all in this sun-smitten peak of Shakespeare's art. Such visionary imaginations far outweigh the minor stressing of Antony's shame or disgrace. For all these effects bear direct relevance to the protagonists: they ever force us to fix our attention, to direct our emotions, to certain qualities, and to refuse any but minor recognition of incompatible suggestions. To read the play as an indictment of reckless love, for instance, is to see one corner foundation—no more—of its structure. The massed structure which is the whole play, though firmly resting on certain moral laws—and these are duly noticed for us, such as Antony's necessary failure in practical affairs, his necessary disgrace in the eyes of men, whilst spelled by Cleopatra's fascination—makes a single, far more profound, statement, reveals a single and happier vision. To refuse this integrity of the poet's statement is to miss its more important and profound meanings. Without shirking any ugly facts or colourings of 'realism' the poet expresses the finest delights of his vision. Within this whole vision the dualisms so starkly divergent in the sombre plays are all resolved, dissolved, melted into a sublime unity. We must be prepared to see all elements herein of sordidness resolved in a total beauty. And not till we see the play as a whole do we recognize the significance of its parts. The whole structure is like a wide window: look at it obtusely—from the strictly ethical and didactic view—and you see little beyond it; draw nearer to the centre, view it as a vivid human tragedy, and you see much more, though not all; but once take your stand directly opposite, attend simultaneously to its imaginative and narrative qualities, and you stare full in the face of the sun-kissed expanse outside: its rich plains, its shadowed chasms, and glistening mountain peaks.

To conclude, I quote two passages which finely illustrate this welding of imaginative 'atmosphere' with the individual protagonist: though, of course, there is really no 'welding' except to intellectual analysis, since the two are not originally distinct. The word serves merely as a metaphor, to suggest rather our own, not the poet's, unification, to close the hiatus caused by the abstracting intellect in its work upon the artistic unit. In these my final quotations those effects which I have analysed are twice compacted finely in a single visionary unit. First there is Enobarbus' description of Cleopatra's meeting with Antony:

> *Enobarbus.* I will tell you.
> The barge she sat in, like a burnish'd throne,
> Burn'd on the water: the poop was beaten gold;
> Purple the sails, and so perfumed that
> The winds were love-sick with them; the oars were silver,
> Which to the tune of flutes kept stroke, and made
> The water which they beat to follow faster,
> As amorous of their strokes. For her own person,
> It beggar'd all description: she did lie
> In her pavilion—cloth-of-gold of tissue—
> O'er-picturing that Venus where we see
> The fancy outwork nature: on each side her
> Stood pretty dimpled boys, like smiling Cupids,
> With divers-colour'd fans, whose wind did seem
> To glow the delicate cheeks which they did cool,
> And what they undid did.
> *Agrippa.*   O, rare for Antony!
> *Enobarbus.* Her gentlewomen, like the Nereides,
> So many mermaids, tended her i' the eyes,
> And made their bends adornings: at the helm
> A seeming mermaid steers: the silken tackle
> Swell with the touches of those flower-soft hands,

That yarely frame the office. From the barge
A strange invisible perfume hits the sense
Of the adjacent wharfs. The city cast
Her people out upon her; and Antony,
Enthron'd i' the market-place, did sit alone,
Whistling to the air; which, but for vacancy,
Had gone to gaze on Cleopatra too
And made a gap in nature.   (II. ii. 195)

Here is a microcosm of the play's peculiar vision, crystal
clear. Nearly all the veins of imagery I have noticed recur.
We have a sensuous languor and beauty, a richness and
splendour, fabric of purple and gold, 'silken tackle',
'divers-colour'd fans', metals gold and silver; an emphasis
on human features, 'dimpled boys', 'flower-soft hands'—
again reference to flowers and the idea of 'softness'—the
'delicate cheeks' of Cleopatra; the emphasis on ships, and
water, and nautical terms—the poop, sails, tackle, oars,
wharfs; the still, lake-like surface reflecting the barge,
whose gold thus melts into the liquid deeps, still water,
its further blue just stirred into silver by the feathering
strokes of silver oars; the 'air' and 'wind' suggestion, the
'love-sick' winds, the 'sense' hit by 'a strange invisible perfume'—again 'strange'; and Antony, enthroned, 'whistling
to the air'; the thought of 'nature' transcended, or nature
thrall to love—the very winds, usually in Shakespeare
things of senseless cruelty, enemies of love, are 'love-sick',
the water 'amorous', the air 'but for vacancy' had made a
gap in 'nature' to gaze on Cleopatra. Nature transcended
we noticed in the play merging into human art, 'music':
here Cleopatra is like a work of art where 'fancy' outworks
'nature'. In that higher vision, known in love or art, she
is beyond 'nature', a goddess, a Venus; again the divine
association—so, also, her handmaids surpass humanity,
spirits of water-element, 'Nereides', 'mermaids'; her boys
are 'Cupids'. Finally, there is again music, 'the tune ôf
flutes'. There is motion in this description; but, as in a
picture, it is a motion within stillness. There is mystery
and something beyond 'nature'; yet it is crystal clear. Like

our whole vision, it is set in a limpid, translucent medium, like strange and lovely flowerings seen swaying lazily through solid, transparent deeps of water.

The other passage gives us Cleopatra's dream-vision of Antony. Again, our recurrent themes of imagery blend in an exquisite poetic unit. She speaks as in a trance, unheeding:

Cleopatra. I dream'd there was an Emperor Antony:
  O, such another sleep, that I might see
  But such another man!
Dolabella.   If it might please ye,—
Cleopatra. His face was as the heavens; and therein stuck
  A sun and moon, which kept their course, and lighted
  The little O, the earth.
Dolabella.   Most sovereign creature,—
Cleopatra. His legs bestrid the ocean: his rear'd arm
  Crested the world: his voice was propertied
  As all the tuned spheres, and that to friends;
  But when he meant to quail and shake the orb,
  He was as rattling thunder. For his bounty,
  There was no winter in 't; an autumn[1] 'twas
  That grew the more by reaping: his delights
  Were dolphin-like; they show'd his back above
  The element they liv'd in: in his livery
  Walk'd crowns and crownets; realms and islands were
  As plates dropp'd from his pocket.
Dolabella.   Cleopatra!
Cleopatra. Think you there was, or might be, such a man
  As this I dream'd of?
Dolabella.   Gentle madam, no.
Cleopatra. You lie, up to the hearing of the gods.
  But, if there be, or ever were, one such,
  It 's past the size of dreaming: nature wants stuff
  To vie strange forms with fancy; yet, to imagine
  An Antony, were nature's piece 'gainst fancy,
  Condemning shadows quite.   (v. ii. 76)

---

[1] The Folio reading is not 'autumn' but 'Anthony'. There seems no reason for the alteration. 'Autumn' is, of course, implied. I have seen it observed that 'Anthony' is related to the Greek ἄνθος, a flower. See Hudson's edition of the play, p. 221.

In *Othello* and *Timon* a vast universal symbolism replaced the lost human love: here the human love and the wide symbolism, which throughout the play were interlaced in the clinging mesh of our pattern, are now blended to the last, inseparate, unified. Antony is 'dead'. But Cleopatra dreams yet an Antony himself a universe, a universe itself an Antony. Love has transcended human limits, its fire lit man with such emblazonry that sun and moon and earth are but elements of his glory: or, conversely, the wide universe becomes personal, a lover. Man is divine. His countenance is as the wide face of heaven afire with sun and moon, and this earth but a pin-point to the embracing stature of man transformed. Here again we have an emphasis on physique: Antony's 'face', 'legs', 'arm'. In *Lear*, earth-limited, our world was conceived as 'great' and man honoured by the comparison:

> O ruin'd piece of nature! This great world
> Shall so wear out to nought.   (*Lear*, IV. vi. 137)

But here, where the human spirit stands colossal, the ocean is but a 'gilded puddle' (I. iv. 62) to his dwarfing height, the earth, a little 'O', crested by his arching arm. Thus our 'earth' and 'sea' and 'universe' imagery are at last knit close in the person of Antony, cohering to make out of our other myriad atoms of poetry a new Antony replacing, yet one with, that Antony lost: so they cling together, crystallize into this angel-personification of her dream. Now again we have 'music', before love's solace and companion, this time the music only of love's voice itself, chorister in the quiring voices of the universe, propertied 'as all the tuned spheres'. But his wrath shook the 'orb' with its thunder—yet his heart was ever bounteous as earth's teeming womb at autumn: again, earth's rich foison, and the fruitful season, 'autumn', and 'reaping'; again the nature-reference but an image to limn the bright bounty and generosity of our Antony. Here again we find the 'element' of water, and water-life, the dolphin whose sportive rise and fall within and over the foam images the amplitude and freedom enjoyed by Antony in 'sport': Antony whose joys played in two elements, the waters of sense and the airs of spiritual delight, so that he rose above the lower element, even when pleasure ran most riotous. This Antony was king of kings, 'crowns and crownets' but his retinue—again 'crowns'; 'realms and islands'—again the stress on the dotted Mediterranean, the wide empire-imagery—were but rich plate—again 'gold'—he scorned, metallic, 'dropped from his pocket', heedlessly, when he bartered an empire for a gipsy's love. What was this Antony? Did he, does he, exist? Is this 'nature' or does Cleopatra dream a god? Yet she has but described the Antony the play as a whole has been directing us, forcing us, to see. But dreams are not enough. Antony 'is past the size of dreaming', and there is nothing in 'nature' to compete with the 'strange forms'—again the stress on 'strangeness'—of fancy. Yet here imagination's reality is firm-based as nature, transcends mere 'fancy' as surely as glorious 'nature' itself transcends mere art. For 'nature' is used here in two senses. First, there is the 'nature' of normal uninspired observation; then there is art, revealing vaguely nature's true and intrinsic beauty; finally, there is the life-vision of love in whose alchemy nature is seen to surpass in easy glory the finest and farthest reaches of artistic creation. Art in comparison with the one 'nature' is 'fancy'—both stranger and more beautiful and yet less certain and real than that nature; but with the other, love's artistic fancy is fused, 'imagination' is there the mating of visionary insight with nature's integrity and divinity. So Antony as viewed by love, in life or death, is as much more englorified than by the tinsel dressings of art and fancy, as the fine fancifulness of art transcends the bleak vision of unawakened man, seeing with his senses the ungilded object without the glamour of love's tinct.

These two visionary units both microcosmically reflect the whole. Both are set within a certain pallid and emotionless element: diaphanous, but weighty—as though eter-

nity lays its heavy breath on the wavelets of time, freezing
them in icy stillness. Yet there is nothing cold, or colourless therein: the paradox is vivid. They are both of the
quality known in blissful dream where fiery ecstasy is
miraculously dissolved in utter peace, both extreme, yet
strangely compatible: thus mirroring the diviner hopes of
mankind. So, in these descriptions, we end our analysis of
the varying grades in our imagery. To this still perfection they lead us, to this height: it is the farthest
excelsior of our poet's vision. And these qualities of movement within stillness, sense-forms lucidly floating in pure
spirit, solidity etherealized, which are evident here especially, are yet to be observed throughout the play: which
thought throws back to my remarks on style at the start.

I have now shown that our whole vision is condensed,
crystallized in these single delineations of our two protagonists, both strongly idealized, ablaze with impossible
beauty or infinite in majesty and power. The finite and
infinite are blended in these descriptions. Within the
story element is everywhere blended, mated, with element,
sun with earth or water with air, giving birth to the 'strange
serpent' of Nile, or the strange forms of 'hail', 'snow', or
evanescent and multiform cloud. It is throughout a life-
vision, a mating of essence with essence. Cleopatra is
spiritually and bodily mated to Antony—even Caesar calls
Antony his 'mate' in empire (v. i. 43): there is no room
for any real enmity. Therefore all our 'nature' here is
bounteous, fruitful, life-giving: and its ethereality and
mystery are strongly emphasized to harmonize with the
ethereal mystery of our final revelation. Never were the
pathos and failure of human tragedy so happily blended
with the infinite purposes of human life. The temporal is
sanctioned by the eternal. For, as in our last passages the
finite and infinite are firmly cemented in unity, so we
notice how the ultimate realities of life and that 'thing'
(v. ii. 5) called 'death' are finely mated, so that love in
truth has power to 'quicken with kissing' (IV. xiii. 39),
or a kiss strikes 'gentle' death (v. ii. 296–7), so that

death is but a 'lover's pinch' (v. ii. 298), and man a 'bridegroom in his death' (iv. xiv. 100). From this marriage of life and death a new reality is born—'a better life' (v. ii. 2); and thus the asp at Cleopatra's breast is imaged as her 'baby' (v. ii. 312). Now we feel the pressure of our 'mating' references throughout, the constant stress on 'melting', 'dissolving', 'mingling', till 'strength' of eternity and 'force' of time are inextricably 'entangled' (iv. xii. 48), and 'death', misnamed phantom, but the simplification, the freeing and unloosing of life's 'intrinsicate' (v. ii. 307) knot. Man steps free in death: 'death', portal of infinity, 'enlarges his confine' (iii. v. 13). In death man is triumphant, a 'conqueror' (iv. xiv. 62). Eros, Iras, Charmian, Enobarbus, Antony, and Cleopatra —all die in the full flood and blaze of loyalty or love, so that 'death' is no more a 'nothing' as in *Timon*, but rather the blue seas and teeming earth, the winds and gleaming clouds, the languorous beauties of a tropic night, the silver and gold of moon and sun, all intermeshed to the bridal music of the spheres, and, at the last, all indistinguishable from a human voice, a human form. We see the protagonists, in love and war and sport, in death or life or that mystery containing both, transfigured in a transfigured universe, themselves that universe and more, outspacing the wheeling orbs of earth and heaven. 'Nothing' has in truth become 'all things' to our vision: Timon prophesied not in vain. So Cleopatra and Antony find not death but life. This is the high metaphysic of love which melts life and death into a final oneness; which reality is indeed no pulseless abstraction, but rather blends its single design and petalled excellence from all life and all death, all imperial splendour and sensuous delight, all strange and ethereal forms, all elements and heavenly stars; all that is natural, human, and divine; all brilliance and all glory.

Additional Note, 1968: The music in Act IV serves as an orchestral attunement to the Elysian themes that are to follow.

VIII

THE DIADEM OF LOVE: AN ESSAY ON ANTONY AND CLEOPATRA

I

IN this essay I shall observe the more specifically human qualities in *Antony and Cleopatra*. I have indicated something of the visionary brilliance and sweeping scope of our imagery, wherein man is all but deified through love. This transcendental and ethereal humanism is primary: all else works within it. But there is a stern realism too. *Antony and Cleopatra* is fired by an intenser realism than any play from *Hamlet* to *Timon of Athens*. There is pain, failure, hate, and evil. The poet never shirks the more sordid aspects of things divine. The play's visionary transcendence marks not a severance from reality but a consummation of it. It neglects nothing, and its prevailing optimism is due to emphasis rather than selection. The lovers are old, their passion often called 'lust'. Antony's armour is shown as 'bruised pieces' (IV. xii. 42). Those primary elements of evil and hate turbulent throughout the sombre plays are present here: but they are resolved constituent to a wider harmony, a less partial view. Those were provisional plays: this is complete and perfect. Those earlier themes—death, unfaithfulness, loathing, hatred, and self-begotten evil: they are here too, transmuted to something rich and strange, blending their wild notes in the full chorus of sweeter melodies. There we lived an earth-life canopied by sombre clouds: the leaden hopelessness of *Lear*, the 'sterile promontory' and forbidding gloom of *Hamlet*, the black minatory rack and forked flashing Satanism of *Macbeth*. Here, though our vision often glimpses that shadowed territory, our sight bends oftener to the clouds' reverse, their silver and gold lining, their ethereal and shimmering floor. In *Pericles* we tread that insubstantial gold.

Now in *Antony and Cleopatra* no persons are bad. There

is no one exponent of any pure negation: no Ghost, no
Weird Sisters, no Thersites, Iago, Edmund, nor Apemantus. In no play is the moral outlook so irrelevant as a
means to distinguish the persons: it is rather an im-
possibility, has no meaning. Analysis reveals that all the
chief persons reflect identical spiritual rhythms: from
positive to negative, negative to positive. Personification
is thus levelled under a single ethical colouring: so that
there are no ethical distinctions—not even the most
purely artistic—between the chief persons. We watch as
though from the turrets of infinity, whence the ethical is
found unreal and beauty alone survives. Though the
individual himself shows a systole and diastole of 'good',
yet, since all the primary persons equally share this ebb
and flow, it is clearly impossible to condemn any one person as 'bad'. Rather we must watch these varying rhythms
and expect to find their significance: which will be
similar in all the persons. Our negation here is disloyalty;
our excellence, loyalty (see pp. vi, 326), with striking
examples of each: but often conflicting loyalties render
our impressions very complex. Here is an example:

> *Antony.* I did not think to draw my sword 'gainst Pompey;
>   For he hath laid strange courtesies and great
>   Of late upon me: I must thank him only,
>   Lest my remembrance suffer ill report;
>   At heel of that, defy him.   (II. ii. 160)

Every one here is friendly at heart: circumstances force
friends and lovers apart. But there is no ill will. Now
Antony's problem is acute. It is the same with Octavia:

>   ... A more unhappy lady,
>   If this division chance, ne'er stood between,
>   Praying for both parts:
>   The good gods will mock me presently,
>   When I shall pray, 'O, bless my lord and husband!'
>   Undo that prayer, by crying out as loud,
>   'O, bless my brother!' Husband win, win brother,
>   Prays, and destroys the prayer; no midway
>   'Twixt these extremes at all.   (III. iv. 12)

Loyalty is our theme: but loyalty is not shown as easy. Often the persons fall from faith or love, but they fall to rise again. There is a strong predominance of the positive essences in each: they are all, at the last, true to their deepest loyalty. Therefore the play of action leaves scant feeling of victorious evil. Evil—here, of course, disloyalty—is ever melted in the prevailing delight. In so far as the play reflects human affairs, the problems of mortality are answered and the questing mind is at peace.

The first effect to be noticed in these persons is a certain strange—the word is apt, the idea of 'strangeness' being frequent in the play—a strange see-saw motion of the spirit, an oscillating tendency, back and forth; a 'varying'. This appears in Antony's wavering between the twin loyalties at Rome and Alexandria; in Cleopatra's hesitation at the end between Antony and Caesar; in Antony's consequent swift changes from love to loathing. The persons seem uneasily balanced, swaying, first one side, then the other. It was the same with Hamlet: like him, they each contain the dual principles, positive and negative, locked in a single personality. With *Hamlet*, this incertitude was the controlling force of the play: his world wavered with the oscillation of his mind. Here the whole is not unsteadied by those actions which compose it: there is a constant sense of surety and safety, a motion within stillness, temporal successions building a strange eternity. The technique, as in *Lear*, is massively spatialized. But in *Lear* the sense of conflict, the opposing parties in the dramatis personae, the conflicting assurances in Lear's mind; and, again, the stark contrast between Lear's reunion with Cordelia and her brutal death—all these forbid quite that harmonious stillness, as of a silence holding all sounds in vassalage, which we find here. Here there are changes, but no proper conflicts; the opposing armies are led by staunch friends, Antony and Caesar, forced only by circumstance to military rivalry. The root antagonists of the play are the two

supreme Shakespearian values—War or Empire, and
Love: there is no question of any ultimate denial or
cynicism. All wide antinomies are melted, fused in unity.
In *Lear* there is a double climax: Lear's reunion with
Cordelia in love, next her death and his. Here these two
realities are always synchronized. Eros, Iras, Charmian,
Enobarbus, Antony and Cleopatra—all die at the height
of love or loyalty: death and love blend in each. All dualisms here are less vital than the unities they build. I will
now notice certain such dualisms, clear enough when isolated, in the more purely subsidiary persons: and from
them pass to Antony and Cleopatra themselves.

Pompey, Caesar, and Antony draw lots as to who shall
feast the others to celebrate their amity. A feast is held on
Pompey's galley, off Misenum. Pompey is thus the host.
During the revelry, Menas draws him aside, suggests
that the cable be cut, the ship set adrift, and the guests
slaughtered at sea: then Pompey will be 'lord of the whole
world' (II. vii. 67). Here is Pompey's reply:

> Ah, this thou shouldst have done,
> And not have spoke on 't! In me 'tis villainy;
> In thee 't had been good service. Thou must know,
> 'Tis not my profit that does lead mine honour;
> Mine honour, it. Repent that e'er thy tongue
> Hath so betray'd thine act: being done unknown
> I should have found it afterwards well done;
> But must condemn it now. Desist, and drink.
>
> (II. vii. 79)

This is a curious blending of sophistry and honour; of
frank nobility and ignoble treachery. Treachery is very
evident in the play, and Pompey's fall from hospitality
and honour—in so far as this speech lowers him in our
eyes—is a reflection of other similar falls. The movement
is typical. Notice, too, the stress laid on personal loyalty:
in Menas this act would have been 'good service'. This,
too, is typical. There is a strong feeling throughout that
loyalty to an individual may outweigh common sense,

abstract virtue, honour: the human element, we must remember, being strongly idealized, more potent than all less concrete incentives. Abstract virtue has much less autonomy here: the significant choice is between one loyalty and another, or loyalty and treachery. An odd sort of treachery occurs naturally. Pompey with a curious readiness is here all but willing to slip the cable of his new-trothed pact: there is no strong evil intent, nor any burning ambition—just a sudden absence of loyalty. Another example occurs in Caesar's conduct at the end. His treachery towards Lepidus is suggested earlier (III. v). Hearing of Antony's death, his response is noble, generous and, it would seem, profound:

> O Antony!
> I have follow'd thee to this; but we do lance
> Diseases in our bodies: I must perforce
> Have shown to thee such a declining day,
> Or look on thine; we could not stall together
> In the whole world: but yet let me lament,
> With tears as sovereign as the blood of hearts,
> That thou, my brother, my competitor
> In top of all design, my mate in empire,
> Friend and companion in the front of war,
> The arm of mine own body, and the heart
> Where mine his thoughts did kindle,—that our stars,
> Unreconciliable, should divide
> Our equalness to this. (v. i. 35)

At this point a messenger comes from Cleopatra, asking Caesar his intents towards her. He replies:

> Bid her have good heart:
> She soon shall know of us, by some of ours,
> How honourable and how kindly we
> Determine for her; for Caesar cannot live
> To be ungentle. (v. i. 56)[1]

---

[1] The Folio reading is '... Caesar cannot *leave* to be ungentle'. Dr. S. A. Tannenbaum defends this as a blunder of Caesar's intended by Shakespeare. See Shakespeare Studies, No. 1, *Slips of the Tongue in Shakespeare*, New York, 1930.

The messenger is dismissed, and he continues:

> Come hither, Proculeius. Go and say,
> We purpose her no shame: give her what comforts
> The quality of her passion shall require,
> Lest, in her greatness, by some mortal stroke,
> She do defeat us; for her life in Rome
> Would be eternal in our triumph . . .   (v. i. 61)

Then he seems somewhat ashamed:

> Go with me to my tent; where you shall see
> How hardly I was drawn into this war;
> How calm and gentle I proceeded still
> In all my writings: go with me, and see
> What I can show in this.   (v. i. 73)

Was Caesar's first flood of sentiment insincere? I do not think so. We are constantly shown a sincere emotion suddenly giving place to an ignominious and selfish policy. Pompey's troth-plight was sincere: but he could have wished his followers to smirch it with treachery. Both Caesar and Pompey have a streak of the *Macbeth*-evil. Pompey 'would not play false and yet would wrongly win', and Caesar 'makes his face a vizard to his heart, disguising what it is'. The *Macbeth*-evil, once titanic and overpowering, is here a minor element: a sinister ripple, indicative of potential black typhoon, on the smooth heaving ocean of this play's resplendent humanism. The evil here, however, exercises no continual power over the personality which is its channel: it comes by fits and starts, intermittent. Events always render it ineffective. Menas' treachery does not materialize, Caesar's plans for Cleopatra are short-circuited by her death. At the end, Caesar's nobler quality is forced into prominence:

> Bravest at the last,
> She levell'd at our purposes, and, being royal,
> Took her own way.   (v. ii. 338)

This is more typical: but the other is present. There is a dark unvalued strain of dross which curiously interlines the rich one of nobility, bounty, and loyalty.

We meet it again in Enobarbus. Through the early acts he is very lovable, faithful to Antony, his caustic and illuminating commentary never quite hiding his warmth of heart. Often he is a chorus to the action: from time to time he voices that common-sense wisdom which is usually forgotten in the visionary brilliance. He both favours and criticizes Antony's reckless love. He, too, wavers, like the others. He can cry:

> Bring in the banquet quickly; wine enough
> Cleopatra's health to drink.   (I. ii. 11)

But he can also advise Antony:

> Under a compelling occasion, let women die: it were pity
> to cast them away for nothing; though, between them and
> a great cause, they should be esteem'd nothing.
>   (I. ii. 146)

Yet again, soon after, he defends her:

> *Antony.* She is cunning past man's thought.
> *Enobarbus.* Alack, sir, no; her passions are made of nothing
> but the finest part of pure love . . .   (I. ii. 156)

She is 'a wonderful piece of work, which not to have been blest withal would have discredited your travel' (I. ii. 164). He even persuades Antony that

> . . . the business you have broached here cannot be without
> you; especially that of Cleopatra's, which wholly depends on
> your abode.   (I. ii. 185)

Notice the contrasts—between 'women' and 'a great cause'; or the 'business' of state (I. ii. 183) and the 'business' referred to by Enobarbus, the business of love. The conflicting calls of these two are at the heart both of this play and *Coriolanus*. The values of War or Empire and Love are ever twin supremities in Shakespeare; more crudely, we can name them 'efficiency' and 'sentiment'; more nobly, the great spiritual heritages of West and East. So apt in this play is Charmian's cry: 'O Eastern Star!'—the star of the eternal feminine burning through mists of masculine ambition, unfaith, doubt: to this star our study of Shakespeare's tragedies leads us. Enobarbus thus early reflects our wavering antagonism. In II. ii. he speaks his fine descriptions of Cleopatra's magic fascination; but later he sternly opposes Antony's rashness. He is the spokesman of enlightened common sense, both appreciative and critical. Often he sees the truth whilst his superiors blunder at cross-purposes. The Triumvirs forget private quarrels to unite against Pompey:

> *Enobarbus.* Or, if you borrow one another's love for the instant, you may, when you hear no more words of Pompey, return it again: you shall have time to wrangle in when you have nothing else to do.
> *Antony.* Thou art a soldier only: speak no more.
> *Enobarbus.* That truth should be silent I had almost forgot.
> *Antony.* You wrong this presence; therefore speak no more.
> *Enobarbus.* Go to, then; your considerate stone.   (II. ii. 103)

Later, when Antony and Caesar are opposed, he urges strongly that Cleopatra should not take part in the war:

> Your presence needs must puzzle Antony;
> Take from his heart, take from his brain, from 's time,
> What should not then be spar'd.   (III. vii. 11)

He insists with vehemence that Antony should fight by land, not by sea. His warnings are proved wise by the event. The sea-fight is a disaster. Cleopatra flies, Antony follows. His soldier's heart is disgusted:

> Mine eyes did sicken at the sight, and could not
> Endure a further view.   (III. viii. 26)

Though Antony's cause is hopeless, he at first remains loyal. 'Six kings' show Canidius the way of yielding (III. viii. 43). But Enobarbus recognizes that loyalty may be called to rule common sense:

> Mine honesty and I begin to square.
> The loyalty well held to fools does make
> Our faith mere folly: yet he that can endure
> To follow with allegiance a fall'n lord
> Does conquer him that did his master conquer,
> And earns a place i' the story.   (III. xi. 41)

He remains loyal while he can feel the glamour of Antony's love. Always he has been sensitive to Cleopatra's rich fascination. He will die with his master in such a cause. But, when he sees Cleopatra herself descend to treacherous betrayal—then, it is as though our whole fabric of love's vision is smirched, blackened: we, and Enobarbus, feel it:

> Sir, sir, thou art so leaky,
> That we must leave thee to thy sinking, for
> Thy dearest quit thee. (III. xi. 63)

He tells Antony of her betrayal. Antony rages at her—then accepts her excuses, recaptures his hopes, becomes recklessly valorous and merry. Enobarbus, not so easily satisfied, now knowing love's ship to be unseaworthy and not trusting Antony's rash optimism, finds the situation intolerable. Cleopatra is treacherous, Antony a fool. He has all reason on his side. Antony is 'frighted out of fear' (III. xiii. 196):

> . . . and I see still,
> A diminution in our captain's brain
> Restores his heart: when valour preys on reason,
> It eats the sword it fights with. I will seek
> Some way to leave him. (III. xi. 197)

Enobarbus' desertion is more than a personal disloyalty. It is a symbol of the protagonists' tottering romance. While Antony's love-cause is intact, Enobarbus would 'earn a place in the story': now that storied romance bids fair to be a farce. He believes the evidence of his eyes, and it is hard to blame him. Here the rightness of his course depends largely on whether his judgement of Cleopatra's integrity is sound. But there is no doubt of her treachery: he is emotionally excused. Moreover, Antony's rash conduct, kissing away all chances of success for the sake of an unprincipled and disloyal woman, will ruin not only himself but his followers. What duty binds a follower to a madman? He is rationally excused. But events, as always in this play, press Enobarbus on to

realization of his true self. He deserts. He finds de-
serters coldly received by Caesar. Alexas was hanged.
(IV. vi. 16). Canidius and others have 'no honourable
trust' (IV. vi. 18). Now he knows his fault:

> I have done ill;
> Of which I do accuse myself so sorely,
> That I will joy no more. (IV. vi. 18)

A soldier brings news that Antony has sent his treasure
after him with 'his bounty overplus' (IV. vi. 22). Now
knowledge of his baseness inrushes, and he shivers in
naked shame:

> I am alone the villain of the earth,
> And feel I am so most. O Antony,
> Thou mine of bounty, how would'st thou have paid
> My better service, when my turpitude
> Thou dost so crown with gold! This blows my heart:
> If swift thought break it not, a swifter mean
> Shall outstrike thought: but thought will do 't, I feel.
> I fight against thee! No: I will go seek
> Some ditch wherein to die; the foul'st best fits
> My latter part of life. (IV. vi. 30)

Too late he finds the worth of common sense and reason
in a world so ruled by the diademed principle of love.
Outward events urge him thus to knowledge of himself.
Now he cannot understand his baseness—it is as a
madness. Loyalty returns, a thousandfold more potent
for his renegade act. Alone the villain of the earth, he
speaks confession to the watery eye of heaven's moonlight,
opening his soul to the infinite spaces, unburdening the
infinity of his sorrow:

> *Enobarbus.* Be witness to me, O thou blessed moon,
>   When men revolted shall upon record
>   Bear hateful memory, poor Enobarbus did
>   Before thy face repent!
> *First Soldier.*   Enobarbus!
> *Second Soldier.*   Peace!
>   Hark further.
> *Enobarbus.* O sovereign mistress of true melancholy,

The poisonous damp of night disponge upon me,
That life, a very rebel to my will,
May hang no longer on me: throw my heart
Against the flint and hardness of my fault;
Which, being dried with grief, will break to powder,
And finish all foul thoughts. O Antony,
Nobler than my revolt is infamous,
Forgive me in thine own particular;
But let the world rank me in register
A master-leaver and a fugitive:
O Antony! O Antony! (IV. ix. 7)

Enobarbus has throughout been a common-sense commentary on the action: this is the action's commentary on common sense. Moreover, this story of Enobarbus exactly reflects our primary strands in the play, the stories of Antony and Cleopatra; it is therefore most valuable to our general understanding. Enobarbus wavers between personal loyalty and reason; at a crucial moment takes the path dictated by his puny wisdom; is next wrenched back by events and by his own heart to a sudden and shattering realization that all expediency is dust and ashes beside the living flame of his love. He cannot fight against the universe. The whole universe ranges itself against his turpitude, in panoply of that moon and glimmering dark in which his soul repents. Now his only life is in death. Death is synchronized with uttermost loyalty. This is the way our joyous universe makes music from the wilful unfaith and wayward purposes of man. There is an unseen power at work forcing each in his own despite to realize a consummate beauty in life and in death, ever pressing the richest liquid from the vines of his soul. Each thus dies for love or loyalty—Eros, who slays himself to 'escape the sorrow of Antony's death' (IV. xii. 95), Enobarbus, Iras, Charmian, and the two protagonists themselves. But there is no fall to death. Death is a rising. We watch a crescendo of the soul to death, itself the aim, the canopy, climacteric, and crown of life. In Enobarbus, in Antony, in Cleopatra,

10

the same theme rings out: a wavering, a failing of trust in
love's unreason, a swift and beauteous recovery in death.
Each life-story is as a wild twang of harp-like music,
whose ringing and swiftening vibrations rise, sweeping
ethereally beyond sound.

II

This wavering, this ebbing and flowing of love's vision
is apparent in Antony. It is an all-important element in
the play, and is reflected in typical passages. There is the
curious image:

> This common body,
> Like to a vagabond flag upon the stream,
> Goes to and back, lackeying the varying tide,
> To rot itself with motion.   (I. iv. 44)

Again,

> . . . the swan's down-feather,
> That stands upon the swell at full of tide,
> And neither way inclines.   (III. ii. 48)

And observe Cleopatra's

> O sun,
> Burn the great sphere thou movest in! darkling stand
> The varying shore o' the world.   (IV. xiii. 9)

'Varying' again: either because of the alternation of light
and dark, or the ebb and flow of ocean whose ceaseless
interaction with earth is in Shakespeare a typical image of
temporal change. Antony is always varying. First we
find him swearing an heroic love for Cleopatra compared
with which 'kingdoms are clay' (I. i. 35). A messenger
from Rome reminds him of other ties, and he changes to:

> These strong Egyptian fetters I must break,
> Or lose myself in dotage.   (I. ii. 125)

Fulvia's death is reported. Like Enobarbus, after his
desertion, Antony finds the event has a quite different
taste from its pre-imagined quality:

> There 's a great spirit gone! Thus did I desire it:
> What our contempt doth often hurl from us,

We wish it ours again; the present pleasure,
By revolution lowering, does become
The opposite of itself: she 's good, being gone;
The hand could pluck her back that shoved her on.
                                        (I. ii. 131)

The same thought is echoed by Caesar:

It hath been taught us from the primal state,
That he which is was wish'd until he were;
And the ebb'd man, ne'er lov'd till ne'er worth love,
Comes dear'd by being lack'd.   (I. iv. 41)

And Agrippa:

            . . . strange it is,
That nature must compel us to lament
Our most persisted deeds.   (v. i. 28)

There is continually this wavering, ebb and flow, of the
spirit, a shifting, varying psychology. It recurs with great
force later: the death of Fulvia forecasts the reported
death of Cleopatra in Act IV, the same rhythm of a
sudden regret at the impact of loss is apparent in both.
Such reversals occur throughout. On receipt of this
Rome-news Antony swerves from reverberating pro-
testation of his love to criticism of Cleopatra. 'She is
cunning past man's thought' (I. ii. 155). Cleopatra taxes
him with inconstancy; but he leaves for Rome, still
assuring her of his love:

            . . . I go from hence
Thy soldier, servant; making peace or war
As thou affect'st.   (I. iii. 69)

Yet, once away from Cleopatra, he is less governed by her
magic. At Rome he is offered Caesar's sister, Octavia, to
be his wife. Policy advises it. He accepts quite readily.
He slips easily and naturally into the contract with a
curious perversity. And all the time we endorse Enobarbus' prophecy:

Maecenas. Now Antony must leave her utterly.
Enobarbus. Never; he will not . . .   (II. ii. 241)

An invisible bond binds the protagonists, heart to heart.

Though Antony may not always know it—albeit, however, he soon realizes that 'i' the East my pleasure lies' (II. iii. 40)—it is true and clear to us as to Enobarbus. The strongest thing in Antony is his love for Cleopatra; the strongest thing in Enobarbus his loyalty to Antony. Both try to break free from themselves. They can no more do it with any permanence than a man can upspring from the earth whose centre draws his weight.[1] Antony speaks, perhaps at the time sincerely, to Octavia:

> My Octavia,
> Read not my blemishes in the world's report:
> I have not kept my square; but that to come
> Shall all be done by the rule. Good-night, dear lady.
>
> (II. iii. 4)

But his burning passion for Cleopatra remembered, the contrast is pitiful. The marriage only widens the split between Antony and Caesar. The interplay of human intention, action, and event is ever strange here; yet again resulting finally always in a strange and unforeseen beauty. Enobarbus sees clearly the probable future: he knows Antony better than he knows himself:

> . . . He will to his Egyptian dish again: then shall the sighs of Octavia blow the fire up in Caesar; and, as I said before, that which is the strength of their amity shall prove the immediate author of their variance. (II. vi. 134)

We cannot analyse the exact responsibility for the breach when it occurs. Each blames the other: which refusal to allot explicit blame is throughout a quality in this play. Such realism is vital: real life witnesses the same futility of surface 'causes', the same complexity of inimical loyalties and loves, the meaningless ineptitude of 'rights' and 'wrongs'. The deep things have their way, and appearances are froth. One thing is clear: Antony returns to Cleopatra. And that is natural and necessary.

From now on, Antony and Caesar oppose each other.

[1] Compare *Romeo and Juliet*, II. i. 1:
> Can I go forward when my heart is here?
> Turn back, dull earth, and find thy centre out.

Now Antony's swift oscillations from despair to reckless courage, from loathing to love of Cleopatra, are emphasized. He insists on fighting at sea. He leaves the battle to follow Cleopatra's flying ship. Shame engulfs him:

> Hark! the land bids me tread no more upon 't;
> It is asham'd to bear me! Friends, come hither:
> I am so lated in the world, that I
> Have lost my way for ever.   (III. ix. 1)

He is 'unqualitied with very shame' (III. xi. 44). Cleopatra is grieved, did not guess he would follow:

> Egypt, thou knew'st too well
> My heart was to thy rudder tied by the strings,
> And thou shouldst tow me after: o'er my spirit
> Thy full supremacy thou knew'st, and that
> **Thy beck might from the bidding of the gods**
> Command me.   (III. ix. 56)

He struggles vainly against this unresisted power bearing him toward his destiny.   Antony loses his wisdom, challenges Caesar to single fight. He is jovial, melancholy, reckless by turns. The fleeting insubstantiality of psychic modes is vivid: shifting, dissolving, reforming essences, and nothing permanent save Antony's preoccupation with Cleopatra, either in love or loathing. For now he finds Cleopatra making private terms with Thyreus, Caesar's envoy. He is as a wild beast in his fury:

> Approach, there! Ah, you kite! Now, gods and devils!
> Authority melts from me: of late, when I cried 'Ho!'
> Like boys unto a muss, kings would start forth,
> And cry 'Your will?' Have you no ears? I am
> Antony yet.   (III. xi. 89)

He abuses Cleopatra violently:

> You have been a boggler ever:
> But when we in our viciousness grow hard—
> O misery on 't!—the wise gods seel our eyes;
> In our own filth drop our clear judgements; make us
> Adore our errors; laugh at 's, while we strut
> To our confusion.   (III. xi. 110)

This is how Antony sees his love: filth, vice, error. We remember:

> Kingdoms are clay: our dungy earth alike
> Feeds beast as man: the nobleness of life
> Is to do thus . . . (I. i. 35)

What has happened? Which is it to be, filth or all the stars of a new heaven ablaze with uncomprehended glory? So swift our interspaced modes of consciousness succeed, so sure they exclude each other. Like Hamlet, Troilus, Othello, Lear, and Timon, Antony is brought to the extreme test. This is the thing which makes Hamlet cry: 'I loved you not'; which wrenched from Troilus the distraught agony of, 'This is and is not Cressid'; which turned the Othello-music to 'Goats and monkeys!' So, too, Lear was transfixed by an unbearable knowledge, the rending tear of his heart's fabric—'Your old kind father, whose fond heart gave all . . .' This it is which attains what grandeur it may in Timon's universal anathema of hate:

> Hate all, curse all, show charity to none.

Not individual persons—no, nor 'dramatic situations'—are here at stake. Heaven and Hell are playing for the validity of the romantic vision. Is that vision true, or is it false? In this resplendent universe will Antony succeed where others fail—yes, in the face of such steel-cold treachery in love's perfected embodiment, Cleopatra, Eastern Star of Love? Now Antony's imperial palace of romance melts, insubstantial, a delusion and a cheat: and the austere Caesar and wronged Octavia look down from their ice-heaven of reason, condemning, scorning. The world may be well lost for love: but for this? Enobarbus' loyalty breaks. Antony's abuse is hideous. Now Cleopatra is a 'morsel cold upon dead Caesar's trencher', a 'fragment of Cneius Pompey's' (III. xi. 117). He disgraces her in brutal words, flings on her memory of lustful intemperance. Cleopatra, 'our terrene moon', is 'eclipsed', portending Antony's fall (III. xi. 153). The

word is apt. The shadow passes. Antony is 'satisfied' by
Cleopatra's answer. Now he is 'brave' again:

Cleopatra. That's my brave lord!
Antony. I will be treble-sinew'd, hearted, breathed,
    And fight maliciously: for when mine hours
    Were nice and lucky, men did ransom lives
    Of me for jests; but now I'll set my teeth,
    And send to darkness all that stop me. Come,
    Let's have one other gaudy night: call to me
    All my sad captains; fill our bowls once more;
    Let's mock the midnight bell.
Cleopatra.   It is my birth-day:
    I had thought to have held it poor; but, since my lord
    Is Antony again, I will be Cleopatra.   (III. xi. 177)

The contrast is violent: there is a sudden change of
consciousness in Antony. The lustful faults for which he
blamed Cleopatra were known to him before: facts are not
here so significant as Antony's attitude towards them.
Love floods again in his heart: perhaps he willingly deceives himself that Cleopatra was not sincere in her
betrayal. This swift oscillation of the spirit from positive
to negative and back again is markedly emphasized
toward the end of Antony's story.

Next Antony bids his servants farewell:

Antony.   Give me thy hand,
    Thou hast been rightly honest;—so hast thou;—
    Thou,—and thou,—and thou:—you have served me well,
    And kings have been your fellows.
Cleopatra.   What means this?
Enobarbus. 'Tis one of those odd tricks which sorrow shoots
    Out of the mind.   (IV. ii. 10)

'Odd': throughout the play we meet a strange beauty, in
tragedy as in mirth or love. This is a new facet of Antony
—Antony generous and warm-hearted to his followers.
In this scene—and at other instances of his 'bounty'—
we are irresistibly reminded of Timon and his servants.
Both heroes are given a setting of rich magnificence and
Oriental display, apt frame to their rich nobility of soul,
their generosity and bounty: both enjoy the feasting and

the music, both are dedicate alike to love. Antony continues to expand this farewell:

> *Cleopatra.* What does he mean?
> *Enobarbus.* To make his followers weep. (IV. ii. 23)

Antony continues. Enobarbus interrupts, urges that the others weep and he is himself 'onion-eyed', that Antony is transforming them to women. Antony recovers himself.

> Ho, ho, ho!
> Now the witch take me, if I meant it thus!
> Grace grow where those drops fall! My hearty friends,
> You take me in too dolorous a sense;
> For I spake to you for your comfort; did desire you
> To burn this night with torches: know, my hearts,
> I hope well of to-morrow; and will lead you
> Where rather I'll expect victorious life
> Than death and honour. Let's to supper, come,
> And drown consideration. (IV. ii. 36)

Again, we are sensible of a wavering, a tremulous rise and fall, like a boat tossing idly on a vast sea: the deep current of that sea bears Antony on.

Next we rise to a high pinnacle of triumphant love. For the first time we meet the two great values, Love and War, perfectly blended in two personalities and one victorious event. Cleopatra buckles on Antony's armour, and he returns in triumph, his warrior-strength and love-ardour at their meridian of glory. At the start, before the battle, he is a little dashed by news of Enobarbus' desertion:

> Say that I wish he never more find cause
> To change a master. O, my fortunes have
> Corrupted honest men! Dispatch.—Enobarbus!
> (IV. v. 15)

Then he returns miraculous in strength, Herculean in love and war:

> We have beat him to his camp: run one before,
> And let the queen know of our gests. To-morrow,
> Before the sun shall see 's, we'll spill the blood
> That has to-day escap'd. (IV. viii. 1)

He clasps Cleopatra to him, adoration of her and pride in his victory blended in a noble phrase:

> *Antony.*   ... O thou day o' the world,
> Chain mine arm'd neck; leap thou, attire and all,
> Through proof of harness to my heart, and there
> Ride on the pants triumphing!
> *Cleopatra.*   Lord of lords!
> O infinite virtue, comest thou smiling from
> The world's great snare uncaught?
> *Antony.*   My nightingale,
> We have beat them to their beds. What, girl! though grey
> Do something mingle with our younger brown, yet ha' we
> A brain that nourishes our nerves, and can
> Get goal for goal of youth.   (IV. viii. 13)

Antony's 'brain' or spirit is young, his body old. Throughout we have this contrast: spiritual romance, material realism. Both Antony and Cleopatra are old. Notice, too, the curious game-metaphor 'goal'. So love's victory in arms is to be celebrated right nobly, in triumphal and processional magnificence:

>   Give me thy hand:
> Through Alexandria make a jolly march;
> Bear our hack'd targets like the men that owe them:
> Had our great palace the capacity
> To camp this host, we all would sup together,
> And drink carouses to the next day's fate,
> Which promises royal peril. Trumpeters,
> With brazen din blast you the city's ear;
> Make mingle with our rattling tabourines;
> That heaven and earth may strike their sounds together,
> Applauding our approach.   (IV. viii. 29)

So high exultation rides on the crest of this wave of victory. But now our oscillation is both fast and violent. An *Othello*-image is apt—from a scene where warriorship and love are mated for a short while finely as in this scene of *Antony and Cleopatra*:

> And let the labouring bark climb hills of seas
> Olympus-high, and duck again as low
> As hell 's from heaven.   (*Othello*, II. i. 189)

One such movement of the spirit is the whole drama of
Othello, Lear, Timon. It is but an event within the many
other waverings and wide visionary spaces of our present
paradise: but the analogy is important. The coarse agonies
of those sombre plays are being ground into rich flour in
this whirring, spindling, soft-voiced, unerring mechanism
that tops the tortured progress of Shakespearian tragedy:
here those agonies will be resolved, melted in the one
'heavenly mingle' of our new vision. So again Antony's
love and hope sink low. No longer drunk with success,
cold fears besiege him intermittently:

> Antony
> Is valiant, and dejected; and, by starts,
> His fretted fortunes give him hope, and fear,
> Of what he has, and has not.   (IV. x. 19)

Again, there is failure by sea: now again Cleopatra is
suspect—she is 'foul Egyptian' (IV. x. 23), and 'triple-
turn'd whore' (IV. x. 26). He will have it she has sold
him to Caesar:

> Betray'd I am:
> O this false soul of Egypt! this grave charm,—
> Whose eye beck'd forth my wars, and call'd them home;
> Whose bosom was my crownet, my chief end,—
> Like a right gipsy, hath, at fast and loose,
> Beguil'd me to the very heart of loss.   (IV. x. 37)

Cleopatra enters, and he hurls the vilest abuse at her. He
would have Caesar disgrace her:

> . . . Let him take thee,
> And hoist thee up to the shouting plebeians:
> Follow his chariot, like the greatest spot
> Of all thy sex; most monster-like, be shown
> For poor'st diminutives, for doits; and let
> Patient Octavia plough thy visage up
> With her prepared nails.   (IV. x. 46)

He drives her from him; then swears she shall die. His
love-vision is now bright or dimmed according as he
prospers in fight. This is only superficially irrational.
Beneath all superficies and outward varying shows, the

theme of these love-tragedies is one: the failure of love—
the fact that it is here a sea-failure is significant—to assert
its royalty in the temporal scheme. Therefore it is often
associated with war, a symbolic value of practical
efficiency. When Love and War embrace harmonious, as
in *Othello* or our recent scene here, then Feminine and
Masculine, East and West, are blended in a universal
concord. But in so far as love and world-success are
antagonistic, love has failed, and meets condemnation.
Wherever or however it be condemned matters little:
justly, for unfaith, in *Troilus*; unjustly in *Othello*; for lack
of generosity in *Timon*, of sentiment in *Lear*—these
differences are surface deep. All we know is that twice,
in *Othello* and here, love and world-victory are seen
together. It is the destruction of that unity which
maddens Antony: he is metaphysically justified, even
without our memory of Cleopatra's former attempt at
betrayal. So she must die, like Desdemona, lest love's false
gilding 'betray more men' in a world that denies the validity
of the romantic vision:

> The witch shall die:
> To the young Roman boy she hath sold me, and I fall
> Under this plot; she dies for 't.   (IV. x. 60)

If this play is to solve our earlier dualisms, it yet shirks
nothing of their essence.

Now at the extremity of despair, Antony sees himself a
shifting, unreal substance, forming, dissolving; purposeless and derelict. He is like the phantasmagoria of sunset
skies, whose essence is mutability:

> That which is now a horse, even with a thought
> The rack dislimns, and makes it indistinct
> As water is in water.   (IV. xii. 9)

The liquidity of 'life' is to melt within the elemental
liquidity of 'death'. This is now Antony:

> My good knave Eros, now thy captain is
> Even such a body: here I am Antony;
> Yet cannot hold this visible shape, my knave. (IV. xii. 12)

Death is visaged as the dissolution of life, mutation whose artistry is strange and mysterious as the multiform pencillings of a vesper heaven. In this life-vision death is not, even at the depth of despair, quite like the 'nothing' of earlier plays: rather a change of mode, a breath scattering and dissolving the wisp of smoke that for a short while claimed individual form and direction. Antony's experiences have ever wavered, unsteady. Now he would end these swift changes from unreality to unreality by the last alternation from the flux of life to the flux of death.

At this point Mardian enters, reporting Cleopatra's supposed death:

> . . . the last she spake
> Was 'Antony! most noble Antony!'
> Then in the midst a tearing groan did break
> The name of Antony; it was divided
> Between her heart and lips: she render'd life
> Thy name so buried in her.　　　　　(IV. xii. 29)

We have just been shot to the lowest depths of despair: love's failure has made Antony's purposes a mockery, his defeat a shame unexcused, his life a vapid and lunatic thing of hazy incertitude. There was only death, itself vaporous as life. Heaven and Hell gamble for man's Love. Antony's soul has been tossed and rocked, first heaven-high, then to tartarean depths. Now, when all seems lost, Heaven plays its final card, the single ace of Cleopatra's death:

Antony.　　　　　Dead then ?
Mardian.　　　　　　　　　　Dead.　　　　(IV. xii. 34)

This is one of the strangest, simplest, most beautiful and most transparent dramatic movements in Shakespeare. There is no flight more swift or sure. This is our last violent alternation. The sun swims back on a blackened universe, Life's sun itself more radiant in panoply of Death, no longer life's antagonist, but rather its robe, its sceptre, and its crown. For now death is no vain dissolution, but charged with an almighty significance. There is no rational sequence, the swelling flood of love's vision has no shallow 'reason' any more than Antony's loathing could defend itself in terms of sharp logic. At this news his anger is not denied, its 'causes' are no less real than before, nor is Cleopatra excused of treachery. His anger, its reasons, still exist: but they are straightway as a raindrop fallen in the ocean of his love, lost therein, meaningless; love's ocean-infinity mingling now with the infinity of Cleopatra's death. The symbol of love, itself infinite, has taken infinity as its territory. In terms of that eternity Love, not War, emerges victor: therefore—

> Unarm, Eros; the long day's task is done,
> And we must sleep. (IV. xii. 35)

Two things agonized Hamlet: faithlessness and death. Here they cancel out, like a fractional calculation, and instead of a baffling complex of figures we are left with $\frac{1}{1}$, itself unity. We are thus beyond all provisional negations: 'infinity' even is inept. We face rather a simple and positive unity, resultant from a calculation in terms of minus quantities. Even our old positive good, 'War', becomes meaningless now. Antony throws off his armour. He knows, like Enobarbus, his purpose, his direction. All else was froth, now the deep surges claim their own:

> Off, pluck off:
> The seven-fold shield of Ajax cannot keep
> The battery from my heart. O, cleave, my sides!
> Heart, once be stronger than thy continent,
> Crack thy frail case! Apace, Eros, apace.
> No more a soldier: bruised pieces, go;
> You have been nobly borne. From me awhile.
> I will o'ertake thee, Cleopatra, and
> Weep for my pardon. So it must be, for now
> All length is torture: since the torch is out,
> Lie down, and stray no farther: now all labour
> Mars what it does; yea, very force entangles
> Itself with strength: seal then, and all is done.
> Eros!—I come, my queen:—Eros!—Stay for me:
> Where souls do couch on flowers, we'll hand in hand,

And with our sprightly port make the ghosts gaze:
Dido and her Aeneas shall want troops,
And all the haunt be ours . . .   (IV. xii. 37)

Dido and Aeneas are apt here. The Vergilian hero sacrificed love for empire; the Shakespearian, empire for love.
This is the dying of our practical value War, or Empire,
the ascent of the immortal value, Love. War, so bright-
honoured in terms of time, holds less prestige in that
eternity to which Love steps as into the element for which
it is born, as the cygnet takes to the waters with untutored
ease. And Antony's vision is now a vision of eternity.
Recently he would slay Cleopatra: then one brief facet,
one little segment, one hour of her, was in his consciousness. Now death silhouettes both her personality and his
warrior-story in perfect completion; but against its darkness she is lit by the greater light.

Since Cleopatra died,
I have lived in such dishonour, that the gods
Detest my baseness.   (IV. xii. 55)

Here love, not empire or warriorship, has the monopoly
of 'honour'. Only in death is the finite thing complete.
Nor is this death an ending. It rather circumferences
and silhouettes its theme, throwing out the whole loved
essence in a bold and rounded perfection. And it is more
—its mystery casts a new glamour, so that our central
figure is not bounded by a rigid line, but rather mingles
with the surrounding unknown, every contour blended
with its setting, like the magic nimbus which haloes the
fine word of poetry, or the bright-haired sun-corona
flashing its brilliance to melt in heaven's blue. This is the
mating of finite and infinite in death: good and ill, ugly
and beautiful, blending in the one perfection. All 'length',
all temporal duration, is now 'torture'. Blind 'force' of
earthly life is entangled with the mastering and purposeful
'strength' of eternity, itself visioned as a brighter life, the
prize of love; no shadowed Hades, but a mode whose
grand Elysium transcends the flowery foisons of our
little O, the earth. Now death is Antony's bride:

> . . . I will be
> A bridegroom in my death, and run into 't
> As to a lover's bed.   (IV. xii. 99)

Death and love become identical.

I have stressed the alternating movements in Pompey and Caesar, where they are less distinct; and in Enobarbus and Antony where they are extremely vivid. Antony and Enobarbus both show a wavering and interchange of consciousness, the sweep of their oscillations getting wider and faster till the final equating of death with loyalty or love. This death is no cadence: death is rather the meridian of that embracing unknown which holds 'time' and 'eternity' as twin quadrants of its arching glory. Life is here deserted for love, itself 'Time's best jewel' (Sonnet LXV), and, since that love is now equated with death, life—or all that is most significant in life—and death are mated. This blending, interfusing, of life and death is echoed often before, the climax sending back reverberations, rippling movements of casual speech, into the preluding acts. Note Enobarbus' words on Cleopatra:

> . . . I do think there is mettle in death, which commits some
> loving act upon her, she hath such a celerity in dying.
>
> (I. ii. 152)

Antony spoke truer than he knew when he referred to making death 'love' him (III. xi. 193); or when he said that in the next day's fight, he would rather expect 'victorious life than death and honour' (IV. ii. 43). I have already observed how Antony's reception of the news of Fulvia's death exactly prefigures the later announcement of Cleopatra's:

> . . . she 's good, being gone;
> The hand could pluck her back that shov'd her on.
>
> (I. ii. 135)

A pale reflex of the later movement; but a neat comment on the 'varying' psychology I have noticed. I noted, too, another such comment:

> . . . the ebb'd man, ne'er lov'd till ne'er worth love,
> Comes dear'd by being lack'd.   (I. IV. 43)

When Antony tells Enobarbus of Fulvia's death, the resemblance to the later report of Cleopatra's is especially clear: the word 'dead' sounding with a leaden simplicity similar in both.

Antony. Fulvia is dead.
Enobarbus. Sir?
Antony. Fulvia is dead.
Enobarbus. Fulvia!
Antony. Dead.   (I. ii. 167)

The theme of death's sudden revelation is thus recurrent. Another early passage curiously forecasts the triple association of death, love, and life which forms the climacteric of Enobarbus', Antony's, and Cleopatra's stories. Cleopatra speaks:

              . . . and great Pompey
    Would stand and make his eyes grow in my brow;
    There would he anchor his aspect and die
    With looking on his life.   (I. v. 31)

Here life and love blend in a kind of death; and in the later action love and death blend in a kind of life. Death and Antony are, towards the end, lovers; for death is kind in this play, a positive, not a negative, reality: death 'enlarges' life's 'confine' (III. v. 13). But it should also be observed that Antony, finding Cleopatra still alive, knowing he is to leave, not meet her, reverts to troubled retrospect of his end, asking Cleopatra to think of him as when he was 'the greatest prince of the world' (IV. xiii. 54). We can yet see his end as a 'miserable change' (IV. xiii. 51) in terms of temporal affairs, the while he is lifted up to the waiting arms of love. The more perfect and joyful blending of death with love is left for Cleopatra.

The oscillation we have observed is no dynamic antagonism: there are not two hostile elements coexistent yet incompatible as in *Troilus*, *Macbeth*, *Lear*. It more nearly resembles the swift single alternations of *Othello* and *Timon*: yet here there is a continual, less irrevocable, succession, almost placid in its gentle varying. The *Macbeth* or *Lear* modes might be compared to the atom with its opposing protonic elements, negative and positive. Recently it has been suggested that this is a false analysis: that the atom is the ultimate unit, itself varying between positive and negative, alternately charged with interchanging significance. Though this appears a provisional and not quite satisfying statement, yet it exactly reflects the mature humanism of *Antony and Cleopatra*: it is in this sense that our play presents a unity in place of the former dualisms. Moreover, these alternations result in an awareness of timelessness. The persons throughout endure the present mode without vivid reference to past or future: the cloud passes, leaving no shadow on the sun it eclipsed. The recollection of past incompatibility with the present mood appears to be at the root of all psychic conflict. Here there is no such conflict, quite: the persons submit first to one, then the other, mode. There is an ebb and flow, a systole and diastole, of positive vision. There is no clear time-continuum of cause and effect: all 'causes' are surface deep, sometimes perhaps non-existent, certainly non-evident. Here the sombre or treacherous or distrustful mood falls, like Keats's melancholy, 'sudden from heaven, like an angry cloud': causeless, self-begotten, mysterious. It was similar with Hamlet. It is so in our own lives. Both *Antony and Cleopatra* and *Hamlet* present in this way a more vital realism by which other plays appear artificial. Here there is little significant feeling of any time-succession, the events are otherwise related and woven. This is clear also in the death-theme; a timeless instant of death and love synchronized opening vistas eternal. By synchronizing death, the most absolute of all negations, with the positive aspect of life, love, we are left with a sense of peace and happiness, an apprehension of pure immortality. Later I shall revert to this timeless quality, noting the massively spatialized technique of the whole. I shall next attempt analysis of Shakespeare's most amazing and dazzling single personification.

III

Cleopatra is baffling in the remarkable combination of diversity and unity. She has, far more than Hamlet, all qualities potential in her. All colours blend in a rich fascination, a single impact, a myriad tints: like some sky-rainbow of humanity she circles the solid humanism of former plays, containing all their essences, but, in sweeping curves of the spirit, outdistancing their varied experiences with ethereal compass. She is by turns proud and humble, a raging tigress and a demure girl; utterly deceitful, she is yet faithful to death; compact of highest regality, she is skittish as a shop girl on a bank-holiday; expressly feminine, she loves to engage in war; all woman's gentleness is hers, yet she shows the most callous and inhuman cruelty. Finally, though she is woman's loveliness incarnate, beauty enthroned beyond the shores of time, set above the rugged map of imperial splendour and down-watching the fighting princes below—herself the only prize of valour, another Helen of Troy, fit to glorify a Caesar's triumph with 'eternal' (v. i. 66) splendour, or crown an Antony with immortality, with all this there is in her a streak of mysterious and obscene evil. She is at once Rosalind, Beatrice, Ophelia, Gertrude, Cressid, Desdemona, Cordelia, and Lady Macbeth. Moreover, since the Antony-theme clearly reflects the essence of the former Shakespearian love and hate antagonisms, it will appear that *Antony and Cleopatra*, among its other amazing subtleties, contains the main elements of the sombre plays: not, as elsewhere, presented as negations, but viewed from the reverse, all fused and united in a single vision of universal and positive assertion, all equally blended in a finely-wrought, harmonious, complexity.

Cleopatra's first words are expressly feminine in their desire to hear love's accents reiterated:

> If it be love indeed, tell me how much.   (i. i. 14)

She urges Antony to hear the messengers from Rome. In a mingle of jealousy and mockery, perhaps meaning to

sound his faith and play on his affections, she calls to mind
the precariousness of their love, the Roman turbulences
that may threaten their paradisal Egyptian dream:

Cleopatra. Nay, hear them, Antony:
 Fulvia perchance is angry; or, who knows
 If the scarce-bearded Caesar have not sent
 His powerful mandate to you, 'Do this, or this;
 Take in that kingdom and enfranchise that;
 Perform 't, or else we damn thee.'
Antony.   How, my love!
Cleopatra. Perchance! nay, and most like:
 You must not stay here longer, your dismission
 Is come from Caesar; therefore hear it, Antony.
 Where 's Fulvia's process? Caesar's I would say? both?[1]
 Call in the messengers. As I am Egypt's queen,
 Thou blushest, Antony; and that blood of thine
 Is Caesar's homager: else so thy cheek pays shame
 When shrill-tongued Fulvia scolds.   (I. i. 19)

She gets her desire: a noble apostrophe to their love. Yet
she is not satisfied. Intuitively, she fears Rome:

     Excellent falsehood!
 Why did he marry Fulvia, and not love her?
 I'll seem the fool I am not; Antony
 Will be himself.   (I. i. 40)

Antony will not attend to Rome—he, luxuriating in love's
'soft hours' (I. i. 44), would continue nothing but 'sport'
(I. i. 47). Cleopatra is insistent, she would 'hear the
ambassadors' (I. i. 48). She senses danger and cannot
rest. Antony brushes her mood aside:

    Fie, wrangling queen!
 Whom every thing becomes, to chide, to laugh,
 To weep; whose every passion fully strives
 To make itself, in thee, fair and admir'd!
 No messenger, but thine; and all alone

---

[1] Again, Dr. Tannenbaum suggests as a better punctuation:
 'Where 's Fulvia's process? "Caesar's" I would say!—Both?'
which seems an improvement. See *Slips of the Tongue in Shakespeare,* as
quoted in my former note.

> To-night we'll wander through the streets, and note
> The qualities of people. Come, my queen;
> Last night you did desire it. (I. i. 48)

The spectroscopic variety of Cleopatra is thus early observed. Next we find her anxiously searching for Antony, afraid:

> He was dispos'd to mirth; but on the sudden
> A Roman thought hath struck him. (I. ii. 90)

Yet, on hearing of his approach, the searcher would hide: she is like a wild animal, suddenly scenting danger. Now throughout we must be ready to observe two things: her ability to act any part to gain or retain hold over Antony's heart; and the deep sincerity of love beneath these surface insincerities. With exquisite subtleties she plays on Antony's affection when she can win, but changes her tactics as soon as her power appears to be failing. Her integrity is questioned by Enobarbus:

> . . . Cleopatra, catching but the least noise of this, dies instantly; I have seen her die twenty times upon far poorer moment. (I. ii. 149)

But when Antony bitterly admits her 'cunning', he continues:

> Alack, sir, no; her passions are made of nothing but the finest part of pure love: we cannot call her winds and waters sighs and tears; they are greater storms and tempests than almanacs can report: this cannot be cunning in her; if it be, she makes a shower as well as Jove. (I. ii. 156)

So closely is play-acting woven into her love. She is a mixture of truth and falsehood, and the complexity is often baffling: passion and premeditation are curiously entwined in her. She is an adept in love's cunning, and so she tells Alexas:

> See where he is, who's with him, what he does:
> I did not send you: if you find him sad,
> Say I am dancing; if in mirth, report
> That I am sudden sick: quick, and return. (I. iii. 2)

When Charmian advises her rather to 'give him way, cross him in nothing,' she answers:

> Thou teachest like a fool; the way to lose him.   (I. iii. 10)

It is all thought out, carefully planned.

There follows the important scene of Antony's farewell to her. Cleopatra's changes throughout are very significant. First she pretends to be ill, asks Charmian to help her away, tells Antony to stand far off. Then, in withering scorn, she speaks:

> *Cleopatra.* I know, by that same eye, there 's some good news.
>   What says the married woman? You may go:
>   Would she had never given you leave to come!
>   Let her not say 'tis I that keep you here:
>   I have no power upon you; hers you are.
> *Antony.* The gods best know,—
> *Cleopatra.*   O, never was there queen
>   So mightily betray'd! yet at the first
>   I saw the treasons planted.
> *Antony.*   Cleopatra,—
> *Cleopatra.* Why should I think you can be mine and true,
>   Though you in swearing shake the throned gods,
>   Who have been false to Fulvia? Riotous madness,
>   To be entangled with those mouth-made vows,
>   Which break themselves in swearing.   (I. iii. 19)

She continues to taunt him: tells him to go, if so he will, without patching excuses. Then she flings down the noble petulances of her love:

> Nay, pray you, seek no colour for your going,
> But bid farewell, and go: when you sued staying,
> Then was the time for words: no going then;
> Eternity was in our lips and eyes,
> Bliss in our brows' bent; none our parts so poor,
> But was a race of heaven: they are so still,
> Or thou, the greatest soldier in the world,
> Art turn'd the greatest liar.   (I. iii. 32)

Then again—

> I would I had thy inches; thou shouldst know
> There were a heart in Egypt.   (I. iii. 40)

Antony at last tries to stem the liquid fire of her thwarted passion inblazing at his readiness to leave her. Hearing of Fulvia's death, she bitterly reproaches him for lacking proper sorrow: so will her own death be received. She is unfair, quite irrational, typically feminine. But all these shows are projections of one central reality: her burning passion, fierce tigress-love, for Antony. Now Antony protests his love's integrity: he goes to make war in her name, her knight. His words are a little facile and perfunctory. Still, the delicious assurance draws from her:

> Cut my lace, Charmian, come;
> But let it be: I am quickly ill, and well,
> So Antony loves.   (i. iii. 71)

Love is ever the pivot of her gyrating personality, the light which illumes the phantasmagoria of her shifting moods. Again Antony assures her that his love is firm. Now again she taunts him, less bitterly; rather with a touch of satiric playfulness, bids him to weep and play one scene 'of excellent dissembling' (i. iii. 79). Antony's patience begins to fail: he has done all that could possibly be required by way of masculine adoration. She has not responded by submitting to his wider duties:

> *Antony.* You'll heat my blood: no more.
> *Cleopatra.* You can do better yet; but this is meetly.
> *Antony.* Now, by my sword,—
> *Cleopatra.*   And target. Still he mends;
> But this is not the best. Look, prithee, Charmian,
> How this Herculean Roman does become
> The carriage of his chafe.   (i. iii. 80)

Envenomed anger is dissolved by a moment of love satisfied—'I am quickly ill, and well, so Antony loves'—and is solidified again to half-playful mockery, which then alters gradually to this laughing Rosalind love: an exquisite gradation, like an April sun from out showery clouds, an unanalysable movement like the meltings of sunset. For now, partly due to Antony's rising impatience, partly as though these surface impersonations can no longer mask her passion's simplicity, she breaks down in the jewelled statement of their love, a sweet finality beyond words:

> Courteous lord, one word.
> Sir, you and I must part, but that 's not it:
> Sir, you and I have lov'd, but there 's not it;
> That you know well: something it is I would,—
> O, my oblivion is a very Antony,
> And I am all forgotten.   (I. iii. 86)

We remember Enobarbus' apt phrase: 'her passions are made of nothing but the finest part of pure love' (I. ii. 151). It is seen true in this sudden abandon, a roseate sincerity swiftly unfurled, the flower to which her other moods are as unopened buds.   As he reproaches her with 'idleness', she answers:

> 'Tis sweating labour
> To bear such idleness so near the heart
> As Cleopatra this.   (I. iii. 93)

But now she is gentle, plays properly woman's part of relinquishing her man to his duty:

> But, sir, forgive me;
> Since my becomings kill me, when they do not
> Eye well to you: your honour calls you hence;
> Therefore be deaf to my unpitied folly,
> And all the gods go with you! upon your sword
> Sit laurel victory! and smooth success
> Be strew'd before your feet!   (I. iii. 95)

Cleopatra angles for her Antony; giving out when necessary, drawing in when possible. She would draw him to her bosom from that world of stern action which is his sphere. She is typical of woman trying to hold man from other interests, other calls. Throughout this scene it will be observed that she is the primary force in their love, its origin and strength, while he is perfunctory, hasty, anxious to be gone:

> Let us go. Come;
> Our separation so abides, and flies,
> That thou, residing here, go'st yet with me,
> And I, hence fleeting, here remain with thee.
> Away!   (I. iii. 101)

A usual Shakespearian love-thought: but not elsewhere presented so casually. Cleopatra fights for his love. But she knows the limitations of her magic, works within them, employing a conscious artistry to serve her instinctive passion. Always, however, till near the play's end, we must observe that love is the only root of her actions. She is thus undivided, a trader in love alone: whereas Antony serves two gods: 'love' and 'honour'.

Now Antony is gone and she is alone with her girls. But she is still all in Antony; would drink mandragora to sleep out the 'great gap of time' which is Antony's absence (I. v. 5). Every moment is weighted with love's memory:

> O Charmian,
> Where think'st thou he is now? Stands he, or sits he?
> Or does he walk? or is he on his horse?
> O happy horse, to bear the weight of Antony!
> Do bravely, horse! for wot'st thou whom thou movest?
> The demi-Atlas of this earth, the arm
> And burgonet of men. He's speaking now,
> Or murmuring 'Where's my serpent of old Nile?'
> For so he calls me: now I feed myself
> With most delicious poison . . .   (I. v. 18)

Alexas enters, brings news of Antony. He presents to her an 'orient pearl', kissed by Antony, an ambassador of love. He repeats Antony's reverberating message:

> 'Good friend', quoth he,
> 'Say, the firm Roman to great Egypt sends
> This treasure of an oyster; at whose foot,
> To mend the petty present, I will piece
> Her opulent throne with kingdoms; all the east,
> Say thou, shall call her mistress.'   (I. v. 42)

Such is the imperial glory of our love-theme: for our material splendour is generally, as here, but the suits and trappings to a spirit-passion out-scintillating the diadems of empire. But Cleopatra takes no note of resounding phrases. Kingdoms are clay. She would hear rather of her Antony alone:

Cleopatra.   What, was he sad or merry?

Alexas. Like to the time o' the year between the extremes
    Of hot and cold; he was nor sad nor merry.
Cleopatra. O well-divided disposition! Note him,
    Note him, good Charmian, 'tis the man; but note him:
    He was not sad, for he would shine on those
    That make their looks by his; he was not merry,
    Which seem'd to tell them his remembrance lay
    In Egypt with his joy; but between both:
    O heavenly mingle! Be'st thou sad or merry,
    The violence of either thee becomes,
    So does it no man else.   (I. V. 50)

Cleopatra's world, despite her queenship, is a woman's
world: her mental horizon close bounded by love's infinity.
So she sends messengers daily to Antony. Alexas met no
less than twenty. Antony blazes in her thought, hour by
hour. Nor even music relieves her longing. Like Orsino,
she would bid music, love's solace and companion,
assuage her loneliness:

Cleopatra. Give me some music; music, moody food
    Of us that trade in love.
Attendant.   The music, ho!
Cleopatra. Let it alone . . .   (II. V. I)

Cleopatra 'trades in love'; so beauty ever lives by ab-
sorbing strength, woman by allure of man. The phrase
does not apply to Cleopatra alone, nor even to a feminine
type: it goes deeper, and to misread it is to forgo the fine
scope of our vision. Cleopatra is not one, but all, woman,
waiting for man. She is another Dido, as Vergil writes
down the story; or as Milton's Eve—'He for God only,
she for God in him'. She waits with her girls for Antony.
They generously humour her restlessness. Poor Charmian's arm is sore with billiards (II. V. 4). Cleopatra and
her girls at Alexandria are as the Eternal Femininity
waiting for Man. A certain eternity broods over this
still, languorous Alexandria. The wars of Caesar and
Antony seem a little childish by these deeps of love: what,
to Cleopatra, are the empires of Antony's promise, to the
look of his eye, his joy or sorrow, his divine humanity?

So Cleopatra, her maids, her eunuch Mardian, talk and think of Antony, play billiards, go fishing: a life still as a windless sea, bronzed tropically by heaven's wide arch of melting flame; a life of ease, but charged to breaking with love's burning weight. And again, this silent Alexandria is a place of eternal peace, calling man back to rest among its olives from the heat and dust of battering days. All here is translucent and bright, pure as the Nile waters:

> . . . we'll to the river: there,
> My music playing far off, I will betray
> Tawny-finn'd fishes . . .   (II. v. 10)

Cleopatra is incarnate queen of music and romance; her Alexandria eternity inspaced on earth.

But there is merriment here, in this eternity. It holds no chill solemnity. Charmian recalls how she once made sport of Antony's 'fervency' and warrior-prowess:

> *Charmian.*   'Twas merry when
> You wager'd on your angling; when your diver
> Did hang a salt-fish on his hook, which he
> With fervency drew up.
> *Cleopatra.*   That time,—O times!—
> I laugh'd him out of patience; and that night
> I laugh'd him into patience: and next morn,
> Ere the ninth hour, I drunk him to his bed;
> Then put my tires and mantles on him, whilst
> I wore his sword Philippan.   (II. v. 15)

So much for masculine 'fervency'. Alexandria is a paradise of feast, fun, and love. This is a myriad-qualitied heaven: a warrior's Valhalla, but also a paradise brimming with the merriment of Shakespeare's own Beatrice, and the mystic wells of romantic light that gleam in Dante's. Alexandria calls Antony from imperial turbulence, would have him relinquish the childish all-too-serious quarrels of Rome and join in the glinting laughter of love. Why must he take things so deadly earnest? Cleopatra, woman-like, cannot admit an Antony's ambitions as all-worthy, would laugh at them: watches them, as Asia diademed with ages of spiritual insight might tolerantly watch

Europe proudly flaunting her war-dinted and plated helmet to the skies. Cleopatra is 'riggish' (II. ii. 245); Enobarbus once saw her 'hop forty paces through the public street' (II. ii. 234). Sportiveness is strong in Antony's and Cleopatra's love. To this happy paradise she would recall him.

But she is a very tigress in wrath. A messenger brings news of Antony's marriage. She strikes him, again and again:

> What say you? Hence,
> Horrible villain! or I'll spurn thine eyes
> Like balls before me; I'll unhair thy head:
> Thou shalt be whipp'd with wire, and stew'd in brine,
> Smarting in lingering pickle.   (II. v. 62)

Next she draws a knife and all but slays him. She is merciless, a Jezebel of wrath. She dismisses him at last, is 'faint', and through her tigress-wrath we again see the purely feminine weakness and love:

> Lead me from hence;
> I faint: O Iras, Charmian! 'tis no matter.
> Go to the fellow, good Alexas; bid him
> Report the feature of Octavia, her years,
> Her inclination, let him not leave out
> The colour of her hair: bring me word quickly.
> Let him for ever go:—let him not—Charmian,
> Though he be painted one way like a Gorgon,
> The other way 's a Mars. Bid you Alexas
> Bring me word how tall she is. Pity me, Charmian,
> But do not speak to me. Lead me to my chamber.
>   (II. v. 109)

Cleopatra is a match for the Roman Empire, yet weak as a child. Later she sends for the messenger, again questions him minutely, with a finely feminine inquisitiveness about her rival. The messenger is tactful.

Cleopatra. Is she as tall as me?
Messenger.   She is not, madam.
Cleopatra. Did'st hear her speak? is she shrill-tongued or low?
Messenger. Madam, I heard her speak; she is low-voiced.
Cleopatra. That 's not so good: he cannot like her long.

Charmian. Like her! O Isis! 'tis impossible.
Cleopatra. I think so, Charmian: dull of tongue, and dwarfish!

(III. iii. 14)

Cleopatra continues by a suggested comparison of her own 'majesty' with Octavia's bearing:

Cleopatra. What majesty is in her gait? Remember,
If e'er thou look'dst on majesty.
Messenger.   She creeps:
Her motion and her station are as one;
She shows a body rather than a life,
A statue than a breather.   (III. iii. 20)

So finely is the contrast pointed. Octavia's whiteness is as paste, or deathly alabaster, compared with Cleopatra's vital sun whose single fire is blent of all passion's varying colours, shifting, opalescent, dazzling. Cleopatra is all womanly things, good or evil. There is danger in her, danger and violence, as in her reception of the messenger, in her desire to distract Antony from all things but herself. She has a serpent's grace, a serpent's attraction, dangerous as Eve, serpent-beguiled. She is well-named 'The Serpent of Old Nile'. Sometimes her love appears violent and selfish and almost evil; at others, it is pure and innocent as the frosty light of a Christmas star. She is one way a Medusa, the other a Madonna of serenity and peace. Now she is reassured by the messenger's details. She cannot fear this puppet, Octavia. She praises the messenger's insight and judgement. She continues:

Cleopatra. Guess at her years, I prithee.
Messenger.   Madam,
She was a widow,—
Cleopatra.   Widow! Charmian, hark.
Messenger. And I do think she 's thirty.
Cleopatra. Bear'st thou her face in mind? is't long or round?
Messenger. Round even to faultiness.
Cleopatra. For the most part, too, they are foolish that are so.
Her hair, what colour?
Messenger. Brown, madam: and her forehead
As low as she would wish it.   (III. iii. 29)

Now she asks the messenger not 'to take her former harshness ill'; she regrets that she so 'harried' him; agrees he is a 'proper' man. Her opinion of him varies according to the news he brings. She is not fair. She does not control and unify her impressions by any cool reason. She is a sapling swaying to every breath of her passionate desires. But those passions harp so fine a natural music as they pass, that there is no incongruity, no lack of beauty: rather an ever-harmonized music of passionate discords.

When Caesar and Antony oppose each other in the third act, Cleopatra assumes another role. Now she is an Amazon. Like Desdemona she will not be 'a moth of peace' when her lord goes to fight. Though Enobarbus strongly attempts dissuasion, she is angered:

> Sink Rome, and their tongues rot
> That speak against us! A charge we bear i' the war,
> And, as the president of my kingdom, will
> Appear there for a man. Speak not against it;
> I will not stay behind. (III. vii. 16)

Now she would be a proper general, practical and efficient as any man, a veritable St. Joan. When Antony is amazed at Caesar's sudden proximity, she is incisively critical:

> Celerity is never more admir'd
> Than by the negligent. (III. vii. 25)

Now she boasts, prideful of her navy. There is really no limit to her repertory. But the feminine basis of her varying shows is never long forgotten. Here, as usual, it reswims into our vision, asserts itself. Always this is our unifying principle in analysis: every strong passion and violent assertion, with a varying, see-saw motion, returns, as with Lady Macbeth, to pure femininity. We noticed this rhythm in Act I; it was vivid in her meeting with the messenger. So, now, her Amazon courage melts into a woman's fear. She would aspire to man's courage, she would have Antony all hers: if he cannot leave the world of turbulence for the crowned peace of love, then she, queen of love, will share this action with him. So her woman's heart ruins his manhood. He follows her flying sails.

The interplay of the sexes, their respective weaknesses and strengths, is always finely pictured. The play throughout shows not only the blending of sex, but also its necessary antagonism and mutual hindrance. Antony never quite forgets his soldiering till the end: he and Cleopatra never blend perfectly till death. The theme of the action is thus the antagonism of those values, the masculine and the feminine, which we have observed already: War, or Empire, and Love. Both these high Shakespearian values, positive and rich in romantic colour and suggestion, contend together; and their contest is as the impact of angelic forces. Not Caesar against Antony, rather Antony the soldier against Antony the lover. Here the love-value finally wins—indeed, one short scene (iii. i.) exists partly (not wholly) to show a strain of ugly self-glorification, Coriolanus-wise, in our Antony's soldiership, decreasing its worth in comparison with his adoration of Cleopatra. Now the wrench apart, and blending, of these elements is the repulsion and attraction of sex. Nor any theme outspaces this. For, in a final judgement, our story is the story of the universal differentiation, the separation and multiplicity, the retraction to unity; the ebbing and flowing of God Himself into His universe. But, whereas in *Timon* after the agony of differentiation unity is reached by utter severance, here it will be attained by sex with sex blending, and death blent with life. Death and Life are the sexes of the absolute: Death, the feminine, calls back the adventurer, Life, to her bosom. So Cleopatra awaits Antony; and so Antony finally dies into the arms of Cleopatra's love. And this sudden raising of our protagonists' love and death story into so universal and titanic a meaning is no extravagance in a play where all elements are ever seen to blend and mingle in a fruitful matrimony, where man himself in love is drawn as a colossus overtopping the spheres of heaven. For, in the meanest and smallest atom the eternal systole and diastole is at work; and this play shows us that same see-saw alternation, that waking and sleeping of vision, that pulsing of eternity, pumping life-blood into the tingling veins of time.

After her fatal action and Antony's shameful retrograde captaincy, Cleopatra is all repentance, distracted, asking pardon:

> O my lord, my lord,
> Forgive my fearful sails! I little thought
> You would have follow'd. (III. ix. 54)

Now she is femininely weak, all bowed to man's strength which that weakness has ruined. But next there is Caesar's offer of peace if Antony be delivered, followed by Antony's challenge to single combat. Thyreus attends Cleopatra alone, and personally offers her safety and protection, if she will betray Antony's cause. He gives her every chance to do so easily:

> *Thyreus.* He knows that you embrace not Antony
> As you did love, but as you fear'd him.
> *Cleopatra.* O!
> *Thyreus.* The scars upon your honour, therefore, he
> Does pity, as constrained blemishes,
> Not as deserved.
> *Cleopatra.* He is a god, and knows
> What is most right: mine honour was not yielded,
> But conquer'd merely. (III. xi. 56)

This is truly a pivot moment, not only of this play, but of the whole sequence of Shakespeare's later visions. Love is at stake. On Cleopatra depends the integrity to Love's cause of Antony, Enobarbus, Iras, Charmian—and Caesar, too, who must laugh to see Antony's prostitute queen desert him. Octavia and all Rome will scorn this love-madness of a once noble soldier, now gipsy-betrayed. She is another Delilah to his Samson, man again is betrayed by woman's cheating lure. Cleopatra is clearly the origin of our love-vision, all other loves and allegiances depend on her integrity; she is Queen of Love, Alexandria Love's palace home. Moreover, where Ophelia, Desdemona, Cressid, Cordelia, all failed through a certain weakness

intrinsic to their limited personalities, here, in the infinite
love-spaces of our present play, in Cleopatra's infinity, we
might expect success. Those heroines we pitied, or, if we
loved, then, with our Cleopatra now known, we realize we
loved them but in 'our salad days', when 'green in judgement' (I. v. 73). Cleopatra's rich profusion and 'infinite
variety' makes them cloy to our taste: they are all merest
Octavias beside her. For Cleopatra is all womankind,
therefore all romantic vision, the origin of love, the origin
of life. The universe is compacted embryonic in the womb
of her divine and unlimited femininity. If she fails, it is as
though the origin of life itself were poisoned at its source.
With an inscrutably evil callousness Cleopatra now proceeds to fail:

> Most kind messenger,
> Say to great Caesar this: in deputation
> I kiss his conquering hand: tell him, I am prompt
> To lay my crown at 's feet, and there to kneel:
> Tell him, from his all-obeying breath I hear
> The doom of Egypt.   (III. xi. 73)

The Serpent of old Nile. This is the primal Eve in
Cleopatra. It is a serpentine evil, an utterly selfish streak
of bottomless evil. She will try to win Octavius. She even
takes pleasure in reminding the messenger of her other
conquests, how great Julius Caesar loved her:

> Your Caesar's father oft,
> When he hath mus'd of taking kingdoms in,
> Bestow'd his lips on that unworthy place,
> As it rain'd kisses.   (III. xi. 82)

Pompey (I. v. 31), Julius Caesar, Antony—and now,
perhaps, Octavius. The murmured remembrance is sweet
to her. Antony is put aside. 'Policy' wins, unutterable
baseness, love's ripening apple worm-eaten at the core.

Antony enters: Enobarbus had left to tell him of
Cleopatra's treachery. He directs his fury first on
Thyreus, then on Cleopatra. He abuses her with all
possible foul invectives. His ideal is now filth, his loathing
knows no limit. It is the old story of Hate from *Hamlet* to

Timon. Cleopatra for long can get no word in to stem the torrential abuse. At last:

> *Cleopatra.*   Not know me yet?
> *Antony.* Cold-hearted toward me?
> *Cleopatra.*   Ah, dear, if I be so,
>   From my cold heart let heaven engender hail,
>   And poison it in the source; and the first stone
>   Drop in my neck: as it determines, so
>   Dissolve my life!   (III. xi. 157)

Are we to accept this excuse? It is all we get. Antony is 'satisfied'. It is as though her fascination wins us to a changed outlook, willing to question no further. Perhaps Cleopatra has persuaded herself even that she was not dallying with treachery. Antony recovers his spirits. All is now again new-born hope, splendid and festive. Again our rocking motion swings back on to our vision the positive essences, love, hope, ardour:

>   It is my birth-day:
>   I had thought to have held it poor; but, since my lord
>   Is Antony again, I will be Cleopatra.   (III. xi. 185)

The eclipsing of our 'terrene moon' (III. xi. 153), Cleopatra, is past. Again she shines refulgent.

Next day, before the battle, she is Antony's faithful woman, solicitous for his health and comfort. She would have him 'sleep a little' first (IV. iv. 1). Then, since he will arm straightway, she would help:

>   Nay, I'll help too.
>   What 's this for?   (IV. iv. 5)

Now Samson's Delilah has become an Andromache, bidding her Hector to battle. Antony laughingly praises her:

>   Thou fumblest, Eros; and my queen 's a squire
>   More tight at this than thou.   (IV. iv. 14)

Here love and warriorship blend finely, each gilded by the other. The rigid dualisms of the sombre plays crossed at right angles, making each a crucifix of torture. Here there is no such pain. The two supreme values are like lines inter-

11

secting and gently diverging at acute angles. Here is the
point of intersection, the highest point of pure life-joy
reached in the play, love and warrior-strength blended:

> O love,
> That thou couldst see my wars to-day, and knew'st
> The royal occupation! thou shouldst see
> A workman in 't.					(IV. iv. 15)

He returns, victor. Cleopatra's phrase of love floods out
in:

> Lord of lords!
> O infinite virtue, comest thou smiling from
> The world's great snare uncaught?		(IV. viii. 16)

But there is next more failure at sea. Antony believes
Cleopatra has betrayed him, the universe is again blackened,
love's lamp-flame oil and smoke malodorous. Antony is
mad as a trapped animal, swears she must die. Cleopatra
is baffled:

> O, he is more mad
> Than Telamon for his shield . . .		(IV. xi. 1)

Her cunning comes to aid her:

> To the monument!
> Mardian, go tell him I have slain myself;
> Say, that the last I spoke was 'Antony',
> And word it, prithee, piteously: hence, Mardian,
> And bring me how he takes my death . . .	(IV. xi. 6)

Now she hears he is dying, and her tragic passion is richly
inwrought:

> All strange and terrible events are welcome,
> But comforts we despise; our size of sorrow,
> Proportion'd to our cause, must be as great
> As that which makes it.			(IV. xiii. 3)

And, as Antony is carried to her:

> O sun,
> Burn the great sphere thou movest in! darkling stand
> The varying shore o' the world. O Antony,
> Antony, Antony! Help, Charmian, help, Iras, help;
> Help, friends below; let 's draw him hither. (IV. xiii. 9)

She is strangely efficient and practical as she gives direction for lifting Antony up to the monument; and withal still more strangely cheerful, as though this snow-crest of tragedy catches a glittering brilliance of delicate merriment from a source unseen:

> Here 's sport indeed! How heavy weighs my lord!
> Our strength is all gone into heaviness,
> That makes the weight: had I great Juno's power,
> The strong-wing'd Mercury should fetch thee up,
> And set thee by Jove's side. Yet come a little,—
> Wishers were ever fools,—O, come, come, come;
> And welcome, welcome! die where thou hast lived:
> Quicken with kissing: had my lips that power,
> Thus would I wear them out.   (IV. xiii. 32)

Death is showered with love's quickening kisses. So she abandons herself to love, and then anger:

>   . . . let me rail so high,
> That the false housewife Fortune break her wheel,
> Provok'd by my offence.   (IV. xiii. 43)

When he dies, the world is 'no better than a sty' (IV. xiii. 62):

>   . . . young boys and girls
> Are level now with men; the odds is gone,
> And there is nothing left remarkable
> Beneath the visiting moon.   (IV. xiii. 65)

Love gone, the world is now a barren promontory extending its naked irrelevances to a staring moon. At the climax of grief she faints. When she revives there are swift changes in her passionate words. First, we are drawn to observe that primary element of pure femininity, something not unlike the weakness of Lady Macbeth:

> No more, but e'en a woman, and commanded
> By such poor passion as the maid that milks
> And does the meanest chares.   (IV. xiii. 72)

In an ecstasy of wrath she next opposes her regality to heaven:

>   It were for me
> To throw my sceptre at the injurious gods;
> To tell them that this world did equal theirs
> Till they had stol'n our jewel.   (IV. xiii. 75)

But she recognizes the futility and puerility of all passion:
now death only makes meaning to her, it alone has positive
significance. Throughout this scene her passion sings so
sweet its varying melodies that we find her supreme in
sorrow as in 'love' or 'sport':

> All 's but naught;
> Patience is sottish, and impatience does
> Become a dog that 's mad: then is it sin
> To rush into the secret house of death,
> Ere death dare come to us?   (iv. xiii. 78)

Suddenly she is strangely bright-hearted, an April
brilliance smiling through tears and cloud. Throughout
we note how merriment is here a ripple on the tragic
waters, ruffling their sombre deeps to reflect sun-ward a
myriad laughters:

> How do you, women?
> What, what! good cheer! Why, how now, Charmian!
> My noble girls! Ah, women, women, look,
> Our lamp is spent, it 's out! Good sirs, take heart:
> We 'll bury him; and then, what 's brave, what 's noble,
> Let 's do it after the high Roman fashion,
> And make death proud to take us.   (iv. xiii. 82)

There is an exquisite variety in her glinting, shifting,
evanescent moods of passion; aglow with the pulsing
blood of her radiant femininity, compact of meekness and
infinite pride, of strength and weakness intertwined.
Throughout this scene there has, too, been a strange
serenity refusing all black Satanic effects, a strength of
wing on which the Ariel spirit of poetry towers above
tragedy, its eagle-eyes up-raised. So Cleopatra is strange to
us, pure woman as she is, like some foreign bird of similar
form to ours, yet surpassing them in its rich variance of
plumage; most surely of our world, most strangely
different; most radiant and peaceful even at the climacteric
of grief.

On casting retrospect over Cleopatra's tale we are
struck by her variety. It surpasses that of any other
Shakespearian person. In this way she is all womankind,

rather than a single woman: or again, we may say she is universal in the sense that any one person, or, indeed, any one object of any sort, becomes a symbol of universal meaning and content if properly understood. And Cleopatra's 'variety' is so vividly depicted that it is easy to understand. Her two primary qualities are: (i) the essential femininity we have continually observed, and (ii) her profuse variety of psychic modes: which two are clearly one, since a profound and comprehensive delineation of essential woman is necessarily very varied, and built of contradictions. Our analyses have without straining made reference, not only to Shakespeare's previous heroines, but to Eve, Jezebel, Helen of Troy, Amazons, St. Joan, Dido, Delilah, Andromache, Dante's Beatrice, Medusa, the Madonna. All women of legend or literature combine to make our Cleopatra. She is a silk shot with dazzling, shifting, colours. The same is true of the play as an artistic whole. She, more than any other, is the play. Hence the femininity in the vowel-sounds and the style generally, which I have noted already, and its shifting, dazzling, opalescent interplay of imagery. Now it will be clear that Cleopatra is the divinity of this play in the sense that Desdemona is the divinity of *Othello*. Her trans-cendent divinity and beauty are stressed in Enobarbus' description of her in her barge. The sombre plays all revolved on such ideals: Hamlet's father, Isabella, Helen of Troy (in *Troilus*), Desdemona, Duncan and the English King in *Macbeth*, Cordelia, Timon himself: all are at some time vividly idealized, all but equated with divinity. Such divinity was ever divine by nature of a certain limited perfection, a certain limited beauty. Cleopatra is divine by nature of her divine variety and profusion. Queen of romance, she is yet, like Antony, old: 'wrinkled deep in time'. The contrast is the same as that between the two theological conceptions of a God containing all qualities good and evil, and a God partial and exclusive: God the Father, and God the Son. The same contrast is reflected in the ethic of the Duke in *Measure for Measure*, who knows both good and evil within himself, and that of Angelo who prides himself on a false, because exclusive, sanctity. Here Cleopatra has beside her Octavia to point the same contrast: and Octavia is a thing of cardboard in this comparison. Now since Cleopatra is so comprehensively conceived, it will be clear that the streak of serpentine evil in her is part of her complex fascination: and, though real and as truly part of her as any other quality, it will be found to melt into her whole personality, enriching rather than limiting her more positive attractions. A limited perfection is sand on which to build: thus Isabella was exposed to shame, her very virtue turned against her when it claimed all-importance. Troilus could not accept Cressid's faithlessness as hers; Desdemona's purity could not save her in a world where an Iago exists. In Cleopatra we find a personification blent of 'good' and 'evil', a Cordelia with a streak of Lady Macbeth. The perfection flowers from totality, not exclusion. From any limited view, her treachery is nauseating; but, from the view of eternity, the whole and all its parts observed, the 'evil' is seen otherwise, as part of a wider pattern. This is why Antony, when his anger is thrown suddenly into relation with death's eternity, so completely alters: his rage abates, its 'reason' now meaningless. Enobarbus speaks truth of Cleopatra:

> Age cannot wither her, nor custom stale
> Her infinite variety: other women cloy
> The appetites they feed; but she makes hungry
> Where most she satisfies: for vilest things
> Become themselves in her; that the holy priests
> Bless her when she is riggish. (ii. ii. 240)

Her power to assimilate all qualities and gild them with the alchemy of her rich personality was observed, too, by Antony. She is one

> Whom every thing becomes, to chide, to laugh,
> To weep; whose every passion fully strives
> To make itself, in thee, fair and admir'd! (i. i. 49)

She is, indeed, 'a most triumphant lady' (ii. ii. 193): and

she triumphs where others failed. I conclude, therefore, that the Cleopatra-vision, without shirking the problems of the sombre plays, yet answers them imaginatively. It remains to indicate how this completer creation, Cleopatra, proceeds through the final scenes to vindicate this statement, and assert the rights of her 'infinite variety' to that imperial diadem of love denied by the poet to other more limited and therefore less perfect divinities. Cleopatra excels by virtue of her psychic infinity, which necessarily includes evil: she wins by her very capacity to fail, and, herself infinite, steps the more naturally to the infinities of death.

So our final act here is as the crest not only of this play but of the whole Shakespearian progress. All this consummate artistry has been lavished on Cleopatra that she may assert the power of love to enclose not only life, but death, in its vision. Her Antony dead, she faces Caesar and his powers alone. She has determined on the 'better life' of death:

> My desolation does begin to make
> A better life. 'Tis paltry to be Caesar;
> Not being Fortune, he 's but Fortune's knave,
> A minister of her will: and it is great
> To do that thing that ends all other deeds;
> Which shackles accidents and bolts up change;
> Which sleeps, and never palates more the dung,
> The beggar's nurse and Caesar's.   (v. ii. 1)

'Death' is not here even named. It is 'a better life','that thing. . . .' Here, where we are directly to catch some awareness of 'death's' mystery, the word itself, with its sombre associations, inevitably blurs somewhat our vision. The root idea of this pregnant passage is the sharp juxtaposition of 'time' and 'eternity'. Caesar, with his worldly success, is 'paltry', tossed hither and thither on the rough flux of 'fortune': so much for world-success. For Cleopatra there is 'that thing', the ender of all other deeds. First we are pointed to its 'ending'—the death of Lear. And we are shown its essential 'greatness' or grandeur, its aesthetic appeal: so, too, in *Lear* death, by its majestic and grand impact, left us with a sense of peace. Next we see how it is master of 'accidents' and 'change', that is, time. Eternity nullifies time at one stroke, prisons it, renders it harmless; that thief 'injurious time', thing of 'robber's haste', ever ready to 'cram his rich thievery up' and escape with it (*Troilus*, iv. iv. 44). So far we have noted death's effect from the side of life: now we pass to its own essential sovereignty. First, it is like sleep; second, it tastes no longer that 'dungy earth' (i. i. 35) which is unworthy of its child; finally, it is nurse alike to Caesar in his glory and the beggar in his penury—a kindly presence, dear nurse to life, eternity calling back the child of time to its bosom. We have passed from its aesthetic appeal to a quick and tight analysis of its apparent effects, and finally we contemplate its more personal, moral, attitude to man: that of a nurse to a child. Is this 'death'? What is the 'death' of *Antony and Cleopatra*? Not that the word itself is elsewhere absent: but it is continually welcomed as something of positive worth and sweet nourishing delight, like love:

> Where art thou, death?
> Come hither, come! come, come, and take a queen
> Worth many babes and beggars!   (v. ii. 46)

So cries Cleopatra when she is surrounded by enemies. They have taken the dagger from her hand, and she has been deprived even of death 'that rids our dogs from languish' (v. ii. 42). Proculeius has falsely promised her Caesar's 'grace', but she does not believe him. In torrential passion she swears she will some way die. She will 'eat no meat', nor drink, nor sleep (v. ii. 49–51). She will not go as a prize to Rome:

> Rather a ditch in Egypt
> Be gentle grave unto me! rather on Nilus' mud
> Lay me stark naked, and let the water-flies
> Blow me into abhorring! rather make
> My country's high pyramides my gibbet,
> And hang me up in chains!   (v. ii. 57)

Her changes are again swift. All this follows closely after her regal reception of Caesar's embassy:

> If your master
> Would have a queen his beggar, you must tell him,
> That majesty, to keep decorum, must
> No less beg than a kingdom: if he please
> To give me conquer'd Egypt for my son,
> He gives me so much of mine own, as I
> Will kneel to him with thanks.   (v. ii. 15)

But now she is wild, entrapped. All the message she will send to Caesar is

> Say, I would die.   (v. ii. 70)

Proculeius leaves her with Dolabella. She recounts now her dream of Antony.

Out of her varying moods, passions, experiences, one fact emerges: her serene love of Antony. This, among all else fleeting, is, ultimately, changeless and still, the centre and circumference of her personality, of the play. Here she is tranced by a breathless tranquillity as she rehearses her marvellous dream. She, who is herself all things potential, knows Antony now as all things accomplished. In death, by love, transfigured, he is the universe and more:

> His face was as the heavens; and therein stuck
> A sun and moon, which kept their course, and lighted
> The little O, the earth.   (v. ii. 79)

Cleopatra, in splendour of love's imaginings, holds earth and its sun, heaven and all eternities in her gaze. So image succeeds image in placid miraculous succession, wondrous. And Cleopatra is tipped with orient fire, the mouthpiece of a revelation beyond earthly sight:

> His legs bestrid the ocean: his rear'd arm
> Crested the world . . .   (v. ii. 82)

In this blazing love-sight, Cleopatra, herself infinite woman, is being mated to the infinity of Antony dead. They, who were not married in life, will find their bridal in death. As a butterfly from its chrysalis she slowly wakes, and is spreading roseate wings to the dawn. But first Caesar comes to her, delays her flight.

A curious dialogue follows. There is a long and elaborate fencing of insincerities, Cleopatra all humility, Caesar all generous bounty: neither is honest. Caesar means to add Cleopatra to his trophies of victory. Cleopatra knows well his purposes, forewarned by Dolabella, but she is trying her last hope: she would fascinate him, add him to her triumphs of love. Caesar deceives her, she deceives him, especially in her proffer of an inventory of her wealth, its falsity disclosed by her servant, Seleucus. Once again her wrath burns at Seleucus' betrayal, at the end dying down to womanly pathos:

> Prithee, go hence;
> Or I shall show the cinders of my spirits
> Through the ashes of my chance: wert thou a man,
> Thou would'st have mercy on me.   (v. ii. 172)

Now all hope of Caesar's favour is dispelled. Both played with the other, played for a rich prize. Caesar for Cleopatra, a jewel in the crown of his triumph, Cleopatra for Caesar's love, another fine emerald to set beside those other victories, Pompey, Julius Caesar and Antony.

So, even at this last moment, the Serpent of old Nile pursues a wavering course. That she sincerely tries to ensnare Caesar is evident enough from her deceit regarding the treasure. But circumstances force her on, as ever in this play, to the final immolation on love's altar. She fails with Caesar, and knows it:

> *Cleopatra.* He words me, girls, he words me, that I should not
>   Be noble to myself: but, hark thee, Charmian.
> *Iras.* Finish, good lady; the bright day is done,
>   And we are for the dark.   (v. ii. 191)

Cleopatra is to be 'noble to herself': in their death for love, Eros, Enobarbus, and Antony, too, are noble to that which is most stalwart and irresistible in themselves. Now Cleopatra is steadfast in her course of dying. She will not go to Rome to have Antony 'brought drunken forth', before her, or to see

> Some squeaking Cleopatra boy my greatness
> I' the posture of a whore.   (v. ii. 220)

Rather she will 'fool their preparation' and 'conquer their most absurd intents' (v. ii. 225). She now speaks from heights overtopping the childish glorification of empire. She has the dignity of a Clytemnestra—but set, not on murder, but self-immolation. Though compact of variety and waverings, she assumes a steadily increasing grandeur of immobility. She is again in the still consciousness of her dream: her 'variety' is now 'infinity', and infinity means death and love, Antony and all the stars sun-blazing to make of one night's darkness a myriad brilliant days. So she will deck herself for the bridal morning of death:

> Now, Charmian!
> Show me, my women, like a queen: go fetch
> My best attires: I am again for Cydnus,
> To meet Mark Antony: sirrah Iras, go.
> Now, noble Charmian, we'll despatch indeed;
> And, when thou hast done this chare, I'll give thee leave
> To play till doomsday. Bring our crown and all.
>
> (v. ii. 226)

Iras and Charmian have throughout been supporters of Cleopatra's love, waiting with her for Antony, recalling old merriment in the empty days of Antony's absence, now urging Cleopatra to step to Antony, to 'finish' and set out 'for the dark'. They are faithful to love's cause always. Now at last Cleopatra is raised beyond wavering, beyond incertitude. She hears that a 'rural fellow' is at hand with figs:

> *Cleopatra.* Let him come in. What poor an instrument
> May do a noble deed! he brings me liberty.
> My resolution 's placed, and I have nothing
> Of woman in me: now from head to foot
> I am marble-constant; now the fleeting moon
> No planet is of mine.   (v. ii. 236)

Death is 'liberty'; it 'enlarges' the 'confine' (iii. v. 13) of even her infinity. Cleopatra's pulsing variety begins to show a marble stillness; and, after our long pageantry of empire, it rests with a 'rural fellow' to bring Cleopatra the key to a wider empire, to speak her sailing orders as she puts out on the brighter seas of death. This short dialogue is important.

First, the clown in blundering Shakespearian rusticity emphasizes again that quality of our death theme here that I have so stressed:

> *Cleopatra.* Hast thou the pretty worm of Nilus there,
>   That kills and pains not?
> *Clown.* Truly, I have him: but I would not be the party that should desire you to touch him, for his biting is immortal; those that do die of it do seldom or never recover.
>
> (v. ii. 243)

'His biting is immortal': so, too, Cleopatra echoes the word shortly after, she has 'immortal longings' in her. Now the clown, rude instrument of truth, proceeds to speak of the most profound difficulty in our understanding of Cleopatra, this play, or, indeed, the whole Shakespearian sequence. Within Cleopatra there is, as I have noticed, a vein of pure evil; necessary in so rich a feminine creation. This is the evil of Lady Macbeth, or Eve.[1] In the Shakespearian and Biblical visions of the birth of evil, man is influenced through woman by a supernatural evil: so Satan tempts Eve, and the Weird Sisters, themselves feminine, tempt Macbeth, but succeed rather through Lady Macbeth who herself, after reading of their prophecy, addresses satanic prayer to the 'powers that tend on mortal thoughts'. At the root of the Shakespearian agony seems ever a dark feminine evil. It is, less strongly, apparent in Gertrude and Cressid, where it is little more than weakness, and in Goneril and Regan, where it is somewhat colourless. Perhaps it is even more ultimate than masculine cynicism—as in Hamlet, Iago, Apemantus —since it so often appears to precede and condition such cynicism. In Shakespeare woman is both the divine ideal and the origin of evil: because she is more eternal than man, more mysterious, the mysterious origin of life. On

[1] I find Mgr. Kolbe also compares Lady Macbeth with Eve: 'We no more shrink from Lady Macbeth than we do from our first mother Eve.' I think this comparison—to which mine may be partly indebted—important.

that dualism the past agonies revolve. Woman, rather than man, is the creative essence, the one harmony, from which man is separated, to which he aspires. On her ultimate serenity and sweetness, not denying but over-swamping her evil, depends the sanity of religion, and the universal beauty. And at this last moment the clown slowly, incisively, speaks, acts as the embassy of the heavenly spheres which ask now from Cleopatra a music to rise and mingle with their own:

Cleopatra. Rememberest thou any that have died on 't?
Clown. Very many, men and women too. I heard of one of them no longer than yesterday: a very honest woman, but something given to lie; as a woman should not do, but in the way of honesty: how she died of the biting of it, what pain she felt: truly, she makes a very good report o' the worm; but he that will believe all that they say, shall never be saved by half that they do . . .   (v. ii. 249)

Two thoughts are apparent: (i) the dishonesty of woman, and (ii) the queer ' report'—as though still living—of a dead woman on her own death. But the ultimate purpose of this dialogue is more exactly stated a little later. Here clearly is expressed the twin potentialities of woman: the divine and the satanic—Desdemona and Lady Macbeth—two qualities which, as we have seen, blend in Cleopatra. Thus up to our very last moment the dualism is empha-sized:

Cleopatra. Will it eat me?
Clown. You must not think I am so simple but I know the devil himself will not eat a woman: I know that a woman is a dish for the gods, if the devil dress her not. But, truly, these same whoreson devils do the gods great harm in their women; for in every ten that they make, the devils mar five.
Cleopatra. Well, get thee gone; farewell.
Clown. Yes, forsooth: I wish you joy o' the worm.
                                                            (v. ii. 272)

That speech is not 'comic relief': the clown fixes his gaze on Cleopatra, drives in word on word into her heart, warning her. Now, at the last, we are to watch the long issue decided. That dialogue limns it clear for us, exact. We knew it, from other plays, and remember. And it is well that the champion of the divinely feminine is no pulseless abstraction to lie like Desdemona unjustified in death and pitiable, but rather a Cleopatra blended of all varieties: eternal woman, strong in all womanly passion, all evil and love intrinsicate. Cleopatra has ruined Antony: it is left to her to justify Antony's sacrifice to love. We shall see whether the orient star of woman's divinity, so long questioned, is a cheat, whether it, so oft the origin of evil, will here accomplish a triumph proportional to all past burdens of shame; whether the Arabian perfume of a Cleopatra's death can at last sweeten to all eternity the nightmare agony of that other blood-stained hand; whether the romantic vision, which sees through 'evil' appearance into the blazing heart alone, is a deception, an Octavia more blest than Cleopatra. In Cleopatra's death is involved no single event only, but rather the justification of that starry hope beyond good or evil, that vision which is poetry in all its guiltless profusion, that trust that unity, not duality, is hearted in the universal breast; that all things blend into a single glory in the universal Cleopatra.

At this point Cleopatra becomes love absolute and incarnate. Caesar, not being Fortune, is only 'Fortune's knave' (v. ii. 3). With love it is different. The perfect lover becomes love. Nor is there any contrast here between temporal failure and love as with Antony. Cleopatra melts naturally into love's eternity. Therefore the poet, ascending to this point, flings out the death of Cleopatra across the page like an upward tongue of fire, and earth-bound tragedy, so long our occupation, now lifts its wings and first takes the airs of immortality:

Re-enter Iras with a robe, crown, &c.
Cleopatra. Give me my robe, put on my crown; I have
  Immortal longings in me: now no more
  The juice of Egypt's grape shall moist this lip:
  Yare, yare, good Iras; quick. Methinks I hear
  Antony call; I see him rouse himself

To praise my noble act; I hear him mock
The luck of Caesar, which the gods give men
To excuse their after wrath: husband, I come:
Now to that name my courage prove my title!
I am fire and air; my other elements
I give to baser life. So; have you done?
Come then, and take the last warmth of my lips.
Farewell, kind Charmian; Iras, long farewell.
Have I the aspic in my lips? Dost fall?
If thou and nature can so gently part,
The stroke of death is as a lover's pinch,
Which hurts, and is desir'd. Dost thou lie still?
If thus thou vanishest, thou tell'st the world
It is not worth leave-taking.
Charmian. Dissolve, thick cloud, and rain; that I may say
The gods themselves do weep!
Cleopatra.   This proves me base:
If she first meet the curled Antony,
He'll make demand of her, and spend that kiss
Which is my heaven to have. Come, thou mortal wretch,
With thy sharp teeth this knot intrinsicate
Of life at once untie: poor venomous fool,
Be angry, and dispatch. O, could'st thou speak,
That I might hear thee call great Caesar ass
Unpolicied!
Charmian.   O eastern star!
Cleopatra.   Peace, peace!
Dost thou not see my baby at my breast,
That sucks the nurse asleep?
Charmian.   O, break! O, break!
Cleopatra. As sweet as balm, as soft as air, as gentle,—
O Antony!—Nay, I will take thee too:
What should I stay—
Charmian. In this vile world? So, fare thee well.
Now boast thee, death, in thy possession lies
A lass unparallel'd. Downy windows, close;
And golden Phoebus never be beheld
Of eyes again so royal! Your crown 's awry;
I'll mend it, and then play.   (v. ii. 283)

Even death is 'play'. The guard rushes in, and Charmian
applies an asp to herself:

First Guard. Where is the queen?
Charmian.   Speak softly, wake her not.
First Guard. Caesar hath sent—
Charmian.   Too slow a messenger.
     O, come apace, dispatch! I partly feel thee.
                                             (v. ii. 322)

Asked if this act is well done, Charmian answers:

     It is well done and fitting for a princess
     Descended of so many royal kings.   (v. ii. 329)

Then she, too, falls. As the guard tells Caesar:

     I found her trimming up the diadem
     On her dead mistress; tremblingly she stood
     And on the sudden dropp'd.   (v. ii. 345)

So Cleopatra is attended in death by her girls, Iras and
Charmian. Throughout this scene there is insistence on
the crowned regality of Cleopatra's death; its softness,
gentleness; its positive nature, loosing life's complex knot;
on the absurdity of temporal things—an 'ass unpolicied';
on the ascension from 'baser elements' to air and fire; on
life, the 'baby', and the star of dawn; above all, on Antony
—for 'death' and Antony are one. This is the love inter-
course of life and death.

     We are reminded throughout of humanity's spiritual
wavering, a torch-like flame flickering, buffeted in the
winds of time; extinguished, it would seem, one moment,
then again bright-flaring. At the death-moments of the
chief persons it burns with a steady brilliance. There is a
graded ascent: the death in bitter remorse of Enobarbus; the
twining of tragedy with love at the death of Antony; and
now, our final resplendent vision. Here the bright palace of
love falls; like a falling star, its lambent arrow-flame
shooting whitely through the night. Cleopatra, Queen of
Love's Eternity, has been attended throughout by her
girls, Iras, Charmian, twin pillars of this palatial love,
Cleopatra. We have seen them with her, stilly waiting at
Alexandria, beyond the turbulence of imperial contest,
eternal feminine beauty outwatching the glories of time.
Iras and Charmian stabilize and solidify the marbled theme

of Love above the flux of change. But now Cleopatra dies, diademed imperially with the crown of Life, to meet her Antony, attended by her girls, whose dying with her, before and after, makes a silent melodic succession, a triple cadence, one death on either side her death, harbinger and escort of her approach.[1] The marble palace of Love falls, piece by piece, dissolves, a visionary Taj Mahal, its fabric melting in the Phoenix fire of its own immortal beauty. Thus an unearthly glory is snatched from heaven, Promethean blaze, to light on Iras, Cleopatra, Charmian in their dying: like the sudden gilding by a horizontal sunset of a myriad pools on sand, before unnoticed, now gold beside a golden sea, till all is alive with fire, and earth itself unplaneted, a burning, tranquil star.

Caesar, symbol of temporal sway, of Western power, stands dazed by this Orient beauty in death. He has wavered between admiration and despisal of love's disciple Antony. He has himself resisted Cleopatra. But there is to be no dissentient voice in our final massive unity. He, like the rest, bows finally to love. Cleopatra, who could not win him in life, wins him in her death. Dazedly he looks on her, crowned and robed for another Cydnus:

> . . . she looks like sleep,
> As she would catch another Antony
> In her strong toil of grace.   (v. ii. 349)

Again events have so fashioned his course that, reft of all hope of an ignoble desecration of Cleopatra's majesty to swell his triumph, himself he speaks the last epitome of her, and Antony's, glory:

> Take up her bed;
> And bear her women from the monument:
> She shall be buried by her Antony:
> No grave upon the earth shall clip in it
> A pair so famous. High events as these
> Strike those that make them; and their story is
> No less in pity than his glory which
> Brought them to be lamented.   (v. ii. 359)

[1] We find an imaginative parallel in the Crucifixion.

Here, where all dualisms are blended, the intrinsic unity of tragic peace is thus set down for us by the poet. High events strike those that make them: the positive purpose of the event is conditioned by the death of the protagonist. That is why here, as never elsewhere in Shakespeare, there is finally no suggestion of tragic pain, so that we freely and joyfully

> let determin'd things to destiny
> Hold unbewail'd their way.   (III. vi. 84)

Destiny is here kind: it ever wrenches man from his perversity, forces him, in his own despite, to reach his heritage of love's immortality. So Antony 'dies' where only he has 'lived'—in Cleopatra's arms (IV. xiii. 37). The spirit of man is each a string vibrating to the sweeping arm of an unseen eternity.

IV

I have concentrated on the human element in this essay, tracing the stories of individual persons. But they, like our former strands of imagery, are only provisionally to be abstracted. The play, as a whole, is to be understood only by these various approaches assimilated in a single vision. A comprehensive view shows it to be amazingly constructed, with so infinite a care that, though we are concerned largely with an historical tale, yet we have a vision far transcending the narration of any single series of events. The technique of scene arrangement is especially noteworthy. There are no long dramatic movements. The massively expanded and spatialized technique forbids any prolonged single swirl of passion. The most powerful emotional movements are all compressed, both by the 'wavering' psychology which presents alternation rather than development, and by the scene variation. This variation of scene applies a break to the action. The vision is diffused over a very wide space, so that the short scenes, with the vast distances between their locations, convey not only an impression of empire, but a still more powerful impression of space as opposed to time. They tend to crush time, to render it subordinate to simultaneity, which eternity envelopes, and encloses the action like a moveless sphere englobing an oiled mechanism smoothly working within.

And this element of stillness is to be related especially to the love-element, as the movement and the action are related to the war-theme. Love is omnipresent universally in our numerous images of element mated with element, the sun fecundating the Nile basin, cloud-forms dissolved in the air, the melting, blending, mingling; and in the sexual conversation of Cleopatra's retainers. Love is imperial over empires. All the persons tend to cohere, to make peaceful societies, as when Antony cements his friendship with Caesar by marriage, or the triumvirs celebrate their new amity with Pompey by feasting and music. This is the natural tendency, only disturbed by the wavering, the alternations, in the persons, perversely spoiling happiness. This love-eternity stilly overwatches the flux of time, its action and imagery interpenetrate the whole action. And Antony alternates from one to the other, between the eternity of love and the temporal glories of empire. Hence the stillness of Cleopatra's palace at Alexandria. It is static, in a world of movement, waiting. Though the action be far-flung we are never left to forget that Cleopatra and her girls hold the destinies of the empire in their eyes. Alexandria encloses the action, frames it: our first and last scenes are necessarily laid there. Moreover, this motionless quality related to action's movement is finely developed in Acts II and III. In ii. v. Cleopatra hears of Antony's marriage and drives the messenger from her. The following scenes are at Misenum, Pompey's galley, Syria, Rome. In iii. iii we are again at Alexandria. Cleopatra is sending for the messenger she has just dismissed. Hardly any time has elapsed. A few minutes at Alexandria enclose—it is logically impossible since Caesar and Antony appear in three of the interposed scenes— a vast and varied stream of action in the outer world. Therefore we have an impression of stillness over-

watching motion, eternity outstaring time; and so our
total effect is one of Love at the start supreme, Antony and
Cleopatra together at Alexandria; next, that love interthreads, encloses, watches and waits for the protagonists
of empire; lastly, draws them back within its own quality,
as Caesar follows Antony to Egypt and Cleopatra at the
end. To understand the play aright we must be prepared
to see Antony as a very human lover, Cleopatra as love
itself. Hence the exquisite contrast of Antony's death, its
quality of tragedy and failure, subtly differentiated from
Cleopatra's dissolving immortality. So we watch love
calling man to her bosom; and death, gentle and soft as a
nurse's love, drawing the wanderers, life, and last love
itself, back to its peace. Accordingly our love-theme,
which ranges equally through all the natural imagery, is
shown as a force not to be denied, more potent than kings,
controlling their actions by its own passivity. We watch
the dualism of East and West, spirit and action, death
and life: and all are finally blended in love. And it must
be remembered that Eastern splendour is closely associated in Shakespeare with love's ideal, which ideal is
often imaged as set beyond a sea: hence the consummate
symbolic accuracy of Cleopatra, Love's Queen, at Egypt,
contrasted with Caesar, empire-symbol, at Rome. Between
these two Antony wavers. His final surrender to love and
death completes the pattern of his story. Time is
annulled. At his dying, 'the star is fall'n' and 'time is at
his period' (IV. xii. 106).

But, though East and West—I use the terms purely to
assist my present attempt—eternity and time, feminine
love and masculine warriorship, are opposing values here,
there is no strong dualism. ˙ The final effect is a blending,
a melting, with a victory for the finer, over the cruder,
ideal. And this points us to a final statement about the
play. I have noticed that the varying psychology of the
play is true to human normality in a way that the
cataclysmic psychic eruptions in *Macbeth*, *Lear*, and *Timon*
are not: since our life is usually a sequence of such alterna-

tions, such systole and diastole of vision. And yet in no former play is humanity so finely idealized. I have also remarked that, though the poet here uses very sensuous and emotional, even coarse, essences, yet the result is not exactly sensuous cr emotional: all is constricted, rarefied by a fine control, a sifting of any but the purest gold-dust of vision. The play presents opposing aspects of its love-theme: the crude and the ideal. Moreover, the lovers are old, Cleopatra 'wrinkled' (I. v. 29), Antony's head is 'grizzled' (III. xi. 17). There is no excess of physical beauty, as in *Romeo and Juliet*. There is a violent, sometimes a harsh, realism in *Antony and Cleopatra*. Human love is battered, weary, yet divine. These opposing aspects we view alternately. It is the opposition of our own lives. No play is more true, and, finally, none more beautiful. It is written from a height overlooking every essence which is employed: it is not only a vision, but a vision understood, and continually interpreting itself. It relates to *Romeo and Juliet* exactly as *The Tempest* relates to *A Midsummer Night's Dream*. Every negation in the play is subservient to the total unity. I have also noticed the peacefulness, and merriment even, which here accompanies tragedy. So that we find a rarefied, unemotional, and happy vision of essences coarsely material, immoral—remembering Antony's unfaithfulness to Fulvia and Octavia—passionate, and tragic; one in which humanity seems at once more tragically real and more divinely ideal than elsewhere; something beside which the dualistic modes of the sombre tragedies appear not only as morbid, but essentially partial and provisional; which, as nearly as any work in literature, solves by direct and truthful life-presentation and immediate understanding, that is, without resorting to 'myth', the dualisms of love and evil, life and death; which more perfectly than any other work of literature blends a myriad diversities of person, place, image, and thought, in a single and harmonious oneness. I conclude that *Antony and Cleopatra* is a dramatic microcosm of human, and other, life viewed from within the altitudes of conscious Divinity; that we have here our most perfect statement of the real; that, whereas the sombre plays are aspects of 'appearance', in *Antony and Cleopatra* we touch the Absolute.

Additional Note, 1951: There is no doubt that the phrase 'terrene moon' (at III. xi. 153) applies directly to Cleopatra. See my letter in *The Times Literary Supplement*, 14 July, 1950.

1965: Before my own essay in 1931 J. Middleton Murry had already in 'The Nature of Poetry' (*Discoveries*, 1924) observed briefly the themes of dying for loyalty and of death as a sweetness in *Antony and Cleopatra*, and also the play's prevailing calm. There was, too, an early phrase of his about 'dying into love' which I cannot trace. See above, pp. vi, 264–6; also p. 341 note, below.

Murry's *Shakespeare* appeared much later, in 1936. I have described my literary relations with Middleton Murry in *Of Books and Humankind* (Essays presented to Bonamy Dobrée, ed. John Butt, 1964).

IX

MACBETH AND ANTONY AND CLEOPATRA

I HAVE remarked elsewhere that 'in point of imaginative profundity *Macbeth* is comparable alone to *Antony
and Cleopatra*', and that '*Macbeth* forces us to a consciousness more exquisitely unified and sensitive than any of the
great tragedies but its polar opposite, *Antony and Cleopatra*'.
Here I shall expand and justify the implicit assertion that
these two plays have a certain powerful similarity of exact
opposition.

Both plays are clearly dominated by a woman. In no
other play do we find just this relation existent between
hero and heroine. Lady Macbeth and Cleopatra each
possess a unique power and vitality which are irresistible
and, in both, expressly feminine: their mastery is twined
with their femininity. Each is very feminine: we might note
that both faint at crucial moments. Each rules her man
in somewhat similar fashion and with somewhat similar
results. In Macbeth and Antony we find, too, a very
definite masculine weakness and strength alternate. Both
are fine warriors, both are plastic to their women. They
fail in warriorship and practical affairs in proportion as
they absorb and are absorbed by the more spiritual forces
embodied in their women. Antony grows strong in love,
Macbeth in evil. Macbeth is aware of the similarity.
Banquo—we might aptly substitute Macduff or Malcolm
—is his Octavius:
                              . . . under him,
  My Genius is rebuk'd; as, it is said,
  Mark Antony's was by Caesar.   (*Macbeth*, III. i. 55)

In point of world affairs both become weak, though they
endure spirit-adventures which quite dwarf the superficial successes of Octavius and Malcolm. Those two are
similar in youth and inexperience. Compare

                    I will not yield,
  To kiss the ground beneath young Malcolm's feet . . .
                         (*Macbeth*, v. vii. 56)

with

> To the boy Caesar send this grizzled head,
> And he will fill thy wishes to the brim
> With principalities.   (*Antony and Cleopatra*, III. xi. 16)

There is reference in both plays to the disgrace of being captured alive, relating often to Cleopatra in the one play, and Macbeth, exhibited as 'rarer monsters are' (v. vii. 54) 'to be baited with the rabbles curse' (v. vii. 58), in the other. Macbeth again explicitly stimulates our sense of similarity by his words on suicide, his determination not to 'play the Roman fool' (v. vii. 30). We observe a somewhat similar conquest of hardened but weakening prowess by youthful integrity in each. Yet, in spiritual adventure, both Macbeth and Antony are indeed rich, and ripened for death. Macbeth is 'ripe for shaking' (IV. iii. 237), he is fallen 'into the sear, the yellow leaf' (v. iii. 23). So, too, Antony cries that his followers

> . . . melt their sweets
> On blossoming Caesar, and this pine is bark'd,
> That over-topp'd them all.
> (*Antony and Cleopatra*, IV. x. 35)

Which again insistently recalls Lennox's words on Malcolm. Caithness speaks:

> Meet we the medicine of the sickly weal,
> And with him pour we in our country's purge
> Each drop of us.

To which Lennox replies:

> Or so much as it needs,
> To dew the sovereign flower and drown the weeds.
> (*Macbeth*, v. ii. 27)

Caesar and Malcolm are both like 'flowers' to be watered by their followers' support. Caesar wears 'the rose of youth upon him' (III. xi. 20). Antony is like an old lion dying (III. xi. 95), Macbeth like a bear at the stake (v. vii. 1). Antony is seen to sacrifice all reason to love just as Macbeth sacrifices all reason to evil. And these tre-

mendous spiritual principles are bodied exactly in their
women. The one pair of protagonists are 'in love with'
each other, both together blended in a reality transcending
persons; the other pair are similarly 'in evil with' each
other. We should observe that Macbeth and Lady Macbeth are joint partners in evil: it is twined with their
love, itself a kind of unholy love. Macbeth partly commits
his crime through his wife's influence over him, his love for
her: and it has been often remarked that she desires it
primarily for her lord's, not for her own, sake. After the
crime the evil bond is yet for a while strong between them.
It is impossible clearly to dissociate their evil from their
love. Their love gives place to evil, which is itself powerfully binding as love; and yet eventually drives them, it
seems, apart. Thus a mighty spiritual force broods over
each pair. They are lost in it, through and in each other
and themselves: yet it is greater, more universal, than
they. This force is radiant and life-giving in the one play,
black and death-dealing in the other. In *Macbeth* the
intellect is baffled and the emotions at every turn troubled.
In *Antony and Cleopatra* the intellectual and emotional
elements are closely harmonized, and both contribute to a
single positive directness that makes the optimism of all
high tragedy here explicit. The intellect is satisfied, the
emotions pleased. Moreover, the one vision fills, the other
empties, its own universe. The two visions may be ranged
as opposites.

There are further imaginative correspondences, not
very easy to characterize. Cleopatra has something of the
paralysing, serpentine, grace and attraction of the
Macbeth-evil, which further relates her to Lady Macbeth
and the Weird Sisters. Lady Macbeth prays to 'spirits' in
her invocation to evil; and those spirits, as they appear to
Macbeth, are feminine. The *Macbeth*-evil clearly has its
roots in femininity. Cleopatra is called a 'witch' (IV. x. 60;
and see p. 247 above), a 'great fairy' (IV. viii. 12). There
is a recurrent 'serpent' suggestion in both plays. Lady Macbeth urges her lord to be 'the serpent' under 'the innocent

flower' (I. v. 66). She is herself serpentine, a temptress, like Eve, serpent-beguiled, serpent-propelled. Serpents and similar reptilian or poisonous creatures are often suggested in *Macbeth* (III. ii. 13; 36; III. iv. 29; IV. i. 6, 12, 14, 16, 17). So, too, Cleopatra is the 'serpent of old Nile'; and crocodiles, serpents, and 'the worm of Nilus' are frequently mentioned in *Antony and Cleopatra*. Here they are not nearly so powerfully impregnated with evil as in *Macbeth*, and are often purely picturesque. In exactly this sense, evil in *Antony and Cleopatra* is subdued to a strange beauty.

Moreover, both plays stress 'air' and air-life. Such references I have already observed in *Antony and Cleopatra*. In *Macbeth* we have a large proportion of air-life in our animal-suggestion: sparrows, eagles, the raven, owl, falcon, hawk, the 'crow' and its 'rooky wood', 'night's black agents' preying, 'maws of kites', maggot-pies, choughs, rooks, 'howlet', the wren fighting the owl, the hell-kite swooping on chickens, the 'temple-haunting martlet', the bat and his 'cloister'd flight', the 'shard-borne beetle'. These are either evil, or sweet in contrast. We also have violent and ominous, or sweet, air-imagery. We have Macbeth's vision of innocence desecrated:

> And pity, like a naked new-born babe,
> Striding the blast, or heaven's cherubin, hors'd
> Upon the sightless couriers of the air,
> Shall blow the horrid deed in every eye,
> That tears shall drown the wind.   (*Macbeth*, I. vii. 21)

Both good and evil spirits ride on the wind, and disorder in the elements is violent. The Weird Women 'hover through the fog and filthy air' (I. i. 12). Again Macbeth cries:

> Infected be the air whereon they ride . . .   (IV. i. 138)

The winds of chaos are loosed:

> This night has been unruly; where we lay,
> Our chimneys were blown down; and, as they say,
> Lamentings heard i' the air; strange screams of death . . .
>   (II. iii. 59)

Macbeth draws a picture of wholesale destruction in
terms of wind:

> Though you untie the winds and let them fight
> Against the churches . . .   (IV. i. 52)

And later:

> Though bladed corn be lodg'd and trees blown down . . .
>
> (IV. i. 55)

All which is naturally an aspect of the usual Shakespearian
'tempest'. But here especially 'air' and 'wind' are stressed.
And this leads on to the thought of 'vast regions' observed
by Miss Spurgeon, who notes as a typical *Macbeth*-idea
'the reverberation of sound echoing over vast regions,
even into the limitless spaces beyond the confines of the
universe', and quotes a passage where heaven itself rings
with the horror of Scotland's suffering, and another where
words of Macbeth's crime should

> .   . . . be howl'd out in the desert air,
> Where hearing should not latch them.   (IV. iii. 194)

Air, wind, and vast spaces—all are then common to both
Macbeth and *Antony and Cleopatra*. And they are as unruly
in the one play as they are still and harmonious in the
other. My analysis of *Antony and Cleopatra* has already
explored this elemental suggestion, and the correspondence, together with the obvious divergences, will be
clear. Sea-imagery, so vivid in *Antony and Cleopatra*,
also occurs in *Macbeth*; but its preponderance is not
sufficient in view of its Shakespearian universality to
justify our stressing it in this connexion, except to
note the same contrast of calm and chaos already
observed. Moreover the *Macbeth*-vision, being so
essentially a vision of 'spirit' or 'nothing', lends itself
rather to imagery of vast emptiness and rushing winds
(like those of Claudio's hell), and evil birds a-wing on the
impenetrable dark. It is a play of 'flighty purpose' (IV. i.
145)—or purposeless flight. It is all spiritual, dizzying,
swift, insecurely poised and immaterial. Thus the solidity
of the 'sure and firm-set earth' (II. i. 56) must not hear and

repeat the steps of wraithly murder whose Tarquin strides fall echoless at the hour when 'nature' itself 'seems dead' (II. i. 50).

Speed and intangibility peculiarize *Macbeth*. Miss Spurgeon notes here 'the action of rapid riding which contributes and emphasizes a certain sense of rushing, relentless, and goaded motion, of which we are very conscious in the play', and quotes examples of such 'riding' action in the imagery. Elsewhere I show in detail that 'speed' is a recurrent thought in Shakespeare in connexion with the heightened awareness of poetry, love, and, we may add, lunacy.[1] 'The lunatic, the lover, and the poet'

---

[1] I quote from my letter to *The Times Literary Supplement*, Thursday, 17 January, 1929:

'. . . Shakespeare continually refers to the swiftness of abstract thought or "meditation". . . . This pure mental activity is compared in point of swiftness with "thoughts of love" or love in many passages of Shakespeare: e.g. *Hamlet*, I. v. 29–30; *Love's Labour's Lost*, IV. iii. 330; *Troilus and Cressida*, IV. ii. 13–14; *Romeo and Juliet*, II. v. 4–8; and, in a negative sense pointing the comparison most clearly, *Othello*, III. iv. 174–9. The swiftness of thought is referred to in *Henry V*, Prologue to Act III, 1–3; and in the Prologue to Act V, at lines 8, 15, 23; in *Antony and Cleopatra*, IV, vi. 35–6; in *King Lear*, III. ii. 4. And the swiftness of love is referred to in *The Two Gentlemen of Verona*, II. vi. 42; in *Romeo and Juliet*, II. ii. 118–19; in *A Midsummer Night's Dream*, I. i. 143–9. The poetic image is "lightning". So much for the swiftness of meditation and love. Now the imaginative connexion of love and poetry in Shakespeare is apparent. The lover, like the poet, is "of imagination all compact" (*A Midsummer Night's Dream*, v. i. 8). Love sees with the eyes of art (*A Midsummer Night's Dream*, II. ii. 104–5). Creative literature is born of the erotic impulse—the statement is clear and vivid in *Love's Labour's Lost*, IV. iii. 291–365. Here the speed imagery is insistent:

> For when would you, my liege, or you, or you,
> In *leaden* contemplation have found out
> Such *fiery* numbers as the prompting eyes
> Of beauty's tutors have enriched you with?
> Other *slow* arts entirely keep the brain . . .

See also *Antony and Cleopatra*, v. ii. 96–100. It is clear, then, that love and poetry may be said to induce a consciousness which "apprehends" a swift reality beyond the lagging attempts of intellect to "comprehend" (*A Midsummer Night's Dream*, v. i. 4–6).'

To which I might add that the 'swift thought' of *Antony and Cleopatra*, are thus, in respect of swift consciousness, to be related to each other. And the extreme of lunacy is to be associated with the idiot-apprehension of the *Macbeth*-evil:

> I'll haunt thee like a wicked conscience still,
> That mouldeth goblins swift as frenzy's thoughts.
> *(Troilus and Cressida*, v. x. 28)

In *The Wheel of Fire* I have written: 'The states of extreme evil and supreme love have a definite imaginative similarity. They stand out from other modes in point of a certain supernormal intensity, a sudden, crushing, conquering power, a vivid and heightened consciousness. In these respects they seem to transcend the hate-mode, except where that touches madness. *Macbeth* and *Antony and Cleopatra* are thus supreme in point of imaginative transcendence'. That comparison will now be more clear. Moreover, it is not surprising that the two poems written by Shakespeare in his youth, wherein clearly he had absolute freedom in choice of subject, should reflect the two most intense and powerful of his tragic visions. *Venus and Adonis* shows us *Antony and Cleopatra* in embryo. In both the feminine element dominates the action. Venus' prophecy about love at the close is a valuable commentary on Shakespearian love-tragedy. Similarly *The Rape of Lucrece* is a commentary on and foreshadows *Macbeth*. The two visions are, imaginatively, exactly similar. As I have observed, Macbeth's crime, is, or may be considered, a kind of self-love like Tarquin's lust. Cleopatra is compared to Venus in Enobarbus' description, Macbeth compares himself to Tarquin. We are, in fact, here faced with the positive and negative extremes of Shakespearian vision.[1] Thus *Macbeth* and *Antony and Cleopatra* stand

iv. vi. 35–6, may be paraphrased 'passion'. Any passionate thinking is 'swift'. Words may be 'winged swift' in 'scorn' so that they 'outfly apprehensions' *(Troilus and Cressida*, II. iii. 123). The drink-consciousness induces 'swift' images. See *2 Henry IV*, iv. iii. 92–127.

[1] On the plane of popular fiction we find reflections of these two modes: the love-story and the 'thriller'. We might also observe the themes of Greek tragedy. Murders and marriages have a lasting appeal—and meaning.

out from the other great tragedies by their excessive intensity, which is to be related to the idea of 'speed'. For the *Macbeth* 'speed' is but a branch of Shakespeare's usual 'speed' thought with respect to poetry, love, and madness. It is the whirling agony I have suggested, metaphorically, to point the quality of Lear's madness.[1] In *Macbeth* it is even swifter, more unbearably swift, like the gyroscopic spin of consciousness in certain forms of nightmare. And what, then, of *Antony and Cleopatra*? The play is still, not swift. But this is a stillness which encloses motion, a stillness growing out of motion, as a swiftly rotating and multicoloured top is abnormally and strangely still, its varied colourings whitened by speed. It is still, that is, to the spectator; not to an insect that tries to lodge thereon. So, too, in *Antony and Cleopatra*, we who watch observe a stillness overpowering, yet one with, speed; an eternity enclosing, yet born from, time; an ethereal uncoloured beauty which is yet blent of the *Macbeth* red, black, and gold, and a shimmering sea-blue of its own. From the height of our vision action becomes static like Wordsworth's cataract, 'frozen by distance'.

The frenzies and phantasms of *Macbeth* range a world itself void and insubstantial. Each play shows us a nature reptilian, volatile, airy. It is hard to find exact words for this common element of spirituality and supernatural strangeness. 'Nature' in both plays is transcended. The dominant spirit quality in both forbids a pure naturalism such as we find in *Lear*. In *Macbeth* what 'nature' there is is mostly distorted, in *Antony and Cleopatra* it is outdistanced. Therefore both 'natures' are 'strange': the word is used in both plays. The one is strangely beautiful, the other strangely evil. Both are beyond the natural. *Macbeth* has its 'air-drawn dagger'; a phrase clearly referring 'air' to the spirit-forms of imagination. So the Weird Women vanish:

> *Banquo.* The earth hath bubbles as the water has
> And these are of them: whither are they vanish'd?

[1] *The Wheel of Fire.*

Macbeth. Into the air, and what seem'd corporal, melted
   As breath into the wind.   (*Macbeth*, I. iii. 79)

Notice the 'water' suggestion, which supports my understanding of the water-element in *Antony and Cleopatra* as a spirit-medium, element of life strange to man; and the word 'melted'; and the 'air' and 'breath' ideas, which, with the 'fog and filthy air', may remind us of 'cloud' imagery in *Antony and Cleopatra*. Now in *Antony and Cleopatra* there is one powerful effect of supernaturalism: the mysterious music that preludes the final defeat of worldly things and the ascension of love:

Fourth Soldier. Peace! what noise?
First Soldier.   List, list!
Second Soldier. Hark!
First Soldier.   Music i' the air.
Third Soldier.   Under the earth.
            (*Antony and Cleopatra*, IV. iii. 12)

Again, 'earth' and 'air'. Different as they are in quality, in point of pure supernaturalism these two incidents are also strangely similar. The two plays have this common element of the immaterial (in the one) and super-material (in the other). It may be called 'spirit'; spirit rich, attractive, dangerous: with a nightmare fascination in the one and a fascinating beauty in the other. This 'spirit' element also occurs in the prophecies. *Antony and Cleopatra* shows us a naturalism so expanded to infinite proportions that it just touches the supernatural; hence the one fine supernatural effect of unearthly music. Whereas the *Macbeth*-evil is wholly supernatural. So, too, the prophecies in *Antony and Cleopatra* are only slightly supernatural. The soothsayer words his skill aptly: 'In nature's infinite book of secrecy a little I can read' (I. ii. 9). Nature's infinity, that is our vision here. As for the other prophecy, in Act II, the soothsayer tells Antony no more than he knows himself: that Caesar's luck and personality both dominate him. But in *Macbeth* the future is crudely, suddenly, presented naked to the present moment. We are 'transported' beyond 'the ignorant present' and feel 'the future in the instant' (I. v. 57). But both plays are powerfully 'spiritual'. And these two spirit-worlds are clearly enclosed in the persons of Lady Macbeth and Cleopatra. Each woman is ultimate in her play: she is the whole play's universe, with its rich fascination and serpentine grace, as Macbeth and Antony are not. They are in it; their ladies are of it: 'it' being 'evil' and 'love' respectively.

We may, then, observe a certain elusive similarity between the essences of these two plays. Next I shall attempt more clearly to show how exactly they may be considered opposites. In *Macbeth* we have noted life-themes of imperial splendour, feasting, and nature's creative innocence. These are, in one way or another, ranged against the evil, the death-consciousness, the dark. They have but insecure place in the *Macbeth*-world. But these life-themes are vividly fulfilled and realized in *Antony and Cleopatra*. Imperial magnificence scintillates throughout the play, and receives a finer expression than elsewhere in Shakespeare. Nor is it here strongly opposed to the love-force. It both blends and contrasts with it: as may be seen from the passage, of clear symbolic meaning, which describes Antony and Cleopatra throned together in imperial magnificence and princely love. The contrast with *Macbeth* is clear: these are the very things Macbeth cannot grasp; they appear only to vanish, elusive. Feasting, too, is a major theme, whether in the fine scene on Pompey's galley, Enobarbus' description of Alexandrian revelling, or Antony's speeches in Act IV. So, too, in *Macbeth*, is feasting vivid: in the entertainment of Duncan, the Banquet scene, and the death-banquet of the Weird Women. There feast is desecrated by evil: the contrast is again vivid. With nature, as I have observed, the same contrast persists. In *Macbeth* nature is deformed, dislocated: in *Antony and Cleopatra* it is fulfilled and transfigured. In *Macbeth* the lovely passage on the breeding martlet with his 'procreant cradle' suggests nature's rich profusion of life; the thought is stressed again in Lady Macduff's words about the wren; and such ideas—blending with 'baby' themes—are clearly the direct antagonists of the evil, suggesting life and birth as opposed to death. Macbeth is without children; and his 'fruitless' crown is to be contrasted with Banquo's 'issue', or Duncan's. We may observe the description of Antony and Cleopatra throned in glory with their 'unlawful issue'. In *Antony and Cleopatra* we have constant suggestion of the mating of element with element, Antony's description of the Nile harvesting, the crocodile bred out of the Nile ooze; which thoughts blend with the sex-conversation of Cleopatra's girls, and harmonize with the main theme of love. Nature here is endued with splendour and happy success. The spirit of evil disorganizes and distorts life-forms in *Macbeth*; the spirit of love illuminates and fulfils them in *Antony and Cleopatra*. In *Macbeth* the evil has two modes of appearance: (i) spirit realities, essentially outside natural law; and (ii) natural life distorted, derelict, without 'form'; either without organic form, as the bits of bodies used for the cauldron ingredients, or without the form of obedience to laws of kind, as in the strange behaviour of Duncan's horses 'beauteous and swift, the minions of their race' (ii. iv. 15)—we should contrast this with the vivid 'horse' themes in *Antony and Cleopatra*—or the inverted relation of falcon and owl. 'Spirit' is, in both modes, seen to be rudely disjointed from 'matter': 'form' being the effect of 'spirit' or 'soul' in—to use the Shakespearian word—the 'shapes' of matter. Thus the evil in *Macbeth* is essentially formless, whether it appear as 'spirit' or in shape of 'nature'. Exactly the reverse is true of *Antony and Cleopatra*. There all life-forms are vividly fulfilled and spiritualized, inflated by spirit to the extreme limits of nature, thence transcending nature and widening into infinity. In *Macbeth* the lights of heaven are 'strangled': star, moon, sun. In *Antony and Cleopatra*, the nights are 'shiny' (iv. ix. 3), stars, moon, and sun bend their love-light on earth. The extreme of this especial vision wherein the

12

finite is rendered infinite by spiritual apprehension is apparent in Cleopatra's description of the universal Antony. In *Antony and Cleopatra* the universe is full, packed full of life-forms. But *Macbeth* is empty, void with a dread infinity, a ghastly vacuum which yet echoes 'strange screams of death'. In *Macbeth* all nature, all life-forms of birth, feast, honour, and kingly glory are opposed by this nothingness, this death. In *Antony and Cleopatra* the universal fires blaze down on earth, and earth reflects that glory, flashes it back from its own imperial splendour. Here we encounter vastness in form of sea and land, empire, earth and air and fire: in *Macbeth* we encounter vastness too; but only a vast abyss of a spiritual 'nothing'.

We see then how *Antony and Cleopatra* in reality contains and surpasses all that is in *Macbeth*: surpasses that vision by showing its elements not in disharmony, but harmony, spirit mated to forms of life. Hence, as I have observed, Cleopatra has in her something of the Lady Macbeth evil, woven into the rich and strange loveliness of her 'infinite variety'. We may note further that in *Macbeth* the evil is opposed not only by natural life-forms but by a wholly supernatural 'grace', and thoughts of angels and divinity generally. In *Antony and Cleopatra* there is no exact correspondence here: any powerful divine suggestion is blended with things natural and human. The 'gods' and 'fortune' are vaguer than in *Lear*. The life-vision is expressed in terms of life and death as we know them: it recognizes no supernatural divinity, except such as may be closely harmonized with life and death, as we know them. The divine blends with the human, the human becomes divine. And yet we must, of course, never forget that the persons, ultimately, are not human at all, but purely symbols of a poetic vision. Finally, we may observe two similar speeches that contrast our two visions neatly with reference to the life-image of babyhood. Lady Macbeth speaks:

> I have given suck, and know
> How tender 'tis to love the babe that milks me:

I would, while it was smiling in my face,
Have pluck'd my nipple from his boneless gums,
And dash'd the brains out, had I so sworn as you
Have done to this.   (*Macbeth*, I. vii. 54)

Compare:

                    Peace, peace!
Dost thou not see my baby at my breast,
That sucks the nurse asleep?
                    (*Antony and Cleopatra*, v. ii. 311)

In the one, a death force is conquering life instincts; in the other, a life-instinct, love, conquers death. So, too, Cleopatra's paradisal dream contrasts exquisitely with Lady Macbeth's agonized sleep.

The bond between Antony and Cleopatra makes them rise above, and scorn, imperial sway; that between Macbeth and Lady Macbeth is servanted to ignominious desire for glory. The one pair are united first by imperial position and advance thence to love; the other, first by love, and advance thence to imperial position. For we should observe, what is a too easily neglected effect in *Macbeth*, the fine love which binds the protagonists. The domestic note is powerful in the early action. 'My dearest love . . .' Macbeth addresses his wife on his first return. 'My husband!' is her greeting to him after his hideous crime. Ironic in their beauty of thought, too, are Duncan's words on Macbeth's 'love' for his wife:

                    . . . but he rides well;
And his great love, sharp as his spur, hath holp him
To his home before us.   (*Macbeth*, I. vi. 22)

This natural love they desecrate for world-glory: Antony and Cleopatra spurn world-glory for love. The one story illustrates crime, action unfitted to the universal purpose; the other play shows us a story which receives universal sanction. Humanity is distorted in the one story: hence Macduff enters with Macbeth's head, the protagonist hideously decapitated. In the other, Cleopatra dies crowned and beauteous in a death which is but an added glory to life.

I conclude with a few remarks on *King Lear*. *King Lear* is to be mentally set between *Macbeth* and *Antony and Cleopatra*. The sequence is clear with reference to 'nature': (i) nature formless; (ii) pure naturalism in a limited sense; and (iii) nature infinite. Or again, as follows: (i) supernaturalism (we have observed how the supernatural evil necessitates a similar supernatural 'grace'—as in the ghost scene in *Hamlet*); (ii) naturalism; and (iii) what I have termed 'universalism'. Now in *Lear* nature is both cruel and sweet. Mr. Edmund Blunden[1] has observed how toward the end the wintry effects of the middle action give place to the more summery images of the fourth act. This movement is related to Lear's reunion with Cordelia: 'nature' is fulfilled by love, and sweet natural effects accompany love here and elsewhere in Shakespeare. Here, however cruel and violent nature may be—in tempest or animal references—it is never distorted: natural laws are not broken. Goneril, Regan, and Edmund are all naturally wicked, Lady Macbeth unnaturally wicked[2]—hence her own torment, the disease-agony of fevered sleep, the sleep-walking scene. In *Lear* the bad persons endure no unrest even: they are merely fulfilling their natural impulses, and, though this may draw on them criticism of unnaturalness, and indeed often does do so, yet we never witness the motiveless and paradoxical subjection to evil that is at the heart of *Macbeth*. Only once does the *Macbeth*-nature directly touch the *Lear*-nature: the murderers in the one, and the captain in the other, both, in similar circumstances, regarding evil as natural (*Macbeth*, III. i. 91–103; *Lear*, v. iii. 38). Elsewhere the divergence is fairly rigid. But, though *Lear* shows us a

[1] In his Shakespeare Association Lecture: *Shakespeare's Significances*.

[2] Lady Macbeth has a streak of natural goodness in her even at the climax of her evil-possession; just as Cleopatra shows a streak of evil within her love. The 'good' in *Macbeth* is always one of 'nature', family affection, allegiance, and all social ties. Hence the point of Lady Macbeth's:

> Had he not resembled
> My father as he slept, I had done 't.   (II. ii. 13)

more natural state than *Macbeth*, it falls far short of
Antony and Cleopatra in general optimism. It is a tragic
vision, a sombre statement. Dr. Bradley has well called it
'bleak' in comparison with the more vivid effects of
Macbeth. *Macbeth*, like *Antony and Cleopatra*, has colour:
the red of blood, the gold of kingship, fires and glaring
spectres, white radiance of divinity. *Macbeth* and *Antony
and Cleopatra* are both, in opposite ways, 'spiritual'; *Lear*
is 'realistic'. *Lear's* naturalism in comparison with *Macbeth*
can be seen from the fact that all within it blends harmoniously: there is no such striking positive-negative contrast
as in *Macbeth*. Good and ill are spectral figures here, indecisive in comparison with the grace-evil contrast. All
is levelled under a single view regarding human existence
as a tragic struggle in which the good finally conquers, but at
appalling sacrifice. *Lear* is, in fact, a symbolic pattern of
human affairs exactly correspondent to any philosophy which
is limited to a strict 'naturalism': pessimistic but stoic.[1]
This is the exact quality of *Lear*: bleak, colourless, limited,
naturalistic. Hence it is pagan through and through. In
Lear our vision is constricted to the earth: this is exactly
what I mean by a 'limited naturalism'. So here the world
is conceived as great—'the thick rotundity o' the world'
(iii. ii. 7), 'this great world' (iv. vi. 137). In the uni-
versalized vision of *Antony and Cleopatra*, the world is the
plaything of princes. It is shown as their lawful property,
the heritage of man, a toy bandied from one to another.
Finally, it becomes 'the little O, the earth' (v. ii. 81). Our
vision is infinity itself. So in *Macbeth* the sun is blackened:
in *Antony and Cleopatra* it is finely mated to earth's bounty.
In *Lear* it is blurred—associated with 'fen-suck'd fogs' (ii.
iv. 169): a doubtful blessing.

In the matters of love and empire we shall again find
that *Lear* is set midway. In this essay I have shown that

[1] The *Lear*-vision appears to me as a life-view corresponding closely
to that expressed by Mr. Middleton Murry's *God*. And yet some of
Mr. Murry's remarks on *Antony and Cleopatra* at one time stimulated
my understanding of the play.

the other two plays present respectively a love-empire rhythm and an empire-love rhythm. Here, where human nature endures, in its painful evolution, an uncertainty, a sight of grotesque incompatibility, we find a corresponding neither-one-thing-nor-the-other in the matter of love and empire. Lear is both king and not king, and both aspects are twined with love-themes. He expects authority without office. Does he love any of his daughters, and if so, which? Do any of his daughters love him, and if so, which? Such questions torment Lear. He resigns his kingship for an old age of love, then destroys his love because his authority is questioned. Much of this is reflected in the Gloucester-Edgar-Edmund theme. All these sons and daughters either sacrifice filial love for ambition or suffer distress or degradation in the cause of true love. The France-Burgundy contrast in point of love and ambition is also apposite. Toward the close we watch Edmund all-out for ambition, and Goneril and Regan, to do them justice, all-out for love. The general effect of the whole play is, then, mostly indecisive, with a victory at the close for love. *Macbeth* shows us a world in chaos, existence itself tottering, the child of peace and life struggling to be born amid the ravages of active death. *Lear* shows a disorder without chaos, a wrench from peace, a contest painful and labouring, and, at long last, victory; in *Antony and Cleopatra* contest and division, life and death, disorder itself, create together a whole of perfect harmony. Death is seen conquering life in *Macbeth*. In *Lear* death and life are correlative, interdependent; death is the sweet end of suffering, the completion of life: 'Break, heart, I prithee break.' The extreme beauty of love, in the Lear-Cordelia reunion, comes before the extreme tragic agony of the close: which two, love and death, are synchronized in *Antony and Cleopatra*. In *Antony and Cleopatra*, death is the consummation of life, itself 'a better life', in truth no death at all, but life. Here life conquers death.

X

A NOTE ON ANTONY AND CLEOPATRA

I ADD some quotations which further illustrate what I take to be the significance of this play. The first three are from F. H. Bradley's *Appearance and Reality*, a book which has aided my interpretation. The Absolute is thus described:

> . . . Such a whole state would possess in a superior form that immediacy which we find (more or less) in feeling; and in this whole all divisions would be healed up. It would be experience entire, containing all elements in harmony. Thought would be present as a higher intuition; will would be there where the ideal had become reality; and beauty and pleasure and feeling would live on in this total fulfilment. Every flame of passion, chaste or carnal, would still burn in the Absolute unquenched and unabridged, a note absorbed in the harmony of its higher bliss (Ch. **XV**).

The following has direct relevance to the temporal aspect of Antony's tragedy (I hardly feel there to be a 'temporal aspect' of Cleopatra's):

> . . . Time is not real as such, and it proclaims its unreality by its inconsistent attempt to be an adjective of the timeless. It is an appearance which belongs to a higher character in which its special quality is merged. Its own temporal nature does not there cease wholly to exist but is thoroughly transmuted. It is counterbalanced and, as such, lost within an all-inclusive harmony. The Absolute is timeless, but it possesses time as an isolated aspect, an aspect which, in ceasing to be isolated, loses its special character. It is there, but blended into a whole which we cannot realize. But that we cannot realize it, and do not know how in particular it can exist, does not show it to be impossible (Ch. **XVIII**).

The Shakespearian vision, perhaps, will help us to this realization. We may remember how vividly, in *Macbeth*, we have a sense of time 'isolated'.

Another passage on 'nature' is exactly apposite:

> . . . Again the infinity of Nature, its extension beyond all limits,

we might call Nature's effort to end itself as Nature. It shows in this its ideality, its instability and transitoriness, and its constant passage of itself into that which transcends it. In its isolation as a phenomenon Nature is both finite and infinite, and so proclaims itself untrue. And, when this contradiction is solved, both its characters disappear into something beyond both (Ch. **XXII**).

In *The Varieties of Religious Experience* William James writes of certain higher intuitions in terms that apply excellently to our play:

> . . . Looking back on my own experiences, they all converge towards a kind of insight to which I cannot help ascribing some metaphysical significance. The keynote of it is invariably a reconciliation. It is as if the opposites of the world, whose contradictoriness and conflict make all our difficulties and troubles, were melted into unity. Not only do they, as contrasted species, belong to one and the same genus, but *one of the species*, the nobler and better one, *is itself the genus and so soaks up and absorbs its opposite into itself* (p. 388).

From which we may be reminded of the necessity to give proper attention to all the coarser and darker effects of *Antony and Cleopatra*, yet seeing them ever as 'absorbed' in the bright vision of the whole. Now *Antony and Cleopatra* presents a positive life-vision which is the very antithesis of the death-theme of *Hamlet* or the evil in *Macbeth*. A passage from Count Hermann Keyserling's *The Travel Diary of a Philosopher* illustrates this opposition:

> . . . This explains, too, the old belief in the two schools of white and black magic, and finally the belief in Ormuzd and Ahriman; this ultimately accounts for the content of truth in the ideas of absolute Good and absolute Evil. At a certain depth of profundity the soul is in fact faced by two apparently equivalent alternatives: the soul may radiate the same elementary force, either positively or negatively. All compromise seems impossible. This position, however, is not the most extreme. It is the most extreme from the angle of the will, for will is blind, but recognition goes beyond this

point of view. The wise man realizes that the difference between good and evil is fundamentally the same as the difference between life and death, that only positively active forces are backed by life, and that they alone are continually supported by an eternal will (p. 128).

So, also, is the love-theme in *Antony and Cleopatra* 'backed by life' throughout. Count Keyserling has another interesting passage relevant to the sense of 'merriment' I have observed as peculiarizing this 'tragic' vision. He writes of creation as a game. 'Thus the existence of a God is conceivable only as play' (p. 331). Dr. Hugh Brown, in an article ' "Playing the Game" as Divine' (*The Hibbert Journal*, Oct. 1929), has, I believe, discussed the same theme. Next Keyserling refers aptly to Shakespeare's comedies, whose spirit, as I have observed, mingles with the tragic essences of *Antony and Cleopatra*. We must not neglect this element of joyousness in Shakespeare's tragedy. It is part of the whole varied harmony. A passage from Mr. Aldous Huxley's *Do What you Will* exquisitely suggests the richness and profusion I have observed in *Antony and Cleopatra*:

> And yet the life-worshipper is also, in his own way, a man of principles and consistency. To live intensely—that is his guiding principle. His diversity is a sign that he consistently tries to live up to his principles; for the harmony of life—of the single life that persists as a gradually changing unity through time—is a harmony built up of many elements. The unity is mutilated by the suppression of any part of the diversity. A fugue has need of all its voices. Even in the rich counterpoint of life each separate small melody plays its indispensable part. The diapason closes full in man. In *man*. But Pascal aspired to be more than a man. Among the interlaced melodies of the human counterpoint are love songs and anacreontics, marches and savage dance rhythms, hymns of hate and loud hilarious chanties . . . (p. 309).

Those are all to be found in *Antony and Cleopatra*.

Shakespeare's remarkable sublimation of death in this play has parallels in both Goethe and Keats. I quote from the admirable study, *Goethe and Faust* (by F. Melian Stawell and G. Lowes Dickinson):

> At the close of *The Singer's Book*, in the stanzas that he called, successively and significantly, 'Self-surrender', 'Fulfilment', and 'Sacred Longing', the poet returns to a thought dominant in his early dramatic fragment of *Prometheus*, the thought that love and death are mysteriously allied, that the sacrament of sex, tearing two individuals out of themselves to unite them in the shock of a life-giving surrender, is only the symbol of a vaster union unattainable save by the supreme surrender of dying. When love has drunk deepest of human rapture, it discerns, dimly, this something more that is to be. The Unknown Eros touches the soul of the lover with his wings. Far away, beyond the dim light of the shadowy bed-chamber, there burns a flame that draws the chosen to itself. It awakens a thirst only to be appeased in death, but that alone gives light to life:

> > Tell no man, tell wise men only,
> >   For the world might count it madness,
> > Him I praise who thirsts for fire,
> >   Thirsts for death, and dies in gladness.
> >
> > Thou wast got, and thou begattest
> >   In dewy love-nights long ago;
> > Now a stranger love shall seize thee
> >   When the quiet lamp burns low.
> >
> > Thou art freed and lifted, taken
> >   From the shadow of our night,
> > Thou art drawn by some new passion
> >   Towards a nobler marriage-rite.
> >
> > Distance cannot weight thee, soaring
> >   Where the far enchantment calls,
> > Till the moth, the starfire's lover,
> >   Drinks the light, and burns, and falls.
> >
> > Die and grow! Until thou hearest
> >   What that word can say,
> > The world is dark and thou a wanderer
> >   Who has lost his way.

Such heaped-up thought and emotion went to fill some of the finest passages in the second part of *Faust* . . . (p. 56.)

The relevance of this to *Antony and Cleopatra* is clear. Keats, too, expresses this intuition of death's consummation. There is the sonnet 'Why did I laugh to-night?' with the conclusion:

> Why did I laugh? I know this Being's lease,
>> My fancy to its utmost blisses spreads;
> Yet would I on this very midnight cease,
>> And the world's gaudy ensigns see in shreds;
> Verse, Fame, and Beauty are intense indeed,
> But death intenser—Death is Life's high meed.

The fourth line of my quotation, 'the world's gaudy ensigns', insistently recalls the empire-theme in *Antony and Cleopatra*. The war-value, or empire-theme, in Shakespeare corresponds to Keats's 'Fame'. The potential sweetness of death is given lovely expression in the *Ode to a Nightingale*:

> Darkling I listen; and, for many a time
>> I have been half in love with easeful Death,
> Call'd him soft names in many a mused rhyme,
>> To take into the air my quiet breath;
> Now more than ever seems it rich to die,
>> To cease upon the midnight with no pain,
> While thou art pouring forth thy soul abroad
>> In such an ecstasy!
> Still wouldst thou sing, and I have ears in vain—
>> To thy high requiem become a sod.

There death is blended not with love, but bird-music. 'Birds' and 'music' are both close to 'love' in Shakespeare. The contrast between sweet death and the cold body ('sod') is close to a similar suggestion in *Antony and Cleopatra*: 'The case of that huge spirit now is cold'. The finest example of this intuition in Keats occurs in the 'Bright Star' sonnet, perhaps his finest poem. I quote it in full, the themes of death and love, and the universal imagery of star, sea, snow, and earth, all being so close to the Shakespearian vision in *Antony and Cleopatra*:

Bright star, would I were steadfast as thou art—
  Not in lone splendour hung aloft the night
And watching, with eternal lids apart,
  Like nature's patient, sleepless Eremite,
The moving waters at their priestlike task
  Of pure ablution round earth's human shores,
Or gazing on the new soft-fallen mask
  Of snow upon the mountains and the moors—
No—yet still steadfast, still unchangeable,
  Pillow'd upon my fair love's ripening breast,
To feel for ever its soft fall and swell,
  Awake for ever in a sweet unrest,
Still, still to hear her tender-taken breath,
And so live ever—or else swoon to death.

There is a variant of the last line: 'Half-passionless, and so swoon on to death'. The blending of finite and infinite, ceaseless movement and eternal stillness, love and death, the alternating, varying, 'soft fall and swell'—all is exactly Shakespearian. The poem is a miniature of *Antony and Cleopatra*. It was written on a blank page in Shakespeare's Poems, facing *A Lover's Complaint*. Nor is this theme peculiar to *Antony and Cleopatra* in Shakespeare. It occurs at *2 Henry VI*, iii. ii. 388:

If I depart from thee I cannot live,
And in thy sight to die what were it else
But like a pleasant slumber in thy lap?
Here could I breathe my soul into the air,
As mild and gentle as the cradle babe,
Dying with mother's dug between its lips.

A passage whose imagery is reminiscent of *Antony and Cleopatra*. A fine passage in *Troilus* (iii. ii. 19) is relevant:

I am giddy; expectation whirls me round;
The imaginary relish is so sweet
That it enchants my sense: what will it be,
When that the watery palate tastes indeed
Love's thrice repured nectar? death, I fear me,
Swooning destruction, or some joy too fine,
Too subtle-potent, tuned too sharp in sweetness,
For the capacity of my ruder powers:

I fear it much; and I do fear besides,
That I shall lose distinction in my joys;
As doth a battle, when they charge on heaps
The enemy flying.

Here extreme love-consciousness is considered a kind of
death as in *Antony and Cleopatra*:

> . . . great Pompey
> Would stand and make his eyes grow in my brow;
> There would he anchor his aspect and die
> With looking on his life.   (I. v. 31)

There is a critical moment in *Troilus* when Cressida is taken
from Troy and Troilus cries:

> Hark! you are call'd: some say the Genius so
> Cries 'come' to him that instantly must die.
>
> (IV. iv. 52)

Probably Troilus speaks as in a trance. In death there is
no unfaithfulness. Troilus forecasts the vision of *Antony
and Cleopatra* in thus associating death and Cressida: in
that vision, by death, the dualism of *Troilus and Cressida*
is resolved. Moreover, this is the very theme of *The
Phoenix and the Turtle*. The mystic profundity of that
poem has lately been admirably analysed in Ranjee's
Towards the Stars. I quote a passage:

> . . . The divinity of love and constancy has passed beyond
> our ken for their rightful place far above our futilities of
> speech and sorrow. They have sought the judgment of the
> Eternal. But it is not two who have gone—it is *one* . . .
> (p. 40).

Again:

> The mist that shrouds the meaning is illumined by an inner
> fire—like the mystic fire in the heart of the opal (p. 60).

This fine poem has too long been neglected. *The Phoenix
and the Turtle* and *Antony and Cleopatra* are reciprocally
illuminating:

> Phoenix and the Turtle fled
> In a mutual flame from hence.

Nor is this matter unimportant. Their vision is—I quote again from Ranjee's Essay on *The Phoenix and the Turtle* —a 'fearless, uncompromising assurance'. It is an assurance of immortality, in terms of 'death' and 'love'. These are shown as synchronized, mated in time. That is probably our easiest way of apprehending the mystery in temporal terms. Hence, Christianity is led to stress the importance of dying whilst in a state of 'grace'. Which is an exact correspondence in terms of orthodox dogma.

XI

THE PROPHETIC SOUL

A NOTE ON *Richard II*, v. v. 1–66

MUCH of Shakespeare's later work is curiously reflected in this interesting soliloquy. Richard is alone
in prison. In his final despair and failure, his mind is
thrown back on pure contemplation and he sinks on to the
restful sweetness of impersonal and wandering thought.
In so doing, he finds that he has made a small world of his
own: which state is now exactly analogous to the creative
consciousness which gives birth to poetry. The first lines
which he here speaks outline a Shakespearian aesthetic
psychology and are interesting as a poet's commentary on
the creative act:

> *Richard.* I have been studying how I may compare
> This prison where I live unto the world:
> And for because the world is populous,
> And here is not a creature but myself,
> I cannot do it; yet I'll hammer it out.
> My brain I'll prove the female to my soul,
> My soul the father; and these two beget
> A generation of still-breeding thoughts,
> And these same thoughts people this little world,
> In humours like the people of this world,
> For no thought is contented.

Creative thought is born from a union of 'brain' with 'soul'.
The statement is similar to Keats's in a letter (to George
Keats, 15 April 1819) of his 1819 letter-journal:

> Not merely is the Heart a hornbook. It is the mind's Bible,
> it is the mind's experience, it is the teat from which the Mind
> or Intelligence sucks its identity.

In another letter (to George Keats, 19 March 1819)
Keats refers to an interesting psychological experience as
follows:

> This morning I am in a sort of temper, indolent and supremely

careless . . . My passions are all asleep, from my having slumbered till nearly eleven, and weakened the animal fibre all over me, to a delightful sensation, about three degrees on this side of faintness. If I had teeth of pearl and the breath of lilies I should call it languor, but as I am I must call it laziness. In this state of effeminacy the fibres of the brain are relaxed in common with the rest of the body, and to such a happy degree that pleasure has no show of enticement and pain no unbearable frown . . . This is the only happiness and is a rare instance of advantage in the body overpowering the mind.

On this passage Mr. Middleton Murry comments in *Keats and Shakespeare*, p. 137:

It is clear that this condition was very far indeed from being a condition of laziness or effeminacy. Out of it directly sprang one of the two profoundest of all Keats's letters; and Keats himself was aware that the condition was truly creative. It is precisely this condition of subordination of the mind to the instinctive being, which, at the climax of his letter, he declares to be 'the very thing in which consists Poetry'. This is the condition in which the faculty of pure poetic perception can work, and it works in that letter with a sovereign power.

Analogous descriptions of this state will be found, I think, in the works of many poets and philosophers. It recurs in Wordsworth's *Tintern Abbey*:

> . . . that blessed mood,
> In which the burthen of the mystery,
> In which the heavy and the weary weight
> Of all this unintelligible world,
> Is lightened:—that serene and blessed mood,
> In which the affections gently lead us on,—
> Until, the breath of this corporeal frame
> And even the motion of our human blood
> Almost suspended, we are laid asleep
> In body, and become a living soul.
> While with an eye made quiet by the power
> Of harmony, and the deep power of joy,
> We see into the life of things.

(Tintern Abbey, 37–49)

Such descriptions are, indeed, remarkably similar. But Keats's reference to 'effeminacy' is not a difficulty. Shakespeare's passage illuminates his meaning. So also does another piece, from Keyserling's *Travel Diary of a Philosopher* (p. 339). I italicize two words:

> Traits of my being come into evidence while I am ill, which as a rule remain hidden; the *feminine* aspect gains supremacy, with the result that the world appears in a different, more personal and more friendly light. During such times I am without will, without wishes, and I think of my habitual efforts which express themselves often so violently, with that gentle, amiable sympathy with which women watch man's unreasonable ambition.
>
> For the time being I am convalescent; this is a condition which always affords me the keenest enjoyment. As a rule, I feel my body as something extraneous, given to the mind as some inalienable matter, without inner connection with myself. But now my mind is completely passive, while the regenerating physical forces are all the more busily at work; and consciousness, now being centred in the body, enjoys the blissful feeling of uninterrupted *productiveness*.

This is like the state of Yoga in which, to quote another of Keyserling's poignant sentences:

> The collected intellect does not only allow the intuitions to pass through it, it serves them as a pliant organ, so that ultimately the whole soul becomes a means of expression for the inmost light (p. 270).

The correspondence with Keats is striking. It is what Richard means by 'proving the brain the female to the soul'. It is essentially both tranquil, and 'productive', or creative: perhaps 'the very thing in which consists poetry'.

In Bergsonian phraseology this psychic state will be that condition in which the mind falls back on 'pure duration':

> The more we succeed in making ourselves conscious of our progress in pure duration, the more we feel the different parts of our being enter into each other, and our whole personality concentrate itself in a point, or rather a sharp edge, pressed against the future and cutting into it unceasingly.
>
> (*Creative Evolution*, translated Mitchell, p. 212)

Again, we have:

> ... The more the feeling is deep and the coincidence complete, the more the life in which it replaces us absorbs intellectuality by transcending it (p. 211).

In Bergson's description this creative union of the instinctive and intellectual parts of man seems, indeed, a more self-conscious, artificial, process. But I think the state is in reality the same. It is essentially creative:

> ... as soon as we are confronted with true duration, we see that it means creation (p. 362).

Now it is the intellect, not the instinct, which in Bergson traffics with materiality. The hard shapes of the material are, as it were, originally carved out by intellect for its own especially practical purposes: which shapes are therefore not necessarily exact signposts of reality. Yet poetry is partly intellectual since it deals in 'shapes'. Poetry devoid of concrete imagery tends towards the vague rhapsodies given us by unprofitable mysticism: since the true mystic must, it appears, express his intuition in action or in some legitimate art form. Richard, as a person in the play, does neither. Hence his unrest later. He almost experiences pure 'duration', his thoughts are 'minutes'. But, for our present purpose, the words he speaks must be taken as 'shapes' of intellect. The true poet seeks expression in words, imagery, and, usually, a certain logical coherence: and these elements are, in the Bergsonian system, intellectual implements. Yet, though these are necessary, they are not the originating power, they are not the poetic essence: that wells from the unconscious, instinctive being: the 'soul'. Shakespeare describes the poetic process clearly enough:

> The poet's eye, in a fine frenzy rolling,
> Doth glance from heaven to earth, from earth to heaven;
> And as imagination bodies forth
> The forms of things unknown, the poet's pen
> Turns them to shapes, and gives to airy nothing
> A local habitation and a name.
> > (*A Midsummer Night's Dream*, v. i. 12)

'Nothing' in Shakespeare can frequently be equated, un-reservedly, with that which he elsewhere names 'soul'; the 'unconscious mind' of modern psychology. The conscious intellect receives imagination's 'forms', and, in the act of poetic creation, turns them to 'shapes'. And this is the exact equivalent of the passage in *Richard II*:

> My brain I'll prove the female to my soul,
> My soul the father.

Moreover, Richard explicitly tells us that his thoughts

> people this little world
> In humours like the people of this world . . .

I will therefore conclude that, having regard to the similar passages I have noticed in Keats, Wordsworth, Keyserling, Bergson, and *A Midsummer Night's Dream*, we may definitely assert that Shakespeare has here temporarily endued his dramatic protagonist with a psychic state closely analogous, if not exactly equivalent, to the process of poetic creation. From this emerges an interesting series of facts.

My purpose is now to indicate the relation borne by Richard's next thought-succession to the future sequence of tragedies. The beginning is 'religious':

> The better sort,
> As thoughts of things divine, are intermix'd
> With scruples and do set the word itself
> Against the word:
> As thus, 'Come, little ones'; and then again,
> 'It is as hard to come as for a camel
> To thread the postern of a small needle's eye.'

Much of *Hamlet* and *Measure for Measure* expresses religious pain. Hamlet and Claudio are tormented by fears of death and the orthodox teaching of eternal punishment. In *Measure for Measure* Christian ethics are subjected to a profound and careful examination. These two problem plays are clearly marked by the presence of (i) a predominating atmosphere of orthodox religion, and (ii) religious pain and intellectual difficulty. And these qualities are very clearly present in Richard's first thought.

Next follows a passage closely reflecting the stoic philosophy that characterizes *Lear*, and containing many references which further suggest the incidents of *Lear*:

> Thoughts tending to ambition, they do plot
> Unlikely wonders; how these vain weak nails
> May tear a passage through the flinty ribs
> Of this hard world, my ragged prison walls,
> And, for they cannot, die in their own pride.
> Thoughts tending to content flatter themselves
> That they are not the first of fortune's slaves,
> Nor shall not be the last; like silly beggars
> Who sitting in the stocks refuge their shame,
> That many have and others must sit there;
> And in this thought they find a kind of ease,
> Bearing their own misfortunes on the back
> Of such as have before endur'd the like.

No one acquainted with *Lear* can fail to recognize an intimate poetic relation. It is in the word 'ambition': Lear's passion, at its highest, is the ambition of suffering man who challenges heaven with injustice. It is in the phrase 'hard world', recalling Edgar's:

> World, world, O world!
> But that thy strange mutations make us hate thee,
> Life would not yield to age.   (*Lear*, IV. i. 10)

It is, too, evident in the words 'beggar' (we remember Tom o' Bedlam) and the reference to 'stocks', reminding us of Kent's punishment and his apostrophe to 'fortune':

> Fortune, good-night: smile once more: turn thy wheel!
>   (*Lear*, II. ii. 180)

Thoughts 'tending to content', too, are found broadcast on the suffering world of *Lear*: the implicit philosophy is often stoic, resigned. Cordelia voices a thought exactly corresponding to Richard's:

> We are not the first
> Who, with best meaning, have incurr'd the worst.
> For thee, oppressed king, am I cast down;
> Myself could else out-frown false fortune's frown.
>   (*Lear*, V. iii. 3)

Lear falls from kingship to a beggarly estate, outcast in
the storm, companioned by Edgar and his few retainers:
yet he touches in this misery a more exquisite perception
of himself, of man, and the purposes of destiny, than ever
he appears to have done as king. Richard's next lines
continue to suggest *Lear*:

> Thus play I in one person many people,
> And none contented: sometimes am I king;
> Then treasons make me wish myself a beggar,
> And so I am: then crushing penury
> Persuades me I was better when a king;
> Then am I king'd again; and, by and by,
> Think that I am unking'd by Bolingbroke,
> And straight am nothing.

These lines do, in fact, trace the exact curves of Lear's fortunes. The 'treasons' of his daughters make him wish himself
a beggar. Confronted with the naked 'poor Tom', he cries

> Here's three on's are sophisticated. Thou art the thing
> itself . . . Off, off, you lendings!   (*Lear*, III. iv. 110)

Lear's sufferings are, however, remedied by Cordelia's
return. He is temporarily restored to security and his
daughter's mothering pity for his past agony, mental and
physical, only to be 'by and by' again cast down from any
hope of happiness until he becomes the 'nothing' which is
death. Strange as it may seem, these lines of Richard's
speech (18–38) do in fact suggest not only the events and
philosophy of the great tragedy to come, but also the
rhythm of the story. Now *Lear* is followed, according to
my interpretations, by *Timon of Athens*. *Timon* marks an
advance on *Lear* in the mystic understanding of death. In
Lear death is purely the ender of pain: in *Timon* it becomes
a positive good. This I have demonstrated elsewhere. The
lines which most clearly indicate the death philosophy of
Timon are:

> My long sickness
> Of health and living now begins to mend,
> And nothing brings me all things.
>
> (*Timon of Athens*, v. i. 189)

This faith is, no doubt, irrational: it is the faith of high tragedy, however, and rooted firmly in many religious philosophies. Death, which is a 'nothing', yet is the harbinger of 'all things'. (One might compare Bergson's close reference of 'nothing' to 'all'.) *Timon of Athens* shows a vision of the human soul, infinite in its longing, unsatiated by the temporal and the limitations of earthly existence. Itself infinite, it aspires only to the infinite; which infinity it reaches in the 'nothing' of death. Now the philosophy of *Timon* is also exactly expressed in Richard's following lines. They are:

> . . . but whate'er I be,
> Nor I nor any man that but man is
> With nothing shall be pleas'd, till he be eas'd
> With being nothing.

No more perfect commentary on the essential meaning of *Timon* could be found. It is an exact microcosm of the play's statement.

But this negation is not final in Shakespeare. We must consider *Antony and Cleopatra*. The negation is pressed far until 'nothing' becomes Nirvana as in Buddhism. The reversal is then swift. If Nirvana be better than life, then Nirvana is itself a better life. If life be, as in *Timon*, the negation of human aspiration, then death automatically becomes its satisfaction. Even if it be nothing, death cannot, as life, be less than nothing. We are cast back to Claudio's words, spoken after the Duke has in detail analysed the purely negative aspect of temporal existence:

> *Claudio.*   I humbly thank you.
>   To sue to live, I find I seek to die;
>   And, seeking death, find life: let it come on.
>   (*Measure for Measure*, III. i. 41)

Like Antony, he will 'encounter darkness as a bride' (III. i. 84). In *Antony and Cleopatra* death mysteriously becomes life. Thus the extreme of negative philosophy worked out in the sombre plays leads to *Antony and Cleopatra*. But this vision of death's excellence may seem

true in so far only as life is bad. Now it is wholly bad to
Hamlet, *Macbeth* and *Timon*, the three purest negative
statements: to such a consciousness death must be wholly
good. Hamlet begins to see this clearly at the end:

> Absent thee from felicity awhile,
> And in this harsh world draw thy breath in pain,
> To tell my story . . .   (*Hamlet*, v. ii. 358)

Macbeth tries to turn life into death; but eventually he, too,
knows he has 'lived long enough'. Timon renounces life
for death. Life's very partiality sublimates death. But, in
so far as life is good, clearly death need not be desired.
Therefore both life and death may become variously charged
with positive meaning. This is what happens in *Antony and
Cleopatra*. Nor need we adversely argue against this dual
optimism that the good things of life are mercilessly slain
by death and therefore they too are smirched with partiality: since in so far as we know them as positive delights
only and regard them in and for themselves, we know no
death; and only in so far as we give attention to death, or
death-forces, are we forced to recognize the partiality of
life, which, however, leads on next to recognition of death's
goodness. Or again: 'Death', being a negation, is rejected
by intellect. Yet, in proportion as we give it reality, it
blackens life, as in *Hamlet*; distorts it, as in *Macbeth*; re-
deems it, as in *Lear*; and becomes itself wholly good, as
in *Timon*. Death always eventually contradicts itself.
Carlisle's words in *Richard II* are apt:

> Fear, and be slain; no worse can come to fight:
> And fight and die is death destroying death,
> Where fearing dying pays death servile breath.
>   (III. ii. 183)

Death is what we make it. Or, again, even more to the
point:

> Poor soul, the centre of my sinful earth,
> Foil'd by these rebel powers that thee array,
> Why dost thou pine within and suffer dearth,
> Painting thy outward walls so costly gay?

Why so large cost, having so short a lease,
Dost thou upon thy fading mansion spend?
Shall worms, inheritors of this excess,
Eat up thy charge? is this thy body's end?
Then, soul, live thou upon thy servant's loss,
And let that pine to aggravate thy store;
Buy terms divine in selling hours of dross;
Within be fed, without be rich no more:

So shalt thou feed on Death, that feeds on men,
And Death once dead, there's no more dying then.

(*Sonnet* cxlvi)

But we have only to remember the joys of life to find these, at their best immediacy, our proper hope and true delight. Hence a comprehensive positive vision of absolute reality must include both life-joys presented as positive delights; yet also elements of failure and insufficiency to justify and give positive colour to death. And this is exactly the vision of *Antony and Cleopatra*. The positive aspects of both 'life' and 'death'—and all negative aspects of anything are clearly to be rejected whenever possible if we are to argue intellectually at all—are therein blended. This is more profound even than the marriage of Heaven and Hell: it is the marriage of Life and Death.

In Shakespeare's work the opposition of life and death is the most profound opposition but one. 'Good' and 'evil', 'heaven' and 'hell', are surface antinomies, surface aspects of 'life' and 'death'. In the same way, even 'life' and 'death' are surface aspects of the 'music'-'tempest' opposition. But in *Antony and Cleopatra*, where the life-aspect of life and death succeeds the death-aspect of death and life expressed in the sombre plays, we find the waters for once stilled and 'tempest' dissolved in music. Besides the ordinary music themes, there is the direct music-symbolism in Act IV, replacing the direct tempest-symbolism of earlier tragedies. We may now return to Richard in his prison. Richard's thought-sequence ends in music:

Music do I hear?

We must consider the music which is indicated to con-

tinue for some appreciable time. Then we shall see that
the movement in Richard's thought which I have been
tracing is a thing strangely beautiful and uniquely interesting. Starting from religious perplexity, developing
through agnostic pain and stoic acceptance to a serene
faith in death's essential goodness, it finally makes 'a swan-
like end fading in music': it fades into music, is lost in
music, those melodies which express more than the mind
may speak in words, music which is the utterance of a
consciousness understanding the ineffable, and drawing the
veil which hides that unity distorted by our conventional
dualism of 'life' and 'death'. Richard's thought-voyage in
the darkened prison is a supremely beautiful thing: and
it is an exact forecast of the movement expressed over a
period of seven or eight years by the greater plays which
followed.

Nor is this really strange. I do not suggest that
Shakespeare evolved, in writing this speech, a philosophy
of immortality: rather the thoughts followed one another,
no doubt, as Keats said that poetry should come to the
poet's pen, 'as naturally as the leaves to a tree'; or, as
Shakespeare puts it:

> A thing slipp'd idly from me.
> Our poesy is as a gum, which oozes
> From whence 'tis nourish'd.   (*Timon of Athens*, I. i. 20)

Thus music, surely, is no strange addition: it is the
natural, because the most beautiful, end to a beautiful
sequence. But the simplest things in the category of
'beauty' may indeed have most complicated analogies on
the plane of 'truth'. I suggest that the sequence of plays
to follow illustrates the subtleties, the depths, and the
visionary heights, which are implicit in this tiny movement
in *Richard II*. The 'soul' in Shakespeare is often called
'prophetic'. It is so here. Shakespeare's poetic and
dramatic genius is such that, wishing to endue his protagonist here with something of artistic contemplation, he
first outlines a metaphysic of creative art, and then so

perfectly enters into the creative thought of Richard, that
Richard becomes a poet, and a poet moreover tracing
the future spiritual history of Shakespeare himself: that is,
more truly a poet and a prophet than Shakespeare at the
time could have guessed. The pain of *Hamlet* was yet
unwritten; the purgatory of *Lear* was no more than a
cloudy spectre on the fringes of consciousness. But there
are more things within the soul than are dreamt of in our
philosophies. Here we see how the poet writes not from his
mind, but from the uncharted deeps which feed it; deeps
of the soul, of unconsciousness, bottomlessly enfathomed
in a world beyond analysis. It is often observed that
Shakespeare does not philosophize, or speak of his art:
but in truth there is philosophy implicit in all he says,
and he often phrases explicitly in intellectual form the
mysterious process of creation. Here we can observe how
Shakespeare forcasts the aesthetic or metaphysic of such
masters as Keats, Keyserling, and Bergson. All assert the
unconscious, instinctive, yet essentially valid and visionary
nature of that creative mood in which bright fountains
closed to the intellectual consciousness break free. It is,
perhaps, characteristic of Shakespeare that he not only
states his thesis with a finer compression and clarity than
the others, but, if we have regard to the plays which
followed, in the same poetic act proves the validity of his
statement. For Shakespeare does not 'describe': he is one
in essence with the objects of his attention. So Richard,
in poetic mood, becomes a true poet, a miniature of the
future Shakespeare, his thought turning on that very axis
about which the visionary sequence of plays unwritten
was destined to revolve. This is the perfect mating of
mind and soul.

But Richard's soliloquy does not end there. After
listening for a while, he breaks out in nervous excitement
and irritation:

> Ha, ha! keep time: how sour sweet music is,
> When time is broke and no proportion kept!
> So is it in the music of men's lives.

And here have I the daintiness of ear
To check time broke in a disorder'd string;
But for the concord of my state and time
Had not an ear to hear my true time broke.

Richard has just been making a kingdom of his own mind
or soul. He was always an individualist, and he has all but
accomplished the individualist's heaven: mysticism. But
suddenly he is reminded of other realities: the turbulence
and rough exacting necessities of the world-order. To
these he has been false. Now 'music' in Shakespeare has
two closely related significances, as I observed in my first
essay; it accompanies, or suggests, both individual and
political harmony. Which two may often conflict.
Richard's wayward individualism loses his crown for him,
but gives him instead an individualistic, and so almost
impregnable, peace. Like Henry VI he is quite ready to
change a crown of gold for a crown of 'content'. I quote
an earlier speech of Richard's:

Mine ear is open and my heart prepar'd:
The worst is worldly loss thou canst unfold.
Say, is my kingdom lost? why, 'twas my care;
And what loss is it to be rid of care?
Strives Bolingbroke to be as great as we?
Greater he shall not be; if he serve God,
We'll serve Him too and be his fellow so:
Revolt our subjects? that we cannot mend;
They break their faith to God as well as us:
Cry woe, destruction, ruin and decay;
The worst is death, and death will have its day.
(III. ii. 93)

Richard knows that
          . . . within the hollow crown
That rounds the mortal temples of a king
Keeps Death his court, and there the antic sits,
Scoffing his state and grinning at his pomp.
(III. ii. 160)

Therefore:
I'll give my jewels for a set of beads,
My gorgeous palace for a hermitage,

> My gay apparel for an almsman's gown,
> My figur'd goblets for a dish of wood,
> My sceptre for a palmer's walking-staff,
> My subjects for a pair of carved saints,
> And my large kingdom for a little grave,
> A little little grave, an obscure grave . . . (III. iii. 147)

In *Richard II* we find the usual Shakespearian dualism of the individual soul's quest, whether for romantic love or religious romance, and the ambitions or calls of world-glory, empire, state-order. Now the hero's weak individualism has sacrificed the latter, but becomes correspondingly strong in failure and tragedy. He is thus a match for tragedy and death, but not for the duties of life. This he now remembers in his soliloquy. Music suggests to him the music of 'state'. His own 'time', that is, his worldly existence ('time' in Shakespeare has a very wide content, but is usually—as we might expect—powerfully suggestive of things 'temporal') has not kept concord with his 'state'. Hence the music later mads him with memory of his failure. Whether the musician is really at fault, or whether Richard's nerves are to blame, need not concern us. True, he is clearly conscious of the beauty and truth of his mystic assurance. It makes death and all eternity a blessed peace. But, unfortunately, he is not dead yet. He is in time, not in eternity. He has misused time when he had it at his command: now he still lives in time, but to a man without freedom or employment, time is an absurd and meaningless thing, wearing him out with inactivity. The fallacy of a purely individualistic mysticism is exposed: just as when Timon found himself hungry. It makes sense of death but not of life. Countered still by the music, Richard now utters the sense of frustration induced by his enjoyment of a practical time-consciousness without the practical activity he has handed over to Bolingbroke:

> I wasted time, and now doth time waste me;
> For now hath time made me his numbering clock:
> My thoughts are minutes; and with sighs they jar
> Their watches on unto mine eyes, the outward watch,

Whereto my finger, like a dial's point,
Is pointing still, in cleansing them from tears.
Now sir, the sound that tells what hour it is
Are clamorous groans, which strike upon my heart,
Which is the bell: so sighs and tears and groans
Show minutes, times, and hours: but my time
Runs posting on in Bolingbroke's proud joy,
While I stand fooling here, his Jack o' the clock.

Richard is, at it were, pure time, like a clock; wnich, in its self-concentration on time, is itself absurdly but necessarily abstracted from all those temporal things whose purposes it serves. Time is, like money or virtue, only good for use. Richard has handed over his own time to Bolingbroke and become Bolingbroke's clock. And all this is set against the music: music first of the soul's eternity, next of that blending of eternity with time which Richard could not attain. Hence it drives him to distraction:

This music mads me: let it sound no more;
For though it have holp madmen to their wits,
In me it seems it will make wise men mad.
Yet blessing on his heart that gives it me!
For 'tis a sign of love; and love to Richard
Is a strange brooch in this all-hating world.

It is true. Richard's mysticism is 'wise'. Yet the music of life may drive the finely-tuned intellect mad. It does so with Hamlet, jangling the bells of a sweet prince's sanity. The individual soul, however sure it may be of itself, may yet be unharmonized with outward things, and madness ensues. Lear gives up world-power and responsibility for an old age of selfish and sentimental love, and helps to plunge his land and himself in all ruinous disorders. This is how the music of spiritual longing may clash with the music of the world and create 'tempests': so here time is 'broke in a disordered string': the music is, to Richard, a disharmony. But when the soul finds itself on a deeper level, as in Lear's reunion with Cordelia, again the music breaks out in undistorted clarity, and then helps 'madmen' back 'to their wits': this level Richard does not attain.

He falls back on sentimental self-love, will not follow to the end the purgatory of self-criticism and self-knowledge which he has started; falls back on thought of the 'love' he has not found, on thoughts of 'this all-hating world'. He cannot compass either the purgatory of Lear or the aristocratic disregard of Timon. He remains an individualist to the last, yet not a pure individualist. He still treasures an instance of love, still regrets the failure of a cruel world to give him happiness.

Our soliloquy, then, not only forecasts the greater tragedies in some detail but also struggles with one of the surface dualisms which vitalize their action: the dualism of the individual and the state. Brutus, Hamlet, the Duke of Vienna—these, and others, must be related to 'disorder' in the community—and hence, in varying degrees, in themselves—due, partly at least, to their own personal intuitions. This personal longing is a religious and ethical perception in *Measure for Measure*; but it may be a death-perception, or a longing for love; it may also be a search for 'honour'. Generally there is a 'tempest', conflict, and disorder. The interweavings and complexities from this view-point are manifold. But from these greater tragedies one fact emerges of primary importance. The personal love ideal wins unconditionally in *Coriolanus* and *Antony and Cleopatra*. In *Coriolanus* personal love is itself shown as an order-force, and warrior-strength transposed to an absurd individualism. Richard is distracted between two realities: the calls of state-duty and his own soul. He is not, in our soliloquy, prepared to follow the 'feminine' principle of religious—or poetic—contemplation to the end, because he remembers how he failed in the 'masculine' task of kingly responsibility. These two elements are strong in the sex-opposition of *Antony and Cleopatra*. The two musics there make one harmony. But love clearly wins a victory over temporal efficiency: though to understand this we must consider both 'death' and 'life'. Antony never ceases to be very masculine. At his dying he is silhouetted against love, not exactly one with it, yet dying where he has lived, in Cleopatra's arms. We must note that Antony and Cleopatra are never actually married in life. We watch love dissociated from ethical and social order; and this, together with other order-forces and empire-forces, impediments their love. They have to dare death to accomplish their final marriage. Hence the fine exactitude and excellence of Cleopatra's phrase:

> Husband, I come:
> Now to that name my courage prove my title!

The forces of 'love' and 'order', the feminine and masculine, are balanced evenly throughout the tragedies. Finally there is a perceptible advantage for the feminine principle. And this is the direction taken by the crowning visions of Shakespeare's latest work.

Additional Note, 1951: A proper appreciation of *Henry VIII* will tend to modify the statement of my last sentence. See my study of the play in *The Crown of Life*.

1965: We may suppose that the music covers the Final Plays as well as *Antony and Cleopatra* and that Richard's return to remembrance of communal responsibilities corresponds to *Henry VIII*.